incubators

incubators

a realist's guide to the world's new business accelerators

COLIN BARROW

JOHN WILEY & SONS, LTD
Chichester • New York • Weinheim • Brisbane • Singapore • Toronto

Other Wiley Editorial Offices

John Wiley & Sons, Inc., 605 Third Avenue,
New York, NY 10158-0012, USA

WILEY-VCH GmbH, Pappelallee 3,
D-69469 Weinheim, Germany

John Wiley & Sons Australia, Ltd, 33 Park Road, Milton,
Queensland 4064, Australia

John Wiley & Sons (Asia) Pte Ltd, 2 Clementi Loop #02-01,
Jin Xing Distripark, Singapore 129809

John Wiley & Sons (Canada) Ltd, 22 Worcester Road,
Rexdale, Ontario M9W 1L1, Canada

British Library Cataloguing in Publication Data

A catalogue record for this book is available from the British Library

ISBN 0-470-84292-X

Typeset by Dorwyn Ltd, Rowlands Castle, Hants.
Printed and bound in Great Britain by Biddles Ltd, Guildford and King's Lynn.
This book is printed on acid-free paper responsibly manufactured from sustainable forestry,
in which at least two trees are planted for each one used for paper production.

Contents

About the author

Colin Barrow is Head of the Enterprise Group at Cranfield University School of Management, and Director of the Business Growth and Development Programme, the UK's most successful programme for entrepreneurs. He is also a founder member of the team that launched 'Cranfield Creates', the business school's own e-business incubator. Colin has also taught extensively on Business School MBA programmes and on management development programmes in countries throughout the world including Malaysia, Singapore, France, Germany, Italy, Spain, Scandinavia and the US.

He was educated at Sandhurst and took his MBA at Cranfield. Before coming to Cranfield to teach, he taught at Stirling University and was Visiting Professor at Suffolk University, Boston. Prior to joining Cranfield he held senior line and staff appointments in industry, including managing directorships with two companies. His research interests are concentrated on the issues that inhibit or encourage the launch and successful growth of independent businesses.

His books on small business and entrepreneurship include: *The Complete Small Business Guide* published by the BBC, *The Pocket Entrepreneur* published by the Economist, *The Essence of Small Business* published by Prentice Hall, and *The Principles of Small Business* published by International Thompson Press. His book, *How to Survive the E-business Downturn*, was published by John Wiley in October 2000.

He acted as an adviser on the Microsoft Business Planner project and two of his books, *The Business Plan Workbook* and *Financial Management for the Small Business*, form the core of this software package, which is incorporated with Microsoft Office 2000. His latest book, *The Business Enterprise Handbook*, written with Robert Brown and Liz Clarke, was published by the Sunday Times in 2001.

Outside of his work at Cranfield, he is a strategic consultant and a non-executive director in a number of companies in both high and not so high technological fields. He is a non-executive director of a high-technology venture capital fund that has offices in the technology parks of both Oxford and Cambridge Universities.

Introduction

Tempting though it might be to believe that business accelerators are an Internet phenomenon, incubators, science parks, innovation centres and technology parks have been around for years. The first serious attempt at incubation, in 1959, is credited to a near-derelict building near New York and the name came into common usage more by way of a joke than a serious description of the task in hand. One of the incubators' first tenants was involved in incubating real chickens. Several waves of accelerators followed this inauspicious start, and by the 1980s several hundred such facilities were scattered around the US, Canada, Europe and Australia. Later incubator progressions took in the developing economies and the Internet variation, which came into being in the mid 1990s, swept across the US, Europe, India, China, Malaysia, Singapore, the Philippines, and elsewhere, bringing the total to some 4000 facilities worldwide. One study (Harley 2001) reports the number of incubators as 3450 in 2000. What was particularly revealing about this report was the split between 'private for profit' incubators and those more established incubators sponsored by the states and universities. In the US, of 950 incubators, some 300 fall into the 'for profit' category. The rest of the world boasted 2500 incubators, but only the same number, 300, are in the 'for profit' category.

Varieties of accelerators and incubators now co-exist in the market, and have radically different aims and objectives. Some, such as those founded by entrepreneurs and venture capital firms, the 'for profit' variety, only want to get rich, by helping entrepreneurs to get rich. That goal at least has the merit of transparency. Some have revenue models that can make the incubator rich without necessarily benefiting anyone else that much. Governments and local governments are more concerned with job creation than wealth, and universities, another major player, want jobs for students and funding for faculty research, rather than riches themselves. Big corporate firms run private incubators to encourage firms who might buy their products or services or create career opportunities for their more entrepreneurial and potentially less fickle employees.

These incubators are havens for entrepreneurs with innovative or technology-based business ideas that need more help than most to be brought to fruition. Such ventures usually have more potential than other business starters, but they are also more risky. No one knows how many entrepreneurs graduate from these incubators each year. But it's a reasonable supposition that each of the estimated 4000 incubators has two or three graduates each year. So 10 000 or so 'eggs' are hatched in a safe environment each year. That's not a big number in terms of business start-ups. Across Europe and the US somewhere between three and four million new businesses are started in most years. But some entrepreneurs who get into an incubator have a better chance of success than if they went it alone. There is not much conclusive evidence to show that the incubator sponsors have done so well.

This book sets out to examine the history of business incubation and to review the main players; their goals, objectives and achievements. It also looks at the range of facilities and services on offer in different types of incubator, and evaluates the likely benefit of those to client companies. The final part of the book is intended to help entrepreneurs to assess whether or not incubation is right for them and, if so, which type of incubator would add most value to their venture. As no one should get into anything they can't see a way out from, the likely exit routes from incubators are also covered in this section.

The book draws on the research findings published in more than 150 authoritative studies of business incubators carried out by recognized experts and practitioners. In that respect, those looking at incubators today are fortunate. Without the groundwork laid by these researchers, much of it conducted only in the past decade, we would only have sketchy anecdotes to rely on for our conclusions. The book also includes the experiences of entrepreneurs in around a hundred business incubators worldwide, thus adding a practical dimension to the theoretical underpinning of all the key propositions expounded.

Whether you are looking for a great place to start your new business, or are in the business of helping others to get their business ventures up and running, this book is intended to provide the insights and knowledge you need to succeed.

Part One

A brief history of business incubation

Incubator (*noun*) apparatus providing warmth for hatching eggs, rearing premature babies, or developing bacteria.

Oxford Dictionary, Oxford University Press

An environment and programme with certain important characteristics: it offers a full array of business assistance services tailored to the client companies; it has an incubator manager on site who co-ordinates staff and outside professionals and organizations to deliver those services; it graduates companies out of the programme (though not always out of the incubator facility) once they meet the programme goals.

The National Business Incubation Association (NBIA), Athens, Ohio

Despite its brevity, the Oxford Dictionary definition of an incubator captures rather more of the essence of the subject than that provided by the organization that has set itself up as the premier 'trade association' for those in the incubator business. However, neither definition gives the full picture of the array of services, motivations and facilities provided by business incubators.

In this first section of the book, we will examine how incubators go about their task and give some insights into why they came about, how they have developed over time, the types of businesses that are most likely to be drawn into their ambit and, in general terms, how effective the incubation process has been so far.

1

How business incubators work

While there is no single model for business incubators, in most cases the concept goes beyond the simple provision of a shared office or workspace facility for small business clients. The hallmark of any effective business incubator programme should be its focus on the added value that it brings to small business 'tenants' in terms of strengthened business skills; access to business services; improved operating environment; and opportunities for business networking, etc. to nurture early-stage small businesses, increasing their prospects for business survival and growth, compared with the situation outside the incubator.

In general, business incubators work through the relationships of a number of stakeholders including sponsors drawn from the local business community, government, and the broader community including venture capital providers, up-and-coming entrepreneurs, and professional incubator management. These all blend their talents to produce sustainable graduate businesses, the benefits of increased income, employment and economic development for the local community and, where appropriate, a return on shareholder investment.

Listed below are some of the critical elements of a successful incubation programme:

- A broad range of supporting stakeholders: Most small business incubators in Australia rely on varying degrees of support (financial and in-kind) from a range of sponsors including Commonwealth, State and local governments, and business- and community-based groups, such as regional development organizations.
- Local demand from entrepreneurs with early stage small businesses: Incubators should service a demand from local entrepreneurs looking

to improve the survival and growth prospects of their early stage small businesses. An effective incubator needs to maintain adequate tenant occupancy to replace the regular graduation of existing tenants. A ready supply of emerging local businesses is essential to the long-term sustainability of any incubator programme.

- Provision of a range of facilities and services to tenant businesses: While the range of facilities and services differs from incubator to incubator, in all cases incubators should seek to nurture the survival of tenant businesses and enhance their growth prospects, rather than passively providing shared office or workspace facilities. Not all incubators will offer a full range of services to tenants. Facilities need to be adequate for the business requirements of prospective small business tenants.

- Effective incubator management: The role of incubator management is crucial in ensuring continuing local support and sponsorship, attracting and evaluating prospective tenants, assisting in the development of existing tenants and facilitating the smooth transition of leaving tenants (successful graduates and others).

- Regular turnover of graduate businesses: The long-term success of any incubator has to be judged against its ability to promote and develop successful graduate businesses. Any incubator programme must balance the needs of continued tenant occupancy against the longer-term business requirements of its tenants and graduates.

- Economic and community impacts: The incubator has to deliver results against the outcomes that the stakeholders want. This may be economic development in the form of new jobs, or it may be valuable experience for university students or profitable investment opportunities for the providers of capital.

WHAT'S IN A NAME?

Science parks, technology innovation centres and various permutations of the words business, incubator, venture, research and programme are all in use to describe the incubation process. One academic has attempted to explain the different roles that innovation centres and incubation centres play (Swierczek 1992). A innovation centre, he claims, is:

> a two-way direction of interaction between the research community and the business community. There is an important openness as to what is happening in the wider environment in the form of new techniques and potentially applicable research acquired through technology scans or in the

form of market needs. For the business incubation approach, the key factor is the entrepreneur and the direction that individual wants to take in the development of the business start-up. If the entrepreneur has a technical background, the business concept will tend to be technology-based. If the entrepreneur does not, then the business concept is likely to be in the service sector, but not usually in technical services.

In Professor Swierczek's paper he indicated that, for research development purposes, countries such as Korea and Japan have favoured science parks as the approach to increasing research-related activities. Research takes priority over any business or jobs that may be created and those that are should be directly related to the science park itself. Countries such as China, the Philippines, Trinidad and Tobago, and Nigeria, with the assistance of the United Nations Fund for Science and Technology Development, have also moved into the business incubation approach. With this approach, job and business creation is paramount. Germany, Taiwan, Singapore, the Netherlands, Ireland and the Scandinavian countries have plumped for the innovation centre route. In this approach, a dynamic relationship is the goal, and entrepreneurs are sought out who may be able to commercialize the output of university or government research. Once again, jobs and business are created, but the main aim is to recover monies spent and to provide a war chest for future research.

However, the world has moved on and the Internet has propelled it forward faster still. Entrepreneurs with limited technological expertise are at the heart of high-technology start-ups and links between the business, research, capital and entrepreneurs have become much more complex than a 'two-way direction of interation'.

In this book no distinction is made by virtue of the name used by an institution provided they are in the business of incubation as defined above. This does not mean that there are not profound differences to be found amongst the various players in this market. It's just that such differences have little or nothing to do with their nomenclatures.

WHY THERE IS A NEED FOR INCUBATORS

There are over 4000 business incubators in operation throughout the world today. From a handful of facilities (40) identified by the National Business Incubation Association (NBIA) in its 1984 Quarterly Roster of Incubators, there are now 800 members in the US alone. There are also hundreds of the newer 'for profit' incubators set up either as standalone ventures or consortia led by major accountancy practices, management consultancies, venture capital providers or major firms such as Microsoft, Cisco Systems, Nokia and Oracle that dominate the high-tech world. The number of new incubators increased by six per month between January and August 1999. After September 1999, growth rates skyrocketed, averaging roughly 25 new incubators per month to December 2000, in the US alone. If to those totals are added the numbers of incubators in other countries around the world (80 in the former Soviet Union; 600 in Western Europe; 210 in Eastern Europe; 50 in Australia; 200 in China; 100 in India), it's not difficult to see how a figure of 4000 incubators operating in 2002 can be arrived at. Figure 1.1 shows the growth of incubators by region and overall.

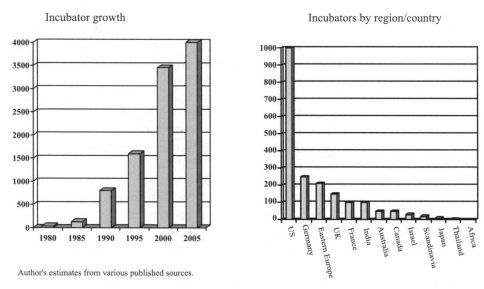

Author's estimates from various published sources.

Figure 1.1   The growth of the world incubator industry.

Two closely related factors have triggered the exponential growth of business incubation and both were discovered, or perhaps a more correct term is 'confirmed' since anecdotal evidence had been around for decades beforehand, by one man. Professor David Birch, in his landmark work emphasizing the importance of new businesses (Birch 1979), demonstrated that it was these fledgling enterprises, employing fewer than twenty workers, that were responsible for over two-thirds of the increase in employment in the US between 1969 and 1976. This revealing statistic was seized upon, especially as it was largely confirmed to be valid for much of the developed world, as the signal for governments, and others, to step up their efforts to stimulate and encourage enterprise.

Small firms had been a neglected part of most countries' economies for most of the post-Second World War years. In the UK the Bolton Committee Report (1971), which was commissioned by the government to investigate the state of the small business sector, had identified that the sector was starved of equity capital and experienced management, but until Birch's paper was published no one accepted quite how important new and small firms were to a country's economic well-being.

Alongside this recognition of the significance of new business, Birch's research also revealed their fragility. He estimated that roughly eight million enterprises operating in the US closed down every year, meaning that 'every five to six years, we have to replace half of the entire US economy'. These findings on small firm failure rates have been confirmed in study after study throughout the world. Birch (1987) returned to the subject to show that, depending on macro-economic conditions, about half of all small firms will survive more than five years. Bates and Nucci (1989) showed that whilst new business creation had increased dramatically in the preceding two decades, failure rates remained high. There was, and still is, a general agreement that two of the main reasons for the failure of small businesses are a lack of management expertise and under-capitalization (Roure and Keeley 1990), as well as the effects of macro-economic mismanagement.

From these twin findings that new firms are both vital and fragile has arisen a plethora of government initiatives to both foster and protect small firms during their formative years. The private sector has not been slow to recognize that if so many entrepreneurs need help, and governments are keen to put money into initiatives, then there must be profitable opportunities for them. Business incubators can be seen as one initiative in an armoury of measures designed to ensure new ventures have an easier passage into the business world.

2

How it all began

Twenty years before Birch published his paper on the problems of new businesses, one entrepreneur was having problems of his own. In 1959 the heirs to a prominent New York family business, Charles Manusco & Son, had just bought another building (McKee 1992). The Manuscos owned a wide range of local businesses in western New York State, where they regularly increased their real estate holdings and investments. Their latest acquisition was a huge multistorey structure amounting to 850 000 square feet. The building dated from 1882 and had originally housed John Harvester and later Massey Ferguson, which manufactured combine harvesters. Along with the building came 30 acres of land. The building, unsurprisingly, had been vacant for a few years, and much of its massive roof needed replacing. The cost of restoring the property would have dwarfed the $180 000 purchase price.

Joseph Manusco, the family member assigned to look after the project, quickly concluded that the property would be impossible to rent to a single tenant. He decided on a revolutionary strategy. He would partition the building and lease it out in small pieces, hoping to find enough tenants to turn a potential white elephant into a money-making proposition.

His first tenant, a sign painter, took 2000 square feet and by the end of the first year he had between 20 and 30 tenants taking 90 000 square feet. Not exactly a wildfire success, but at least the building was paying its way and the capital appreciation was building up as a sweetener for the family firm's coffers. Manusco, who has been credited with inventing the term 'incubator', stumbled on the name by accident. One of his early tenants, a company from Connecticut, incubated chickens. Soon after the firm's arrival, Manusco would joke that he was incubating chickens, when asked what he was doing with his building. From there it was but a short leap before his venture was known as a business incubator.

Today the business is known as the Batavia Industrial Center, with 1000 people working in the building. Some of the early tenants are still in the building and the centre's philosophy is that whilst it continues to encourage new businesses to start up, anyone can lease space and stay as long as they like.

THE NEXT STAGE

Batavia was an early example, albeit an accidental one, of an initiative to make space for small firms to get started. Its focus was property, like that of various government initiatives, such as the Beehive Units fostered in the 1970s in the UK. Beehives were small factory units built in clusters on the edge of towns with all services laid on and easy in and out lease agreements. Established in 1975, the British Steel Industry (BSI) claims to have invented the concept of shared managed workspace, in the UK at least. The BSI was set up to help create employment in areas affected by the scaling down of steel production in Europe. As well as property, BSI went on to add venture and loan capital as well as training and advice to its initiatives to stimulate employment.

About 250 miles east of the Batavia Center and two decades later, what is considered by some to be the first modern incubator was formed. Around 1980 in the city of Troy the business incubator concept assumed greater dimensions. Troy, a city of 55 000 people, is more than 200 years old. Located along the Hudson River east of New York, Troy was a major centre for the industrial revolution in the 1800s, but 150 years later it was in need of a new purpose. It had been the home of the detachable shirt collar, stove manufacturers, textile mills, stagecoach and carriage builders, breweries, bell manufacturers, iron and steel centres, and more. Iron plates for the Civil War ship the *Monitor* were rolled in Troy. Even Samuel Wilson, better known as Uncle Sam, lived and worked in Troy during this time. But little of this activity could help in creating new jobs or encouraging younger citizens of Troy to stay in the area and not search out more exciting opportunities.

Most of Troy's buildings date from the 1700s and 1800s; they are the fine homes of former industrial tycoons, worker and factory housing, and homes of the emerging middle class. They are still used and lived in today, many retaining their original character and features. Wood frame, terracotta, brownstone, and brick houses line the streets of the city. Queen Anne, Mansard, Beaux Arts, Romanesque, Italianate, Greek Revival, Gothic Revival and many other kinds of buildings can be seen in Troy.

In keeping with the city's industrial heritage such buildings became home to the Rensselaer Polytechnic Institute (RPI), the first degree-granting technological university in the English-speaking world. Over the last 175 years, Rensselaer alumni have been the originators of technologies, products and events that have changed our world, such as the Apollo Project, e-mail, and the first pocket calculator. Rensselaer provided at least a hint of future industries; of where wealth might be created in a second industrial revolution. In 1980 George Low, who became president of RPI after directing NASA's Apollo space missions, was searching for ways to expose his students to the business experience, but in a laboratory setting so the Institute could retain a measure of control and direction. The Institute began a networking programme that linked student and faculty entrepreneurs to investors. Business people came to speak about what was required to launch a business. Students were paired with businesses in their areas of technological expertise so that they could gain first-hand knowledge of how businesses function. Then students and professors began to launch their own companies and RPI's incubator project grew in leaps and bounds. Troy's town fathers were not slow to recognize the potential value of the RPI incubator and the role it could play in helping them tackle their own problems in reinvigorating a once vital economy. In many ways the RPI incubator's history mirrors the involvement of local and national government with technological universities in the birth and development of many other incubators all over the US and elsewhere worldwide.

At first in RPI, several early incubator companies operated out of informal incubator space in the basement of a campus academic building. The first permanent incubator building was the H building, a 3500 square-foot, single-storey brick building then used for storage. The H building was renovated into office space using a $50 000 grant from the US Economic Development Administration (EDA), which Rensselaer matched with $50 000 of its own funds. In 1982 the H building was filled with incubator companies immediately following the completion of renovation. It soon became apparent that there was sufficient demand for incubator space to support a much larger facility. In 1981 Rensselaer's 42 000 square-foot J building, formerly a Catholic church home for 'wayward girls', was selected to be the next incubator expansion. The J building required significant renovation, which was financed by a $600 000 loan from the City of Troy Industrial Development Agency and a $200 000 loan from the New York State Urban Development Corporation. Renovations were completed in 1982 and the J building has been almost fully occupied ever since.

Debt service on the two renovation loans for the J building has been fully supported from the incubator operating budget. The New York State loan was paid in full in 1997. The City of Troy loan became due in 1991 with a substantial balloon payment, which Rensselaer paid off and refinanced to the incubator. The incubator 'department' of Rensselaer continues to service and pay off this debt through an internal transfer of funds from the incubator operating budget, which will continue until 2005.

In response to ongoing demand for incubator laboratory space of a type not available in the original two incubator buildings, Rensselaer's administration 'loaned' unused portions of a laboratory building in the nearby City of Watervliet for incubator company use. This 1964 building was originally designed for research and had most recently housed an electronics research centre complete with clean rooms. However, this research was moved to a new state-of-the-art campus facility in 1988, leaving the building largely empty and stripped. The incubator gradually cleaned and reactivated portions of the building as new incubator companies needed lab space.

Since 1992, the incubator has expanded in stages and now occupies the entire 32 000 net square feet of this building, housing seven client companies. In 1997, the building's heating, ventilating and air-conditioning systems were renovated for higher energy efficiency. The bullet list below gives statistics on the companies housed there:

- Greater than 80% survival rate for participating companies.
- Over 150 companies served since 1980. Most have remained in the capital region of New York State.
- 28 current tenants; 230 jobs.
- Occupancy in the incubator typically exceeds 95%.
- Over 2000 jobs created.
- Annual sales of incubator 'graduates' exceeds $200 million.
- Hundreds of RPI students employed.

RPI makes the above claims about the success of its incubator. These claims give a clear indication of the purpose and mission of most state/local government- and university-based incubators: business birth, survival, and that businesses stay and grow close to where they were born. To that might be added reaching a point close to financial equilibrium where the sponsoring institution neither gains nor loses money, and has additional benefits for its students and faculty thrown in.

The mission statement of UBCA (Universitair Bedrijvencentrum Antwerpen), the incubation and innovation centre of University of Antwerp in Belgium, given below, captures the essence of the goal of university and government goals in forming an alliance to start and run a business incubator.

1. To promote, support and enhance the creation of small and medium-sized enterprises in new technologies and related services in the Antwerp region.
2. To offer to its tenant firms an affordable infrastructure, qualitative service and easy access to research centres.
3. To facilitate more effective interaction between university, industry and institutes for higher technical education in the province of Antwerp.
4. To build and sustain the image of the University of Antwerp as the 'interactive' university in Flanders.
5. To create new sustainable employment in the region.

WHERE WE ARE NOW

In the two decades since George Low's Rensselaer Polytechnic Institute incubator got started, there have been a myriad of differing 'business models'. Even Low's model was not unique. Other institutions, corporations and town governments had already recognized the benefits to be gained from the commercialization of high and not so high technology developments by encouraging new business start-ups. The University Science Center, for example, was founded in Pennsylvania with these ideals, in 1964 (Duff 1999). In 1973 the National Science Foundation (NSF) supported a series of experiments with innovation centres through its Experimental Research and Development Programme (National Science Foundation 1985). By 1981, a year before Rensselaer's H building got fully underway, the NSF programme had extended its reach to embrace a total of eleven centres. These served as the basis for future university efforts in launching incubation or, as they were more usually known, innovation centres (Allen and Weinberg 1988).

Universities and local and national government agencies were not the only players in the game. Between 1957 and 1970, the Fairchild Corporation was involved in the start-up of 35 companies, including Intel and National Semiconductor (National Council for Urban Economic Development 1985). Corporate venturing, as this activity has become known (where large established high-technology firms took a stake in new small start-up ventures) has played a fluctuating role in the incubation process. After a run of successes, some well-documented failures slowed corporate America's appetite for involvement with small firms. For example, Kodak established a major corporate venturing programme in the early 1980s and attracted over 4000 internal venture proposals. Some 300 of these received seed funding, more than 100 were commercialized as separate units or adopted internally, and only 14 became new businesses, spun into the holding company, Eastman Technologies. By 1990 only one of these was still operating independently as a Kodak subsidiary, and in 1989 Kodak announced it was discontinuing new venture activity (Ginsburg and Hay 1995). However by 2000 the wheel had turned full circle and corporate venturing was popular once more, particularly with firms that were riding high on the Internet boom. Cisco Systems, the world's most highly-valued business entity, was reported to have raised $1.9 billion between January and August 2000 through initial public offerings (IPOs) of businesses in which the company had taken a founding shareholding (Corporate Venturing Report 2000). Also in 2000, Apple generated $1.3 billion from its corporate venturing investment in Akamai (Gill *et al.* 2000). The incubation process itself has become more complex and all-embracing. From the early days when the equivalent of a warm light over a chicken egg was all that was provided to help small firms get a foothold in the business world, incubators now help to find seed corn funding as well as first and second stage financing. Office services, website design, accountancy, intellectual property, corporate finance, strategic consultancy and networking have all been added to the armoury, whilst, with the advent of virtual incubators, premises have become an optional extra, rather than the raison d'être of the process of incubation.

After the property speculators and developers, local and national governments, universities and big business, a new breed of incubators arrived on the scene in the 1990s. Businesses such as Oxygen in the UK and idealab! in the US were set up solely to make money from the incubation process without the burden of altruistic objectives such as revitalizing an ailing economy, providing an outlet for enterprising students or gaining a window on new and related technologies. Part venture capitalist, part corporate financier and part management consultants, these dotcom factories are more closely aligned to the force-feeding associated with foie gras production than the more natural process of encouraging an egg to hatch by the judicious application of heat. These new incubators are designed to encourage rapid growth and they accept that a high proportion of the companies hurled through the process will never make orbit, let alone outer space. So far the best that can be said of most of these new incubators is that they have fared little better than the firms they seek to help. Some new incubators are little more than companies who have not been successful at one type of Internet activity and want to try their hand at something else before their cash runs out completely. Others have been floated on stock markets on the back of the Internet incubator craze and are busy 'investing' share-holders' money in what is, in effect, little more than a unit trust or portfolio of unquoted Internet and high-tech stocks. The value that these investors are hoping for is the incubator's ability to pick winners, cultivate them quickly and propel them on to a similar, if not the same, stock market that they themselves launched their shares on a few months earlier. That neither the incubator nor their clients were anywhere near making a profit was something that investors took a while to recognize and even longer to react to. Some of these 'new, new' incubators will be and to some extent already are successful. But most probably will not be. And this is certainly a new experience for budding entrepreneurs. Instead of being a safe harbour, their incubator could be as much at sea as they are themselves and every bit as much in need of a lifeboat. At least they should all get some first-hand experience of developing new business models and business plans to try to convince their respective investors they have sound futures.

To add a further, somewhat surreal, twist to the rush of new 'for profit' incubators to the market has come an influx of new businesses whose goal is to help would-be business hatcheries to accelerate themselves into being.

Incubatorincubator.com is so far only a registered domain name, but its owner Jonathon Abrams plans to use it to set up in the business of incubating incubators. He set up an Internet portal in 1999 called Hotlinks, which was partly funded by another incubation business, CMGI. However, even Abrams is already late arriving in the field.

KnowledgeCube set up a network of incubation facilities under the KnowledgeCube umbrella at the end of 1999. In addition to financing, KnowledgeCube aims at providing local incubators with the expertise and connections to get them up and running quickly. KnowledgeCube Group Inc. is a private corporation with corporate headquarters at One Rockefeller Plaza in New York, as well as three offices (in Boston, Seattle, and Brussels). Networks and partnerships around the world supplement these offices, giving KnowledgeCube a presence in the world's technology centres.

Unlike most venture capital firms, KnowledgeCube Group is structured as a holding corporation rather than a limited partnership, so it can retain the flexibility of raising additional capital quickly by issuing stock or debt. KnowledgeCube's funding comes from its founders, managers and strategic investors. These strategic investors include some of the world's most prominent strategists, technologists, financiers and business leaders, among them, according to the information on KnowledgeCube's website: Rajat Gupta (Global CEO, McKinsey & Co.), Andy Stone (Managing Director, CSFB), Ali Hanna (Director, McKinsey), Pradman Kaul (Global CEO, Hughes Network Systems) and Ben Seiver (Managing Director, AIG Global Investment). Over the past year, KnowledgeCube has teamed up with nine e-technology ventures based in Boston, New York and Seattle, to help support their process. These companies develop Internet enabling/infrastructure technologies and knowledge-value-added applications of these technologies. The equity investments range from $500 000 to $5 million. Equity holdings range from 10% to 50%, which provides a useful insight into their business model.

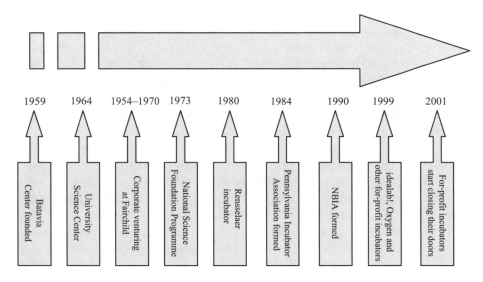

Figure 2.1   Timeline: the development of business incubators in the US.

THE INCUBATOR LIFE CYCLE

Alongside this development of the incubator model has been what Allen (1988) described as the life cycle of the incubator itself. The focus of incubator management attention during the 'start-up' stage is sorting out the physical facility, either through renovation of an existing building or the construction of purpose-built accommodation. Incubator cash flow requirements mean that early tenants are likely to be chosen on their ability to pay rent rather than their growth potential. This stage ends around the time that the facility breaks even financially.

During the second or 'business development' phase, attention is redirected towards nurturing new businesses. Now more importance is placed on developing a business advisory function and business networks. The incubator manager now starts working to build synergies through discussion and trading between tenants. When demand for space is appreciably greater than space available for tenants, and sophisticated, responsive busi-ness advisory arrangements are functioning well, the incubator is ready to move into the 'maturity' phase.

Maturity is when the incubator spreads its span of influence throughout its region or business sector, becoming a focus for entrepreneurial endeav-our. Once demand for tenancy exceeds the available space or other scarce resources such as investment capital, the incubator can become more dis-cerning with its entrance criteria and accelerate the graduation of firms. At this stage, the programme may consider expansion to accommodate the demand for its services. For the new generation of 'for profit' incubators this invariably means raising more money. For the rest, including universities and government-sponsored incubators, this usually means finding more space and buildings. As the incubator moves through the three phases of its life cycle, it is expected that the quality and quantity of development out-comes (e.g. in terms of firms graduated) would get higher.

So the incubator management has to serve several masters and the balance of responsibility to each shifts as the incubator matures and moves through its life cycle. The incubator stakeholders have to be kept happy, whether they are shareholders, venture capital firms, a university or govern-ment department. The physical premises and/or other resources have to be managed and developed. And, of course, the 'tenants' or client business have to be serviced. The patience and understanding of the stakeholders plays an important role in whether or not an incubator can survive long enough to become mature and function effectively. As the timeline in Fig-ure 2.1 shows, the patience of the 'for profits' breed of incubators may not be sufficient for them to last this course.

3

Who goes in for incubation?

This book tells the story of many incubator clients and gives details of their business sector, aspirations and achievements. Like entrepreneurs themselves, they defy universal categorization. Would-be business starters that have gone in for incubation come from all business categories and sectors. It would not even be true to say that all firms that go into business incubation facilities are either small or new. When Cranfield University's technology park was opened two decades ago its first and only client was Nissan, who set up their European research facility there, with an investment of £46 million. So large in fact was Nissan's requirement that they consumed all of the park's first phase of property capacity. It would be more than a decade before any new or small businesses came in to the park. Even that statement is not quite accurate, for, during the decades before the geographic area now known as the technology park came into being, new ventures huddled round the edge of the campus in small shed-like buildings brought into being by professors and teams of students attempting to commercialize their research projects, some with conspicuous success – Cranfield is nothing if not entrepreneurial, having justly earned a reputation for earning more commercial research funding than either Cambridge or Oxford universities, both barely a hundred miles away. Now Cranfield's innovation centre, based on the park, a £1.5 million investment part-funded by the district council, is home to dozens of small and mostly new firms occupying its 250 to 2000 square foot units. The demarcation between the technology park and the innovation centre is too subtle for even an insider to define or recognize with much confidence.

In the science park at Cambridge, England, about which we will hear more later, one entrepreneur is just coming on to the park with his third business venture. Two of his periods of tenure were with the same business, at quite distinctive stages in his firm's development. The third 'visitation' was with a completely new venture. It's not even true to say that all the firms coming on to business incubation facilities have much to do with technology any more. Whether the facility is called a science or technology park or an innovation centre, it will not provide much of a clue as to the firms you might find on it. Cranfield, for example, sets out to attract 'knowledge industries', rather than technology firms *per se*. In Germany, which did not begin setting up incubators until the mid 1980s, many facilities claim to want to 'promote the setting up of those firms which are active in the *areas of the future*' (author's italics). The Fraunhofer Institut für Systematik und Innovation (1985) outlined in its paper on German incubators the following classification scheme (see below). It is certainly a catholic range of enterprises.

- Handicraft-orientated incubators, without co-operation and services.
- Industrial parks with limited company status and technological orientation and limited provision for co-operation and services.
- Technology-based incubators with extensive co-operation and services.
- Incubators that as well as offering services offer space to research departments, institutions and divisions of established firms.
- Research park-like locations for new and established firms, without the provision of services and co-operation possibilities.

The NBIA, in it's 10th Anniversary Survey of Business Incubators 1985–1995 revealed that there were more service sector participants in the incubation process than any other category, with light manufacturing and technology companies neck and neck for second place.

All in all, it seems today that most business incubators are more concerned with finding clients who are in the 'value-adding' business rather than in any particular sector. University incubators want to encourage entrepreneurship amongst their wider student and faculty bodies, not just students in engineering and technology departments. Governments, both local and national, want to create new jobs above almost any other goal. After decades of elevating the 'small businessman' to a position close to that of a deity, the true quarry for all those involved in the incubation business is at last clear. It is entrepreneurs that are needed, rather than 'small businessmen', though for some time these were thought of as being one and the same thing. In truth it seems unlikely that they are even members of the same species yet alone the same family.

The term 'entrepreneur' was introduced into economics by Cantillon in around 1755 and raised to prominence by the French economist J.B. Say around 1800. He used it to describe someone who 'shifts economic resources out of an area of lower and into an area of higher productivity and

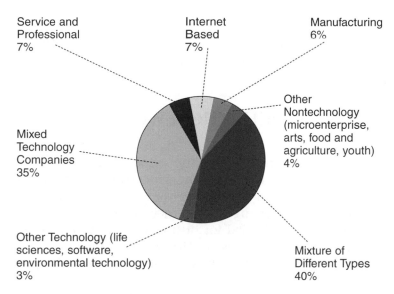

Figure 3.1   Business incubator client companies (2000).
Reprinted by permission of the National Business Incubation Association, from NBIA's 2000 survey of incubation executives.

greater yield'. (Say was an admirer of Adam Smith and translated his *Wealth of Nations* into French.)

Classical economics, with its focus on getting the most out of existing resources, does not provide an adequate vehicle for handling the entrepreneur. Indeed, most classical economists and the modern schools (from Keynesians to Friedmanites) consign the entrepreneur to the ethereal realm of 'external forces' along with the weather, governments, pestilence and war. Although some economists recognize their existence, they simply do not accommodate entrepreneurs in their models of the economy. (You can test this for yourself by reading the index of any ten major economics textbooks. Seven will have no entry at all under the heading 'entrepreneur', one will devote a paragraph to justifying their exclusion, and the remainder will devote no more than a page to the subject.)

Joseph Schumpeter was the first major modern economist to return to Say's ideas. In *The Theory of Economic Development* (1912) he postulated that dynamic disequilibrium induced by the innovating entrepreneur, rather than optimization and the balancing of needs and resources, is the norm in a healthy economy. By this definition, most new business start-ups are not truly entrepreneurial, as many are simply poor copies of existing businesses in that they are not shifting economic resources to an area of higher productivity and greater yield. (At best they are moving sideways and at worst down and out.) But now it is clear. Who every business incubator wants as a client is an entrepreneur. What is less clear is how they can detect entrepreneurs and differentiate them from paler imitations. We will examine this when we look at different types of incubator.

DOES BUSINESS INCUBATION WORK?

This question is clearly central to anyone seriously thinking about entrusting their economic well-being to a business incubator. The same is true for a university, national or local government or venture capital provider that has not already taken the plunge and launched an incubator. Later in this book, when the benefits claimed for business incubation are examined in detail, this question will be addressed. However, even in an introduction to the history of the subject it might be considered too tantalising to leave it unanswered until much later.

There seems little doubt that some incubators give entrepreneurs a terrific deal. Those that offer subsidised rent, shared office equipment and access to tax breaks and grants are clearly a good deal in most cases. It is not so clear that the new generation of 'for profit' incubators who take anything from 5 to 50% of the equity in a new firm offer such great value. Neither is it clear that incubators offer wonderful value for their sponsoring bodies. As we will see later, few 'for profit' incubators actually make a profit and the rest may not deliver much in terms of job creation and extra value in the community providing their support. Campbell *et al.* (1988) examined 60 incubators to determine sales growth and job creation after 'graduation', when the client companies left the incubator. Some three-quarters of graduates who had been away from the nest for at least five years were tracked down. The results were hardly impressive. Their revenues on average were under $1 million and the median number of employees was nine. Reynolds and Mitler (1988) and Storey (1985) uncovered achievements of a comparable or better standard by entrepreneurs unaided by any process of incubation.

Numerous studies around the world have examined the impact of business incubators, but these studies and the literature that dominates the field comes largely from organizations representing incubators or their sponsors, and there are few serious academically credible studies. In fairness, trying to conduct such a study, with innumerable variables to control for and the difficulty of finding a control group, are daunting. Sternberg *et al.* (1997), after analysing all the available material in Germany, came to the conclusion that there is no reliable evidence to show that business incubators do any good. That observation has not, however, discouraged the Germans from getting 200 incubators launched and running, the first having been set up as late as 1983 in Berlin.

Perhaps we should not be too surprised if researchers have difficulty in proving the value of business incubation. One of the most exhaustive studies ever made into small business research (Storey 1994) examined every initiative designed to help small firms in the UK, and came to the conclusion that with one possible exception no government or local government initiative had ever represented any real value to the tax-payers concerned. Nevertheless, many firms and geographic areas have benefited greatly from attracting, stimulating and fostering an entrepreneurial community. It just might be that some aspects of the payback are too vague to assign a monetary value to. That, however doesn't mean there is no value.

Each section in this book contains examples of incubators and their clients. You can judge for yourself if you think the end result is of value or not.

Part Two

Who are the players?

The range of players in the incubator business has grown rapidly in parallel with the growth in incubators themselves. In the beginning, as we have already seen, the market was opened up by for-profit property developers such as the Manuscos and the Batavia Industrial Center in western New York. After, and in many cases alongside, the property developers, came government and quasi-government entities such as the National Science Foundation, the US Small Business Administration, and the US Department of Housing and Urban Development through its Community Development Block Grant programme, all of whom played a part in promoting or funding incubators.

Universities, colleges, venture capital providers, business angels and networking associations have all played a part in providing new incubator models, as have corporate venturers and, more recently, dedicated for-profit seed and growth capital-providing incubators.

Various attempts have been made to cluster incubators into categories in order to better understand their aims and objectives. One study (Midland Bank 1997) identified four main types.

1. *Technopoles*. Within Technopoles an incubator is part of an integrated project involving educational and or research institutions and a range of other organizations interested in creating regional growth.
2. *Sector-specific incubators*. These aim to exploit specific local resources to develop new businesses in a specific sector and so become a focus or nucleus of growth locally, perhaps giving rise to what has become known as the 'cluster effect'.
3. *General incubators*. These cater for a broad range of businesses with no specialization, although there is often a general emphasis on innovation.

4. *Building businesses*. These aim to create businesses by building appropriate management teams to exploit specific commercial opportunities as well as trying to select winners and nurture them.

A later study (PricewaterhouseCoopers 1999) came up with four rather different categories.

1. *Standalone*. An independently owned and operated incubator which does not function as a separate business unit within a larger entity.
2. *Embedded*. An incubator which operates as a business unit within a larger entity, such as a technology park, regional development organization or business enterprise centre.
3. *Networked*. An incubator which operates in formal co-operation with other incubators, either under common ownership or management or through the common provision of services or sharing of information.
4. *Virtual*. An incubator which provides a substantial proportion of support and services to clients through a network of communications from a remote location. Business clients are typically dispersed over a wide geographic area, perhaps over several continents.

Despite the beguiling simplicity of these categorizations, they are neither comprehensive nor very helpful in understanding the roles of the various players in the market.

At least five generic forms of business incubators have emerged over the past 40 years (see Figure below). These were described in some detail by Campbell *et al.* (1985), as follows:

- *Industrial incubators*. These are sponsored by quasi-government and non-profit groups. Their objectives are to create jobs by creating employers (Pacholski 1988) usually in response to job closures or general unemployment. Industrial incubators are most often found in rehabilitated factories, warehouses, schools, office buildings and similar redundant and often run down properties.
- *University-related incubators*. These set out to commercialize the science, technology and intellectual property coming out of university research. The university incubator offers new companies access to laboratories, computers, libraries and the expertise and assistance of its faculty and students. Some of these are directly sponsored by universities, but more usually they are a partnership involving a number of other interested players. (Smilor 1987).

- *For-profit property development incubators.* These incubators provide shared office and workshop/production space, together with shared services. Some property firms have gone in for upmarket developments aimed at image-conscious start-ups in the software, Internet and professional services sectors, for example, where a good address is seen as one of the keys to success. Property developers are primarily interested in rental income and real estate value growth (Nyprop 1986).
- *For-profit investment incubators.* These are often little more than a neat way for venture capital firms and business angels to have firms in their portfolio in the one location. This allows them to give them greater attention and may create synergies in their portfolio, rather as old-fashioned conglomerates sought to do, with somewhat limited success.
- *Corporate venture incubators.* This is one of the fastest growing and most successful of the incubator models. Big firms take in small firms and offer money, facilities and expertise and perhaps sales resources in return for a stake in the firm.

	For-profit property development incubators	Non-profit development corporation incubators	University incubators	For-profit investment incubators	Corporate venture incubators
Main goals	Property appreciation Maximize occupancy Sell services to tenants	Job creation Encourage entrepreneurship Diversify economic base	Faculty–industry collaboration Commercialize university research	Make substantial capital gain, quickly	Get into related markets quickly and inexpensively Have a window on related technologies
Subsidiary goals	Create investment opportunities for more property	Generate sustainable income to break-even point Use vacant premises	Exploit investment opportunities Create goodwill in local community	Develop synergies in investment portfolio	Provide entrepreneurial opportunities for staff Make money

No value-adding capability	Some value-adding capability	Considerable value-adding capability

Business incubator, by type and value-adding capacity.

In this part of the book, we will look at each significant type of player in turn.

4

The property developers

Commercial property developers used to find the balance of risk and return unattractive for spaces smaller than about 150 square metres (1500 square feet). It used to make some economic sense when buildings were old or redundant, and where redevelopment grants were available. But from the new site developer's point of view, prospective tenants for smaller spaces tend not to appear substantial, in commercial terms. Small firms find it difficult to meet the expectations of covenants, guarantees and bank references required to secure a lease, typically for a minimum of three years. In addition, given the relatively large scale of the space against a firm's early needs, moving into available spaces means that new firms must carry a significant cost overhead, particularly if the space requires fitting out.

The flexibility in space provided by incubators results from the incubator offering to lease small spaces (as small as ten square metres), commonly on short-term leases with as little as one month's notice required by either party to vacate. In addition, incubator buildings usually contain spaces in a variety of sizes so that, as a firm grows, there is the potential to relocate to a larger incubator unit. It is less common for incubators to vary the dimensions of individual units. A significant additional innovation by incubators has been the two-page lease agreement which overcomes the intimidation and legal costs inherent in negotiating a standard lease. The start-up firm finds that the terms of the lease mean that costs are avoided and, in turn, from the incubator perspective, the tenant does not develop any rights that they then might want to hold on to. This means it is easier to initiate and end relationships. If the tenant fails, it can get out quickly with minimum cost, and the incubator can get the next tenant in. Yet tenants have security while they are paying their rent. A new generation of commercial developers has found lucrative business in setting up business parks, in units as small as 600 square feet, aimed at a mixture of established image-conscious businesses and new ventures hoping that some of the kudos will rub off on them.

In many ways these are the easiest of the players in the Internet incubation business to understand. They have simply identified small and new businesses as a market segment that needs a 'product', perhaps with a modest amount of tailoring. They also realize that they are in the 'buy in bulk and sell in pieces' business. Property developers can now command much higher rental yield per square foot for small properties than they might get from tenants taking a larger space. They can also site their developments in secondary areas, confident that a small firm employing perhaps just the owner and a few employees will be less concerned about the availability of public transport, local shops and restaurants and the other amenities that a big firm might consider essential.

The biggest player in this market in the UK is MEPC which was acquired in May 2000 by Leconport Estates, a new vehicle jointly owned by GE Capital Real Estate and the BT Pension Scheme. At the end of November 2000, MEPC owned and operated 15 business parks and 5 other business space properties with an aggregate 1.14 million square metres of space, let to 673 different tenants. Eighty-two per cent of their business space assets are in the south-east, but they also have business parks in Glasgow, Liverpool and Cardiff. Their development programme has a potential end value of £576 million and they are currently investing approximately £28 million per month in building it up.

One of MEPC's earlier investments is Milton Park in Didcot, Oxfordshire, which started out as a conversion of an old ordinance factory site and now extends to nearly 3.5 million square feet with 150 tenants employing some 6000 people. Tenants in Milton Park range from high-technology firms such as Bookham Technology, Psion, and Oxford Asymmetry, to firms in the flooring sector and in plumbing. Not all of MEPC properties are as large as Milton Park. Their Axis Park close to Heathrow Airport is only a few hundred square feet and has capacity for around a dozen tenants. Nothing on MEPC's website would suggest they offer anything to their tenants other than shelter from the rain.

MEPC is only in the property business. Any other services or facilities of possible value to new and small businesses locating on an MEPC park are to a large extent accidental. Tenants in Milton Park (and, coincidentally, a few other science parks around the UK) are lucky in having Kids Unlimited as a fellow tenant. Kids Unlimited was founded in 1983 by husband-and-wife team, Jean and Stewart Pickering. After recognizing a need for comprehensive childcare provisions, they opened their first private nursery in Wilmslow, Cheshire. Just two years later, an additional nursery was built in the same grounds. The business subsequently grew out of a recognition that companies were keen to provide the benefit of childcare for their employees. Kids Unlimited now provides a complete range of services for such companies. This ranges from advising organizations on how to assess the demand for childcare among employees to providing the most appropriate solution within a given budget.

Kids Unlimited currently operates from 36 locations and has plans to open a further 20 nurseries over the next 5 years in selected locations throughout the UK. These include nurseries at Cambridge Science Park and Oxford Business Park. A much more recent entry to the property end of the business incubator market is Regus, an international organization and leading worldwide operator of business centres. They have brought together people, property and technology to provide entrepreneurs (and others) with a platform for doing business on flexible terms, whenever and wherever you require. They offer a global network of fully equipped offices and meeting rooms which can be hired for an hour, a day, a month, a year or longer, rather as you would book a hotel. Regus clients range from multinational companies (around 33% of FTSE 100 companies are, or have been, customers of Regus) to start-ups requiring flexibility and convenience at manageable cost. This blend of small and new businesses rubbing shoulders with established and famous businesses is a valuable learning and networking experience in itself.

Established by Mark Dixon, also an entrepreneur, the first Regus centre, overlooking Stephanie Square in Brussels, Belgium was opened in 1989. In 2000 Regus made its initial public offering on both NASDAQ and the London Stock Exchange. Regus is now represented in 50 countries, with a network of 360 business centres offering some 70 000 workspaces. Regus is the largest operator of business centres in Europe and the world's largest provider of 'public access' videoconferencing facilities. They employ over 2800 people worldwide.

Whilst Regus don't offer the range of advisory services or help with raising finance that, say, a university base incubator would offer, their range of facilities, technologies and services is both impressive and valuable (see Figure 4.1).

HOW SUCCESSFUL ARE THE PROPERTY DEVELOPERS?

So the property-based incubators do make money, which after all is the name of their game. MEPC's last accounts show revenue from rents of £306 million in 2000, up from £287 million in 1999. The net worth, or value of

Facilities	Technology	Services
Equipped offices • Hotdesk offices • Executive offices • Team offices • Open plan offices	**Networks** • RegusNet E1/T1 high speed Internet access • LANs: CAT 5 cabled • WANs: leased line, ISDN or Internet • ISDN lines to desktop • VPNs: encrypted connection	**Reception** • Call answering • Mail handling • Couriers • Voicemail • Guest welcome
Shared facilities • Tea and coffee points • Business service points • Reception and waiting area • Cybercafes	**Infrastructure** • CAT 5 cabling • Firewall protection services	**Secretarial** • Faxing • Photocopying • Printing • Word processing • Translations
Meeting rooms • Private lounges • Interview rooms • Meeting rooms • Boardrooms • Training rooms • Conference rooms	**Communications** • Multifunction handsets • PABX systems • Direct voicemail capability • Detailed call logger	**Concierge** • Office supplies • Catering services • Dry cleaning • Travel arrangements
Room formats • Interview • Round table	**Computing** • IT support services • Network printing	

Figure 4.1   Regus's range of facilities, technology and services.
Source: As published on their website, 10 April 2001.

the business to the shareholders, rose from £2189 million to £2346 million over the same period.

Regus, on the other hand, turned in rental revenues of £200 million in 1999 which had more than doubled to £421 million by December 2000. The value of the business to the shareholders rose from minus £24 million to a positive £202 million over the same period.

So we can say with confidence that property firms can make both profit and great shareholder value from providing space and facilities to new and small firms.

5

Government and local government

In the US, the SBA (Small Business Association) has taken the initiative in helping to fund incubators. In Israel, under the guidance and support of the Office of the Chief Scientist of the Ministry of Industry and Trade, a country-wide incubation programme was first implemented in 1991. Through these technological incubators, the government provides entrepreneurs with physical premises, financial resources, tools, professional guidance and administrative assistance, so that during their stay in the incubator 'they may turn their abstract ideas into products of proven feasibility, novelty, advantages, and necessities in the international market place'. Entrepreneurs going into an Israeli incubator could expect to receive grant aid of up to 85% of an approved budget. The government expects that at least 10% of incubator participants' equity will be made available to key staff members other than the entrepreneur themselves.

Unsurprisingly in Israel, and elsewhere (Eire, for example) the incubator programme has undertaken to provide special treatment for recent immigrant inventors, scientists and engineers. Otherwise the incubator sets no barriers as to age, duration of stay in the country, or country of origin. By January 2000, Israeli incubators had graduated 592 business projects, whilst a further 200 remained in incubators. Of the graduates, 308 (52%) have continued under their own steam whilst 284 (48%) have been discontinued. Of the 308 ongoing projects, 225 have managed to attract investments ranging from US $50 000 to US$ 27 million. The surviving companies employ about 1900 people (source: Office of the Chief Scientist, Ministry of Industry and Trade website at http://incubators.org.il).

Korea's Small and Medium Business Administration (SMBA) is following the same path. Until 1994 the country, had no incubators. By the year end, they had two and six years later, one hundred and forty-two were in operation. Plans are in place for a further 160. To date, Korea's incubators provide their tenants mainly with office space, but some also offer management, technical, marketing or legal services. Let's hope they get a more convincing result for their investment than the Israeli government would appear to have obtained.

Government and quasi-government departments rarely work alone in their efforts to stimulate the creation of business incubation facilities. But often they go to extraordinary lengths to imply collaborative partnerships in this area. Often these 'partnerships' are in reality little more than government agencies working alongside each other and transferring funds from one national pot to another, with the inevitable erosion of value brought about by layers of administration and bureaucracy. One interesting example arose in April 2001 when the launch of the Plymouth International Business Park was announced. The business park is owned by the South West of England Regional Development Agency, a relatively new government-sponsored organization. The decision to establish Regional Development Agencies (RDAs) was taken by the government in 1997 following a manifesto commitment to give more emphasis to regional development in England.

The White Paper, 'Building Partnerships for Prosperity', was launched in December 1997 and, following a period of consultation, the Regional Development Agencies Act 1998 was passed by Parliament. The aim is for the RDAs, amongst other tasks, to encourage local business development. The other partner in the business park is Priority Sites, itself a partnership of the public private variety owned by the Royal Bank of Scotland and English Partnerships. The Royal Bank of Scotland is a relatively simple business to understand, but the same cannot be said for English Partnerships. English Partnerships is another quasi-government-sponsored organization, which focuses on national and cross-regional co-ordination, where this adds value to the government's regeneration agenda and the work of the RDAs. Their initiatives are developed alongside the RDAs' economic strategies, and in support of their priorities and programmes. They aim to complement and strengthen the RDAs' work and to make their expertise available to them, through Service Level Agreements and the provision of financial and logistical support.

English Partnerships sets out to provide quality places for people to live and work and provide environmental benefit. English Partnerships aims to deliver the UK government's regeneration and development aspirations at two levels:

- by supporting an urban renaissance;
- by acting as a national force for regeneration and development.

To square the circle of government involvement, the land being used for the business park is a 33-hectare site formerly owned by the army and now redundant. So with the exception of the bank, all the parties to this venture are, in reality, directly or indirectly sponsored by the UK government.

That does not in any way invalidate the value of the park itself. The aim of the park is to send out a message of having high quality and design premises and to refurbish the region's current office and industrial stock, which is fairly old and of low quality. Without the park, the region feels that it will be at a disadvantage in trying to attract new economy and high-tech ventures. The recent success of the nearby Tamar Science Park in attracting research and development companies has provided the RDA with encouragement. That science park has already filled its incubator and is building a further 44 units.

These incubators go a little beyond the stark facilities offered by property developers. For example, the Tamar facilities include a broad range of office, business and scientific support services, and state-of-the-art leased premises on a short- or long-term basis. Tamar currently has 34 self-contained units with unit sizes ranging from 26 to 141 square metres. Sites are also available on the 28-acre Science Park for companies to develop their own facilities. Conference rooms and common rooms are available, as are reception and office services, security, janitorial services, and building maintenance. The offer of direct access to university research support and grant support is also likely to be attractive to new and growing businesses, probably more so than MEPC's lucky 'accident' in having a nursery on site.

Not all government and local government initiatives are so elaborate. Nor are they all focused on the high-tech end of the market. For example, in spring 1993, an incubator was set up in Patricksburg, Indiana, which is a town of 200 people about 50 miles south-west of Indianapolis. Unemployment in that region was 'woefully underreported', according to the Head of Economic Development for Owen County, which includes Patricksburg. The incubator's purpose was the improvement of local natural resources, such as hardwoods and wool, which they shipped out at low prices.

For instance, wool from local sheep was not 'graded' before it was taken out of the county, and so could be sold only at the lowest price. But when the Owen County incubator opened, local farmers could not only shear their own sheep, but also wash the wool, scrub it, curd it, spin it and weave it into a finished product commanding a high-grade price. Businesses were set up in the incubator to provide these services and the local economy got a much needed shot in the arm.

People without a high-school education who had been displaced from agricultural jobs were trained to grade wool. The incubator project provided them with training and a salary, and then with a skilled manufacturing job.

This experience has been replicated many times across the US and elsewhere, as the example below illustrates. Often the attraction of a rural incubator has been little more than having affordable space and available labour, commodities in short supply in cities.

A couple who moved their business from their house into the Indiana County Small Business Incubator did so because 'moving the firm to the apparel centre of New York City would have devoured their earnings'. There they opened a small factory and hired 15 trained seamstresses from the area who had been unemployed for months. Since the move, the firm has grown a sound 20% per year. The proprietors claimed 'We never could have done this the way we have done it, or as successfully, without the incubator'.

HOW SUCCESSFUL HAS GOVERNMENT BEEN?

So have these government-sponsored incubators been the unqualified success that the above small-business proprietor undoubtedly thinks they have?

One study (Roper 1999) of the success of the Israeli incubation project is not too encouraging. He concluded that whilst 'the Israeli incubator programme is a bold and very well funded attempt to address a specific issue (the need for the Israeli economy to absorb and exploit the skills of immigrant scientists and engineers), the evidence to date provides little conclusive proof of the value added or cost-effectiveness of the programme either as a means of promoting high-tech start-ups, immigrant absorbtion or local economic development.' The failure rate of 48% was seen as being higher than comparable figures for small firms generally. For example, in Europe (European Observatory for SMEs 1997) the average closure rate for the first five years was nearer 40%.

The cost per job created was $56 000 allowing for the failure rate and assuming the repayment of grants by successful companies. However, the average cost per new job created in Ireland was only $23 000 and the cost per job from the activities of Scottish Enterprise was a third of that figure (Jackson 1998). In a study on the effectiveness of US incubators (Sherman 1999), the conclusion was reached that 'consistent with past research, we found some evidence that incubators do create jobs, but that many of these jobs tend to be unstable. There is also the question of how many of these jobs are net additions to the community versus substitutes for other business that are not in the incubator.' The researchers did, however, conclude that a more realistic outcome of incubators was to improve the chances of survival and growth rate of start-up firms. They found evidence that firms in incubators had a much lower failure rate compared to the national average. That was not the experience in Israel, for example, and the author of the US study qualified his work with this paragraph:

> The research that has been completed to date in this area has limited value because no one has been able to develop a control group of 'truly' comparable firms that did not participate in the incubation programme. Until we can compare treated firms with non-treated firms, major questions concerning incubation effectiveness will continue to exist.

In Australia a study (PricewaterhouseCoopers 1999) of the 72 business incubators that had received support at national or local government level (State and Commonwealth), whilst not exactly damning, concluded that the incubators had a long way to go to deliver a satisfactory return on their investment:

> The performance of a significant proportion of incubators funded by the Commonwealth government has, to date, been mixed, and steps need to be taken as a matter of priority to remedy existing deficiencies in the administration of the programme and to increase its effectiveness against the outcomes sought.

Between them, government agencies contributed A\$ 40 million, which was over 68% of all the funds required to set up and run the incubators. But even after being in business for five years, over half the incubators claimed they would not be able to run without continued support. Rental income accounted for the balance of incubator funding, whilst corporate sponsorship accounted for just 4%.

6

The academics

Universities have been at the forefront of developing business incubators. By the early 1980s, several hundred campus-based incubators were in operation. A thumbnail sketch of two of these will set the scene for the way events were shaped in the US. Dr Sam Chauncey, a former top administrator at Yale University, persuaded the Olin Company to donate a vacant small arms factory to Yale in 1982. He raised a million dollars from the city, the state and from private sources to remodel the factory into office and work spaces. Within five years he had incubated over 100 companies involved in a broad spectrum of activities, and created 500 jobs. Members of the Yale faculty were involved with many of the businesses.

Also in 1982, the Utah Innovation Center was launched on the back of a National Science Foundation (NSF) grant. A real estate partnership was created to construct a 77 000 square foot building in the university's research park and a broad array of services were offered to clients in return for equity stakes. An independent venture capital firm and a leasing firm became part of the Center and provided those services to incubator clients.

By the time the Yale and Utah incubators were operational, there were few university incubators in the UK or elsewhere for that matter. One exception is the Cambridge Science Park. The development of the science park at Cambridge is a useful illustration of how the process of stimulating new enterprises in general, and business incubation in particular, is undertaken by universities. However, it has to be kept in mind that Cambridge was fairly late into the game. Stanford and a score of other universities had begun such initiatives long before Cambridge had even applied for planning consent.

THE CAMBRIDGE STORY

The land where the Cambridge Science Park is located, on the north-eastern edge of the city of Cambridge, has belonged to the College since its foundation by King Henry VIII in 1546. It was farmland until the Second World War when it was requisitioned by the US Army and was used to prepare vehicles and tanks for the D-day landings in Europe. After the war, the site lay largely derelict until the decision to develop it was taken in 1970.

The development was a response to a report by the Mott Committee, a special Cambridge University Committee set up under the chairmanship of Sir Nevill Mott (then Cavendish Professor of Experimental Physics) to consider an appropriate response from Cambridge to an initiative of the incoming Labour government following its election victory in 1964. Whitehall had urged UK universities to increase their contact with industry with the objective of technology transfer and also to increase the payback from investment in basic research and an expansion in higher education, in the form of new technologies.

The Mott Committee's report (1969), recommended an expansion of 'science-based industry' close to Cambridge to take maximum advantage of the concentration of scientific expertise, equipment and libraries and to increase feedback from industry into the Cambridge scientific community. Trinity College was impressed with the importance of these ideas. The College had a long tradition of scientific research and innovation dating from Newton onwards, and since it had a piece of land available, it decided to apply for planning permission to develop it as a science park, an idea born during the 1960s in the US where the first science park was established by Stanford University.

Outline planning permission was granted in October 1971 and the first company, Laser-Scan, moved on to the site in autumn 1973 following clearance and landscaping of the derelict area, conversion of the old gravel pit dug for wartime concrete standings into a lake, and construction of the first stretch of road.

The growth of the Cambridge Science Park was slow in the first five years. The science park concept was an unfamiliar one in the UK, and companies were mainly attracted to it by a desire to be close to the university's scientific research. Early on, UK subsidiaries of multinational companies started to locate there (LKB Biochrom from Sweden and US laser specialists Coherent were the first two) and the number of companies slowly grew to 25 by the end of the 1970s.

By the early 1980s, a mini-cluster of technologies and people had developed and this, plus the attractions of Cambridge as a centre for research, began to draw in more companies. A period of strong growth followed, and the Trinity Centre was opened in 1984 to provide a meeting place, meal facilities and conference rooms for the increasing number of people working at the park. More starter units and the Cambridge Innovation Centre were built to expand the range of accommodation available, and a squash court was opened in 1986.

During the 1980s, several venture capital companies opened offices on the park, including the regional office of 3i, the UK's leading venture capital company. In the second half of the decade, university academics began to bring companies to the park, encouraged by its success and also because of the breaking in the mid-1980s of BTGs monopoly (British Technology Group, the government-owned agency which had a monopoly on intellectual property originating in UK universities).

The Cambridge Science Park also began to accommodate spin-outs from existing tenant companies such as Cambridge Consultants, and saw the first collaborative venture formed by park companies – Qudos, which was founded by the university's microelectronics laboratory (which was then located at the park), Prelude Technology Investments and Cambridge Consultants.

Incubators for start-ups were established elsewhere in Cambridge. The most significant of these from the incubator industry point of view was the St. John's Innovation Centre. Located on the Innovation Park developed by St John's College, the Innovation Centre opened in 1987, providing business support and accommodation for early stage knowledge-based companies. The Centre set out to differentiate itself from other property developments in the Cambridge area by:

- providing free advice to tenants on business issues through an experienced team;
- supporting tenants and non-tenants by engaging in local programmes with university departments and government bodies to help promote the creation of wealth in the sub-region;
- helping entrepreneurs to access funding; and
- acting as a catalyst in promoting technology locally, regionally, nationally and internationally.

The Innovation Centre, as well as providing business advice to tenants, offered them flexible accommodation in leasing terms and the possibility to share communal facilities including conference rooms and a restaurant.

Centre tenants are aspirational start-up firms operating in a wide range of leading-edge technologies including neural networks, workflow management software, multimedia, fixed and mobile telecommunications, cryotechnology, biomedical imaging, lasers, chromatography, data communications, instrumentation, films and, increasingly, biotechnology. The Centre provides free networking advice to tenants and makes recommendations on:

- sources of assistance in the university;
- product innovation, design and manufacture;
- human resource management;
- the availability of bank finance, venture capital, UK and EC grants;
- marketing and public relations; and
- training and development.

The Centre can provide, on a paying basis:

- company administration (contracts of employment) and staff handbooks;
- company secretarial services (statutory reports); and
- accounting (book-keeping, budgeting).

The 1990s saw many changes in the Cambridge high-tech and science park scene. The cluster of high-tech companies in the Cambridge area grew to some 1200 companies employing around 35 000 people, and demand for space duly increased. More venture capital firms came to Cambridge and a virtuous circle was formed where more start-ups were encouraged by the proximity to funds, followed by more funds in search of enterprising ventures to back.

The life sciences sector has grown strongly and at the Cambridge Science Park is rapidly becoming the dominant technology sector. These, plus fast-growing Internet and telecoms-related companies, and the growth and success of a number of companies which have been at the park for some years, have altered the pattern of space occupation in recent years. There are now fewer but larger, better funded and more successful companies at the park and more of them are being launched on to the UK stock exchange. A new biotech venture capital fund, Merlin Ventures, has recently opened an office there. However, the origins of companies which have recently arrived is much the same as in the past: they are a mixture of spin-outs, developing new ventures from the Cambridge area and elsewhere in the UK, and UK subsidiaries of multinational companies. There are now some 70 companies at the park employing some 4000 people.

Aside from the services on offer at St. John's Innovation Centre, the science park itself is more closely modelled on the property developer model, an accusation they would no doubt deny, citing their reluctance to take just any old tenant during the recession years in the 1980s. But tenants at the Cambridge Science Park are largely just that, albeit with introductions to one of the most influential networks in the world.

CAMBRIDGE CASES

This section discusses three case examples of recent firms to locate on the science park, to give a flavour of the types of business that find the park attractive and why they do so. Some of the language used here is quite technical, so bear with me. In June 2000, Cambridge Drug Discovery, a science park company, was awarded a EU Framework V Grant for over two million Ecus to use its proprietary retroviral display library technology to select novel protease cleavage sites and clone novel proteases that may be implicated in disease states such as cancer. The award demonstrated that clients are at the cutting edge of research and are in a good position to attract international grants and international collaboration.

As well as using the retroviral display libraries, Cambridge Drug Discovery's HTS (high-throughput screening) technology was exploited to form the basis of a novel protease inhibitor screen to target proteases of therapeutic interest. The company is now developing its novel protease inhibitor screens in-house and will file new patents to protect any novel proteases they discover. In addition, Cambridge Drug Discovery has undertaken further collaborations with third parties to screen for inhibitors against proprietary protease targets.

The grant was awarded to a European consortium led by Cambridge Drug Discovery consisting of Dr Mark P. Chadwick (Cambridge Drug Discovery, Project Co-ordinator), Dr François-Loïc Cosset (INSERM, Lyon), Dr Christian Buchholz (Paul-Ehrlich Institut, Langen) and Dr Luis Alvarez-Vallina (Hospital Universitario Clinica Puerta de Hierro, Madrid).

ThirdPhase Ltd, a spin-out from Oxford University which is developing and marketing data acquisition technology for Phase III clinical trials, settled into Unit 292 at the Cambridge Science Park in March 2000. Two of the company's three founder directors, Dr Mark Holt and Dr Timothy Corbett-Clark, are former research students from Oxford's Department of Engineering Science where they were members of its Neural Networks Research Group which was headed by Professor Lionel Tarassenko, a non-executive director of ThirdPhase.

ThirdPhase is utilizing emergent technologies based around the Internet to fast-track the process of clinical trial reporting in Phase III, the most expensive part of the clinical trials programme during which drugs are rigorously tested on a statistically representative group of patients. Its unique database technology will enable pharmaceutical companies to accurately track every transaction in a clinical trial, ensuring that the data supplied to regulatory bodies is of high quality. It employs a proprietary browser technology specially built for use in clinical trial data acquisition. The company has been set up with the help of Isis Innovation, Oxford University's Technology Transfer company, and has so far been funded by private investment.

Tadpole Technology plc., now transformed into a leader in mobile computing solutions for professional markets, returned to the Cambridge Science Park in February 2000, moving into Unit 20/21. Founded in the early 1980s by George Grey, then a recent graduate of Trinity College, Tadpole was one of the earliest UK information technology companies to be listed on the London stock exchange, and has spent two previous periods at the Cambridge Science Park where it established a reputation as a centre of excellence in portable computing design. The company has notched up a number of firsts, such as the design and development of the world's first Pentium-based notebook computer and the development of the first portable workstation, the SparcBook. The descendant of the SparcBook is the recently launched UltraBooklliTM, the most powerful of its mobile workstations to date.

Have they been successful?

Academic studies have been carried out since at least the 1970s first in the US and then in Europe on the effectiveness of science parks. A pioneering study was carried out by Money (1970), who examined the success of US science parks using a qualitative assessment of success. Money's study was later complemented by studies by Danilov (1971), Baughman (1981), Minshall (1984), and Smilor and Gill (1986). In Europe, most of the early studies on science parks were carried out in the UK (Monck and Segal 1983, Moore and Spires 1983, Williams 1984, and Oakley 1984). In Scandinavia, Teräs *et al.* (1985) carried out a study to classify science parks.

Until the early 1990s research showed disappointing results for the performance of science parks, at least when measured against the most optimistic expectations (Monck *et al.* 1990, Massey *et al.* 1992, Kauranen *et al.* 1992). But even by the turn of the decade, studies (Louis *et al.* 1989) were suggesting that universities served a critical role as incubators of new products and processes. This research, for example, showed that in communities where universities received larger grants there was a significantly higher level of entrepreneurial activity than in communities receiving smaller grants. This is not exactly a revolutionary finding and nor does it say much about the efficiency with which that entreprencurial activity was bought. After all, the Israeli incubation programme stimulated lots of entrepreneurial activity, but at four times the cost of creating similar activity elsewhere. However, the Arizona Technology Incubator, for example, has absolutely no doubt that their services provide value for money. Their website contains this sentence: 'We are grateful to the many sponsors of this economic development programme and are proud to be returning $29 to our community for each $1 invested in ATI by them.'

Recently, researchers (Autio and Klofsten 1998) have both challenged the basis of earlier pessimistic research and come up with a more optimistic evaluation of the achievements that can be credited to science parks. Sarfraz Mian (1997), a professor of management at the State University of New York at Oswego, developed and tested a framework for assessing the impact of University Technology Incubators (UTBIs). He studied 4 out of a sample of 35 incubator facilities that had been running for over a year and 29 out of their 84 graduating firms. All the incubators had increased their space, one by as much as fifteen times, which suggests that the universities concerned must have seen the experiment as a success. They also all reported an enhanced public image due to favourable press coverage and site visitors. None reported adverse publicity. However none, of this sample at any rate, saw much internally stimulated enterprise amongst either students or faculty. As far as their clients were concerned, all reported growth in sales and employment, with the range of results between 45–400% for sales and 11–79% for employment. Even so, once again the researcher had to qualify his findings. 'There is no reliable way to identify a comparison group because of a strong selection bias of UTBI tenants.'

Bank Boston (1997) in a somewhat smaller and more esoteric sample, came to the firm conclusion that entrepreneurship can be fostered and encouraged in universities. The study confined itself to Massachusetts Institute of Technology (MIT), about which we will hear more later in this chapter.

THE MIT STORY

In the first national study of the economic impact of a research university, Bank Boston reported that graduates of the Massachusetts Institute of Technology have founded 4000 firms which, in 1994 alone, employed at least 1.1 million people and generated $232 billion of world sales.

If the companies founded by MIT graduates and faculty formed an independent nation, the revenues produced by the companies would make that nation the 24th largest economy in the world. That is roughly equal to a gross domestic product of $116 billion, which is a little less than the GDP of South Africa and more than the GDP of Thailand.

Within the US, the companies employed a total of 733 000 people in 1994 at more than 8500 plants and offices in the 50 states – equal to one out of every 170 jobs in the US. Eighty per cent of the jobs in the MIT-related firms are in manufacturing (compared to 16 per cent nationally), and a high percentage of products are exported.

The report said that the MIT-related companies:

> are not typical of the economy as a whole; they tend to be knowledge-based companies in software, manufacturing (electronics, biotech, instruments, machinery) or consulting (architects, business consultants, engineers). These companies have a disproportionate importance to their local economies because they usually sell to out-of-state and world markets, and because they so often represent advanced technologies.
>
> Firms in software, electronics (including instruments, semiconductors and computers) and biotech form a special subset of MIT-related companies. They are at the cutting edge of what we think of as high technology. They are more likely to be planning expansion than companies in other industries. They tend to export a higher percentage of their products, hold one or more patents, and spend more of their revenues on research and development.

In interviews, MIT graduates cited several factors at MIT which spurred them on to take the risk of starting their own companies – faculty mentors, cutting-edge technologies, entrepreneurial spirit and ideas. The study profiled seven MIT graduates who started companies in Maryland, Massachusetts, California, Washington State, Illinois and Florida. Nearly half of all company founders who responded to the MIT survey maintain significant ties to MIT and to other research universities in their area. The study also revealed that MIT graduates and faculty have been forming an average of 150 new firms per year since 1990; and in Massachusetts, the 1065 MIT-related companies represent 5% of total state employment and 10% of the state's economic base (sales in other states and the world). MIT-related firms account for about 25% of sales of all manufacturing firms and 33% of all software sales in the state.

The study also looked at employment around the nation and the world from MIT-related companies. Massachusetts firms related to MIT had world employment of 353 000; California firms had 348 000 world jobs. Other major world employers included firms in Texas (70 000); Missouri (63 000); New Jersey (48 000); Pennsylvania (41 000); and New Hampshire (35 000).

In determining the location of a new business, the 1300 entrepreneurs surveyed said that quality of life in their community, proximity to key markets and access to skilled professionals were the most important factors, followed by access to skilled labour, low business costs and access to MIT and other universities.

The companies surveyed included 220 companies based outside the US, employing 28 000 people worldwide.

Some of the earliest known MIT-related companies still active are Arthur D. Little, Inc. (founded in 1886), Stone and Webster (1889), Campbell Soup (1900) and Gillette (1901).

UK UNIVERSITIES AND INCUBATION

In a recent survey, the *Financial Times* (2001) detected signs that UK universities are leveraging their intellectual property and world-class research, but still concluded that 'most academics still have one foot firmly in the ivory tower'. The *Financial Times* survey sent questionnaires to 100 universities, and got 59 replies. For the most part, the universities responding to the FT survey are those with science parks or some form of business incubation process in place, which makes them a more useful sample than if all one hundred of those questioned had actually replied.

The survey revealed that only 258 companies had been spun out from the sample in the past three years, while start-ups accounted for a further 138 companies. A spin-out was defined as a company set up to exploit research from the university and which had raised external finance from investors. A start-up was defined as an independent company in which the university had taken a share of equity.

Universities were asked to value those stakes based on funding rounds or actual/potential revenues of the companies. The combined value was £142.9 million. While a handful of institutions, often spurred on by government-backed schemes, had spun off some highly successful companies, 10 had not spun out any companies at all, while 29 had no stakes in start-ups.

Two-thirds had either made no money or less than £1 million from their commercial activities, with 14 valuing their portfolio at between £1 million and £10 million. Only six had a portfolio worth more than £10 million.

Spin-out companies were concentrated in the information technology (IT)/telecoms arena and the industrial sector, with 32 and 33 of the universities having spin-outs in these two areas respectively. Twenty universities had ventures solely in these areas.

Twelve institutions had spun out consultancy businesses, while the London School of Economics (LSE) and Oxford were the only two to have spun out finance and banking ventures. The University of Salford had the most diversified portfolio. It had spun out 12 companies across seven sectors and had taken stakes in 32 start-up companies, valuing its stakes at £2.51 million.

University College London (UCL) also had a wide-ranging portfolio, with 17 spin-offs across 6 sectors. While it had no start-up stakes, the value of its portfolio was £11.2 million.

Another good performer was UMIST – the University of Science and Technology in Manchester. It had built up a £25 million portfolio with 15 spin-outs across 3 sectors – consultancy, IT and telecoms, and industrial applications. The main chunk came from UMIST's 30% stake in Photo-Therapeutics, which was valued at £45 million in November 2000. It also had a 2% stake in the listed Knowledge Support Systems group, a software company founded 12 years ago by Professor Madan Singh which floated in March 2000. UMIST realized £11 million from this investment.

Like UMIST, the London Business School has a venture capital arm dedicated to spin-off funding. Up to April 2001, Sussex Place Investment Management has invested £3 million of its £25 million fund in 20 companies and has made a return of £8.5 million. (We will look in Chapter 17 at Sussex Place, which incidentally is the address of the London Business School, when their incubation process is reviewed.)

Bath University's portfolio was bolstered when BlazePhotonics, a fibre-optic spin-out, raised £6 million in first round of funding in early 2001. Its portfolio is worth £21.8 million, despite having only four spin-offs and a stake in one start-up.

The University of the West of England is a new university which has done better than some of the UK's leading academic institutions, creating a portfolio valued at the time of the survey at £12 million. Instead of incubating and funding spin-outs from the outset, it encourages staff to research and develop ideas in-house, reserving the right to buy a stake once the company is off the ground. They don't waste a lot of money on hundreds of spin-outs, but they claim to 'let a lot of fires burn and see which lasts, then back that one.'

One older university outpacing the rest was Oxford. It has been spinning out companies since 1959 and estimates that its current commercial activities are worth about £2 billion. It has spun out a further 20 companies in the past 3 years – worth £9.5 million – through its commercial arm, Isis, which was founded in 1988. Oxford has a new business school which is concentrating much of its efforts on building links between the university, incubators and science parks and venture capital providers. The pinnacle of their efforts is an annual VentureFest, which we will look at in Chapter 12. Five Oxford-born companies – Oxford Asymmetry, Oxford Instruments, Oxford Molecular, Oxford GlycoScience and PowderJect Pharmaceuticals – are listed on the London Stock Exchange.

Meanwhile, Cambridge, at the heart of the silicon fen, has generated only £5 million from eight spin-outs and two start-ups in the past three years. This is because in the past the university has not taken stakes in spin-outs, focusing instead on the importance of such companies for the economy. Cambridge claims that there are billions-worth of companies that have benefited from research in the university but in which Cambridge does not have a shareholding. In future the university plans to take financial stakes in such companies. This highlights one of the difficulties in evaluating the economic impact of universities in the entrepreneurial process. As most academics don't see this as an important part of their job, they don't bother to account for it.

But science parks continue to get support. Cambridge, for example, has built a potentially lucrative tie with MIT in the form of the Cambridge-MIT Institute (CMI), which was founded in 1999 with a £68 million government grant, which may concentrate academic minds a little more on enterprise development.

The UK government, like governments the world over, is taking steps to foster an entrepreneurial ethos in universities. The latest drive to do so is through initiatives such as the Science Enterprise Challenge, which has earmarked £25 million to set up enterprise centres in UK universities. Essex, which has spun out two companies worth £1.6 million, plans to put that money towards building a science park and thus encourage even more entrepreneurial activity on the campus.

In the US, where science parks began, their worth is already being seriously questioned. Failure rates (Amirahmadi and Saff 1993) for science parks appear to be high there, with about half of all science parks eventually closing down. Few Australian science parks are credited with success (PricewaterhouseCoopers 1999).

7

The corporate venturers

The Confederation of British Industry (CBI), in its report, 'Connecting Companies', published in 1999, defines corporate venturing as: 'A formal, direct relationship, usually between a larger and an independent smaller company, in which both contribute financial, management or technical resources, sharing risks and rewards for mutual growth.' However, as my Cranfield colleague David Molian (2001) points out in his review of the literature, the British were hardly the first to appear on the corporate venturing scene.

Corporate venturing first began to appear in the US in the 1960s and 1970s. By the mid 1970s it was estimated that 25% of America's Fortune 500 companies had a corporate venturing programme (Fast 1978), and the area was sufficiently evolved for writers to be able to identify and classify different styles of corporate venturing or corporate entrepreneurship (a phrase widely in use at this time). Thus Schollhammer (1980) categorizes five different types of corporate venturing:

1. *Administrative*, which is little more than an extension of traditional research and development activity.
2. *Opportunistic*, which is based on scanning internal and external environments, usually via product champions.
3. *Acquisitive*, in which other firms' technical capabilities are acquired (either through outright purchase or through licensing).
4. *Incubative*, which takes place through semi-autonomous venture development units.
5. *Imitative*, which is essentially the creative imitation of other firms' innovations.

After decades in the doldrums, and many false starts, corporate venturing, by latching on to the fourth item in Schollhammer's list, has finally found a real purpose. Figure 7.1 gives some idea of the scale of the growth and how recent it has been.

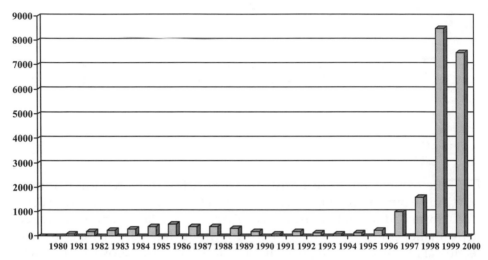

Figure 7.1   US corporate venturing investment.

WHAT'S THE IDEA BEHIND CORPORATE VENTURING?

Molian (2001) advances the theory that corporate venturing came from three big ideas, arriving in waves. This first wave was brought about by the limits to growth reached by large corporations as the expansion in consumer and industrial demand that followed the end of the Second World War levelled off. The oil price shocks of the early 1970s exacerbated these problems and, in the search for renewed growth, large businesses began to cast around for new ideas, one of which was to set up separate new ventures or corporate venturing subsidiaries charged with developing opportunities outside the firm's traditional range of products and technology. Perhaps the best known of these is the personal computing division of IBM, which took the firm out of its mainframe territory and into the territory pioneered by Apple.

However, this first wave of corporate venturing was something of a failure. One researcher, Fast (1978), maintained that nearly all of the corporate venturing activity started in the 1960s and the early 1970s was discontinued towards the end of the decade. Sykes (1986) provides a first-hand account of Exxon's disastrous foray into internal corporate venturing. Between 1970 and 1981 Exxon invested in 19 internally-generated corporate ventures. By the end of 1982 all had been written off, none having reached commercial viability. (By comparison, external Exxon investments made in syndication with venture capitalists generated a collective internal rate of return of 51% in this period.) For those corporations still active in corporate venturing, the death knell was sounded by the highly influential article published by Biggadike (1979), who argued that the typical corporate venture – construed as diversification – took a minimum of eight years in which to produce a return comparable with earnings from the firm's core business.

The second wave took place in the early to mid-1980s, in line with the return to growth of Western economies and the expansion in the independent venture capital market (Chesbrough 2000). The argument advanced by informed observers such as Drucker (1985), Moss Kanter (1985) and Pinchot (1985) was that large companies needed to acquire or reacquire the skills of innovation and entrepreneurship which had created them in the first place.

However, this second wave of corporate venturing also had its high-profile casualties. Fired by enthusiasm and, quite possibly, envy of the rate of innovative new businesses spawned by commercial rival 3M (Molian 2001), Kodak established a major corporate venturing programme in the early 1980s, which ultimately failed (see Chapter 2).

The third wave, and it remains to be seen if it will be third time lucky, started as Western economies emerged from recession in the early to mid-1990s and interest in corporate venturing resumed (Merrifield 1993). Commentators on this wave place particular emphasis on the use of venture capital firms as models for corporate venturers: first, to retain and motivate employees (Chesbrough 2000), and second, to create a window on the development of complementary technologies as in the cases of Adobe, Intel, Lucent, Sun Micro, Texas Instruments and Xerox.

Those arguing in favour of corporate venturing also claimed that it was quicker and cheaper to sponsor an entrepreneur to champion a new project or investment than it was to push them through the corporate treacle.

The biggest change in corporate venturing in this third wave is the overwhelming desire to make profit and a willingness for venture capital firms to be involved in the process from the outset. The coalescing of a number of related big firms in seeking to sponsor the birth of new enterprises has also become a major feature of this latest incarnation. In fact, corporate venturing firms have become so much like business incubators in their way of working that they have even taken to calling themselves incubators.

WHO IS IN THE GAME?

The examples in this section give a flavour of who is playing and exactly what their game is.

Hewlett-Packard's Garage Programme

Hewlett-Packard (HP) has invested $1 billion in what it calls its Garage Programme for new start-up companies. The deal for entrepreneurs is that HP will provide up to $2 million in the form of financing for start-ups of any businesses with e-potential to purchase equipment and services (mostly their own, it has to be said, but they will include some third-party products). The financing, which does not require a down-payment, runs for two years, but payments can be deferred for the first six months.

HP's Garage Programme aims to mimic the atmosphere of a start-up and thus appeal to young, ambitious professionals who are not interested in becoming part of a stale corporate culture. They can get all the thrills associated with building something new and at the same time tap the resources of an established bricks-and-mortar company, including its marketing resources and corporate clout.

The programme is based on the following principles:

- *Build it*. HP offers a wide range of technologies, including Java development offered on the NT, Linux, or HP-UX operating systems, storage, PCs, and mobile devices. A qualified team of HP's e-commerce professionals designs the best combination of infrastructure.
- *Run it*. HP facilitates $24 \times 7 \times 365$ up-time, provides security to the site and capacity for storage, and enables access to HP's Managed Web Solutions and on-Tap e-services.
- *Market it*. HP opens the door for companies on its Garage Programme to millions of corporate clients, increasing their visibility by virtue of association with the HP brand name and by offering joint press releases.
- *Finance it*. HP's own financing unit, called HP Technology Finance (HPTF), offers a portfolio of financing options, including $2 million in financing with a zero down-payment and a six-month payment deferral for basic business start-up costs.

HP stays out of the start-up selection process, a lesson the first wave of corporate venture firms failed to learn. Instead they have partnered a network of investors (including Angel Investors, Divine interVentures, Draper Fisher Jurvetson, and Redleaf Group), who oversee the selection process for them. The VCs get a great reward for carrying out the selection process. For one thing HP-supported start-ups only need a 'few hundred thousand' dollars in venture capital (VC) backing as they have already got $2 million from HP. The HP support network also includes hosting providers AboveNet Communications, Cononus, Qwest, Communications International, and

USinternetworking, and start-ups and value-added service providers (including Allegrix, Boardseat.com, Impresse, In Alysys, Mirror Image Internet, My Contraasts.com, Screaming Media.com, and Zantac.com). Part of the Garage Programme is the E-Scholarship program, which awards a combination of hardware, software, and services to the first-place winners of business plan competitions throughout the world. HP and co-sponsors allocate more than $1.5 million in products and services to 10 worldwide recipients of the scholarship. The first HP E-Scholarship award went to the MOOT Corp. in 1983 for the best new Internet business plan and venture opportunity.

One unique aspect of the HP proposition is that HP's goal is not to take equity stakes in companies – they rarely do that – but to find companies in their early stages and give them whatever they need to ensure that they become successful. By getting a foot in the door with companies which will grow exponentially, they hope to increase demand for their own products. HP has coined the term 'guerrilla growth' to describe what it hopes to achieve. If it is successful, it will help HP to generate more revenues.

IBM-Conxion Dotcom Incubator Programme

The IBM-Conxion Dotcom Incubator Programme provides up to $1 million in Internet technology and services, including servers, software, Web hosting, managed services, tools, training, and round-the-clock support for six months to selected Internet start-ups. Start-ups also get technological help from IBM partners Vignette, Servicesoft Technologies and Mercury Interactive. In this incubator programme, a start-up can choose to buy or lease the technology after a year, or it can simply walk away from the deal. Like HP, IBM uses third parties to screen the start-ups that get into its programme.

LycosLabs

Founded in 1995, Lycos, Inc. is a leading web media company and owner of the Lycos Network, one of the most visited hubs on the Internet reaching nearly one out of every two US web users. The Lycos Network is a unified set of websites, attracting a diverse audience by offering a variety of services, including leading web search and navigation resources; web community and communications services including free home page building, free web-based e-mail, clubs, chat, instant messaging; a personalized My Lycos start page; a comprehensive shopping centre featuring more than 2400 merchants; and an assortment of compelling content such as games, music, news, fun and educational information and activities for kids as well as information about investing, technology, entertainment, sports, small business, and travel. Headquartered near Boston in Waltham, Massachusetts, Lycos has moved into the incubation business in a fairly modest way (see the table on page 64 showing the investments made by corporate venture firms).

LycosLabs aims to provide a focused environment to sustain the entrepreneur and accelerate his or her path through the most critical period of the company's growth: the transition from an idea to a viable business. The LycosLabs ace in the hole is not just access to capital or even useful equipment and software. What is on offer is hands-on counselling from the same team of industry veterans that built the Lycos Network. That's the team that launched the fastest start-up in NASDAQ history and grew audience reach from 14% of web users to 50% in less than a year, attracting more than 30 million unique users every month. They built Lycos into one of the few Internet companies that has turned a profit, exceeded Wall Street's estimates for 15 quarters, and did it in advance of industry expectations. As they say on their incubator website, 'It's not enough to have Internet experience, you have to have successful Internet experience'.

Those in the incubator are provided with fully equipped office space on Lycos' headquarters campus in suburban Boston. They then remove the 'distracting, de-focusing invasions into the creative process that plague other start-ups'. In other words, they take care of their clients' everyday business needs. Finance, human resources, legal, and information technology infrastructure are managed by LycosLabs for the start-ups, providing more time and energy for valuable interaction between entrepreneurs, Lycos managers, and engineers who have successfully negotiated the Internet start-up phase themselves. The entrepreneur is surrounded by the scarcest, most valuable resources – the guidance and expertise of others from Lycos who have succeeded in building companies from scratch. At least that's the theory.

LycosLabs plans to develop several businesses per year, providing start-up funding for each company that they select after a thorough screening process. After the incubation process has been successfully completed, Lycos will be on hand to help their clients with their move to a public offering or other 'liquidity' event, as they coyly term it.

Its first investment was in Boston-based thinkingBytes Technology, Inc., a new wireless provider of applications for the Personal Digital Assistant (PDA) market (e.g. Palm Pilots and Handspring Visors). The thinkingBytes product family enables users to organize and view content from websites and corporate databases. The firm has co-located at LycosLabs offices and the companies are actively working together on developing business strategy, rapid software development, marketing, corporate development, and accelerated hiring. LycosLabs' top wireless strategist has taken a seat on the thinkingBytes board of directors.

Lycos has obviously learnt a thing or two about the value of keeping all its chicks close to the nest. They now insist that all potential incubator inmates must already be located in New England, and should be willing to move on to their campus for approximately six months in order to be considered for funding. Their website issues the firm warning: 'Please do not submit your business plan unless you fit this profile.'

THE SUN, ORACLE AND CISCO JOINT VENTURE

Sun Microsystems, Oracle and Cisco have recently combined their corporate venturing activities and concentrated their efforts into something that looks so much like a standalone business incubator that they have called it just that: 'business-incubator.com'. The initiative backed by three industry leaders whose names are synonymous with the Internet brings together what they claim is 'a unique package for people and businesses who've got great innovative ideas, products and enthusiasm – but just need to let the world know'. Their goal is to prove that the products and services from Sun, Oracle and Cisco are entirely suited to supporting new businesses and the 'incubator' is their vehicle for achieving that goal. You can see from the outset that, like the HP Garage proposition, this is mostly about selling Sun, Oracle and Cisco products, in the first instance at least.

The typical goals of their six-month corporate venture programme are to:

- design in security, scalability and 24×7 operation before 'go-live';
- prove that the proposition works;
- understand the immediate and developing IT requirements;
- identify appropriate products and skills (e.g. web designers, application developers, business consultancies & VCs);
- de-risk the technology stack for VCs, increasing willingness to fund; and
- endorsement from four leading Internet companies prepared to subsidise your start without equity or warrants.

They are trying to reduce time to market, reduce technical risk and make use of their expertise. What is on offer, in a practical sense is access to key Internet technologies – hardware, software, and network architectures, including the following:

- Sun Microsystems server – a robust and scalable Sun Microsystems server plus consultancy (80% of Internet traffic runs on Sun Microsystems);

- Oracle 8i database, development tools and consultancy (69% of the world's e-commerce sites run on Oracle technology);
- Cisco Systems computer network infrastructure enabling secure connectivity via routers and switches (80% of Internet traffic runs over Cisco Systems equipment); and
- Exodus hosting the server, protecting your business and customers with a security firewall, making sure it's on duty day and night.

Entrepreneurs are invited to sign up with business-incubator.com for six months at an initial cost of £15 000, for which they get, in effect, discounted hardware and software with some advice thrown in. And of course there is the implied endorsement of the corporate brands to consider, too. When the client is ready to leave the incubator it should have an operation that is up and running and a business plan in place. If you are not quite ready to fly the nest then the incubator team hopes to be able to identify partners with the appropriate product, skills or money to assist at your current stage of development.

Novell Inc.'s corporate venturing strategy, whilst being every bit as robust as Apple's or HP's, has taken a very different route. Novell Data Systems began life in 1979 as a computer manufacturer and maker of disk operating systems. In January 1983, Raymond J. Noorda and Safeguard Scientific, a venture capital firm, reincorporated NDSI as Novell, Inc. to design and market software and hardware used for data networks. Noorda, an experienced engineer and marketer, became president/chief executive officer. The business moved forward steadily until 1996 when, recognizing that the Internet was beginning to revolutionize the traditional network market, interim CEO John Young initiated a programme to make the company's products Internet-ready. Novell is now recognized as a leading provider of net services software that secures and powers all types of networks – intranets, the Internet and extranets, corporate and public, and wired to wireless, across all leading operating systems.

In 1997 Novell Ventures was formed to act as an in-house venture capital provider. Their goal was primarily to seek out companies that could strengthen the demand for Novell's directory-based networking technology. They generally invest between $1 million and $5 million per deal, and like to keep their stake below 20% of the company being financed. However, if the deal looks right they will invest more. For example in 1999 they put $20 million into Redleaf Group LLC, of Saratoga, California, making them the second-largest shareholder.

Novell Ventures invests in development-stage companies that have:

- demonstrated a strategic fit with Novell;
- a management team with the ability to execute in a changing market;

- at a minimum, developed a fully functional prototype networking or distributed computing software product;
- a business plan that describes a winning strategy, detailing its business model, future development, marketing, sales, production and support; and
- financials that realistically project significant market potential and return on investment.

So far, they have backed over 20 entrepreneurs. Their investments range from Caldera Systems, Inc. based in Utah, who make Linux-based business solutions, to Edgix Corp. in New York who are involved in Internet content delivery, and in California they have a stake in Oblix Inc., who develop automation software. But Novell rarely like to go in alone. In the Oblix deal they went in with VCs Patricof & Co and Lehman Brothers and fellow corporate firm Cisco Systems. Novell Ventures also invests in the funds of other VCs including those of Kleiner, Perkins, Caulfield and Byers, Accel Partners and Advent International.

WHO ELSE IS PLAYING?

Perhaps who else is *paying*, would be a more appropriate phrase. Over 200 companies have active corporate venturing programmes. General Electric, not content with being a star performer itself, is always on the look-out for new entrepreneurs to back. Recently they have backed, Pink Dot Inc., a company which provides a grocery and prepared food delivery service, and Paytrust.com., an online service for paying and receiving bills. It's not just big companies nor high-tech companies, nor those firms from the old economy that think they have lost the plot that are playing in this game. Starbucks Coffee, a successful and expanding business, has taken an interest in Cooking.com, Inc., a Californian online seller of cookware and speciality goods. United Parcel Service (UPS) has taken an equity stake in NetCel360 Ltd., a Hong Kong-based company providing Internet-based e-commerce outsourcing solutions, and Sara Lee Corporation has bought into MadeToOrder.com, a Redwood City-based online source of logo merchandising. These three examples give an interesting insight into the corporate venture firm's strategy. They have plenty of cash and expertise to offer, and in return they need an injection of something that can be in short supply as a business grows up, an event that can happen very quickly in the Internet age: innovative new business ideas, tangential to their current core business, that could become really important in the not too distant future, or new ways of delivering their core products and services. The new corporate venture firms also want much more prosaic outputs: a flow of new compliant customers and a share of what they see as the spoils that accrue to venture capital firms operating in the same arena.

Dow Chemical, rather than start its own incubation programme, formed a partnership with campsix, a San Fransisco-based incubator, in October 2000. For Dow the attraction was two-fold: speed and Internet expertise. campsix had the incubator infrastructure in place, and workspace along with legal, financial, recruiting, engineering and marketing services. Dow spent a year looking internally for e-business ideas and dusting down musty patents generated from their research before deciding on this partnership approach. The joint venture is called iVenturi, and it raised $8 million in its first financing round. No doubt the Dow name helped.

The list below, drawn from David Molian's research (2001) and companies' own public statements, gives an idea of the scale of financial involvement of firms in the incubation sector. (Figures shown in the list are in millions of dollars.)

- Electronic Data Systems   1500
- Andersen Consulting   1000
- PricewaterhouseCoopers   500
- Time Warner, Inc.   500
- Intel Corporation   450
- Cisco Systems   450
- Microsoft   450
- Softbank   350
- News Corporation   300
- Comcast Corporation   250
- Unilever   200
- Sun Microsystems   200
- Novell, Inc.   170
- TransCosmos, Inc.   150
- Cambridge Technology Partners 100
- Adobe   100
- Cannon   100
- Oracle   100
- Readers Digest   100
- Lycos   80
- InfoSpace.com, Inc.   30
- Broadvision, Inc.   10
- Cognex Corp.   10
- Fujisawa Pharmaceutical Co.   5

THE 64 MILLION DOLLAR QUESTION

Corporate venture firms have, according to various industry watchers including the Corporate Venturing Report, a magazine published by Asset Alternatives, about $6400 million riding on this industry. The first two waves of corporate venture investments proved to be something of a dead duck, rather than a powerful way to stimulate new ventures and make money at the same time. Will the third wave be anymore successful? The results so far are mixed rather than conclusive. Both Apple and Cisco have had good results, raising over $3 billion from their combined IPOs of corporate venture investments.

Apple, in particular, seemed an unlikely entrant to the incubation business. After years of confusing its customers with multiple product lines, it has produced a clear strategy based on three ranges; the consumer level iMac, the professional-level G4 and the laptop PowerBook lines. However, to keep its eye on other developments whilst keeping its management team focused on the core business, it took a $15 million stake in Akamai Technologies, the firm whose software tries to keep the web running smoothly even under extra-high traffic demands. Their stake is now worth over a billion dollars, some 10% of Apple's own value, and some would argue it might even one day be a more valuable proposition than Apple itself.

The $550 million invested by Federal Express in 'Zapmail', however, was a stunning corporate venturing failure. Zapmail (basically fax machines at Federal Express offices) reflected FedEx's mistaken belief that customers would eventually abandon overnight delivery of documents in favour of electronic document transfer. Zapmail lost millions and nearly bankrupted FedEx, who were criticized for backing the venture far too long after the marketplace had rejected the concept. Many venture capital firms claim that corporate firms always tend to base their judgements on 'strategic' value, which inevitably will lead to firms reinforcing failure. They become attached to their fledglings, unlike VCs who simply take a hard financial view to second rounds of financing. It's obviously harder to pull the plug on a firm that is tied in closely to your own. It is in order to avoid that type of problem that Novell keeps their product and operations management out of discussions on company valuations, and leaves that to the VCs.

But whatever the results, big businesses seem compelled to keep trying to find the entrepreneurial elixir. Foster and Kaplan (2001) have built a database of 1008 US companies in 15 industries and looked at their performance between 1962 and 1998. Not one of these companies outperformed the market over this period. In fact, the longer the companies survived the worse their shares performed.

The authors claim that their research demonstrates that only two types of company can outperform the market. These are new companies and companies in new industries. These findings will indubitably give the corporate venture incubation process a further shot in the arm, which has to be good news for would-be business starters in search of a free or nearly free ride.

However, the research finding that Foster and Kaplan seem most enthusiastic about is that companies that are likely to do the best are not those that put stock market performance first. The ones that put employees and the community ahead of investors will win every time.

This last point may be one that the most prominent corporate venturing companies have yet to learn. The table below lists some big companies who announced equally big job cuts in 2001. The list has been culled from newspapers and company statements, and is by no means comprehensive. If you now compare that list with those companies heavily involved in corporate venture activities, you will see an uncomfortable overlap of names.

General Electric	**75 000**
Daimler Chrysler	26 000
Procter & Gamble	22 000
Nortel	**21 150**
Lucent	16 000
Motorola	11 000
WorldCom	10 000
Sara Lee	**7000**
Delphi	7000
J.C. Penny	5300
Cisco Systems	**5000**
Intel	**5000**
PricewaterhouseCoopers	**1000**

(**Bold type** denotes those companies with corporate venturing activities referred to in this book.)

In the UK, corporate venturing is still small beer. But it appears to be providing some encouraging results. Research data is still thin, when compared with the US experience. Confirmation of the low rate of penetration of corporate venturing in the UK was provided by the CBI-sponsored study (CBI 1999), which asserted that a worryingly small proportion of multi-nationals were undertaking such activities in the UK. This analysis was begun by sampling the population of SMEs in industries believed to be more prone to small-firm/big-firm relationships. The survey elicited 98 responses from small firms in the pharmaceutical, biotechnology, IT, telecommunications and engineering sectors. Fifty-nine per cent were involved in alliances of various types, the mean turnover of the small firms being £2 million and that of their corporate partners £10 million. Thirty-six of the SMEs and their partnering firms were subsequently interviewed in depth, and a total of 135 alliances of various types was identified.

The encouraging news from the survey was that 80% of the alliances reviewed were operating successfully, with many claimed to have exceeded both parties' expectations. Large firms' reasons for backing these small firms were predominantly linked to the 'softer' issues of finding new ideas, gaining access to the right people and skills, and transplanting into the core business an entrepreneurial culture. For smaller firms, the motives were more concrete, concerned with access to sales and distribution resources, collaboration on commercialization and research, and access to complementary products and processes. In terms of 'hard' results, 70% of the SMEs claimed a growth in turnover as a direct consequence of the alliance (the mean increase being £600 000) and 64% had become more profitable. Forty-nine per cent of all the businesses interviewed had gone on to seek additional joint venture alliances on the strength of their first experience.

From the larger firms with experience in corporate venturing, the study elicited the following investment criteria. They preferred:

- developed technologies over concepts;
- enabling technologies over finished products; and
- management teams over individual entrepreneurs.

This last point gives a valuable pointer to would-be entrepreneurs seeking big-company support in getting their venture off the ground. Get a team together and look less like a one-man band and more like a corporation from the outset. But it is not only technology firms that are involved in corporate venturing, nor is it only start-ups that they want to get involved with. Bass Hotels and Resorts, which has 2800 hotels worldwide under the Intercontinental, Crowne Plaza, Holiday Inn, Express by Holiday Inn, and Staybridge Suites brands, took a stake in lastminute.com (see case example below). Bass also forged a strategic alliance with Site59.com, a US-based company in the same line of business as lastminute.com. Their CEO, Michelle Peluso, had formerly worked as a manager for the Boston Consulting Group (BCG), a global consulting firm known for designing e-commerce strategies for companies and incubating start-up Internet companies. She left to become a White House fellow and was working as a Senior Advisor to the Secretary of Labor, Alexis Herman, when BCG proposed the concept for Site59.com and asked her to lead the company.

lastminute.com

Just a couple of months after its UK listing, with its shares trading at 60% below its March 2000 flotation price, lastminute.com was under new management. The story behind the birth of the new business had been breathlessly peddled around London in a burst of PR activity, aided by a photogenic founder, only a few weeks prior to this. This story turned turnover of under £200 000 per year into a business that was eventually, however temporarily, valued at £400 million.

The idea behind lastminute.com belongs to Brent Hoberman, the less visible of the founders. After a lifetime (aged 31) of trying to book hotels, restaurants and air tickets at the last minute – and being frequently disappointed – he decided that he, and others like him, deserved a better deal. After all, he reasoned, there were millions of empty hotel beds, unfilled restaurants and spare seats on aeroplanes. All that was needed was for the link to be made. Hoberman, who lives in Notting Hill, London, met his co-founder Martha Lane Fox whilst they were both working at Spectrum, a management consultancy.

Fox was not convinced by the idea, nor by the idea of starting a business, and moved on to Carlton to work on its pay-TV channels. Hoberman had helped to launch the British Internet Auction House, qxl.com, and whilst he never empathized with that business, was convinced about Lastminute's concept. After twisting Fox's arm quite hard, they set out to put a business proposal together.

Both the entrepreneurs come from privileged backgrounds – Oxford for both of them, and Eton and Westminster respectively. Both had entrepreneurial families – Hoberman's grandfather started with one shop in South Africa and built up a chain of 250 shops. He claims to have always wanted to be an entrepreneur.

Fox's late grandfather started the upmarket estate agents Lane Fox, and her cousin and aunt are well-established interior decorators in London. Her ambitions leaned more towards being an actress, as her performance in the run-up to Lastminute's UK listing revealed. Despite this privileged background, both had to work hard in getting their plans accepted. Her network helped, but in the end it was learning to write a business plan at Spectrum, and Brent being brilliant at Excel, that really counted.

Both founders have worked hard, putting in long hours and lots of travel, but nothing prepared either of them for the transition from a Notting Hill kitchen table to a stock market player in two years. By the time the company had 700 000 customers and 200 employees, it was becoming clear that the founders needed help. Fox was quoted as returning from Paris having received a shock: Lastminute's Paris office had a staff of 30, whereas when she went there a few weeks earlier there were only 10 people in the office.

On 16 April 2000 the financial pages of London newspapers carried this comment:

> New blood in at Lastminute: Troubled Internet company lastminute.com will announce the appointment of a new tier of senior management to run the business this week. Shares in lastminute.com, founded by Brent Hoberman and Martha Lane Fox, fell to an all-time low on Friday and are now trading at 60% below last month's offer price. The company is bringing in three senior executives to strengthen the management of the business both in the UK and

internationally. Charles McKee has been appointed executive vice-president, David Kelly joins to head the UK team and Helen Baker joins as head of supply for the UK. McKee, who will be responsible for international expansion, was a general manager at Virgin Atlantic Airways with responsibility for global distribution. He joined Virgin in 1992 as vice-president for Asia and the Pacific before being appointed senior vice-president for North America. Kelly, who will be responsible for the day-to-day running of the last-minute.com business in the UK, was the director of customer service at Amazon.co.uk. Baker will work with existing suppliers in the UK.

'These appointments add a great deal of depth to our management team, bolstering the existing senior expertise and freeing up the time of other senior executives to focus on their core roles', said Brent Hoberman, chief executive of lastminute.com.

The dramatic fall in the share price has been embarrassing for both last-minute.com and investment bank Morgan Stanley, which raised the top of the price range on the eve of the flotation. Lastminute was a hugely important deal for Morgan Stanley because, over the preceding year, it had missed out on almost all of the major European Internet flotations. But what was embarrassing for Morgan Stanley was a buying opportunity for Bass, who gained an outlet for 'distressed inventory', as unsold bedrooms are rather quaintly referred to in the trade, as well as an insight into a whole new way of doing business. Intel also have a stake in Lastminute, but whether anyone other than perhaps the Bass and Lastminute's other strategic suppliers will make any money from this investment remains to be seen. Figure 7.2 shows the fall and fall of lastminute.com's share price.

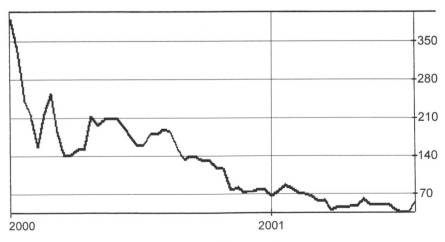

Figure 7.2   lastminute.com's share price (in pence).

8

The entrepreneurs

Aside from the property developers there is another, much more recent, type of business incubator, whose only goal is to make money. Universities want opportunities for their students and faculty, governments want jobs for their voters, and corporate venture firms want to reinvigorate their aging corporate bodies. The NBIA carried out a survey of its for profit members, to which 67 replied, and asked them, amongst other questions, 'From where do you expect to receive your primary source of return?' Only 13% listed rent and other service fees as being a major income source. The rest saw their return as being largely equity-based. There is a view that claims recent ownership of the for-profit incubation process for the pioneers of the likes of idealab!, Brainspark and Oxygen. Whilst these high-profile dotcom factories have certainly captured the media's attention, they were not the first in the field. In the 1980s, Control Data Corporation launched a number of 'Business and Technology Centres' to recruit new businesses so that investments could be made in them. Loren Shultz's 'Technology Centres International' were alongside them as the true pioneers in this arena (Campbell *et al*. 1985). But the original model has been given new zest and a number of new twists. Venture capital firms, business angels, accountancy firms, management consultants and a few entrepreneurs that have failed to make their mark anywhere else have jumped on the bandwagon. The bandwagon itself was propelled into motion by the Internet feeding frenzy indulged in by investors, taking the NASDAQ to new highs and lows in the three years to 2001. Each of the participants has a slightly different agenda and has something different to offer their prospective incubator clients.

THE IDEALAB! STORY

The highest-profile of the investment incubator models is that created by successful and not so successful entrepreneurs, and the most high profile of those was idealab!

No one doubts that Bill Gross, idealab!'s founder, is an entrepreneur. But the jury is still out as to whether his version of business incubation will deliver lasting results. In high school, Gross started Solar Devices, a firm which sold plans and kits for solar energy products. In college at the California Institute of Technology, he patented a new loudspeaker design and formed GNP Loudspeakers, Inc. After graduating, Gross and his brother Larry started GNP Development, Inc., which made a natural language product for Lotus 1-2-3 with the futuristic-sounding name of 'HAL'. In 1995, Lotus Development Corporation acquired GNP. From February 1986 to March 1991, he was a software developer at Lotus Development. In 1991 he started Knowledge Adventure (KA), an educational software publisher that was eventually sold to Havas Vivendi.

In 1994, Knowledge Adventure decided to spin out a new venture – Worlds, Inc. – and founder Bill Gross expected the worst (Gross 1998). He had argued with the board that it was in KA's best interests to maintain a controlling ownership stake in Worlds, whose powerful new software technology had enormous revenue potential. But the board prevailed, and KA took only a 20% ownership in the new company, giving the rest to Worlds' employees. Within a year, the company's performance had surpassed all expectations, and instead of owning 80% of a $5 million business, KA owned 20% of a $77 million business. The arithmetic may have been counter-intuitive, but the lesson was clear. When KA let go of Worlds and gave its employees near total ownership, the company unleashed a new level of employee performance. That, in turn, led to the creation of economic value that more than made up for the equity KA had surrendered. So compelling was this 'new math of ownership' that Gross founded a new company, idealab!, on this principle. The company, which develops ideas for Internet-based businesses and seeds the most promising ones, takes no more than a 49% equity stake in the new ventures and gives at least 1% of ownership to each employee. For Gross, this radical approach to ownership was the key to inspiring stellar performances. In part, employee-owners are motivated by their potential to earn great financial rewards. But the drama of ownership, he argues, is even more important. In that drama, employees become personally involved in the struggle to outdo the competition and emerge victorious.

In addition to capital, idealab! provides a full range of resources to infuse start-up companies with the development strategies and financial support needed to rapidly introduce innovative products and services.

Resources include office space and the accompanying network infrastructure, consulting and services relating to development and technology, graphic design, marketing, competitive research, legal, accounting and business development support and services. idealab! also provides advice on strategy, branding, and corporate structure.

idealab!'s mission is 'to develop individual ideas into highly focused and successful Internet businesses'. idealab! leaders believe that to succeed in the dynamic Internet market, companies must achieve a rapid speed of execution by tapping the services, support and knowledge of individuals and organizations that have extensive experience in starting Internet companies. idealab! combines the best elements of a small and nimble company with the financial strength and wisdom of a much larger organization – sharing these benefits with its operating companies: 'Each business in our integrated, collaborative network of companies uses the Internet to satisfy an unmet market need.'

In March 2000, Gross raised $1 billion in a financing round from major companies worldwide. Investors included BancBoston Capital, Dell Computer Corporation, Hikari Tsushin, Ignition Corp., Investor AB, advised by its affiliate Investor Growth Capital, NY, Kline Hawkes & Co., Petersen Properties, Sumitomo Corporation, T. Rowe Price Associates, Inc., 24/7 Media and entities affiliated with Moore Capital Management, Inc. But by 1998 there were signs that this new model for incubation still had some bugs to iron out. Shopping.com, an idealab! incubator client, went public at the end of 1997 in an $8 million offering underwritten by California investment bank Waldron & Company. Within months the Securities and Exchange Commission had suspended trading in the stock amid allegations of price manipulation. No one suggested that Gross was involved in 'jiggering' the firm's stock. Nonetheless, as chairman of Shopping.com's board and as the company's initial financial backer, some of the press fallout for the chain of events that had resulted in such a fiasco inevitably landed on him.

In October 2000, amid the general NASDAQ consternation with technology stocks, idealab! announced that the company would postpone its initial public offering and focus on new company creation. The company statement signed off under Bill Gross's name as chairman and chief executive officer of idealab! read:

> Over the past several months, we have seen dramatic shifts in the market and determined that it is in the best interests of the company, its employees and investors that we not proceed with the offering during this volatile time. We will continue to do what we have always done best, build great companies. We move forward with an even greater emphasis on creating innovative businesses that deliver sustainable, profitable growth over the long term.

'We have a solid financial foundation. We understand the measurements and criteria that the public markets demand. idealab! companies are based on great ideas, sound business models and will endure as they create value for our employees and investors. When the time is right, we will return to the public markets,' said Gross.

Unfortunately for idealab!, their 'solid financial foundation' has taken a few high-profile knocks since then. Among the first of idealab!'s companies to fold was beauty e-tailer Eve.com., which was founded in June 1999. 'We will be closing our doors on Friday, October 20 (2000)' the posting on their website read. 'We hope that shopping with us has been a "beautiful" experience. Thanks for your support.' Customers who placed orders after 8 am on Friday will not have their orders shipped, Eve.com said. Orders placed earlier will be shipped 'subject to availability of stock.'

Over the last months of its life, the company had improved its gross margins and reduced costs to the point that Eve delivered orders profitably. However, this was not enough to overcome the lack of sufficient scale. After examining every alternative, the company regretfully concluded that liquidation was the only viable option.

More damaging publicity came with eToys, another idealab! incubator firm who had to file for Chapter 11 bankruptcy in March 2001. eToys launched its initial public offering in May 1999, raising $166 million at a price of $20 per share. By October of that year, the stock had hit a high of $84.25. Over Christmas of 1999, eToys drew more customers than the websites of Toys 'R' Us and Amazon.com, according to industry traffic figures. By December, however, the company told Wall Street its revenues would fall dramatically *short* of expectations. At the time, it said it had begun looking into selling the company or its assets. eToys sold its BabyCenter.com website to Johnson & Johnson for $10 million; not much of a return on the $166 million raised only a few months earlier.

idealab!'s regional incubators have not fared much better. In February 2001 the Boston 'office' of idealab! announced that its one investment, Refer.com, had shut down. Visitors to Refer.com's website were greeted with a message saying that the company had been unable to raise additional venture funding and had ceased operations. At its peak the previous year, Refer.com had 35 employees. Over its last few weeks as it wound down the business, it had been operating with just five. Refer.com created a site where, for a fee, employers posted jobs and anyone who successfully referred a friend placed in a job could earn a referral bonus of $1000 or more. But employers shied away from the site, in part because of the difficulties involved in running an external recruitment programme. Programmes relying on company outsiders can attract large numbers of referrals, which can be cumbersome to process. And employers have no relationship with those making the references, a departure from most hiring processes, which are based on trust in the referrer.

idealab! has had its successes but they would appear to have gone into hibernation, along with other similar ventures. The press release in October 2000 announcing the postponement of its IPO was the last to be listed on idealab!'s website (as of 15 April 2001).

Gross was not the only entrepreneur to turn his hand to incubation. The next section will discuss more entrepreneurs who did the same thing.

REACH FOR YOUR CHEQUE BOOK!

'Reach' was created in March 1999 by two successful technology entrepreneurs, Frank Selldorff, founder of Breakaway Solutions (NASDAQ: BWAY) and Peter Cowie, founder of Charter Systems. It later merged with the BISYS Group (NASDAQ: BSYS). The Reach Partner Company management team includes more than 40 professionals with 'deep' functional expertise who are actively involved in managing and launching Reach Companies. The team is backed by an advisory board of technology and business leaders.

Reach creates and launches leading IT companies. Client companies are created by applying strong entrepreneurial expertise and a 'hands-on suite' of management talent to ideas conceived from deep industry experience. Reach claim their approach to business creation and launch dramatically accelerates the growth of valuable new businesses.

Eleven companies have been created to date. Two companies have been launched, of which two have received external funding. They claim to have six more poised for the first institutional round of financing, and the remainder are in pre-launch stages.

The incubator provides all the strategic and infrastructure services companies need to move at Internet speed. Their team of Internet business and technology experts take an active role, providing both the insight and the effort required from the start. Reach claims its environment is so complete that they are capable of launching businesses with nothing more than an idea – they can provide the complete team.

There is little evidence that providing teams to exploit someone else's entrepreneurial concept is a winning formula. This concept is one that has been applied with little success by development agencies in economically poorer regions of advanced economies. For example, the then Highlands and Islands Development Board (HIDB) in Scotland tried in the mid 1980s to form village co-operatives to develop salmon, a natural resource, into a farming business. This idea came from HIDB, as did the funding, management development, business processes and other expertise. All the implanted team had to do was run it, and they had the greatest difficulty in getting motivated, because it was not their idea in the first place.

Brainshark, founded in 1999, was Reach's first graduating incubator client. Their product Enterprise 'optimizes collaboration using on-demand content delivery of time-critical corporate information such as new product introductions, corporate training, sales channel communications, and corporate communications.' Brainshark Enterprise is designed for users to self-author, publish, edit, and distribute content instantly. A basic knowledge of PowerPoint, the most ubiquitous presentation software and the telephone is all that is required. To view content on Brainshark, all users need is an Internet browser and a standard audio player such as RealPlayer® or Windows Media Player. When you have finished making a PowerPoint presentation, simply upload the file to the Brainshark platform. After the presentation is uploaded, the author is randomly assigned a phone number and secure password. Using any type of phone (land line, cellphone, Voice over Internet Protocol (VoIP) etc.) the author calls the Brainshark Audio Presentation Centre to add an interactive voice component to their presentation. The author then records audio to accompany each slide using a voicemail-type phone menu. When the author is satisfied with the presentation, he simply hangs up the phone and the presentation is immediately available. At that point a built-in offline feedback mechanism is activated, allowing the audience to interact one-on-one with the expert who authored the communication.

The product's back-end technology then automatically creates reusable 'knowledge assets' by indexing and cataloguing each slide/audio pair in the presentation. These assets are then added to a searchable database so they can be edited and reused to quickly author future 'rich-media' presentations. In addition, the author can optionally specify a list of authorized viewers and Brainshark Enterprise will automatically create random passwords for each user. The author can then receive reports from Brainshark Enterprise indicating specific details about when and which slides of the presentation have been viewed by each viewer, or group of viewers.

Whilst the NASDAQ was rising, the number of new incubators also rocketed. Across the Atlantic Ocean entrepreneurs took to this new form of midwifery with equal enthusiasm. A typical example was Brainspark, which was set up by three former investment bankers, Stewart Dodd, Richard Davidson and Noah Freedman, from WestLB Panamure. They set up in May 1999 and floated on London's Alternative Investment Market (AIM) soon afterwards. At one point the business was valued at £155 million, on the back of little more than an idea. Brainspark looks to take a 25% stake and in return helps with seed capital of up to £1 million as well as providing help, business advice and networking opportunities. Regular Thursday evening gatherings on their roof terrace in London's fashionable Clerkenwell district munching salami rolls, drinking Bud and listening to music pumping out from loudspeakers was all part of the 'chance to meet great minds'. At one point Davidson, aged just 25, and his colleagues were managing 308 people in a facility that had grown from 500 square feet to 20 000 square feet in little more than 12 months. Over the same period they drew 16 businesses into their incubator. But within a year the buzz had reduced to barely a murmur. Brainspark used to have 30 applicants a day for places in its incubator. That dropped to 20, then 10 and is now a trickle, as the illusion that every man and his dog can become an Internet entrepreneur has faded from the public consciousness.

RUNNING ON EMPTY

Oxygen provides a clear illustration of the dangers entrepreneurs face when they set up incubators. Little of the early magic that made the protagonists' names appears to have rubbed off on their clients, and they have little to show in their balance sheets for the millions spent.

Oxygen was also founded in early 1999 by a group of high-profile media and City investors, including Rupert Murdoch's daughter Elizabeth, PR guru Matthew Freud and Michael Edelson, all of whom have a significant interest in new media and technology. The company was introduced to the Alternative Investment Market of the London stock exchange on 4 February 2000 via a placing. Operational locations currently include London, Cambridge and Manchester. Oxygen specializes in early-stage new media and technology ventures offering both capital and services which include a web development team, software developers, PR, marketing, legal advice and accounting. Capital and services are provided in return for equity.

Funding from Oxygen Holdings gives fledgling companies room to breathe. Targeting nascent web-based content and e-commerce concerns, they set out to provide cash, technical support, and management consulting mainly to young entrepreneurs and students.

Oxygen's current investment portfolio is valued in their latest accounts at £5 030 000, and this comprises investments in 14 companies including Black Book Publishing Limited ('Crushguide') which publishes online guides to going out in major cities, Digiguide, a TV listing programme operating both off- and online, Global Remainders (a business-to-business market exchange), Studylink (an online clearing system), and n-Game, which provides multiplay games for cross-platform gaming in the mobile Internet and interactive television sectors.

The financial facts make sorry reading, but to be fair a score of other entrepreneur-led incubators on both sides of the Atlantic have done little better.

- Oxygen raised £7.86 million after expenses during the period through a combination of its flotation on 4 February 2000 and a subsequent placing in March 2000, of which £5.6 million was used for investments. Investments sold during the period generated proceeds of £328 000 and resulted in a net profit on disposal of £106 000.
- Oxygen made a loss of £4 472 000 during the period (as per their accounts of 31 March 2001). This comprises provisions made against the cost of certain investments (£1 751 000), a charge for the impairment of goodwill which arose on the acquisition of Oxygen Partners Limited (£2 270 000) and losses from ongoing activities (£451 000).
- Cash resources as at 30 March 2001 were down to £550 000.

Curiously, the management have established HotSpot Network with partners in Finland and Israel to 'provide the necessary platform to ensure Oxygen continues to have exposure to global investment opportunities in compatible funds and individual companies.' They also have a stake in UniversiRed.com, a Latin-American vertical portal for college students in Argentina, providing free academic resources, lifestyle content and communication tools.

Oxygen's mix of clients and continents would challenge the abilities of a global giant company from the old economy to manage it successfully. It can be no great surprise to see that its small team have their hands rather more than full.

Despite its sickly share price (see Figure 8.1) and indifferent financial performance, Oxygen has successfully floated off three of its incubated companies on the AIM (Alternative Investment Market). One of Oxygen's 'successes', E-Millionaire show is in the incubation business itself, in a manner of speaking. They run a 'game show' in which they claim to be the only show on television to give away £2 million in venture capital funding. Typically they draw in 7000 applicants for each prize award. A shortlist of entrepreneurs do their stuff on camera and the viewers select the winner. Entrants get some help in putting together a business plan using software downloaded from the show's website. They also expect to get visibility to draw in would-be partners, investors, suppliers and perhaps even clients, for some entrants as well as for the winners themselves.

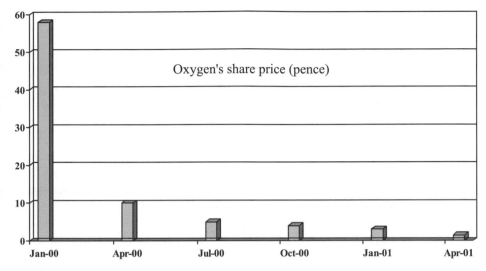

Figure 8.1   Running out of Oxygen?

IF AT FIRST YOU DON'T SUCCEED . . .

In 1998, Las Vegas-based Jackpot Enterprises was a $100 million a year operator of slot machines on the acquisition trail. They were one of the largest gaming machine operators in Nevada. Operating out of headquarters in Las Vegas and a small branch office in Reno, Jackpot's 700 employees placed and maintained more than 4000 slot machines and video poker machines in approximately 400 locations throughout the state. That year, they tried to buy a Canadian competitor, but the deal failed to materialize. The following year Jackpot came close to acquiring casino operator Players, but was beaten to it by another player in the market, Harrah's. With Jackpot's share price stuck at around $8 a share the company, in common with many old economy operators, felt it was going nowhere.

Jackpot's chairman and co-founder Allen Tessler, then aged 63, and Alan Hirshfield, also 63 and a major shareholder, took a long hard look at their balance sheet. Their great strength lay in having $65 million in cash, but in the co-founders' view, they had no growth opportunities. They decided to reinvent the company – as an incubator of Internet business-to-business companies. The two men recruited Todd Meister (29) and Keith Meister (27), Harvard graduates whose Meister Brothers Investments firm had a stake in nine Internet companies with names like Cyberbills and UReach. The Meisters were made co-presidents, and the newly restyled JNet acquired a controlling stake in their company. Meanwhile, JNet bought

35% of Digital Boardwalk Alliance, an Internet technology developer, to add something other than cash to their incubator proposition.

Tessler knew something about this sector, as a former co-chairman of Data Broadcasting and co-founder of CBSMarketWatch.com, both of which provide financial services to web companies. The eighth of March 2000 marked the rebirth of Jackpot as JNet Enterprises, a business-to-business Internet incubator. The news sent its stock soaring 49% in one day. The company retained the investment banking firm of Koffler & Company to advise it on the disposition of its gaming business segment. Between April and June 2000, management formalized its plan to sell the slot machine business and on 8 July the company entered into a definitive agreement to sell its route operations for $45 million in cash.

Now with a war chest over $100 million they were in business. One of their first incubator clients was eStara. This business gives the power of voice to e-business with a simple online solution: point, click, talk. Its web voice solutions claim to humanize the Internet experience, helping e-businesses to attract customers and close sales in real time. eStara OneClick Contact connects website visitors with e-business call centre agents live via a crisp, clear voice call over the web from any PC with microphone and speakers. eStara technology is compatible with existing customer contact solutions and call centre systems and requires no new hardware or software. Early adopters of eStara included J.Crew, Allfirst Bank and the NHL's Washington Capitals. eStara has also received *Internet Telephony* magazine's Editors' Choice Award for 2001. Whether or not the business will be a commercial success remains to be seen, as is the case for many other ventures in this sector.

The metamorphosis from entrepreneur, successful or not, into incubator proprietor is happening everywhere. But you have to ask the question, if someone has difficulty running their own business, how much help will they be to others trying to get new businesses off the ground? Kroll (2000) reviewed two new converts to the incubator business with less than perfect pedigrees. CyberShop.com, the first company examined by Kroll, struggled, along with many others in the business-to-consumer (B2C) market, at their original business of selling cut-price apparel and home furnishings. The six-year-old company lost $11 million in 1999 on sales of $7 million. In February 2000 it closed its doors to online retailing and reopened as an Internet incubator called Grove Street Ventures, which was later changed to Grove Strategic Ventures. Chief executive Jeffrey Tauber repositioned the company to boost its stock. 'We were impressed by the success of firms such as CMGI and Internet Capital Group and believe our strengths could be leveraged similarly,' he wrote in a press release. The fact that his original business was losing money didn't deter him from telling other entrepreneurs how to run theirs. Tauber's key experiences were in completing an IPO in March 1998 and in merchandising. Prior to founding CyberShop in 1994, he had been president of Avanti Linens. Before joining Avanti Linens, Mr Tauber was a buyer and merchandise manager at Bloomingdale's where his areas of responsibility included bed pillows, blankets, sheets, women's swimwear, and ready-to-wear. (While at Bloomingdale's, Mr Tauber was named Federated Buyer of the Year in 1987.)

Kroll also commented on Vengold's conversion to this new trade.

> Vancouver, BC-based Vengold decided to give up mining for Internet riches. Small wonder, after losing $76 million in just one quarter's trading. In February 2000 the company repositioned itself as an Internet investor, paying $900 000 for an existing incubator, Ideapark, in Vancouver. The new company name: Itemus.'

So does changing places make any difference to the performance of these businesses? Well, Jackpot's share price stood at $4 in April 2001, about half its price before it changed horses. It briefly rose to $14, but it has been all downhill since then. The following sentences from their latest filed accounts reveal the extent of their achievements to date:

> JNet Enterprises, effective March 2000, is in the process of transitioning itself from engaging in the gaming industry into a technology company and manager of technology-related funds. For the six months ended 12/31/00, company reported no revenues. Net loss from continuing operations totalled $12.6 million versus an income of $8.8 million. Results reflect the absence of $11.1 million net fee from terminated merger, and a $4.8 million equity loss in Internet-related businesses.

The accounts went on to say,

> Net income (loss) for the 2000 six months was a loss of $6000 compared with net income of $8.2 million for the 1999 six months. For the 2000 six months, the results reflect the asset impairment provisions and higher administrative and interest costs. These losses, net of associated tax benefit, were almost entirely offset by the after-tax gain from the sale of the gaming machine route operations.

Cutting through the legalese, this is another way of saying that so far they have swapped a stable business making a profit for something that is not only loss-making, but that is consuming the hard-won capital gained from the sale of their slot machine business.

9

The venture capitalists

For most innovative business propositions, venture capital firms are an integral part of every deal. Venture capital is a means of financing the start-up, development, expansion, or purchase of a company. The venture capitalist (VC) acquires an agreed proportion of the share capital (equity) of the company in return for providing the requisite funding.

WHAT DO VENTURE CAPITALISTS DO?

Unlike banks and other sources of debt capital, the equity funds provided by VCs do not have to be repaid by the entrepreneur and, as such, can be seen as risk-free, to the entrepreneur at least, and a particularly valuable asset to acquire.

Venture capital firms often work in conjunction with other VCs and providers of finance in putting together a total funding package for a business. Venture capital has its origins in the late eighteenth century when entrepreneurs found wealthy individuals to back their projects. Now venture capital is a global business with over 600 active VCs in the US and a further 400 or so across Europe and Asia. Traditionally, VCs have been divided into two main camps: hands-off and hands-on. The former believe that the main and perhaps only value they have to bring to the party is money, particularly money free of any interest or repayment burden which could cripple a small firm before it has a chance to take off and show its true potential. Whilst they may put a non-executive director (NED) on the board of firms they invest in, they see this as a stewardship role. The director is there to see that the money they invest is spent in the manner agreed. The hands-on VCs have a different agenda. They believe that their experience is valuable and the entrepreneur should have the benefit of as much of it as possible. In this regard, the economic value added by venture capital firms has been discussed by numerous authors (Bygrave and Timmons 1992; Chen 1983; Sahlman 1990). They also believe that their network can add value and they often look for an experienced business person, especially one with relevant industry experience, to act as their representative on the board, albeit in a non-executive capacity. But in this respect they are often straining the traditional role of a non-executive director close to breaking point. The most visible role of NEDs in big business is when they are dragged into controversies over pay and contracts, or when the managing directors of public companies treat the company's assets as their own. They are also called upon to referee in board disputes and play a major role in hiring and firing the chief executive. Its hardly surprising with those roles in mind that big companies prefer to have at least three non-executives on the board. Small firms are unlikely to have more than one NED and they are unlikely to involve themselves in esoteric corporate governance issues.

This group of hands-on VCs has both expanded in number and extended their involvement in the process of business formation. During the 1990s VCs replaced governments as the main advocates of business incubation and themselves became influential players in this market, with many of them setting up their own business incubators. The funds being invested by venture capital providers exploded in the five years to 1999 (see Figure 9.1). This growth continued into the first quarter of 2000 with over $22.7 billion going into start-ups in the US alone.

A number of factors persuaded VCs that they needed to get into the incubation business and, as usual when it come to money matters, these are

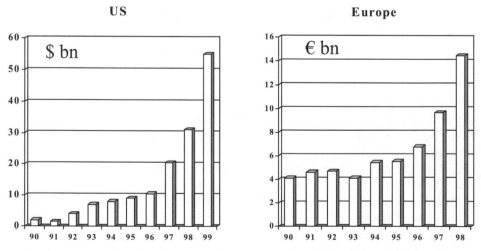

Figure 9.1 Venture capital explodes: annual investment in the US and Europe. Modified from Barrow (2000).

clustered around fear and greed. First we will discuss greed. Until recently, the returns that VCs made were not exactly startling. In the UK (Barrow 2000) the average return on high-technology investments by VCs over the life of the investment was 23%. In the US the average return across all sectors ranged from a low of 2% in 1990 to a high of 44% in 1995. But in 1999 something startling happened. US venture capital firms made a 147% return. That abnormally high return was brought about mostly by Internet and other high-tech investments turning into IPOs less than three years after the investment had been made. This can be favourably compared with the seven years plus that it had traditionally taken for a VC to realize his investment, with the exit route more likely to be a trade sale on a much lower multiple.

Now VCs have a lot more experience of IPOs than entrepreneurs have, or any other party to the investment process, except for possibly the underwriters themselves. So many VCs reasoned that if they could stay close to the entrepreneurs they invest in, get their big idea into the market quickly, and then help entrepreneurs to exit gracefully, everyone would be better off. Everyone, that is, except the general public who would be stuck with overpriced technology stocks. The entrepreneurs would be better off, since instead of working for a lifetime for the chance of making a few million when they retire, they could get out swiftly whilst they were young enough to enjoy their wealth, with hundreds of millions rather than the odd couple of million.

The VCs could play to their strengths by investing big sums of money, for short periods of time, with an IPO as an all-but-certain exit route, irrespective of the profitability of their client. As Table 9.1 shows, there was at

Table 9.1 Valuations of selected IPOs (source: Company filings)

Company	IPO date	Value ($ millions)	Sales (three-months pre-float)	Value as multiple of sales
Stamps.co	June 1999	$454	nil	infinite
Netpliance	March 2000	$1333	$26 000	51 283
b2bstores.com	February 2000	$65	$2200	29 729
CyberCash	February 1996	$251	$22 000	11 413
CareInsite	June 1999	$2153	$213 000	10 110
Ventro	July 1999	$810	$184 000	4177
DSL.net	October 1999	$509	$210 000	2425
PartsBase.com	March 2000	$180	$362 000	443
Envision Development	September 1999	$61	$388 000	130
Frontline Communications	May 1998	$14	$321 700	42

this period an almost perverse relationship between pre-float sales and the multiples used to value a company when it floated on a stock market. Profits were definitely not required and high sales were not that valuable. In short, the investing public only required a sight of the business in action and, the less they could see, the more alluring they would believe the venture might be. This was classic South Sea Bubble material: untold riches of an unspecified nature in a distant land well out of sight. All that was required was a boat and a crew willing to undertake the hazardous voyage.

What better way was there for VCs to keep close to their investments than to have them all close to hand in a dedicated business incubator? The time they usually spent working with their client companies over seven years or more could be condensed into a year or two. Instead of wasting time travelling to different locations to review performance, they only had to walk down the corridor and see everyone in one location. The time formerly spent travelling could also be used to better purpose in advising and adding value to their investments.

But not all VCs are equally as good at picking winners. According to the Yale Endowment Fund (Barrow 2000), the returns they made ranged from the bottom quartile making less than 5%, to the top quartile making over 25% over the 10 years to 1997. This brings us to the second driving force that spurred VCs into business incubation. Worse than making poor returns were the inevitable duds that VCs ended up backing. True, VCs did their best to avoid backing losers. One VC, Accel Partners in the US, went on record to say they received 25 000 business plans each year asking for finance and invested in only 40. VCs also take great care to check out their potential clients. The process of checking out a potential investment is known as the due diligence process, which involves a thorough examination of both the business and its owners. It can usually take several weeks, if not longer. (There is a rumour in the trade that VCs string out the process just to see if the business they are considering investing in is robust enough to survive without them. If it can, then it has at least one of the hallmarks of a winner.) Past financial performance, the director's track record and the business plan are all subjected to detailed scrutiny, usually by accountants and lawyers. Directors are then required to 'warrant' that they have provided *all* relevant information, under pain of financial penalties. The cost of this process is rarely less than a five-figure sum, and will have to be borne by the firm raising the money, but will be paid out of the money raised, if that is any consolation. But how can you evaluate a start-up venture that is little more than a concept or a handful of equations? In any event, the shape and direction of new businesses change so dramatically in the early weeks and months that they can render a business plan and its subsequent evaluation of little long-term value. How much better it would be to have your investments close at hand so you can monitor the subtle signals that will give those vital clues as to the likelihood of success. Being on the doorstep, successes can be quickly reinforced and failures ruthlessly weeded out before too much money has been wasted. Once again a business incubator provides a perfect environment to reduce the chances of failure.

One further factor drove VCs to getting into the incubation business. With a thousand VCs competing in an arena where a decade earlier there had been only sixty or so, the fight to invest in the best opportunities had become fierce. One Internet start-up in the UK, Clickmango.com, succeeded in raising £3 million from Atlas Venture in just eight days. Such was the enthusiasm for the natural health products website venture that an earlier meeting with another VC resulted in an offer of £1 million in just 40 minutes. (Clickmango.com was, as events turned out, a failure.) In the highly competitive environment of backing high-tech and innovative ventures, a VC needed something in its armoury other than money and an appetite for risk. Most VCs had these attributes. But having a business incubator had the twin virtues of lowering their risks and of making them stand out from the herd. It was also a game only the big VCs could play. Having an incubator could help restore their competitive advantage over the new breed of small boutique VCs, who had acquired a reputation for being fleet of foot. Thus it was that VCs moved into what they were slow to realize was a completely new line of business, and one that few of them would succeed in, just as few corporate entities succeed when they diversify.

SUCCESSFUL VENTURE CAPITALISTS

Some of the VCs who are making a success of their incubator projects are briefly described below, together with some examples of their protégés. These activities are not always called incubators, but as the services on offer go well beyond the provision of equity capital, they can properly be seen as such.

Speedventures

This is a venture capital investment firm that started up early in 1998 in Sweden and now has $70 million in its fund. Housed in a five-storey glass-fronted building fitted with moss green carpeting and Ikea furniture, the company took two years to invest the first $6 million of its fund in jump-starting 25 Internet-related firms. Speedventures claims to have written the manual on how to roll out high-tech start-ups on to the international arena within six months of arriving at their incubator. In the form of a PowerPoint presentation, and in many ways similar to a master franchisor's manual for a countrywide McDonald's chain, Speedventures follows the legendary business plan template of Medialab, the Internet consultancy which gained toeholds in sixteen countries in just two years. In addition to advice and capital, they offer access to their international contact network, including lawyers, human resources managers and public relations experts, and access to Speedventures' offices in London, Milan, Amsterdam, Munich and Helsinki.

Matrix Partners

Matrix Partners, based in the US, has been in venture capital since 1977. Their mission is 'helping our founders and management teams build the next great companies of tomorrow and often entire new industries'. In 1995 they extended their offer to include 'entrepreneur space', a dedicated facility and resource to provide hands-on help to the companies they invest in. Not every investment gets this treatment, but so far a dozen have. Since bringing Entrepreneur Space online in 1995, Matrix has hosted 12 companies including beFree Inc., Cadia Networks, Inc. (acquired by FORE Systems, Inc.), Convergent Networks, Inc., FirstSense Software, Inc., Redstone Communications, Inc., (acquired by Siemens Corporation), Sycamore Networks, Inc. and iWant.com, Inc.

SilverStream Software, Inc., founded in June 1996, utilized the Matrix Entrepreneur Space before permanently settling in Burlington, Massachusetts. The company's product, the SilverStream Application Server, is one of the industry's most comprehensive application servers which claims unmatched integrated development tools, high-performance server and complete web functionality. In August 1999, SilverStream Software, Inc. completed an initial public offering.

Kleiner, Perkins, Caufield and Byers (KPCB)

KPCB have been involved in the venture capital longer than almost anyone else in the business. Based in the US, in 1972 they began to offer entrepreneurs what they called a 'broader philosophy of value-added investing'. Their proposal was to provide access to people with the necessary knowledge and insight to help their client firms achieve stunning results. They termed their new model the Keiretsu, loosely modelled on the Japanese concept of the same name. Their model is described as 'a really compelling aspect of doing business with the firm. It's a really powerful feature. You can call the partners up and get information about a firm. And as they foster and incubate a series of small companies in unrelated fields, synergies develop.' They offer the following examples of significant collaboration within KPCB's network of companies:

- AOL and Sun jointly buy Netscape.
- Amazon.com invests in Drugstore.com, WebVan (through Home-Grocer), and WeddingChannel.com.
- Siara and Zaffire work with BroadBand Office (BBO) on product features and early qualification on their network.
- CoSine partners with Qwest on product definition, performance and testing prior to Cosine's initial product release.
- Intuit Netscape and Concentric to offer home banking via the Internet.
- America Online (AOL) and Intuit announce strategic alliance to bring electronic banking to AOL subscribers.

Accel Partners

Accel Partners, a leading US-based venture capital firm with expertise in Internet start-ups, and Kohlberg, Kravis Roberts & Co. (KKR), a leading private equity firm with expertise in building value at large corporations, joined forces to create a joint venture that provides financial and intellectual capital to companies seeking to integrate their online and offline strategies to create more rapid growth and value. The joint venture is composed of leading operating executives from physical and Internet businesses whose main focus will be the development and implementation of new ideas that enable more efficient and effective integration of Internet and physical assets. The Accel/KKR venture also invests in these companies seeking to merge the Internet and physical assets, and so provide them not only with capital but also with broader and better access to management expertise, networking opportunities and accelerated speed-to-market capabilities.

Draper Fisher Jurvetson (DFJ)

Gotham Ventures, the incubator arm of DFJ, the venture capital provider, is located in the heart of Silicon Valley in California. Their investment focus is on early-stage IT companies in Internet technology, broadband and wireless communications, networking infrastructure and solutions, enterprise software and IT services. The primary location for their investments is the east coast of the US, in particular New York and the surrounding regions. They also invest in Israeli venture-stage IT companies, which are increasingly relocating to the east coast.

Their ideal investments are 'in companies run by entrepreneurs with a "can't lose" attitude'. Typically they invest $1–5 million initially in a company and reserve sufficient capital for follow-on investments. They prefer huge markets or markets entering a hyper-growth phase. They look for the market leaders with breakthrough solutions or approaches to fundamental market needs. DFJ Gotham takes an active role in each company in which they invest. Their partners take board seats and use their extensive operating and financial experience to guide their young companies towards success in developing products and business strategies, raising money, hiring key executives and ultimately in creating enduring value.

They work very closely with all of the partners at DFJ as well as with the other funds within the network. The DFJ network of funds benefits their portfolio companies by providing them with the opportunity to form valuable strategic relationships with other DFJ portfolio companies, of which there are some 250.

They claim that their limited partners include some of the most successful technology entrepreneurs, technology companies and financial institutions in the US as well as in continental Europe, Israel and Japan. The global network of these limited partners also benefits their portfolio companies.

One of the firm's star investments, and an interesting insight into their corporate style, is the Hotmail case example below.

JavaSoft/Hotmail

In September 1988, Sabeer Bhatia arrived at Los Angeles International Airport. He had won the transfer scholarship to California Institute of Technology (CalTech) by being the only applicant in the entire world (there are usually about 150 who give it a try) in 1988 to get a passing score on the notorious CalTech Transfer Exam. Sabeer had scored 62 out of 100. The next highest score was a 42.

Sabeer intended to get his degree and then to go home to work, probably as an engineer for a large Indian company. He was following the modest path of life as set by his parents. His mother had been an accountant at the Central Bank of India for her entire career, and his father spent ten years as a captain in the Indian Army.

But as a graduate student at Stanford, Sabeer was drawn to the basement of Terman auditorium. There, the speakers were entrepreneurs like Scott McNealy, Steve Wozniak and Marc Andressen. Their fundamental message was always the same: You can do it too. Sabeer knew that famous people always said such things. They want to be inspirational. But Sabeer's impression of these successful entrepreneurs was that they really were fairly ordinary smart guys, not much different from him and his classmates.

When he graduated, Sabeer did not want to go home. So, along with Jack Smith, he took a job at Apple Computer. Sabeer could have worked at Apple for 20 or 30 years, but he got swept up in the decade's fever: You haven't lived until you've gone solo.

Sabeer then met a man named Farouk Arjani who had been a pioneer in the word-processing business in the 1970s, and had since become a special limited partner of Sequoia Ventures. The two hit it off well, and Arjani became Sabeer's mentor. What set Sabeer apart from the hundreds of other entrepreneurs for Arjani was the size of his dream. Even before he had a product and before he had any money behind him, he had become completely convinced that he was going to build a major company that would be worth hundreds of millions of dollars.

In mid-1995, Sabeer began taking around a two-page executive summary business plan for a net-based personal database called JavaSoft. When Jack Smith, by now a partner in the venture, albeit a reluctant one, and Sabeer came up with the Hotmail idea in December, JavaSoft became, in effect, the front for Hotmail. Sabeer knew that Hotmail was an explosive concept, and he didn't want a less-than-ethical venture capitalist to reject him, then turn around and copy his idea. He kept showing JavaSoft and showed Hotmail only to those VCs he had gained respect for:

> It was fine that they were rejecting JavaSoft. But in so doing, I got to see how their minds worked. If they rejected JavaSoft for stupid reasons, then I said thank you and left. If they rejected it for the right reasons, then I showed them Hotmail.

Sabeer presented his business plan to Steve Jurvetson of Draper Fisher Jurvetson. Jurvetson remembers:

> . . . Sabeer's revenue estimates as showing that he was going to grow the company faster than any in history. Most entrepreneurs have that trait, but they are also concerned with looking like a fool. Sabeer's projections were dismissed outright, but Sabeer's passionate belief was unchanged and he was right. He grew the subscriber base faster than any company in the history of the world.

One might have presumed that since Sabeer had been rejected by 20 previous VCs and was a nobody, he would be grateful to accept Draper, Fisher, Jurvetson's $300 000 on their terms. The VC made the perfectly reasonable offer of retaining 30% ownership on a $1 million valuation. Sabeer held out for double that valuation – their cut was 15 per cent. Their negotiations got nowhere, so Sabeer shrugged, stood up, and walked out of the door. His only other available option was a $100 000 'friends and family' round that had been arranged as a back-up and was not nearly enough money. If he had gone that route, Hotmail would not exist today.

Draper and Jurvetson relented; they called Sabeer the next day to accept their 15% cut of the business. They were confident that they could add sufficient value to the venture to make the deal work, even at what for them was a much higher price.

It took enormous confidence to do what Sabeer did: first, to hide his real idea, and second, to hold out for the valuation he thought the company deserved. But Sabeer gives the credit to the culture of the Valley itself.

> Only in Silicon Valley could two 27-year-old guys get $300 000 from men they had just met. Two 27-year-old guys who had no experience with consumer products, who had never started a company, who had never managed anybody, who had no experience even in software – Jack and I were hardware engineers. All we had was the idea. We didn't demo proof-of-concept software or a prototype or even a graphic printed on a piece of paper. I just sketched on Steve Jurvetson's whiteboard. Nowhere in the world could this happen but here.

On New Years Eve 1997, Sabeer sold Hotmail to Microsoft in exchange for 2 769 148 of their shares. At that time those shares were worth $400 million. It was barely nine years since Sabeer had stepped off his flight from Bangalore, India, with $250 in his pocket, the maximum amount allowed by Indian customs officials.

CHANGING THE MODEL

VCs are constantly searching for ways to differentiate their incubation offer. Since its launch in January 2000, LabMorgan has set up incubator facilities in India and Singapore, as well as more obvious destinations in Europe and the US. In January 2001, LabMorgan merged with Chase's e-finance unit, Chase.com. Chase.com had been established in 1999 to facilitate the development of e-commerce strategies and Internet opportunities by acting as a catalyst for Chase's core lines of business. Unlike most venture funds or private equity investors, LabMorgan claims to bring what it calls 'operational traction' as well as money to strategic partnerships in three key ways:

1. LabMorgan can significantly enhance an emerging company's revenue by directing J.P.Morgan Chase's own business to the entity. The

Lab's business strategists work with each partner company to create a path for technology adoption within the corporation.

2. At the same time, this strategic relationship 'credentials' a new company's technology as J.P.Morgan Chase actually implements and utilizes the technology to enhance the competitive market position of a specific line of its business. In addition, The Lab co-brands or otherwise publicizes that effort to further enhance the company's profile among key communities.

3. The Lab uses scalable components from J.P.Morgan Chase's own IT portfolio and leverages corporate content expertise to help fine-tune the value proposition and improve a partner's market acceptance. Not only can this accelerate a new entity's technology build, but it can also reduce associated build risks.

DOES BUSINESS INCUBATION PAY FOR VCs?

There is no easy answer to this question. VCs don't derive their money from incubation alone. Even VCs who are heavily involved in the incubation process make hands-off investments and have the occasional lucky break. But one fact is not in dispute. The VC industry is in the worst financial shape it has ever been in. It is hard not to correlate its current hangover with the binge of Internet and high-tech investments made in recent years. Let's look first at how the industry is doing as a whole, and then at one relatively new VC who is closely associated with the incubation process.

The world has changed since the heady days back in 1998 or 1999 when venture capital funds were making triple-digit returns on their investments. Venture capital fund returns declined in the fourth quarter of 2000 for the fourth consecutive quarter, and finally dipped into negative territory, with a –6.3% return for the quarter (Shread 2001). The negative return in the fourth quarter of 2000 was the first negative quarter the industry has seen since the third quarter of 1998, when the IPO market shut down during the Russian debt crisis. It was also the single largest quarterly decrease the industry has seen since the Venture Economics quarterly performance series began in 1980. Since 1984, there have been only six quarters with negative results.

While in Shread's opinion VC losses compare favourably to the 32.7% loss sustained by the NASDAQ in the fourth quarter of 2000, he believed that venture capital returns will not fully reflect the 'tech wreck' for some time to come. He went on to state that:

the only holdings that reflect current valuations are those in publicly traded companies. VCs won't be writing down the value of their private company holdings until their valuation changes in the next funding round or IPO. Meanwhile, many inflated private company valuations remain on the books, even some holdings that are being carried at cost.

To understand the significance of that statement you need to know something of how a VC 'values' his portfolio. Figure 9.2 shows the value of a fictitious VC's investments in three companies. When he took them into the incubator the seed funding valuation of the portfolio was £40 000. A year later those same companies received second-round financing from, say, another VC. The price of that round of financing will be used to value the original VC incubator's portfolio. In our example this shows a new value of £80 000, double our original stake – an impressive result by any standards.

Investment	Shares taken	Price	Value when taken into incubator (2000)	Price at second round financing (2001)	Value at 2001
Amazing	10 000	1	10 000	2	20 000
BooHoo	5000	2	10 000	4	20 000
Clunkmango	20 000	1	20 000	2	40 000
Portfolio value			£40 000		£80 000

Figure 9.2   Valuing a VC's portfolio.

But you have to be alert to the fact you can't spend or deposit this increase in portfolio value. This year-over-year, rolling-rate-of-return percentage does not measure real money for VCs and their investors. As the saying goes, 'it's not over until the fat lady sings'. For a VC the fat lady is a 'liquidation event', which means an IPO, trade sale or any event which brings the fund cash in return for its original stake. Of greater concern is the doubtful models used to value the various rounds of financing an incubator investment (or any other unquoted company investment, for that matter). A comprehensive study (Barrow et al. 1999) was conducted into the way VCs and underwriters value high growth business in the US, Canada, France and the UK, and the findings were presented at an international conference in Lyon, France, in 1999 to an audience of practitioners and academics. The conclusions, presented below, cast an interesting and disturbing light on the methods used.

CONCLUSIONS OF AN INTERNATIONAL COMPARISON OF BEST PRACTICES BY VENTURE CAPITALISTS AND UNDERWRITERS INTO VALUING HIGH-GROWTH POTENTIAL COMPANIES

This study constitutes the first investigation of valuation practices for high growth potential firms by underwriters and venture capitalists in four major markets (UK, France, US and Canada). The objective was to document the valuation processes and methods used to value the new 'gazelles' of the economy and identify any differences between these two groups of players and across countries. The evidence, gathered on a representative sample of some 174 valuation cases across 82 venture capitalists and underwriters, supports the view that (1) both VCs and underwriters rely primarily on comparable-based valuation methods; (2) they often complement these valuations with discounted cash flow approaches, particularly so when confronted with situations where adequate comparables are tough to find, such as with very young firms with no established markets and revenues but facing huge potential growth rates; (3) the valuation levels by both parties are significantly different for similar firms, which (4) seem to be explained mainly by differences in the perceived risk levels associated with differing stages of development; (5) valuation-specific knowledge development and dissemination activities are actually quite limited at this point. More sophisticated valuation methodologies, such as economic value added and real options, are so far shunned by most venture capitalists and underwriters, who appear to rely more on *ex post* contractual tweaking of the payoff functions than the *ex ante* optimization of the investment valuation. This behaviour could actually be very rational to the extent that the nature of these early-stage, high growth potential firms makes them inherently difficult to value. It may be a better investment of efforts to focus on the covenants of the contractual arrangements than the actual value of the deal.

With the constant evolutions in the valuation methodologies and the potentially strategic nature of any advantage gained in this domain for both venture capitalists and underwriters, one would expect to see more novel approaches translated into practice in the near future. Many firms interviewed, for example, were very cognizant of the latest techniques but had so far failed to translate them into policies, mainly because of a lack of time in the heady equity markets of the late 1990s. The lull in equity markets in the second half of 1999 may have provided many of these firms with just the opportunity to revise their practices and implement some new approaches.

One of the key limitations of such studies is the perceived proprietary nature of valuation methodologies by many firms. If indeed a firm is able to develop a better 'mousetrap', as indicated above, it would constitute a significant competitive advantage, which to some extent could even be sustainable if undisclosed. In other words, there are very few incentives for firms to disclose intimate details of their procedures. We attempted to by-pass these limitations here by navigating at relatively innocent levels of generality, but it would clearly be exciting to be able to obtain more precise information, for example, on the methods used to determine discount rates in discounted cash flow (DCF) approaches.

The study concluded, in effect, that there was no real science to valuing high growth high-tech business and the same process used for valuing more conventional firms was largely still in use.

The Canadian, UK and US VCs interviewed assert there has been 'little change' in the evaluation process over the previous five years (70%, 90% and 80% respectively) whilst the French opening up of capital markets has been more recent, providing too narrow a window to witness material change in processes.

So at the macro-level it will be some time yet before we know if the VCs' incursion into value-added incubation has been worth the effort and if they have delivered any better results than their more relaxed 'hands-off' brethren.

CMGI: A NEW, NEW, WAY TO LOSE MONEY

CMGI, Inc. is a relatively new VC and it set their stall out to attract only high-tech, high growth entrepreneurs, and offer them an incubation pro-cess to accelerate their growth. In addition, CMGI has floated and sold off more than 20 of its stakes in those entrepreneurial ventures, so the results of a full cycle of their value-creating activities can now be seen.

In 1995, CMGI @ Ventures was formed. With its $45 million fund it claimed to be the world's first Internet-only venture firm focusing solely on that sector. The following year CMGI took majority stakes in Engage and NaviSite. Engage offers profile-driven Internet marketing solutions for targeted web marketing whilst NaviSite is an application service provider (ASP) providing Internet outsourcing solutions. In 1997 CMGI acquired Accipiter, an advertising technology platform, and merged it into Engage. With the acquisitions of InSolutions and OnDemand Solutions and the subsequent merger of those companies into SalesLink, CMGI strengthened its e-commerce and fulfilment offerings, and from then onwards had in effect a full service incubation process to offer entrepreneurs.

CMGI @ Ventures invests across the full range of Internet and information technologies, with an emphasis on the areas of infrastructure and emerging technologies. CMGI's network of companies aims to provide the entrepreneur with an 'exceptional' research and development environment and integration platform. According to the their literature, 'CMGI's expertise in helping grow businesses fast can be clearly seen in the numbers: Over the last five years, 72 companies have received funding from CMGI @ Ventures, with 52 currently in the portfolio. There have been 15 company sales and nine initial public offerings.'

They certainly have an impressive record of attracting entrepreneurs and then helping them get their businesses off the ground, into orbit and then either sold off or floated through an IPO. The list below contains a veritable Who's Who of the new economy world, and also shows the shorthand used in firms' stock market listings.

IPOs
GeoCities (NASDAQ:) GCTY (now YHOO)
Lycos (NASDAQ:) LCOS
Critical Path (NASDAQ:) CPTH
Silknet Software (NASDAQ:) SILK (now KANA)
Chemdex (NASDAQ:) CMDX (now VNTR)
MotherNature.com (NASDAQ:) MTHR
Vicinity (NASDAQ:) VCNT

Liquidity events
GeoCities sold to Yahoo! (YHOO)
Ikonic sold to USWeb/MarchFirst
Netcarta sold to Microsoft (MSFT)
TeleT sold to Premiere Technology (PTEK)
PlanetAll sold to Amazon.com (AMZN)
Reel.com sold to Hollywood
Entertainment (HLYW)
TicketsLive sold to Advantix
(Tickets.com) (TIXX)
Softway Systems sold to Microsoft (MSFT)
Promedix sold to Chemdex (now Ventro) (VNTR)
Raging Bull sold to AltaVista
Silknet Software sold to Kana Communications (KANA)
Half.com sold to eBay (EBAY)
eGroups sold to Yahoo! (YHOO)
FindLaw sold to West Group

They started in 1997 with the sale of NetCarta to Microsoft and in 2000 they concluded the IPO of Vicinity on the NASDAQ, before the public appetite for high-tech stocks had evaporated. Their expertise as a VC incubator *par excellence* is not in doubt. But the fact is that as an operating business they have not yet made a profit as a VC. Figure 9.3 is extracted from their last filed accounts (CMGI 2000 Annual Report). Over the five years of their life they have lost a cumulative $912 812 000. Whilst for three years out of five they made an operating profit, their loss-making years, particularly the last year, more than wiped out the profitable years.

(in thousands, except per share) Year ended July 31	**2000**	1999	1998	1997	1996
Consolidated Statement of Operations Data: Net revenue	**$898 050**	$186 389	$92 197	$67 306	$20 873
Cost of revenue	**737 264**	179 553	82 021	42 116	14 353
Research and development expenses	**153 974**	22 253	19 108	17 767	5412
In-process research and development expenses	**65 683**	6061	10 325	1312	2691
Selling, general and administrative expenses	**694 056**	89 054	46 909	45 777	16 812
Amortization of intangible assets and stock-based compensation	**1 436 880**	16 127	3093	1254	–
Operating loss	**(2 189 807)**	(126 659)	(70 259)	(40 920)	(18 395)
Interest income (expense), net	**(15 096)**	269	(870)	1749	2691
Gains on issuance of stock by subsidiaries and affiliates	**80 387**	130 729	46 285	–	19 575
Other gains, net	**525 265**	758 312	96 562	27 140	30 049
Other income (expense) net	**113 385**	(13 406)	(12 899)	(769)	(746)
Income tax benefit (expense)	**121 173**	(325 402)	(31 555)	(2034)	(17 566)
Income (loss) from continuing operations	(1 364 693)	423 843	27 264	(14 834)	15 608

Figure 9.3   CMGI 2000 annual report, abbreviated income statement.

It's hardly surprising that CMGI's share price has mirrored their profit performance. Like the Grand Old Duke of York, they have marched their shareholders to the top of the hill only to take them back down again very quickly (Figure 9.4).

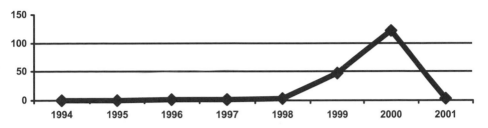

Figure 9.4   VC incubators: up the hill and down again.

It remains to be seen how much comfort will be gained by CMGI's shareholders, and for that matter those of all the other VCs in the high growth incubation business, when they read their firms' annual reports. CMGI, at any rate, seems to be comfortable with its achievements, as the folowing extract from their message to shareholders seems to indicate.

DEAR FELLOW SHAREHOLDERS:
In a year of many significant events at CMGI, the one that stands out most occurred after the close of our fiscal year: the reaffirmation of CMGI as a company dedicated to growth, leadership and profitability. We demon-strated this in September by organizing our operating companies into five segments that, together with our venture capital affiliate, make it patently clear that CMGI is a healthy, flexible and strategically managed business, expertly navigating the environment in which we operate – the Internet – even as it changes our personal lives, our company and the world around us.

10

The business angels

The term 'angel' was first coined, in business parlance, to describe a private wealthy individual who backed a theatrical production, usually a play on Broadway or in London's West End. By their very nature, such 'investments' were highly speculative in nature, as shows tend to either soar or bomb. The angel would typically have a personal interest in the production, the arts in general, or perhaps in a member of the cast. He or she may also have wanted to play some role in the production itself or in negotiating an aspect of the business relationship between the players and the theatre or some other outside party. In any event angels were (or indeed are, for theatrical angels still exist) determined upon some involvement beyond merely signing a cheque. There is no rational way to calculate either risk or reward in such ventures. A great writer and a great cast are not guarantees of success. In the same way total unknowns can also triumph. The chances of losing money are high.

Business angels are a similar breed. They are informal suppliers of risk capital to new and growing businesses, often taking a hand at the stage when no one else will take the chance. Figure 10.1 describes their risk/reward profile, but it does not completely describe their motivation. But whilst they often lose their shirts, they sometimes make serious money. One angel who backed Sage with £10 000 in their first round of £250 000 financing, saw his stake rise to be worth £40 million.

INCUBATORS IN THE MAKING

Business angels perform a role very similar to that of a business incubator. They provide help and guidance to their 'clients', and, in addition (unlike many incubators except those run by VCs) they put up cash too. Observation by industry watchers such as the European Business Angels network

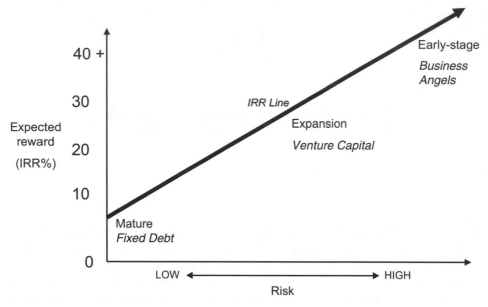

Figure 10.1   Business angels: risk versus reward.

(Cave 1999) suggests that business angels get heavily involved in helping their investments get off the ground. On average they spend 10 hours a week in dealing with each of their investments. That is more than many full-time incubator managers spend on the business affairs of *all* the firms in their incubator. The majority of angels' time is spent administering the incubator, fund-raising and dealing with the incubators' various sponsoring bodies. As the case example below shows, business angels can also get physical.

Cache Box

Cache Box, Inc. has been a provider of high-tech systems since 1988. Their original mission was to help businesses migrate from old 'cash register' technology to electronic point-of-sale (EPOS) computer technology. Today, Cache Box designs PC-based point-of-sale software and hardware that sets the standard for functionality and style. Cache Box claims to be the largest and most successful supplier of food and beverage POS systems to the military. Worldwide, there are over 1000 installations of Cache Box equipment. In addition, Cache Box holds a 10-year contract with Amtrak to automate its on-board food services.

Using its government contracts as a foundation, Cache Box has taken advantage of the unique position it holds in the marketplace by aggressively pursuing the commercial market. An important first step to this expansion was the establishment of dealerships throughout the US and abroad to resell and support its products. The company has set up dealers in the largest US markets as well as establishing a distributorship in Europe.

Its core product, Virtual Diner, allows restaurants to verify online ordering, display daily specials, and post menus, wine lists, parking information and directions. The online table-management feature allows consumers to enter the desired date, time and number of guests and, while they wait, the system checks availability and confirms if the desired time is available. If there is a conflict, the feature offers other options.

The company grew from a consulting firm with two employees and revenue of $100 000 in 1994 to a firm with 30 employees and revenue of $9 million by 1999.

In 1999 Cache Box decided to become an angel incubator to Wealumni.com by providing 1300 square feet of space in their offices in Arlington, Virginia. By offering office space at a reduced rent with no lease, telephone, voicemail, computer network, photocopier and Internet connection, and administrative support and use of their accounting system, they eliminated the need for Wealumni.com to struggle through the usual start-up pains. Not having to spend precious time dealing with the chore of setting up an office – negotiating a lease, buying or leasing office equipment, and soliciting equipment bids – meant that Wealumni.com could spend more time developing a customer base and fine-tuning its products/ services. And, being close at hand, Cache Box can keep an eye on their investment and perhaps even influence how the company will grow.

Wealumni.com was a young, energetic company with its finger on the pulse of trend-setting technologies. Cache Box was a 12-year-old company that needs to continually take a fresh look at its products to stay ahead of its competitors. Wealumni.com has the energy of youth – an energy that serves to revitalize its staff. Cache Box has stability and the experience of age. It is a win–win situation that plays itself out every day in a mutual mentoring capacity.

ANGELS GO WHERE OTHERS FEAR TO TREAD

Angels have another great strength, as this example shows. The CEO of a $10-million software company in Utah had a sobering realization late on Christmas Eve 2000: sales weren't picking up fast enough to enable him to pay all his staff. It was a temporary problem exacerbated by a late payment from one major customer. The chief financial officer made a late-night call to an angel with whom the company had a long-standing relationship. The angel, confident that he was hearing the truth – he'd always been kept informed – wrote a cheque for $100 000 to cover the salaries of the company's 30 employees.

That kind of eleventh-hour rescue could come from only one type of investor. Distinctions may blur between VCs, corporate venture firms and university incubators, but one fundamental difference remains: because they are investing their own money, only angels are equipped to take decisive, even heroic, actions. Angels, no matter how much they have evolved, are still free to act on their feelings. 'It's a great company,' the angel backing the software company in this example explained. 'They have integrity.' That's as far as he needs to go in explaining his decision to bail the firm out.

HOW MANY ANGELS ARE THERE?

Informal venture capital provided by business angels has been investigated most intensively in the US. Three authoritative studies have been conducted since the early 1980s. Four studies (Gaston 1989; Wetzel 1983, 1987; Wetzel and Freear 1988) estimated that the total equity investment from informal sources was between two and five times greater than that from the formal venture capital industry – itself the largest venture capital market in the developed world. In the UK, research conducted by Harrison and Mason (1992, 1996) estimated the informal risk capital pool to be in the range of £2–4 billion, a figure endorsed by Cave (1999) and Mason and Harrison (1997).

In truth, no one knows the amount of capital business angels either have or are prepared to invest. Two relatively new developments have almost certainly made the size of the business angel pool of risk capital greater, more international and more incubator-like in its way of operating. First, the rise of Internet-based services designed to bring firms and angels together (such as Garage.com) is bringing a new breed of talented expertise to the angel market. Guy Kawasaki, former 'chief evangelist' of Apple Computer started Garage.com in 1998. They filter business plans vigorously and then send the best to prospective angels, venture capitalists and corporate investors. This permits e-mail exchanges between angels and companies seeking finance (Greco 1999). It also raises some interesting challenges to the traditional angel model. For example, angels are characterized as 'invisible' people (Creagh 1999) who value their privacy, yet on the Garage.com website there are a series of named would-be investors. Moreover, some of these people are not merely wealthy individuals but are presidents, chairmen and former CEOs of major corporations such as Compaq. Although they are seeking to invest as individuals it is clear from their willingness to be named that they are encouraging companies which may have need of their extensive industry experience to approach them.

Garage.com seeks to raise between $1 to $4 million per firm – amounts that are too small for traditional venture capital firms. Not just anyone can be an investor – potential angels must meet strict US Securities and Exchange Commission (SEC) guidelines as accredited investors and have a net worth of at least $1 000 000 as well as demonstrating experience in start-ups. In the US at least, there are hundreds of stock option millionaires who are very familiar with the Internet and new technologies and media industries. They may be more comfortable than traditional angels in investing in high-tech companies and providing their managerial experience down an electronic link rather than travelling to the physical site of the company.

This sector has not been seriously researched and no one has yet estimated how much money or other resources are available for the right proposition.

The second factor is an earlier development: the formation of Business Angel Networks (BANs), in which groups of angels cluster together to pool investments and expertise. One effect of this is to bring into play larger sums of money. On her own, an individual angel is unlikely to put up more than £50 000 (see Figure 10.2). That sum is hardly likely to make a great impact on the total sum needed to get a high-tech or Internet venture off the ground. But grouped together in syndicates angels can and do put millions into new ventures.

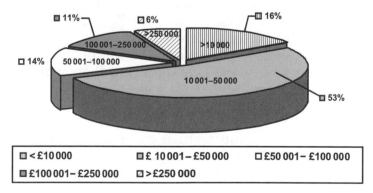

Figure 10.2 Amounts invested by UK business angels. Modified from Cave (1999).

BANs don't just provide pooling arrangements. They act as magnets to draw new angels in and they provide knowledge and education to give them greater confidence in doing deals. BANs are currently exploding in numbers in Europe. Like angels themselves, BANs are hard to keep track of, but a trawl of sites using various search engines in April 2001 came up with 156. The UK and Germany had the largest number of networks, with 65 and 72 respectively. Angels have also discovered that pooling resources and sharing due diligence make for greater efficiency. Brand-name groups like the Band of Angels in the US or the Business Angel Forum in Germany have helped legitimize angels as a breed.

RECOGNIZING ANGELS AND WHAT THEY WANT

Harrison and Mason (1992) identify three main sampling approaches used by North American academics. First is the use of large-scale surveys of high-income individuals. Second is to use the firm that has received the investment as the basis for contact with the investor. Third is to use the snowball effect which uses the fact that investors are often linked by social or business networks and that the identification of one angel can lead to others. They acknowledge that all these methodological approaches present difficulties around the area of representativeness, and makes comparisons between different studies difficult. However, the picture researchers have come up with (see Cave 1999, Creagh 1999 and Mason and Harrison 1995) looks something like this:

1. Business angels are generally self-made, high net worth individuals with entrepreneurial backgrounds. Most are aged 45–65. Nineteen per cent are millionaires.
2. Only 1% of business angels are women.
3. Typically business angels invest 5–15% of their investment portfolio in this way. An example supporting these statistics is Robert Wright, a Cranfield MBA, who founded a small UK airline, City Flyer Express. He became a business angel when he sold out to British Airways for £75 million in 1999. He has built up a portfolio of six investments and has committed less than £1 million to his angel activities. Two of his investments are in the high-tech area, and one of those is being run by two other Cranfield MBAs.

   A business angel's motivation is, first and foremost, financial gain through capital appreciation, with the fun and enjoyment of being involved with an entrepreneurial business an important secondary motive. A minority are motivated in part by altruistic considerations, such as helping the next generation of entrepreneurs to get started, and supporting their country or state.

4. Business angels invest in only a very small proportion of investments that they see: typically at least seven out of eight opportunities are rejected. More than 90% of investment opportunities are rejected at the initial screening stage.

5. Around 30% of investments by business angels are in technology-based businesses.

6. The majority of business angels invest in businesses located close to where they live – two-thirds of investments are made in businesses located within 100 miles of their home or office. They are, however, prepared to look further afield if they have specific sector-related investment preferences, or if they are technology investors (see the Paul Allen case study below).

7. Ninety-two per cent of angels had worked in a small firm compared, for example, with only 52% of venture capitalists who had similar experience.

8. Most angels will also tell you that they avoid investing in industries they know nothing about, as this quote in an article on angels by Jeffrey Seglin (1998) illustrates. 'It's easy enough to lose money investing in areas where you have some knowledge,' says Stephen J. Gaal, founding member of Walnut Venture Associates, a group of 15 investors that includes a professor at Harvard Business School. 'We want to go into businesses where we're not the dumb ones.'

9. Angels basically back people rather than propositions. (Which makes it hard to see how Paul Allen's model, which is designed to avoid meeting as many people as possible, can be made to work.) An observation in Seglin's (1998) article sums it up neatly: 'You seem to think we invest in businesses. We do not. We invest in people.' Gaal and his group look for 'very smart people with very high integrity'. An avid angel who is involved in at least 40 companies insists, 'I also bet on the jockey, not just the horse'.

10. Business angels are up to five times more likely to invest in start-ups and early stage investments than venture capital providers in general.

Paul Allen, business angel – a case study

Microsoft co-founder and Portland Trail Blazer owner Paul Allen makes it easy to find him and exactly what type of investment he is prepared to back by posting his investment criteria on his website, the Wired World of Paul Allen. He tells you right off what's *not* on Paul Allen's hot list: film production, scripts or concept papers; themed amusement parks or restaurants, music acts, or record companies.

Allen believes a surplus of ideas can cause a shortage of focus, so he is on the lookout for innovations that exploit the unique characteristics of new technology. In particular, he is looking for:

- ideas that help people work, play, or learn better. Allen invests in products and services that people will find useful. The Wired World is the real world, not a private domain of technologists.
- ideas that connect people to information and let them personalize it. The microprocessor is more than cheaper, smaller computation power. When you combine it with a communication channel, you get the possibility of personalized information, a quantum leap in value for the user.

Entrepreneurs looking for backing are encouraged to complete and submit Allen's online equiry form which asks, among other things, you to categorize your business. Entrepreneurs must also submit a rationale for why their idea fits into Paul Allen's Wired World strategy, in about 200 words. That done, stand by your e-mail, since Wired World personnel will contact applicants within 30 days if they're intrigued. They will then ask for proposals to be submitted in standard business plan format, including an executive summary describing company operations and business model. They ask for this proposal in writing, delivered by US mail, and due to the large volume of enquiries he receives, Allen cannot consider requests for meetings or phone calls to present or discuss proposals.

FOLLOWING THE RULES

Business angels have had a benign regulatory ride in the US. Normally selling shares in unquoted companies is tightly regulated. Regulation D (a.k.a. 'Reg D') is an SEC rule governing exemptions from private placement offerings – i.e. sales of securities directly to 'accredited investors' such as high net worth individuals, as well as to institutional investors, such as banks, mutual funds, insurance companies, pension funds, and foundations. Such offerings do not have to be registered with the SEC, provided the securities are bought for investment purposes rather than for resale, as specified in the investment letter.

Under the Securities Act of 1933, any offer to sell securities must either be registered with the SEC or meet an exemption. Regulation D provides three exemptions from the registration requirements – Rules 504, 505 and 506 – allowing some smaller companies to offer and sell their securities without having to register the securities with the SEC.

While companies using Reg D exemptions are not required to register their securities, and usually don't have to file reports with the SEC, they must still file what's known as a 'Form D' after they first sell their securities. Form D is a brief notice that includes the names and addresses of the company's owners and stock promoters, but contains little other information about the company. The position in the UK and elsewhere is less clear, but as most angels now operate in networks that have accredited investor status, a way through the red tape can usually be found.

HOW SUCCESSFUL ARE ANGELS' INVESTMENTS?

Not very, would appear to be the conclusion. It would seem from the research that the entrepreneurial and independent spirit that drives their investments may lead them to regret their choices. More recent research (Creagh 1999) concluded that angels suffer a partial or complete loss on 40% of their investment portfolio and that angels' greatest regret was not conducting more pre-investment due diligence. They are, then, inexperienced investors when compared with venture capitalists, but they take a much more 'hands on' approach to the firm they have invested in. They found that 50% of angels conducted minimal or no sector research, met their entrepreneur an average of 5.4 times before investing (compared with venture capitalists who met on average 9.5 times) and 54% of angels neglected to take up independent personal references compared to only 6% of venture capitalists.

But it's not all doom and gloom. Enough business angels are successful to inspire others to stick with it and new entrants to be drawn into the market. The following list

- One in five investments had an average annual return of 50%.
- On average, investors sell their shareholding in the most successful investments after four years (and 75% sell after seven years). Conversely, half of the investments in which business angels lost money had failed within two years of the investment being made.
- The method of exit from their investment is: written off – 40%; trade sale – 26%; sale to other shareholders – 16%; sale to third party – 10%; flotation – 8%.

A LAST WORD ON ANGELS

Angels play several roles in the business incubation process. They can act as incubators themselves, as in the Cache Box example. They can offer hands-on advice, as most do. Or as with Paul Allen (Microsoft's co-founder) or the aspirant angels from the band of presidents, chairmen and former CEOs in major corporations such as Compaq, they can offer access to unrivalled business networks.

But as the case study below shows, angels can also work in conjunction with conventional incubators as part of those incubators' networks of funding sources and expertise. It would not be difficult to relate several hundred other examples of similar cases of such relationships between entrepreneurs, business incubators and business angels resulting in a new business getting funding and resources, where in other circumstances they may not have fared so well. There is little doubt that business angels have an important and growing role to play in the incubation of new and growing businesses throughout the world.

Focus Solutions

Focus Solutions Group plc (formerly Focus Solutions) started out in 1995 with five people crammed into a small room in a Warwickshire village in the UK. The company supplies software products and e-commerce tools which enable large organizations in the financial services sector to control and manage their business on networked computers via the Internet and other emerging channels such as digital TV and worksite marketing. Insurance companies are divesting themselves of their paper-based and outdated computer systems and are gearing up to electronic systems that maximize the benefits of e-commerce.

In 1997, a shortage of cash coincided with the realization that the company must move quickly to seize opportunities in the marketplace. Although the management team was highly regarded, they needed additional resources to accelerate the development of the business and undertake a full market launch. At that point they entered the ambit of the University of Warwick Science Park's incubation programme. As well as helping the business through its formative period, the incubator team introduced them to a business angel who would bring them complementary management skills as well as some capital. After publicity in *The Bulletin* (the Science Park's newsletter) a relationship was formed with a business angel who was a former senior partner at KPMG. His involvement provided the catalyst for an initial investment of £800 000 followed by a subsequent investment of £600 000.

In 1999, flotation of the Focus Solutions Group on the AIM raised £10 million additional capital to speed up the development of new products and their application in overseas markets, particularly the US.

11

The consultants

The latest additions to the incubator family are the service-for-equity arrangements adopted by consulting and accounting firms, which have shown their willingness to provide expertise for a stake in the action. McKinsey, BainLab, Andersen, PwC and others are precursors to this latest generation of business incubator companies. But these models also open the door to interesting new dilemmas, in particular in terms of conflicts of interest, so much so that the accounting standard board in the US has already stepped in to remind all parties of the absolute necessity to maintain arm's-length relationships with audit clients. Similar concerns are bound to appear with respect to consulting firms, lawyers and other professionals taking equity stakes in their clients.

These professionals may not have money of their own to put into incubator clients, but they have, or at least claim to have, something even more valuable – business savvy. These firms have worked with some of the most successful firms in the world and alongside some of the greatest business managers. If stars such as these have to have the likes of McKinsey or Bain close to hand as they make strategic choices, surely all firms need their help? This proposition sounds attractive, but it probably has less substance than it would at first seem to have. The key challenge for the superstar consultants is that their expertise lies in working with big established firms and government departments, rather than with individual entrepreneurs and small start-up firms. A glance at McKinsey's website, for example, comes up with this list of their most recent and important assignments, which have been turned into reports on their worldwide activities.

> Helping Korea Change Course: A McKinsey Global Institute report generates government attention and public interest.

> Weathering the Russian Crisis: Micky Obermayer talks about how the Moscow Office has responded to the nation's financial problems.

Corporations of the Future: Large corporations can make structural changes that allow them to act like small upstarts, yet take full advantage of scale, scope, and global reach.

Improving Criminal Prosecution in the Bronx: When the District Attorney's Office in the Bronx, a county in New York City, asked McKinsey to help improve the quality of trial preparation and boost the morale of the Assistant District Attorneys, our team observed that cases typically moved through the courts like product orders in a poorly run factory.

Making Human Services Human: A Chicago team helps a state rethink its social services, and has what one top official calls a 'major impact' on citizens' lives.

If these reports are indicative of the direction big consultants see their money coming from, it's hard to see what they can offer small firms that is distinctive and valuable. Their key skills seem to be in the field of revitalizing ossified or confused big organizations and in the areas of brand building, mergers and acquisitions, and market leadership and domination. Later in this chapter we will examine the usefulness of these strategic advantages to most new firms.

Ernst & Young, however, as we will see later in this chapter, have found a way round this potential pitfall by partnering with a much smaller incubator. In this way they hope to get the best of both worlds. A small-scale incubator to get the business off the ground and a big incubator to accelerate the business through the stages of growth and on to an early exit. In fact, most consultants have chosen 'accelerator' as the word to describe their business incubators (see Figure 11.1). They see that as the key benefit they can bring to young companies and it is one we will look at more closely when we examine the true worth of an incubator to an incubator client.

WHO ARE THE BIG PLAYERS?

Let's start with McKinsey, as they are recognized as one of the founding members of the business consultancy business. Their ability to innovate and exploit new opportunities started in 1937 when Marvin Bower, McKinsey's legendary managing partner, redefined management consulting with a one-page strategy statement that concluded McKinsey would offer a 'career profession' for young people rather than an end-of-career vocation for wise old men. What these young people would bring to the party, Bower argued, was not wisdom but intelligence and problem-solving skills. They would be guided by what James O. McKinsey described as a top management perspec-

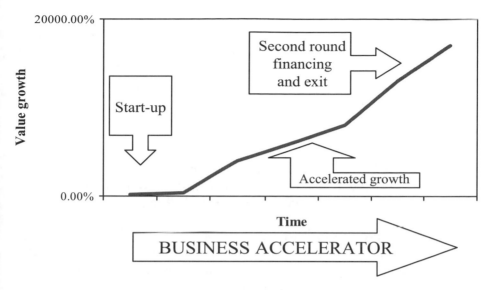

Figure 11.1   The accelerator model of business incubation.

tive which was very different and much more exciting than the time-and-motion perspective of management consulting then dominant. McKinsey didn't get around to implementing Bower's strategy until after the Second World War, when most of their 'wise old men' were fired. In the early 1950s, McKinsey became the first consulting firm to recruit at Harvard Business School. In 1985 McKinsey added a new goal to its mission statement: the need to 'attract, retain and develop' truly outstanding people. In that way, McKinsey reckoned it had anticipated the 'war for talent' by over a decade.

However, in choosing Harvard as their main recruiting ground they unwittingly presented themselves with a new and unexpected problem. Harvard changed from being a school that turned out fodder for big businesses and government to one that sought to foster entrepreneurial talent. So successful was Harvard at achieving this goal that by the mid 1990s Harvard forecast that by 2010 80% of its alumni would be running their own businesses. The corollary of that was that fewer talented people would be available for the likes of McKinsey. In fact the change was even more dramatic than that forecast. It was rumoured that 80% of the Harvard MBA class of 1999 not only wanted to start up on their own, but they wanted to do it immediately on graduation, rather than in the subsequent decade, as Harvard had expected. Furthermore, they only wanted to start dotcoms. At the very least, they wanted to work in an Internet company and secure a stake in what looked then very much like an old-fashioned gold rush.

McKinsey's response was to establish Accelerators in 1999 their service to turbo-charge the launch and growth of new e-businesses worldwide. They aimed, using Internet vocabulary, at combining their deep and focused e-business expertise with the experience and reach of the company's 500 e-business consultants. Also on offer was access to their extensive network of 'best in class' third-party service providers and their Fortune 500 client and alumni database. McKinsey's Accelerators offer four main types of assistance:

1. Intensive business building (six to twelve months): For ventures that need to move at maximum speed McKinsey offer a large team to provide day-to-day execution of the marketing plan, including product launch.
2. Targeted projects (one to six months): Accelerator teams provide in-depth analytical services to enable start-ups to pinpoint their market opportunities, position and vulnerabilities. They can also screen merger and acquisition projects.
3. Burst services (two days to two months): Based on the hypothesis that few start-ups have the resources for lengthy analysis and drawn-out marketing studies, McKinsey consultants can provide rapid market data and other targeted analysis needed for short-term decision making.
4. Senior counselling (as needed): Access to McKinsey partners for open, unbiased dialogue on any key business issues.

McKinsey now have standalone Accelerators in Amsterdam, Atlanta, China, London, Miami, Munich and Silicon Valley in California.

There has been little publicity about Accelerator clients or the take-up of the incubation process in general. McKinsey's UK website offers two examples; one, a brick-and-mortar financial services industry leader who needed help in developing and implementing a new B2B portal from its existing business. The other was an independent TV and film company who needed help in 'leveraging' the best of its current assets to build a series of new e-businesses.

There is not much in these to inspire an entrepreneur to get in touch, but as the latter of these examples would be turned away by Paul Allen, perhaps they have a niche to go for after all. McKinsey's Accelerators are physical centres where start-ups can work with experienced e-business consultants, web designers and technical experts under one roof. That has to be a valuable experience, even if there is no hard cash on offer.

bainlab

Bain is a much younger, but no less visible, firm than McKinsey. They came to unwanted prominence in the UK through their involvement as advisers to the Guinness managing director, Ernest Saunders, during the ill-fated take-over battle for Distillers. Founded by Bill Bain and a number of former Bain & Company partners in 1984, the firm's challenge was to 'put our money where our mouth is'. They have their own venture capital arm, Bain Capital, which bases its investment philosophy on the same approach of delivering results through strategy that Bain & Company offers its clients. Bain Capital's perfor-mance has been phenomenal, with an average annual internal rate of return (IRR) exceeding 100% and over $20 billion in portfolio revenue.

Bain can justly claim to be one of the world's leading global manage-ment consulting firms, with offices in all major cities throughout the world. They employ 2400 people operating out of 26 regional offices. Bain have worked with over 1500 major corporations from every economic sector, in every region of the world, to improve and help sustain bottom-line results. Quantum leaps in performance are a frequent outcome of the customized, creative and often breakthrough strategies that Bain develops for its clients. They claim to track the results of all their assignments and show that Bain clients outperform the market by 3 to 1.

bainlab, their incubator, was started about the same time as McKinsey's Accelerator. It draws from more than six years experience of developing win-ning e-business strategies. This experience includes more than 100 e-commerce projects and over 1000 strategy projects helping clients initiate new businesses.

bainlab's focus is helping Internet start-ups succeed. They claim their world-class e-commerce expertise allows them to identify and refine Inter-net business models and work with management to transform those ideas into ultimate online success. bainlab works with e-commerce start ups – both entrepreneurs and dot.com spin-offs of bricks-and-mortar corpora-tions – as well as providing technical and management expertise to late stage private e-commerce companies. Global in scope, bainlab has incu-bated and funded businesses in the US, the UK, Germany and Hong Kong. In addition, it has identified a select network of resources to provide services critical to the development of early stage web businesses, such as web de-sign, public relations and interim management. They also provide the fund-ing necessary in the early stages of a company's growth.

bainlab has six basic criteria when looking for potential entrants to its incubator:

- large market;
- opportunity to fundamentally enhance customer experience and economics;

- opportunities that will dramatically improve the efficiency and effectiveness of an industry supply chain;
- passionate commitment from the founders to the success of the venture;
- broad and deep industry experience in management team; and
- internet expertise.

Two companies that have had the bainlab treatment are Wishstream and Takira.com.

Wishstream claims to have been the first e-billing application service provider (ASP) in Europe. Their service harnesses the full power and reach of the Internet to enable businesses that post large volumes of recurring bills on paper, to present them to their customers electronically via the Internet. Using Wishstream, companies can use their billing process to 'create new online revenue opportunities, increase customer retention and substantially reduce costs'. With billers having no systems to manage and no capital expenditure, Wishstream's service represents the quickest and most cost-effective solution for many small- and medium-sized businesses who wish to present their bills electronically. Wishstream target their service at both the business-to-consumer (B2C) and business-to-business (B2B) markets.

Peter Whent, co-founder of Wishstream, also founded Transmit International in 1991, a leader in the UK electronic document distribution market. Following the successful sale of Transmit in 1995, he worked in various roles at facsimile service providers Xpedite Systems. His roles included sales director, managing director and director of international operations for Europe, the Middle East and Africa, a post he held until October 1999.

Co-founder and Vice President of Sales Miles Quitmann has held several senior sales management posts. In the early 1990s he was a successful manager in the sales organization at The Candle Corporation. Other roles include the post of sales director at data mining software vendor Active Analysis and Sales and Marketing Director at Systems Integrator, ISIS.

Another bainlab client, Takira.com, was formed in May 1999 in order to capitalize on the rapid migration of the offline direct marketing industry to online marketing via the Internet. Headquartered in San Francisco, Takira.com unites technology with professional services to help companies increase the effectiveness of their direct marketing campaigns.

ENTER THE ACCOUNTANTS

As well as the management consultants, the big accountancy practices are also joining the incubation business in a big way. PricewaterhouseCoopers

(PwC) is a case in point. PwC announced the launch of its own incubator in March 2000, pitched at both external entrepreneurs and its own staff. PwC claimed the incubator programme was backed by $500 million to fund expansion across Europe. To begin with, they launched in London and Paris, with offices in Amsterdam, Hamburg and Oslo following close behind.

PwC allows its own staff to develop ventures during three-month 'sabbaticals', should the firm believe the business plan stands up. After the first three months, if a venture looks likely to succeed, PwC consultants would be expected to run the start-up full-time and PwC would take an equity stake in it. The company cites clients such as QXL, 365 (see case example below) and Scottish Power spin-outs as their initial projects.

365

Dan Thompson, the founder of 365 Corporation, started his business on the back of his belief, shared presumably by the stock market who valued the firm at £285 million when it floated, that people have passion centres. Thompson, an Oxford graduate and chartered accountant, had previously founded and run his own computer games and software company, Renegade Software. Aged 35 he sold it to Time Warner for £5 million, netting about £1 million himself. The first service he offered was Football365, which provides personalized football content and news aimed at people who are passionate about football. The company is following the sector's tradition by having accelerating losses, £14.6 million in the year to March 2000, up from £1.2 million the preceding year. Whilst Thompson believes his passion centre belief is right and the Internet is a 'fantastic medium for making money', 365 is *not* making money. However, at the last count its cash reserves, helped no doubt by expert advisors, PwC included, was not in question, which is more than could be said for Oxygen, a business incubator itself (see Figure 11.2).

Apart from the explosive earning potential of an incubator – should any of its projects be successful – consultancies have another agenda in launching incubators. One is the desire to be seen as an integral part of the new economy, the other, frequently cited by outsiders and the consultants themselves, is the desire to retain key staff who might otherwise be lured away by the 'scent of equity'. Consultants across Europe are extracting greater flexibility from their employers when working with start-ups, as well as being given room to develop their own ideas, as some consultancies struggle to retain expensively trained staff.

Ernst & Young's Business Accelerator, also launched in 2000, works with early stage companies in order to rapidly grow their business, obtain

Company	£ million cash in bank (estimate)
lastminute.com	130
StepStone	127
QXL	80
gameplay.com	80
Freeserve	76
3i	75
The Exchange Group	60
Scoot.com	55
Just2Clicks	50
365 Corporation	50
freecom.net	40
NetStore	40
Paradigm	21
Letsbuyit.co	20
Affinity Internet	19
Oxygen	8

Figure 11.2   Cash reserves at the end of 2000.

critical funding and bring them to market, often taking a risk-sharing approach by accepting an equity stake. The preferred areas of focus are companies in the B2B market and enabling technologies, but they are also prepared to take on companies with existing business models looking to roll these out into global markets.

Their Business Accelerator team provides a mentoring service offering advice, guidance and support on issues ranging from the traditional Ernst & Young financial advisory services (fund-raising and business planning) to the wider areas of marketing, logistics, and helping CEOs to build their team. They believe in sharing the risks and rewards with their clients and are willing to consider innovative and flexible fee arrangements to help meet the needs of the new breed of businesses. *We will put our money where our mouth is* is their motto, at least as far as incubator companies are concerned.

Ernst & Young can provide all the services needed by fast-growing early-stage businesses utilizing both their internal network and external alliances. They have built up alliances with market leaders and best of breed companies within the 'early stage business market' in order to provide a complete service. They take a partnering approach and want to immerse themselves in the businesses they incubate. Partnering rather than client and service provider, holistic rather than specialist, virtual rather than concrete, and bespoke rather than off-the-peg, is the vocabulary they use to describe this relationship.

Within months of launching the Accelerator, Ernst & Young joined forces with Xworks, a London based e-business incubator. Wisely, Ernst &

Young appear to have recognized the mismatch between what a global giant can offer to an entrepreneur at the start-up stage. The two companies collaborate in the development and testing of business plans through a company's start-up and growth phase. Xworks provides practical services including technology and marketing and the development of online relationships. Ernst & Young Business Accelerator provides the essential strategic advice and support to enable fund-raising, business planning, team-building and structuring for the growth and development of the enterprise.

Xworks provides management and services for companies at start-up and incubator stage. As the business grows and the complexity of financial management requirements increases, Ernst & Young will provide the incubated companies with business advice on a larger scale. This includes fund-raising, business systems and planning for expansion, prior to enabling an exit strategy or third-stage funding. In effect, Ernst & Young are using Xworks, and others, as a pre-incubator before deciding if the opportunity is big enough for their 'big guns' to get involved.

Xworks, at the time they joined forces with Ernst & Young, were incubating six companies, five of which had already launched. Four of these companies are now generating revenue and three are in profit (see list below).

Xworks Incubator clients

- OntheBox.com, a platform-agnostic electronic TV listings guide.
- World Motor Sports Ltd, which has launched formula-1.co.uk, one of the UK's leading Internet destinations for fans of Formula 1 motor racing.
- Quantum Research, a profitable web-enabled outsource call centre.
- Space, an e-business solutions company.
- Careerplus, a recruitment agency operating in the IT and new media sectors.
- Chemserve, an electronic trading platform for the chemical industry.

EVERYONE IS AT IT

It is not only big management consultants and accountancy practices that are running incubation services for start-ups and small firms. Internet fever has brought almost every provider of services into the game. As the case example below demonstrates, there are lots of people who believe they have an invaluable resource that no small firm should be without. And they are prepared, just like their more conventional incubator competitors, to offer that resource or service on easy terms to selected clients.

EmployeeService.com

In 1998, when Jay Whitehead founded EmployeeService.com, a human resources firm in San Francisco, he set aside 5% of the shares to pay bills. His bank wanted equity before they would lend him money. Both his landlords asked for equity in the firm before they would rent him office space. He gave equity to people who referred business to him, and equity to the firms that leased him office equipment. Cisco Systems wanted stock valuation information before it would even send a salesman to see him, and equity to put him on a priority list for new equipment.

Then it was Jay Whitehead's turn. When he offered his firm's services to Internet start-ups he topped off his fee with equity in his clients: he took the cost of his firm's work in cash, and the profit in equity. Before long he was sitting on a portfolio of equity in more than a dozen firms, hoping more would go public than go bust, just like venture capitalists who once had this world of early-stage private equity to themselves.

A typical technology start-up will pay for legal services in part with equity (see Figure 11.3). Its public relations (PR) firm will take equity in lieu of some fees; so will its management consultants. There are venture branding firms, venture advertising firms, even venture building engineers. Software companies will offer licence fee discounts for equity. Venture head-hunters now try to take a third of a placed executive's first-year stock options along

Law firm	Number of clients in which it has an equity stake	Total equity value
Wilson, Sonsini, Goodrich & Rosati	34	230
Venture Law Group	16	62
Cooley Godward	17	45
Gunderson, Deffmer, Stough, Villeneuve, Franklin & Hachigian	11	31
Brobeck, Phleger & Harrison	12	22
Gray, Cary, Ware & Freidenrich	4	8
Fenwick & West	6	7

Figure 11.3   US law firms taking stakes in Internet clients.

with a cut of his salary. In tight office-space markets such as San Francisco and New York, a venture landlord may take equity equal to 3% of a rent over the term of the lease, on top of the rent itself.

A start-up may trade equity for advertising space in magazines; it may even give equity to a television network for airtime. Equipment vendors are willing to cut a deal for equity; even the cleaning firm that comes in at night will discount its fees for stock.

For start-ups too, there are risks as well as benefits. One benefit is that an equity stake aligns the interests of the service provider with those of the start-up, cementing a long-term relationship and reminding the service firm that the goal is to see the start-up succeed, not just to milk it for cash.

One risk, however, is that start-ups which give away equity indiscriminately in their early days may find that they do not have enough to keep their employees later. The smart ones pay cash for short-term relationships – a naming consultant, for instance – and save their equity for business marriages, such as their law or PR firm. Those that trade equity for a cheap database licence may feel locked into a single provider's technology. And any firm that gives away a percentage or two of the company to a headhunter may find in a year or two that it has conducted the most expensive executive search in history.

HAVE INCUBATORS BEEN A SUCCESS FOR CONSULTANTS?

Accelerators are a small, and arguably becoming smaller, part of these firms' business. They don't account separately, in published figures at any rate, for incubator activities. However, there are several indicators that early experience has not been good for consultants. In the first instance, many have made it all but impossible to find their incubator websites and many that can be relatively easily found have not been updated since the NASDAQ began its plunge to territory below the 2000 mark from its 4000 high when the incubator fever was at its peak. There was a flurry of press coverage in early 2000 covering the launch of their accelerators, but during the last quarter of 2000 and the first quarter of 2001 there has been almost a complete press blackout. There are few examples of consultants taking in new businesses and pushing them up the growth curve to an early IPO, making a fortune for their partners in the process.

But at least one problem has gone away. It's no longer difficult to recruit and retain great staff. The stampede from business school to Internet start-up has slowed to less than a trickle. A number of high-profile consulting executives who fell in love with the process of 'Accelerating' Internet and other high-tech firms are licking their wounds. The case study below illustrates that the skills that go into making great consultants, do not transpose easily into helping entrepreneurial ventures break into profitable territory.

George Shaheen, Andersen Consulting

In September 1999, George Shaheen, managing partner and chief executive at Andersen Consulting, was less than a year from being able to sail off into the sunset a rich man. He could retire early in 11 months and pocket a bonus of about $10 million. If he stayed around a little longer, he stood to reap a potentially juicy payout from his group's venture investments, plus a possible windfall of $50 million or more from a plan to separate the consulting division from its accounting sibling, Arthur Andersen. (The consulting arm split off a year later, and rebranded itself under the name Accenture.) Shaheen became an Andersen man right out of college in 1967 and rose to the head of the consulting business in 1989.

But there is a big difference between having a few tens of millions and having a billion in the bank. Shaheen got a call that month from David Beirne, general partner of Benchmark Capital, a big investor in Webvan, a three-and-a-half-year-old profitless online grocer that was about to go public. The company was looking for a high-profile CEO. The brain-child of Louis Borders, the father of mega-bookseller Borders, Webvan had stockpiled some $400 million in venture capital. Now it needed a high-profile executive to deliver the goods and give it some clout on Wall Street. It wanted Shaheen. The lure was 1.25 million shares of stock, plus 15 million options. Given the astronomically high share prices of the dotcom IPOs of the day, a billion-dollar payoff for Shaheen was not unimaginable. And so, after 32 years at the firm, having built its consulting business into a juggernaut with $9 billion in annual revenues, at 55 years of age Shaheen became a one-man incubator.

Two years later, the situation has turned decidedly sour. Webvan is seen by some investors and analysts as a living monument to the delusions formerly surrounding online retailing. Webvan shares peaked at $34 on the day of its IPO in November but started to slide in December; they hit $4.375 in April 2000. By April 2001 the shares were down to just ten cents and NASQAQ wanted to delist them from the index. More than $5 billion has been cleaved from Webvan's market capitalization and it has piled up $291.6 million in losses.

The grocery market is huge, at $650 billion annually. Online grocery selling has been a tiny part of that, with sales of $513 million last year, according to Forrester Research (2000). The company's shares may have been unfairly lumped in with the rest of the online grocery players – industry pioneer Peapod, Streamline.com – and other e-tailers the stock market has savaged. Shaheen had his sights on the elusive 'last mile' of e-commerce, the golden pathway into the consumers' home that everyone from Amazon.com (who is suing Webvan for $6.25 million over an alleged breach of an advertising agreement), to Wal-Mart, to Fred Smith's FedEx have sought in vain. Bridge the last mile, they all believe, and fabulous riches await. The goal for Webvan was to bring home the bacon and whatever else the customer requested, by refrigerated truck, within 30 minutes of the appointed hour. They can do that easily now and under Shaheen's leadership the company has met or exceeded every performance milestone it set for itself: sales growth, customer satisfaction, repeat users, gross margin. But his time has run out. Whilst Webvan is not George Shaheen's first experience in the grocery game (his first job was bagging groceries and trimming beef part-time with his identical twin brother, Gerald, at their father's U-Save grocery store near Elmwood, Illinois) it will almost certainly be his last.

On 17 April 2001 Shaheen announced his resignation as chairman and chief executive of Webvan. He was quoted in the UK *Daily Telegraph* that day as saying, 'Webvan is an innovative business model which redefines the future of retailing and the way people shop. Unfortunately, changes in the capital markets have altered the timetable and operating approach. A different kind of executive is needed to lead the company at this time.'

But it wasn't just changes in the capital markets that caused Shaheen's problems. Webvan itself had moved beyond its entry business model and was selling pet food, office supplies, electronics, and almost any merchandise that could be transported in a van. It stocked nearly 4000 non-grocery items, and did virtually everything except make money.

Shaheen may have found his headline coverage on 17 April distressing, but that was nothing to what he must have felt when he read this widely reported press story just two days later.

Dallas, 19 April 2001

Accenture announced today that its partners have voted overwhelmingly to proceed with an initial public offering. Accordingly, it has filed a registration statement with the Securities and Exchange Commission for a proposed offering of Class A common shares.

Accenture's newly issued shares will be offered by an underwriting syndicate led by joint book-running managers Goldman, Sachs & Co. and Morgan Stanley. Joe W. Forehand, Accenture managing partner and CEO, said, 'Our partners' decision reflects our organization's commitment to enhance our long-term growth, strengthen our ability to deliver the highest-value solutions to our clients and continue to provide competitive rewards to motivate and attract the best people.'

Accenture is the world's leading provider of management and technology consulting services and solutions. More than 70 000 people in 46 countries deliver a wide range of specialized capabilities and solutions to clients across all industries. Under its strategy, Accenture is building a network of businesses to meet the full range of client needs – consulting, technology, outsourcing, alliances and venture capital.

12

Variations on a theme

Not all business incubators or incubation processes can be easily pigeonholed. Universities, venture capital firms, business angels, consultants, accountants and the corporate venture departments of big firms often combine, coalesce or collaborate in all manner of ways to change their offering and gain an advantage, however temporary, in the incubator marketplace. You have to remember that all these organizations are hunting the same quarry, the real entrepreneur, and they are operating in waters that have already been overfished. And in some of the international waters that new incubators are now fishing in, there were few fish to begin with. A 10-nation study by the London Business School and Babson College found a big gap between entrepreneurship in North America and Europe. Based on surveys of 10 000 people in spring 1999, one in 12 Americans is trying to found a new business, compared with just one in 30 Britons, one in 45 Germans and one in 67 Finns.

Anyone can get involved in helping people to get a business started, but to be truly successful an incubator needs to lure in people who could probably succeed without their help. But with it they might just get there a bit faster or do things on a bigger scale. Here are some of the players who have different kinds of incubator offering, each aimed at a particular market segment.

FOCUSED INCUBATORS

Most of the incubators we have looked at so far will take on most types of high-tech business with high growth prospects, and some are even less fussy than that. Some incubators set out to appeal to a certain group of enterprises, or at least to a narrow segment. The logic here is that you can't be all things to all men. If your institution has a particular strength, then why not emphasize it? Whilst doing so may narrow the funnel of potential entrants, the value that can be added to those selected should be correspondingly greater. This incubation strategy has been researched and reasonably well understood for some time (Galante 1987), but appears to be enjoying a new popularity, not least with those incubators concentrating only on Internet business for their prospective client base. But even lumping technology, including the Internet and industry-focused, between them they account for fewer than one in five incubators (PricewaterhouseCoopers 1999, and see Figure 12.1).

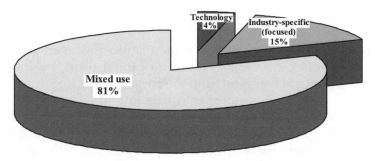

Figure 12.1   Incubator focus.

This section gives some examples of focused incubators and how they operate.

Project Hatchery

Operated by CALSTART, the US's first advanced transportation consortium, this incubator is only open to business ideas relevant to the transportation field. The 'Entrance Gates', as the entry criteria are called by Project Hatchery staff, invite applicants only if they pass six hurdles:

- you must be proposing an advanced transportation product or service;
- you should be commercially viable within three years;
- you can leave the incubator at any time, but you may only stay longer than two years by special arrangement;
- you must have a viable business plan (how this is different from the second point is not made clear!);
- you should have the potential to create jobs in California; and
- you should be able to pay all participation costs.

Hatchery offers shop and office space to get work done, machine and hand tools to fabricate prototypes and pilot production runs, legal, accounting, business and management support services, network access to over 200 member organizations, product and programme support through marketing and media access, industry news and information, ongoing notices of technology funding opportunities, and guidance in technical and financial proposal preparation.

Based on the former Alameda Naval Air Station at Alameda Point in California, the incubator is only twenty minutes by ferry across the bay from San Francisco's financial district, and fifteen minutes from Oakland International Airport. It is also a place of great and unexpected natural beauty. Almost half the area is a wildlife preserve, which has stunning views of the Bay, the Bay Bridge and the San Francisco skyline. The Golden Gate is just visible in the distance.

Even the incubator itself is sub-segmented into even tighter focus areas. WestStart, for example, is the area where emerging companies in the clean air transportation industry can get all the help they need to grow and succeed. Included in the low rental here is access to furnished conference rooms, a kitchen, a lunch room, machine shop, fax and high-speed copier.

Also located on the site at Alameda is ACET, the Alameda Center for Environmental Technologies, a business incubator helping environmental and biotech start-ups. Here they aim for 'a collegial atmosphere so entrepreneurs can meet and network with each other'. ACET has a co-operative arrangement with a French incubator, Savoie Technolac, giving their clients 'fast-track access to European Union markets and to emerging European technologies'. ACET is also affiliated to Berkeley National Science Laboratory at California State University. Their link with the Oakland office of the Department of Energy helps with grant funding and expert advice. ACET's graduate companies include Baffin, Inc., who licence advanced wastewater treatment processes, and Biometrology, Inc., who provide out-sourced scanning and analytical services for the biomaterials, biomedical, pharmaceutical and polymer industries.

Palo Alto Research Center (PARC)

In 1970, Xerox Corporation gathered together a team of world-class re-searchers and gave them the mission of creating an 'architecture of informa-tion'. The scientists at the PARC, which was based in Palo Alto, California, lived up to this challenge by inventing personal distributed computing, graphical user interfaces, the first commercial mouse, bitmapped displays, an ethernet, client/server architecture, object-oriented programming, laser printing and many of the basic protocols of the Internet. In the years since

Xerox established the Palo Alto Research Center, PARC technologies have changed the computing world.

The PARC is a magnet for people interested in commercializing any of its three areas of technological excellence, and businesses are constantly being started up and spun out.

The work of PARC centres loosely around three areas.

- *Smart matter*: Future software and hardware systems will be characterized by modularity, dynamic reconfiguration, collaboration between a large number of entities, and the blurring of boundaries between the physical and computational worlds. The Smart Matter theme encompasses a broad range of research to enable new classes of products that optimize the use of microscale technologies and create a tight coupling between computational and physical functions. The research space spans communication, computation, control, device design and fabrication, and systems integration.
- *Networks and documents*: PARC has a legacy of deep understanding of networking and large dynamic systems. Work in this theme builds on that understanding as well as drawing on PARC's world-class competence in security, programming languages, and systems design.
- *Knowledge ecologies*: PARC's work in knowledge ecologies spans Internet, communication, computation, systems integration, and knowledge. The resulting technologies are used in a broad range of knowledge management, knowledge sharing and e-commerce applications, either as discrete components or integrated into application suites or solutions. Experts consider the standard of PARC's knowledge ecologies work to be world-class; Xerox has won numerous international awards for work originating in this area.

The Women's Technology Cluster (WTC)

This has, as its name implies, two filters on the types of businesses it wants to attract. In the first place, their services are aimed at women, and only at women with technology-based business ideas. Based in San Francisco, like Project Hatchery and a few dozen more business incubators, WTC is the brainchild of Cate Muther, a former senior vice-president at Cisco Systems. They have raised about $550,000 from public groups such as the city of San Francisco and from private firms such as Pacific Gas and Electric.

The WTC was founded as an entrepreneurial community of technology businesses in which women have a principal ownership stake. They only take in start-up business in IT-related areas such as business software, multimedia, Internet, infrastructure, telecommunications, wireless, digital media, business process automation and so on. Each company receives market-rate office space with shared facilities, as well as management assistance and mentoring to enhance its success.

The central objective of the WTC is to help women entrepreneurs get access to capital. They base their argument that women get a raw deal in this area on the research findings of the National Foundation of Women Business Owners (1996). They report:

> . . . that of the nearly eight million women-owned businesses in the US, only 1% have used venture capital financing. Technology companies represent the majority of venture capital deals. Over 30% of all newly formed women-owned businesses are in the technology-based sector. Yet women received only 1.6% of the $33.5 billion invested by venture capitalists over the five years to 1996.

And that is despite the fact that 37% of those graduating with MBAs in the US, are women, a high proportion of whom are probably working in the same venture capital firms that are turning down women-managed business proposals!

A second major objective of the WTC is educating entrepreneurs to give back to the community. The WTC planned to establish a culture and value system of giving back, influencing entrepreneurs in the formative stages of their businesses. WTC graduates would establish a pattern of philanthropy.

Each new business entering the WTC contributes a small percentage of the firm's equity into a Venture Philanthropy Fund. The Venture Philanthropy Fund becomes an indexed portfolio of stock options in the businesses that join the WTC community and its network of community and business partners. The Fund is an asset of the non-profit-making WTC. Within the venture capital return horizon of between seven and ten years, they expect the Fund to hold equity in some successful public companies. As WTC companies achieve liquidity through merger/acquisition or an IPO, funds can become available for social investment in the non-profit sector. Income from the Fund goes to provide grants to sustain the WTC and to support other non-profit programmes in the community addressing social and economic change. The Venture Philanthropy Fund is the vehicle for entrepreneurs to give back, and the sustainability model for the future of the WTC.

So far, WTC has accepted less than 10% of business applicants into the incubator, and WTC companies raised $61 million in private equity in the first 16 months of the incubator's operation.

The WTC provides incoming companies with facilities and resources, increased access to venture capital, and a team of technology, marketing, recruiting and finance specialists. By aggregating the key elements of successful business development under one roof, the WTC creates a collaborative environment that allows entrepreneurs to focus on building their businesses.

The WTC provides members with the following core facility services: a month-to-month lease including furnished office space, professional facility management, 24-hour access, shared conference rooms, multimedia projection equipment, copy and fax equipment and a computer network with high-speed Internet access. Companies also enjoy access to the Panasonic Venture Fund, as well as regular seminars by industry experts.

Four companies graduated in the first 18 months: Latino.com, IDS, MyPsych.com, and AudioBasket.com. Other WTC incubator users are discussed in the following sections.

Vistify   Co-founder Menekse Gencer
Vistify is pioneering the evolution in e-commerce towards an always-on, any-device user experience. Vistify's new e-commerce solution has two distinct features: a single shopping trolley across multiple access devices as well as multiple e-commerce categories, and a database that tracks household behaviour across all categories. Vistify provides a turnkey end-to-end e-commerce offering that network operators and device manufacturers can leverage to bring value-added services to their users.

To date, network operators (cable, DSL, satellite, wireless) have been unsuccessful at extracting incremental revenue from the e-commerce running through their cables. In today's environment, most network and appliance operators extract only flat access fees per customer household. Vistify gives network solutions to enable differentiating, value-added e-commerce services for which they can extract incremental fees.

AgentArts, Inc.   Co-founder Kerri Lee Sinclair
AgentArts, Inc. is a Melbourne- and San Francisco-based company developing personalized entertainment profiling services designed to assist consumers in browsing, navigating, and purchasing entertainment content, starting with music. The company was founded in early 1999, and has recently launched its first-release product, AgentMusic (www.agentmusic.com), a music profiling and referral service.

ComMira E-Solutions Ltd.   CEO Lam Sun
Applying the latest Internet-based technology to revitalize the food and grocery distribution and retail business, ComMira designs, builds,

and operates a unified web-based working environment, incorporating both software applications and hardware appliances, that integrate internal business processes and external collaboration across the food and grocery distribution chain.

LevelEdge   CEO Lisa Henderson
LevelEdge provides database applications and services for amateur and professional sports team management, leading the sports team management market with relationships that include the NCAA, Nike, key high school and coaching associations, professional sports teams, and camp/clinic organizations.

MEconomy, Inc.   CEO Valerie Buckingham
MEconomy, Inc. is a seed-stage privacy-focused infomediary. Their team of online marketing, profiling and security experts have developed a simple, scalable service that incentivizes and empowers individuals to be in total control of their privacy and the market value of their personal information. MEconomy provides permissioned targeted marketing (where users can give or deny permission for information about them to be disclosed), as well as a partner proposition for Portals, ISPs and Ad Networks to access permissioned profiles.

MsMoney.com   CEO Tiffany Bass Bukow
MsMoney.com, Inc. is a financial services Internet company offering financial education to women.

StageSmart   CEO Yola Haddad
StageSmart has created a cost-efficient and sophisticated solution that allows retailers in highly fragmented, information-intensive industries to sell effectively and efficiently online. StageSmart first targeted the high-end audio and video equipment industries, solving a $30 billion problem for 17 000 retailers who can now extract incremental fees.

Focused incubators don't just operate in the US, they abound throughout the world. Some focused incubators are small affairs, but in Malaysia, a rather more ambitious project is under way.

Madness in Malaysia

Multimedia Super Corridor (MSC): In the Malaysian hinterland, flanked by palm-oil plantations that have operated here for decades and close to the international airport for Kuala Lumpur curiously sited miles from the capital itself, a mammoth business incubation project has been established. It is Malaysia's Multimedia Super Corridor (MSC), the brainchild of Prime Minister Mahathir Mohamad. Mahathir set out to build – from scratch – Asia's version of Silicon Valley, a huge zone stretching 750 square kilometres, an area slightly larger than Singapore. The project, started in the mid-1990s, was to cost $20 billion and take two decades to finish. It promised fibre-optic networks, research facilities, tax breaks, and new 'cyberlaws' to any multinational setting up shop. Malaysia would provide the best incubator in the world for high-tech businesses and create an environment in which a native high-tech industry could take root and boost the country into the ranks of developed nations by 2020.

Working with advisers such as Kenichi Ohmae, then a top consultant at McKinsey & Co., the Malaysian leader envisioned an IT nirvana. In a new city called Cyberjaya, Malaysians and foreigners would work side by side in 'intelligent buildings' wired with the latest technology. Mahathir attracted a Who's Who of the IT industry to give the project credibility. Rivals such as Bill Gates of Microsoft, Larry Ellison of Oracle, and Scott McNealey of Sun Microsystems all agreed to sit on a 41-member advisory panel. Coupled with cheap land and an inexpensive, English-speaking workforce, Malaysia stood a chance of passing Singapore as the region's premier technology centre. Mahathir also pledged a new capital city, Putrajaya, where the federal government – including the Prime Minister himself – would work electronically. He drew up a set of 'cyberlaws' to protect intellectual property and prevent computer crime. He proposed a new NASDAQ-style stock exchange, the Malaysian Exchange of Securities Dealing & Automated Quotation, or MESDAQ, to provide capital for local high-tech startups. At one end of the corridor, Mahathir built the world's tallest buildings, the Petronas Twin Towers. At the other, 50 kilometres to the south, was the futuristic Kuala Lumpur International Airport. Travelling the globe to promote the MSC in 1997, Mahathir called the corridor 'a gift to the world', and 'a global bridge to the Information Age'. The aims of the corridor were to create:

- a vehicle for attracting world-class technology-led companies to Malaysia, and developing local industries;
- a multimedia utopia offering a productive, intelligent environment within which a multimedia value chain of goods and services would be produced and delivered across the globe;
- an island of excellence with multimedia-specific capabilities, technologies, infrastructure, legislation, policies, and systems for competitive advantage;

- a test bed for invention, research, and other ground-breaking multimedia developments spearheaded by seven multimedia applications;
- a global community living on the leading edge of the Information Society; and
- a world of Smart Homes, Smart Cities, Smart Schools, Smart Cards and Smart Partnerships.

To achieve these goals, three phases of activity were envisaged:

Phase I: In this phase, the Malaysian Development Corporation (MDC) would successfully create the Multimedia Super Corridor, attract a core group of world-class companies, launch seven flagship applications, put in place a world-leading framework of cyberlaws, and establish Cyberjaya and Putrajaya as world-first intelligent cities.

Phase II: The MDC envisaged that, during this period, it would link the MSC to other cybercities in Malaysia and the world. It will create a web of corridors and establish a second cluster of world-class companies. It would also set global standards in flagship applications, champion cyberlaws within the global society, and establish a number of intelligent globally-linked cities.

Phase III: During this final phase, it is expected that Malaysia will be transformed into a knowledge-based society, a true global test bed for new multimedia and IT applications and a cradle for a record number of multimedia companies. It will have a cluster of intelligent cities linked to the global information super-highway, and become the platform for the International Cybercourt of Justice.

Mahathir's rhetoric may have gone down well in the West, but the Kuala Lumpur taxi drivers knew the truth. Relocating the capital was extravagant madness, whilst the present capital was still a building site. Roads, bridges and rail links in Kuala Lumpur are primitive, to say the least, and in any event the country is driven by ethnic divisions that need more than a Multimedia Super Corridor to link them. The big firms have either withdrawn or scaled back their investment plans. Like the half-finished, almost deserted shopping malls in Kuala Lumpur, that were the hope for economic wealth in the 1980s, the concept of the Super Corridor has a hollow feel to it. (In those shopping malls, pirate copies of Microsoft Office 2000 and almost any other program you cared to name can be had for £1, which makes Malaysia's cyber-laws look a little hollow too.)

The biggest beneficiary of Malaysia's problems has been Singapore, where they have quietly pushed forward with plans to attract multinational companies. Sun Microsystems, for example, has devoted far more resources to Singapore than to Kuala Lumpur. In 2000 Sun had just 30 workers in Malaysia, while it employed about 200 in Singapore. Hong Kong, too, is now trying to steal Malaysia's thunder, by earmarking $1.7 billion to develop a new IT zone; Shanghai also has high-tech plans; mainland China has plans for 400 business incubators, and almost every other country in the region has plans of a similar scale. With a technology downturn occurring in the West, it is hard to see the likes of Cisco or Motorola shedding thousands of jobs in Europe and investing in a risky project like this.

The essence of Silicon Valley is not fibre-optic cables . . . it is its creative, innovative drive and the large numbers of people racing to create new ideas. There is still not much evidence of this happening yet in Malaysia, but the Malaysians are a resourceful and talented people, and a scaled-down and refocused incubator programme may well yet succeed. But with $5 billion already spent and a website that stopped recording the project's milestones in 1999 the signs are not too good.

Interactive Minds

Not all focused incubators are grand follies, nor are they based on university campuses. Interactive Minds (http://www.iminds.com/) is a cross between a virtual incubator with no central location, a genre that will be examined in the next section, and a business angel with a clear view of the sort of entrepreneurs he wants to attract. Established in 1995 by Randy Haykin, a Yahoo! founder, Interactive Minds has its real-world home in Pleasanton, California. Haykin calls his incubator a 'catalyst' because it pumps money into companies preparing for large infusions of venture capital. Unlike traditional seed investing, Haykin's approach involves a hands-on approach. For instance, he personally assists in a company's executive recruitment. Doing this is not easy, however. Haykin estimates that he reviews as many as 750 business plans annually, choosing just five per year – with his firm taking as much as a 30% equity stake in a start-up.

The incubator focuses on prototype and early-stage enterprise software and services companies. They recognize that most new companies not only seek funding but also desire active 'hands-on' assistance. Interactive Minds leverages the extensive operating backgrounds of its principals and their established network of seasoned industry professionals. Such active 'hands-on' involvement has proven to be valuable in helping to launch and accelerate the growth of their client companies.

Interactive Minds only recruits companies based in the western United States and primarily targets companies based in Silicon Valley and the San Francisco Bay area. Their industry focus is enterprise software, including applications, platforms, services, and technologies. They are most keen on supply chain integration and management, knowledge management, e-learning, information management retrieval and storage, and cross-enterprise applications. They are happy to pump anything from $250 000 to $5 million into the firms they back, and will typically invest $500 000 to $2 million in a first round of financing, followed by additional amounts in later rounds.

Over the past five years the incubator has been very successful in attracting clients with businesses that have certainly been worthy of their acceleration process. Some have had successful IPOs and quite a few have been sold on to people Haykin no doubt rubbed shoulders with in his days at Yahoo!

Incubated companies include the following:

CyberStateU.com, an interactive e-learning company providing advanced skills development to the corporations and individuals who drive the Internet. CyberStateU.com has had five years of successful experience in delivering distance learning to over 5000 IT and computer telephony specialists worldwide before coming into the incubator process.

dotBank supplies a person-to-person payment platform allowing individuals to send and receive money over the Internet. The growth in person-to-person sales transactions on auction and classified services has resulted in a demand for a more convenient payment mechanism than bank drafts or money orders.

Freeworks is a business service platform that incorporates management and administrative solutions to support small business processes. The platform accommodates organic workflow business automation technology that enables the rapid introduction of new, integrated services by a provider and simple use by the small business.

Impulse! Buy Network was created to combine the rapid growth of online shopping and e-commerce with the popularity of impulse buying among consumers who seek quality merchandise.

www.eteamz.com, named a 'Hot Site' by both USA Today and Sports Illustrated for Kids, runs an online community for connecting players, coaches, and families to the sports they love. The company aims to bring the excitement of amateur sports to the Internet by providing free league, team and individual player websites, tips and drills, communications tools, commerce and services for sports participants, coaches, officials, families and friends.

iOwn.com, founded in 1996 under the name HomeShark.com, streamlines and facilitates the home buying and refinancing process, while aiming to provide 'the best possible customer experience'. iOwn's goal is to help customers feel confident that they are making the best financial decisions and getting the best deal on their mortgage, often the largest financial transaction of their lifetime. The company distinguishes itself from other similar companies by offering low-cost mortgages, home listings searches and an incomparable level of service.

THE NET WORKERS

A view long held by researchers (Grayson 2000) and entrepreneurs is that, next to money, the key to success is knowing the right people. The right people are not always the top people. They are a group that is hard to define and even harder to contact. They are people, perhaps with money, certainly with knowledge and experience, and with an enthusiasm for new and small businesses. They may even want to move out of their safe job and join an entrepreneurial venture. Every incubator claims to foster networking, even if it is nothing more sophisticated than a chance to talk over your problems with fellow sufferers. However, one type of business incubator has turned networking into an art form. Like Brainshark's Thursday evening gatherings on their roof terrace, these networking incubators have found the way to get the right people to meet each other and get what they want from each other. Whilst some argue that such 'casual' networks may not be effective, they would be flying in the face of both experience and research evidence. Philip Davies and Mitchell Koza (2001) have argued that both weak and new networks can have a big impact, as there are fewer barriers to implementation and no entrenched views to overcome, as is often the case in more formal network structures such as trade or research associations.

The MIT Enterprise Forum is the pioneer in this sector. Based at Massachusetts Institute of Technology in the US, the Forum promotes the formation and growth of innovative and technologically-oriented companies through a series of specialized executive education programmes. Founded in 1978, it operates through a network of 23 chapters in the US and overseas. Member chapters are formed around a core group of MIT graduates. Membership and programme participation is open to all – non-MIT graduates, friends of MIT, local business executives and entrepreneurs. Each chapter is run by a volunteer board of experienced entrepreneurs, corporate executives, university professors and industry leaders.

Forum chapters offer advice, support and educational services for emerging technology-based companies. Programmes may include:

- professional seminars;
- start-up clinics;
- case presentations; and
- business plan workshops.

Perhaps the most valuable feature of Enterprise Forum activities is the opportunity provided to network with a variety of business professionals, including:

- venture capitalists;
- private investors;
- industry experts;
- other successful entrepreneurs;
- bankers;
- accountants; and
- big firm managers looking for a career change.

Over the past 20 years, the MIT Enterprise Forum claims it has assisted approximately 1000 companies by making their business plans more attractive to financial resources, building management teams, focusing on specific markets, developing strategic alliances, and increasing profits. MIT officials say that at least 30 companies, with an aggregate value of $180 million, have been created as a result of the business plan competition alone.

Business plan competitions are held each year, to encourage and stimulate entrepreneurs to write up their business plans by offering some help in the process, a critical audience to evaluate their proposals, and a cash prize for the winners.

The business plan competitions are fierce but friendly. Organizers said that of the 120 entrepreneurs or so that enter the competition each year, only six finalists get to the public judging forum. The close to 500 spectators watched as the teams presented summations of their technologies and business plans.

MIT entrepreneurs are generous as well as ambitious, in a way that would make Cate Muther, founder of the Women's Technology Cluster, proud of them.

At the ninth annual business plan competition held on the MIT campus, in 1990, the winner, Direct Hit, turned down its $30 000 prize. The founder said that as their firm had recently received venture funding, they wanted others to have their winnings. This sum was then split evenly between three also-rans who had not been in line to receive any money. In the same year, an anonymous donor then gave $30 000 to competition organizers when it was learned there were two first-place winners. Thus both winners were awarded the top prize of $30 000. The top prize is now $1 million.

First Tuesday is the global meeting-place and marketplace for start-ups. At First Tuesday events and on its website, entrepreneurs can connect with all the services and goods they need to fuel growth: capital, talent, technology, knowledge and services.

Founded in October 1998 in London, First Tuesday currently hosts events in more than 100 cities across the globe. So far, First Tuesday has helped entrepreneurs to raise over $150 million of seed capital and has over 100 000 members.

First Tuesday takes the entrepreneur's side. They believe that entrepreneurs are made, not born; that an efficient start-up marketplace should exist for entrepreneurs everywhere; and that smart people who do not live in Silicon Valley, who are not already rich, or who have not already created a company, should be able to get funding based on merit – their drive, their passion for their business, their track record, their idea, their energy. First Tuesday help to make this possible.

The First Tuesday community began in October 1998 in the Alphabet Bar in Soho, London, when Julie Meyer, Mark Davies, Adam Gold and Nick Denton brought together 80 friends involved in creating new media companies. The event was a success. Deals were done, friendships forged, and the growth of First Tuesday began, at Internet speed. John Browning joined the founding group in January 1999.

It was to a First Tuesday meeting in April 2000 that Ernst Malmsten, chief executive of Boo.com and Kajsa Leander, the co-founder and former fashion model, took to the platform to tackle, as he said, 'the hot issue'. He said: 'Boo has never revealed any financial information and has been seen as very secretive. This has fuelled speculation about targets, burn rate and our valuation.' To scotch some of this speculation, Mr Malmsten pulled a piece of folded orange paper from his pocket. With a flourish reminiscent of an actor revealing an Oscar prizewinner, he read out Boo.com's sales figures from Monday that week. They revealed that the gross order value of goods sold that day, net of the new 40% discount, was $83 063 (£50 648) from 1078 orders. Visitors viewing the site amounted to 36 381. The conversion rate was 2.96% – not much of a return on an £80 million investment!

Investors, who unsurprisingly are in a very small minority these days, wear red badges and try to avoid being ravaged by dotcom hopefuls, who wear green badges. In the meantime, numerous yellow badges – worn by business services companies, head-hunters and journalists – mill around and get in the way. From the original meeting to today's global network of over 100 000 subscribers, the needs of the entrepreneur have remained at the core of First Tuesday's business. First Tuesday provides:

- Classic events: Open, informal gatherings whose attendees include a mix of investors (red dots), entrepreneurs (green dots) and professional service providers (yellow dots).
- Matchmaking events: First Tuesday dominates the offline, physical matchmaking space for ideas and capital in Europe today. The first matchmaking event was held in London in November 1999, and successful themed events have since been hosted in cities including Zurich, Berlin, Prague and London. Business plans are submitted via the web, evaluated by a team of experts, and matched with investors.
- Wireless Wednesday: events focus on educating entrepreneurs and investors within the wireless industry.
- First Tuesday forum: An online discussion group for the European Internet industry.
- First Tuesday jobs: Currently in 24 cities across Europe, First Tuesday Jobs helps start-ups to find people via email and the web.
- First Tuesday Daily News Round-up powered by moreover.com: Web headlines harvested by moreover.com.
- First Tuesday Offices: an online exchange of under-utilized office space across Europe.

However much would-be entrepreneurs liked the parties, and however successful the networking events, as a financial investment First Tuesday was as much a disaster as many of the firms it fostered. In February 2001 the business was sold to the local organizers of the group's events for £1 million. It was put up for sale in March 2001 by the Israeli incubator Yazam as part of a restructuring programme that led to the closure of its European operations. Yazam paid £50 million for First Tuesday, barely 18 months ago.

But with sponsorship claimed from major companies including McKinsey & Co, Morgan Stanley Dean Witter, Spencer Stuart, Russell Reynolds, Oracle, Sun Microsystems, Excite@Home, NewMedia Investors, Berwin Leighton, Goldman Sachs, CSFB, Robertson Stephens, IBM, Arthur Anderson, VEO.net, Apax, Europ@Web and PricewaterhouseCoopers, First Tuesday could be around for some time yet.

Other networks that work in a similar way are discussed in this section:

Webgrrls (www.webgrrls.org.uk) – established American website for women, with offshoots in many countries, including this UK version. It holds meetings on the third Wednesday of every month.

Digital People (www.digitalpeople.org) – a Silicon Valley group hosting London events for entrepreneurs and venture capitalists.

e-women (www.e-women.org) – a monthly meeting for women in new media.

Internet Alchemy (http://internetalchemy.org) – a meeting on the third Wednesday of the month called Wap Wednesday. This focuses on wireless uses for Internet technology.

Venturefest fair, an annual event run in June, was started up in 1999 in Oxford, England, by faculty members of the newly created Saïd Business School. It is run in much the same way as a computer show would be run. It is held in an exhibition-type venue, though this year it is being held in the UK Atomic Energy Authority's Culham Science Centre, a local powerhouse of high-tech innovation and enterprise in Oxfordshire, England. Culham is not only the centre of excellence for the UK's domestic fusion research and development programme, but also hosts the flagship European fusion experiment JET, the premier facility of its type anywhere in the world. The Culham site is also home to many high-tech businesses, some of which have spun out from mainstream UKAEA fusion activities over the years.

The Venturefest events include specialist seminars, networking events and business competitions. An exhibition runs alongside the fair that allows innovators, new businesses and sponsors to demonstrate new technologies and showcase commercial opportunities. The centrepiece of the event is the business plan competition, run in a similar way to that at the MIT Forum, discussed above. Open to teams or individuals from around the world, it attracts entries from entrepreneurs, innovators, scientists and academics from a wide variety of backgrounds. Sixteen of the submitted entries are selected to attend the final stages of the competition, which are held during the two-day Venturefest fair. Entrants are offered business plan coaching from a team of corporate financiers. The winner this year was an MBA team from Cranfield School of Management, who collected a £10 000 prize, donated by Reuters Greenhouse Fund.

VIRTUAL INCUBATORS

Unlike traditional incubators, which offer a protected, safe environment for start-up entrepreneurs to nurse their fledgling businesses, virtual incubators are typically web-based resources which go some way beyond simply being an e-version of a small business magazine. These incubators help companies in the early stages of development that eventually plan to seek major funding. Members may be start-up companies seeking angel investors, or entrepreneurs in the pre-start-up stage who are seeking legal, accounting, or marketing resources or help in putting together a business plan. Virtual incubators screen entrepreneurs, vendors and investors against a number of criteria and try to create the illusion of a First Tuesday-type event, but over the Internet.

The obvious advantage of a virtual incubator over a networking event is the time you save. The bit that's missing with a virtual incubator is personal contact and empathy. Two examples of well-established virtual incubators from both sides of the Atlantic are EntreWorld and the International Centre for Entrepreneurship and Ventures Development. These will now be discussed.

EntreWorld (http://www.entreworld.org) is designed to increase an entrepreneur's productivity by getting them essential information as quickly and easily as possible. Launched in 1996 as one of the first small business websites, EntreWorld is part of the legacy of one of America's greatest entrepreneurs – Ewing Marion Kauffman. His vision – 'self-sufficient people in healthy communities' – was the driving force behind the Kauffman Center for Entrepreneurial Leadership in the US. They actively seek out and provide content, and have more than 1000 current articles, audio clips, tools, databases and even town-to-town small business event listings. They have created an entrepreneur's search engine which narrows the web down to subjects that might appeal to entrepreneurs. The most valuable incubator assets they have are The Resource Database (The entrepreneur's search engine, which covers more than 1000 web resources for entrepreneurs, selected, reviewed and organized for easy reference. Content is ducted through four main channels – Starting Your Business, Growing Your Business, Rapid Growth and Supporting Entrepreneurship); Peer-to-Peer Learning (Entrepreneur's bylines: EntreWorld successfully engages renowned business founders to share their insights with other entrepreneurs. Each month, EntreWorld offers three to five new Entrepreneur's Bylines through which entrepreneurs explore the difficult but important lessons they've learned in their rise to the top); and Events Calendar (Search by city or date, and pull up listings of nearby small business meetings and conferences where you can network with and learn from other entrepreneurs, provided you are in the US, of course).

The International Centre for Entrepreneurship and Ventures Development (ICEVED) is a very different proposition. It is an initiative of 25 business schools offering global links to other business schools, entrepreneurs, investors and information. The information side of their offer is at least as useful as that provided by EntreWorld, but what is most valuable is their links to distance learning programmes. Here entrepreneurs can learn how to do the books, carry out market research or write up their business plans. Some of these learning packages are free, supplied by ICEVED's sponsors and members. There is also a networking service so that entrepreneurs can show the executive summary of their business plan to VCs and angels. The site can also be used to find students anywhere in the world to carry out market research to validate a business proposition, investigate market opportunities, or size up a distant competitor. The database can also be used for finding employees or business partners. Business schools participating include Cranfield in the UK, Instituto de Empressa (Madrid), London Business School and SDA Bocconi in Milan. There is a strong representation of South American business schools. IBM is the site sponsor. Business angels and VCs looking for high-tech businesses being started up by high-flying international MBA students are heavy users of this incubator networking service. The incubator is open to anyone, not just business school students and alumni, as is the MIT Forum mentioned earlier. You just have to register.

Virtual incubation is not as easy a process as might at first be imagined. matchco.co.uk set out to offer a fast-track service matching electronic business entrepreneurs to funding. The service also offered interactive assessment of ideas and proposals, access to professional advice and a secure environment for developing online business plans with advisors. Established in February 2000, the service was launched by Eurobell, a division of the telecommunications company Deutsche Telekom, who also offer Internet and related services. But by February 2001, the service had been temporarily suspended, which is Internet code for closed down. match.co's slogan was 'turning good ideas into real businesses'. Virtual incubation is a good idea, but even big companies such as Deutsche Telekom can find it difficult to make them work in the real world.

DIY (DO IT YOURSELF) INCUBATORS

Generally, business incubators are formed by one organization to attract other weaker organizations that have something to gain from being under their wing. But it is perfectly possible for small organizations to achieve the same end result for themselves, and so save the erosion of equity that is almost inevitably the price to be paid to incubator 'owners'. In the wider business arena, such structures are known as co-operatives and, as such, rarely have profit maximization as their goal, or high-tech as their medium. But some high-tech firms have succeeded in forming what are in effect self-managing incubators. The story of the birth and development of what is considered to be the founder member of this select club is told below.

A tiny company, Technical and Computer Graphics (TCG), was founded by Peter Fritz and three other computer specialists in Sydney,

Australia in 1971 (Duff 1999). For them all, it was their first attempt to run a business of their own. They gained their start with two significant breaks: first, they had a customer in the form of an order for some programming that one of the partners brought with him from the Commonwealth Department of Supply; second, they obtained a $5000 overdraft from the Bank of New South Wales (now Westpac), which gave them the working capital needed to tide them over their first months. Turnover in the first year was $69 000. The business was a struggle in its early years, as is the experience of many small firms. It changed direction more than once, as opportunities appeared and others disappeared.

The firm's first big break came with the opportunity to create a new computerized stock control system with a car distribution agency, Capitol Motors. This was the first such system using mini-computers in Australia. A second project with a chemical laboratory, California Laboratories, created Australia's first 'turnkey' in-house stock control mini-computer system.

TCG became a group of companies partly by design, and partly by accident. The first separate company was formed in 1973, after the Capitol Motors and California Laboratory experiences, to house the firm's engineering capacity, as TCG Systems Automation. This was done partly to distance the founding firm from the hardware side of TCG, and partly to give the initial head of engineering his own sphere of influence.

Pat Gallagher, another local businessman who had formed his own business, had taken up the Australian distribution rights for the US company Norand. Through this vehicle, Gallagher acquired the Australian rights to market portable computer terminals designed for retail stock control, from the Swedish firm Micronic. Gallagher's operation was too small to get significant contracts from major retailers, and Gallagher wanted to sell the terminals to TCG as a means of obtaining some market leverage. Peter Fritz countered this with a partnership offer and, after negotiation, it was agreed to form a new company, TCG Systems Automation Marketing (TCG SAM), to exploit the Micronic agency.

TCG SAM demonstrated the benefits of networking, in this case the synergy that emerged between a small marketing company with a product to sell, and an organization that could back it up with financial clout, accounting, computer programming and systems engineering expertise, and an established computer maintenance service. The beginnings of a self-assembled business incubator with a particular technological focus had been created, albeit partly by accident.

Further companies emerged in the TCG group through employees becoming directors of their own operations and new start-up businesses being attracted by the leverage to be gained by coming under the TCG umbrella. TCG had by now become expert at securing grant aid and other soft finance for start-ups, as well as providing an aura of respectability that gave bankers comfort. By 1981, TCG group had nine companies within its orbit, with $10 million in annual turnover and 100 employees.

The TCG network consists of independent firms whose relationships are governed by bilateral commercial contracts. It is open to new entrants who are prepared to abide by their rules. There is no internal hierarchy, such as one of the members being the 'lead firm'. Basically the incubator works by everyone agreeing to follow the 'rules', rather as they might if they operated as a co-operative.

The first rule is that member firms must give preference to each other in the letting of contracts. This rule gives the group its identity; without it, TCG member firms would simply be businesses sharing an address and some resources. Tendering and contract letting is done along strictly commercial lines. Preference does not exclude the possibility that contracts will sometimes be let outside the group, against a competitive bid from a member firm, when circumstances warrant it (such as work overload, or as a signal to the member firm that it has to improve).

The second rule for group cohesiveness is that member firms do not directly compete with each other. If one member firm is marketing hand-held terminals, another member firm does not acquire rights to market the same kind of terminals from another supplier. This is a form of 'self-denial' that establishes trust between members. In the absence of such a rule, members would be reluctant to discuss business opportunities with each other, for fear that others would take advantage of the information in a way that undercut the original firm's operations (Miles and Snow 1995).

Member firms don't aim to make profits from transactions amongst themselves. This is the origin of the various forms of 'cost-plus' and profit-sharing arrangements that exist between them. The goal is to maximize profit from dealings with the outside world; dealings with each other are a means towards this end.

The flexibility of the group as a whole comes from member firms being able to respond to opportunities as they see fit. They do not need 'approval' for entering into any transaction or new lines of business, provided their proposed innovation does not breach any other rules. This rule allows for maximum flexibility. There is no overall network 'owner' or controller; there is no holding company 'holding' the TCG network together; nor is there any form of 'central committee' or formal governance structure for the network as a whole. It is cohesive as a result of the commercial ties operating between member firms. Group coherence is also provided through the oversight of transactions by the central accounts department. Member firms can hold equity in each other, as some do, as well as in third-party joint ventures.

Member firms have natural incentives to co-operate with each other, based on the insights of long-term interest maximization rather than on short-term spot transacting (Mathews 1993). These incentives are complemented by the sanction of expulsion if any member wilfully disobeys the rules. It has not not been necessary at TCG to resort to this sanction in all its years of network operation – but it remains a rule of last resort. Expulsion happens simply by severing all commercial ties with the miscreant member.

There are no 'sub-contractor only' firms within the TCG group; each member firm has access to the open market, and is free (indeed is expected) to bring in work from outside. This rule allows the network to expand, without sacrificing the efforts of older members to the improvidence of new entrants. This rule is translated into the requirement that new members obtain capital through bank overdrafts rather than through equity from other member firms. It is the network as a whole that provides the collateral for such a loan – so the new member enjoys considerable advantages in starting its life within the protection of the group. Companies tend to stay within the incubator longer than in more conventional models. This is simply because the TCG model does not require a trade sale or IPO to generate a large capital return to some investing organization. The firms in the incubator in effect invest in each other, and each firm's growth contributes to the general increase in wealth. Companies leave the TCG 'nest' to pursue their own interests when they find this environment is no longer right for them.

There are now some 200 people at work in the incubator. Each company in the TCG network consists of between 5 and 15 professionals. TCG is generally regarded as one of Australia's most successful incubators.

SERIAL INCUBATION

Most incubators, as we have seen, are one-off ventures, the initiative of a university, local government office, consultant or entrepreneur. Some people, however, have made incubation their business and roll out incubators in much the same way as Shell or Esso might roll out filling stations. Once the basic design has been made, all you need is a geographic gap in the market to drop your outlet into. The theory is that, in much the same way as business angels won't spread their investments very far, entrepreneurs will start up on their own doorstep, all other factors being equal. So if an incubator were only to operate in one place, its pool of potential talent would be restricted. It's a difficult and expensive learning process getting an incubator up and running, so why not spread that cost across, say, a dozen incubators rather than just one? For the entrepreneur it's harder to see any great benefits. It's possible to see why a regular consumer might get comfort, and perhaps even value, from using filling stations or hotels of the same brand. If they were happy with a Holiday Inn in Paris, then they should be equally satisfied with the Holiday Inn when they go to Chicago. But entrepreneurs are not regular consumers, as a general rule. Starting a business is a one-off experience for all but a small minority of serial entrepreneurs.

The following three examples, two of which can hardly be considered as success stories and one of which is a shining example, all provide valuable insights to potential incubator entrants and perhaps to anyone else inclined to go into incubation as a business model.

John Kao, 49, is the son of Chinese immigrants who for 13 years taught an oversubscribed class on creativity at Harvard Business School. He focused on applying the process of improvisation to build and invigorate businesses, something close to Schumpeter's concept of 'creative destruction'. In his spare time at Harvard he lived what he taught, both in business and the arts. He founded two small biotech companies, helped finance director Steven Soderbergh's unconventional film *Sex, Lies and Videotape* and was nominated for a Tony award for producing a Broadway play. He gained fame in 1996 for writing a best-selling book on corporate creativity called *Jamming*. He once spent a summer playing the keyboard for eccentric rocker Frank Zappa. He also completed an MD and a residency in psychiatry. That year he left Harvard to test out theories in the marketplace. Starting out working with corporate giants, Kao soon found a niche in the incubation business. Under the brand name Idea Factory, Kao raised a $40 million VC fund and in a leased warehouse in San Francisco started up his first incubator in 1998.

A year later, Kao bought the venerable Ealing Studios, a formerly state-run studio set in four acres close to London. As well as having plans to convert Ealing into a digital entertainment magnet making content for the web in addition to mainstream films, Kao started UK Incubator. His aim at this stage was for Idea Factory to open sibling offices throughout Asia and Europe to launch new dotcoms.

With a Paris-based former Harvard Business School classmate Linda Karma, who was a sales and marketing executive in Europe with Apple, Silicon Graphics and Lexmark, Kao has looked for an open warehouse that could house a local Idea Factory. Kao recruited Leen Zevenbergen to be his Netherlands-based chief executive for the European roll-out. Zevenbergen gave up a $1 million salary running the Dutch operation of European consulting firm Origin to tie his fate to Kao's vision.

The Idea Factory proposition is, as you might expect, strong on business school jargon. Their incubation process starts at the very beginning of a new business with a process Idea Factory calls Venture Creation 101. For all the grandeur of the name, this is in effect a one- or two-day workshop to 'rapidly help you clarify your core business concept, refine the promises you're making to your constituents, and sharpen the relationship between your organizational values, purpose, mission, and strategy.' The proposition for Venture Creation 101 includes 'examining your operating environment and providing a specific agenda for the next steps through a systematic inventory of the talent, technology, funding, and other resources needed to deliver on your promises to shareholders, customers, and employees.'

Another gizmo in Idea Factory's armoury is Customator. This they claim is a 'proprietary customer insight methodology for defining new product, service, and business opportunities in the new economy. Customator uses techniques of ethnographic research, user scenario development, multidisciplinary ideation, lifestyle mapping, and rapid concept visualization to uncover insight into customers' tacit and emerging needs and wants.'

This process sets out to tell entrepreneurs what they most want to know but can't tell you about – the products and services that satisfy tacit needs. These are the needs and wants they have difficulty expressing explicitly, about things they can't imagine until they see them for the first time.

Customator services include Theatre of the Customer – The Idea Factory's project-specific Innovation Workshop – and Customator.com – The Idea Factory's online community of customer collaborators for new product insight. Customer + Collaborator = Customator is the formula used to describe their model. Their website and press coverage offer no clue as to how successful the roll-out has been, nor are details of successful incubator clients readily available.

Divine Interventures, Inc. also set out with a grand plan to set up business incubators around the world. By April 2000 they had facilities in Austin, Texas and Calgary, Alberta in Canada. With backing from Microsoft, Dell and others, the company filed for a $461 million IPO and, according to the filing details, planned to open a third incubator in May 2000. But things have not gone to plan. On 13 February 2001, Divine interVentures Inc.'s Chief Executive Andrew 'Flip' Filipowski told analysts that the company was abandoning its strategy of trying to build an Internet incubator company and instead would become a business software provider for the enterprise information portal market, with a new name, Divine, Inc.

'Until today we were perceived to be an incubator,' Filipowski said at a technology conference sponsored by Robertson Stephens. 'Divine will be perceived by you folks in future as a software company.'

Since going public in mid-2000, the company's stock has nosedived. The company, which owns stakes in 52 B2B Internet firms, has styled itself as an 'Internet Zaibatsu', a concept borrowed from Japanese business to form a network of companies with shared interests. Fifteen of the 52 companies are located in Divine's facilities to promote cross-selling and shared marketing and business support. Now, according to Filipowski, Divine Inc., which will operate divine interVentures as a wholly owned unit, will seek to develop corporate software markets for enterprise portals. The company, according to forecasts in the spring of 2001, expected to become profitable in mid-2002.

One organization that has made a success of incubator roll-out is SPEDD, Inc. who have a network of 18 business incubators in the adjoining states of Pennsylvania and Ohio. SPEDD derives significant economies of scale from this arrangement, spreading the costs of management and service provision across many facilities.

SPEDD, Inc. was formerly known as the South Western Pennsylvania Economic Development District (SPEDD). Up until 1982 it served the economic development needs of 6600 square miles and a population of four million people in a region centred on Pittsburgh, Pennsylvania. Begun in 1967, they gained experience in a wide range of economic development roles including technology parks, vocational training, and technical assistance for both private and public development corporations and governments. With changes in the pattern of government funding in the late 1970s and early 1980s, SPEDD searched for a new corporate rationale and in 1982 started the first business incubator in its region. Over the next six years SPEDD oriented its activities solely toward the development of incubators. In 1988 the SPEDD formed an alliance with a private, for-profit corporation and changed its name to SPEDD, Inc.

Now determined to become efficient, SPEDD focused on the issue of increasing the efficiency with which they treated building and incubator operations issues such as rent collection and fit-out. SPEDD's network of 18 incubator sites provides it with the economies of scale to have a specialist unit look after buildings and operations-related functions. Management of key operations is centralized and, with the aid of the one administrative staff member resident at each site, billing and payments for rent and services are carried out. But the real value to entrepreneurs of locating in a SPEDD incubator lies in being able to participate in what it calls its Passport Programme. This has been developed over time and SPEDD claim that only its extensive experience and wide network make its Passport Programme possible. The programme has been developed in four identifiable stages, which are listed below.

Stage One: Incubator staff and the entrepreneurial network deliver services to clients in a fairly conventional way responding to local needs.

Stage Two: The services are analysed, broken down into their constituent parts and repackaged as 'products'. The product definition process includes developing a product description designed to communicate effectively with an entrepreneur, a clear statement of outcomes delivered by the product and the definition of the amount of time needed to 'consume' the product, and what its price and any related costs will be.

Stage Three: The collection of products is defined as a system which can be refined. Additional products are added and poorly used products are retired from the system. New members in the network are inducted into the system, trained in how to deliver existing products and encouraged to put forward suggestions on how the system might be improved. The Passport Programme is constantly redeveloped to include the most effective sets of products.

Stage Four: The system is deliberately managed to facilitate the transition of incubator management away from delivering introductory products and on to more sophisticated ones. The aim is to maximize the 'value added' delivered by the incubator management team through the delivery of more advanced products. That is, members of the network are encouraged to deliver more of the products, thus allowing the incubator management team to focus the majority of their time and attention on managing the system, developing new products and delivering higher value-added products. In that way the Passport Programme provides the flexibility necessary to allow incubator management to move up the value-added chain of services offered by the network. Network members deliver the products within a managed environment which ensures its quality.

In designing the Passport Programme, SPEDD took the services that were being delivered through the incubator and defined each one as a product. They defined 18 products, for example, marketing products, business plan preparation, accounting and bookkeeping, switchboard services, group purchasing and customized job training. Products are made attractive and offered in a way that encourages entrepreneurial curiosity. Since fees are charged for each product, incubator clients can pick and choose which they need and even non-tenants are allowed access to some services, thus widening the incubator's network and revenue opportunities.

The continuous enhancement and evolution of the Passport Programme gives SPEDD a significant competitive advantage in communicating with entrepreneurs and prospective entrepreneurs – as well as with communities who wish to develop an incubator. This novel mode of communication has given SPEDD significant leverage for growing its business. SPEDD has 300 incubator clients in its programme at any one time, and around 70 active clients in their 18 local communities for its products. Its smallest incubator is 18 000 square feet and its largest is 500,000 square feet. (For the full story on SPEDD see Duff 1999.)

Nothing in the business incubation world stands still for long. With upwards of five million new enterprises struggling to be born each year, two million in the US and 400 000 in the UK, for example, there will always be organizations eager to play a part in smoothing their passage into the business world. Helping small business is a big business. As the Internet for-profit incubator model goes into hibernation, at least until sanity is fully restored to the high-tech sector, other players will regroup and launch new incubator models with new agendas. (The author's definition of sanity in this sector, incidentally, is when Amazon.com makes a real profit or closes down, and when Cisco's shares are on a price:earnings (P:E) ratio of no more than 25:1.)

These are some new incubator developments in the UK, which after the US is the most mature market in this field.

The South East England Development Agency (SEEDA) launched five 'enterprise hubs' in March 2001 in the first phase of a programme to create a network of business clusters across the south-east of England. The hubs – in Southampton, the Isle of Wight, Brighton & Hove, North Oxfordshire and Newbury – will form business networks providing flexible workspace for new companies and will have strong links to universities. With investment of $12.6 million over five years, the hubs will provide up to 250 000 square feet of new workspace, doubling the amount already under development in the region. SEEDA's goal eventually is to create 30 hubs with one million square feet of space for small and growing businesses, which will assist up to 600 start-ups each year.

With a strong focus on innovation and technology transfer, the initiative will provide the physical infrastructure for business incubation and clustering. As well as links to local partners, each hub will have its own experienced director, or 'business champion', and support staff. On the Isle of Wight, for example, Gavin Wonnacott, who ran the Innovation Centre at Cranfield University, is the hub director and Simon Fanshawe, media personality and chairman of Surf FM, heads the Brighton & Hove Enterprise Hub. Entrepreneurs will have access to academic expertise, business advice and public- and private-sector sources of finance. Each hub will have its own focus, which will be linked to local strengths. The Isle of Wight hub, for instance, will concentrate on composites manufacturing, while the one in North Oxfordshire will be linked to the Materials Research Centre at Oxford University and will specialize in nanotechnology, motor sport and media. Others will focus on electronics, advanced engineering and new media and creative industries.

At present, about half of all business start-ups in the UK fail in the first five years. SEEDA aims to raise the survival rate to 80% or more.

Meanwhile, in Scotland, Glasgow is planning to turn a 550 000 square foot brownfield site in the city centre into the UK's first inner-city science park. The project, jointly sponsored by the city council, Scottish Enterprise development agency, and local universities, is one of the most ambitious ever seen in Scotland, and promises to create an $84 million science and technology quarter that will generate up to 3000 jobs over the next five years. Dubbed CityScience, the site will house research and development (R&D) and business facilities for a range of high-tech industries already prospering in Glasgow, including software, opto-electronics, e-commerce and life sciences. Some 400 000 square feet of the site, which is located opposite Strathclyde University, a short walk from the city centre, will be devoted to R&D facilities. Plans for the remaining space include small business incubator units, housing, shops, a café, restaurants, a hotel and a gym.

Also aiming to capitalize on the UK's high-tech boom is incuVest LLC, a New York-based company that specializes in creating leading-edge technology companies. It has already established a European base in London, where it will focus on building European technology-based businesses through what it calls 'enterprise factories', or networks of serial entrepreneurs who are able to identify ground-breaking technologies and commercialize them to create successful companies.

13

Incubator associations

I nevitably a number of 'trade associations' have built up around the process of incubation. The National Business Incubation Association (NBIA) is probably the oldest incubator association. It was formed in 1985 by industry leaders, growing from about 40 members in its first year to about 1130 members in 2001. The Association is primarily composed of incubator developers and managers, but technology commercialization specialists, educators and business assistance professionals are also well represented. Its mission is to provide training, and a clearing-house for information on incubator management, development issues, tools for assisting start-up and fledgling firms.

NBIA ACTIVITIES

NBIA offers professional development activities and specialized training to help business-assistance professionals create and administer effective incubation programmes. The Association's public awareness activities educate entrepreneurs, public sector leaders, corporations and investors on the benefits of business incubation. NBIA also conducts research, compiles statistics, produces publications that provide hands-on approaches to developing and managing effective programmes, tracks relevant legislative initiatives, and maintains a speakers' bureau and referral service. It creates partnerships with leading private- and public-sector entities to further the interests of the industry and its members.

Who belongs to NBIA?

- incubator executive directors, managers and staff;
- incubator developers and researchers;

- business-assistance professionals;
- economic development professionals;
- university-related research park managers;
- corporate joint venture partners;
- industry consultants;
- venture capital investors;
- educational institutions;
- people exploring the feasibility of business incubation for their communities; and
- anyone interested in business incubation!

In the UK the Science Park Association (UKSPA) and the newer UK Business Incubation (UKBI) network vie with each other for the attention of incubators. Both set out to cover similar ground and embrace some of the services offered by the more established NBIA.

These associations don't just look inwards. For example, the United States Agency for International Development (USAID) and the Canadian International Development Agency (CIDA) have worked in conjunction with various other aid agencies and their respective incubator associations to encourage incubators in other countries. One such project helped to found the National Business Incubator Association of Russia in 1997 with 22 organizations operating and/or promoting business incubation, including the Russian Academy of Management. By May 1998 (OECD 1999) this association had 32 members. Their activities are broadly similar to those carried out by their American and Canadian counterparts, but also include a national training programme for potential incubator staff. In one case, 15 Russians were trained in Austin, Texas, in one of the US's leading business incubators. Those 15 Russians then went on to set up and run 12 new incubators with an average of 10 tenants in each, which have gone on to create more than 3240 jobs each year since then. Similar schemes have taken place in China, India, Africa (to a lesser extent) and in other parts of Asia.

Part Three

What do incubators really have to offer?

Incubators come in many flavours. Most include fully furnished and equipped office and conference space at below-market rates, plus reception services. Most add in management consulting functions such as planning, accounting, marketing, and financing, plus opportunities for networking and partnering. Part-time and affiliate incubation is available at some sites.

Bill Gross (1998) of idealab! fame, agonized over exactly what should be done by incubator staff and what should be left to the entrepreneurs. He reasoned that, while some assistance is invaluable, too much is counterproductive. The solution he arrived at was that accounting, legal services, payroll, some design work, and some technology platforms (for example, databases and web-building tools) would be centralized in idealab! Product development, sales, marketing and other core functions would be left to the client companies. idealab! would also provide shared office space. His core staff of 20 worked at any one time with four or five embryonic companies under idealab!'s roof. Those that were 'ready to fly' were hatched into stand-alone enterprises, which had to find their own office space, but continued to receive operational assistance from idealab!. Gross's incubator does not consider its task done until, as he puts it, 'some sort of a liquidity event' takes place. That means that until the client has gone public on a stock market or sold to another business, at a valuation of at least $100 million, a successful incubation job has not been carried out.

SPEDD, the incubator network in Pennsylvania, takes a more hands-on approach to delivering services. It divides its business pursuits into two distinct activities, real estate management and service provision. Services are delivered (1) to clients (incubator tenants) and (2) in teaching others about effective enterprise development strategies (including the incubator industry, municipalities, universities, government, and small business centres). SPEDD directly employs 20 staff to manage its business operations and its 18 incubator facilities. It is not possible to neatly categorize SPEDD staff into discrete roles, since work patterns are fluid and some staff perform multiple duties. In general though, approximately 14 staff are responsible for incubator facility management in three areas, administrative secretaries, maintenance, and security. The balance (six people) are responsible for service delivery to tenants and other businesses as well as for delivering centralized management functions on behalf of the entire SPEDD incubator network (e.g. purchasing, book-keeping). Those managers responsible for tenant and small business services visit multiple incubator sites each week. It is typical for any one manager to visit seven or eight sites per week. Tenants communicate their need for services though their site's administrative secretary.

The main types of facilities provided by incubators are described and explained in Chapter 14, and examples of different incubators are used to illustrate this.

14

Premises

Young companies often struggle to find office space in the competitive London property market. Office rents in the capital are climbing towards all-time highs in West End locations such as Soho. New hot-spots such as Clerkenwell and Farringdon have seen rents rise by 50% in just one year, fuelled by demand from the Internet industry. The same pattern is being repeated in many other markets favoured by high-tech entrepreneurs.

This is creating a problem for landlords and prospective new-economy tenants. The property industry traditionally uses a simple rule of thumb to minimize the risk of taking on occupiers who might struggle to pay the rent. To be an acceptable risk, you have to be earning three times the annual rent in profit, according to London property consultants. Yet the overwhelming majority of high-tech companies are years away from making profit. Many cannot even boast a turnover to match their annual rental payments.

lastminute.com caused controversy early in 2000 when it moved into £1 million-a-year offices in Buckingham Gate, near Victoria Station, shortly after its turbulent stock market debut. Similar West End buildings attract several prospective tenants when they come on to the market. Bidding wars are commonplace, and new firms run the risk of being priced out of the market. Even when they can match the rent offered by competing tenants, landlords often plump for old-economy occupiers, which they see as being less likely to experience financial difficulties.

Reports of high-profile start-ups running out of money have prompted many landlords to treat high-tech firms with caution, and warnings of a continuing new economy meltdown have added to the uncertainty. New-economy companies consequently find it hard to persuade landlords to let them space.

Doubleclick's decision to move into a new office building in the West End was regarded as a landmark deal. Even though Doubleclick is a £1 billion corporation, it had to pay a two-year rental deposit that is believed to have cost the American group well over £2 million. This has set a precedent that looks likely to be adopted as an industry standard. Most landlords now insist that new company tenants pay a deposit equivalent to two years' rent. Others demand that they secure a guarantee from their banks or venture capital backers. Smaller companies can expect to be asked to pay a deposit of 6 to 12 months rent, while companies moving into larger buildings have to find even more cash. For anything over 4000 square feet, bank guarantees with a cash deposit are essential; typically one year's rental deposit and a one-year guarantee.

In the past, landlords have preferred to deal with blue-chip corporations that are prepared to sign long-term leases. But dotcom and other high-tech companies want to ensure maximum flexibility. The inflexible approach adopted by institutional landlords asking small firms to sign 10-year leases when they do not even know where they will be in six months' time is driving more small firms into the more friendly arms of business incubators.

With the exception of virtual incubators, most incubators provide some sort of physical premises. Some, such as Regis, which we have already examined, provide little more than physical assets. Even incubators with high-tech-sounding names can turn out to be little more than landlords in disguise.

HOW TO CHOOSE INCUBATOR PREMISES

As Rice and Matthews (1995) point out, a wrong decision regarding the choice of incubator facility can outweigh right decisions about the financial model, the management structure and other issues in the establishment of an incubator. In that respect it would clearly be wrong to underestimate the importance of the property assets of any incubation service. In their review of the performance of incubators in Australia, PricewaterhouseCoopers (1999) graphically illustrated this point in a number of cases with incubators encountered during their review. In one instance they quote the example of a newly established incubator which appeared to be 'in trouble' despite the efforts of experienced management, strong community backing and $500 000 of Commonwealth (local government) funding. In this case the facility chosen was in a poor location and ill-suited to the practical requirements of tenant businesses. Despite some initial positive signs, the incubator struggled to maintain occupancy and has failed to achieve specified performance targets.

The PricewaterhouseCooper's report listed the following as the key issues to take into account when considering the adequacy of an incubator facility's premises:

- **Location and access:** The incubator needs to be located at a site and in an area which is well suited to sustainable business operation. If incubator facilities are not readily accessible or serviced by adequate parking for tenants, customers and suppliers, the incubator will face an uphill battle to attract tenants and maintain viability.
- **Size:** The incubator needs to be able to flexibly adapt to the requirements of tenants as they grow. While there is no automatic link between incubator size and viability, incubators which have the capacity to provide the appropriate services and space are likely to experience some level of economies of scale, and are therefore more likely to be successful.
- **Fit-out and maintenance:** While many tenants are not looking for premium grade workspace, the presentation and fit-out of an incubator facility needs to be appropriate to the practical requirements of tenant businesses. A facility which is poorly maintained or in need of refurbishment is also going to place an excessive burden on the running costs of the incubator.
- **Flexibility:** The ability to flexibly manage and reconfigure the layout of tenant workspaces as tenant businesses change and grow is a distinct advantage.
- **Land and environment:** The land on which the incubator is located should be suitable. In some instances, reclaimed land is used. Incubator proponents need to be aware of the issues that this may lead to. The costs of dealing with or removing environmental hazards can place a severe and unexpected strain on an incubator budget.

The consultants concluded this aspect of their report by saying: 'The "best practice" incubator needs to locate in a facility which is well suited to the practical business requirements of its tenants.' This may sound rather a bland conclusion, but when you consider that a sizable number of business incubators are located in redundant buildings of one sort or another, prospective users of such facilities might do well to pause and consider exactly why they are redundant.

Example – The Massachusetts Innovation Center

The Massachusetts Innovation Center (MIC) is a good example of what is on offer in terms of premises, and almost certainly meets all of the criteria laid down by PricewaterhouseCoopers. MIC claims in its literature to offer growing businesses appropriate space and access to facilities otherwise unavailable to start-ups or young companies. MIC affiliates have access to spacious conference rooms, along with almost unlimited, affordable and customizable business space within its 300 000 square foot campus at One Oak Hill Road in Fitchburg, Massachusetts. The space has been designed to be state-of-the-art, flexible and cyber-smart. This includes new office space, upgraded electrical and other sustaining systems. Their buildings are Internet-ready, providing MIC affiliates with direct, high-speed access connections via an in-house OC48 fibre-optic cable. According to MIC, few other facilities offer access to this level of high-speed connection. Their telecommunications system is also sophisticated, and claimed to be highly functional and reliable. These advanced capabilities give young businesses the critical technological edge they need to succeed in an e-business, information technology environment.

MIC affiliate businesses have access to space that is: Affordable; customizable and expandable to accommodate business needs and growth; outfitted with dependable and reliable telecommunications; equipped with high-speed (OC48) Internet access (each office has a T1 connection); and ready to occupy.

The MIC business community is just one hour north-west of Boston and just minutes from scenic and historic Massachusetts Route 2. This central location offers close proximity to major highways, including Routes 495 and the Massachusetts Turnpike. Fitchburg is an ideal business location. The city is close to both Boston and Worcester but, unlike the state's two largest cities, the pleasant community offers reasonable office rental costs and freedom from traffic congestion. Young companies gain tremendous value from MIC's combination of shared business resources. They can help new businesses make the most of limited resources by providing access to office reception services and the use of up-to-date office equipment including copiers, fax machines and audio-visual equipment.

LEASES

Incubators usually include easy in, easy out leases and the ability to grow or shrink on the same site. Some incubators have time limits and others have other factors such as size that set a limit on how long a firm can stay in an incubator. Other incubators are rather more accommodating, welcoming the same firm back time and time again as its circumstances change (see Tadpole for example, who are now on their third stay at the Cambridge science park). UBCA, the incubation and innovation centre of Antwerp University will even provide facilities for between one week and six months, although this is rare.

RENTAL RATES

Incubator rental rates are usually close to the market rate for local proper-ties. However, some aim to charge a fraction below the going rate. Other incubators are located in areas that attract government support of some kind. For example, the Science and Technology Park based on the West Bohemian University in Plzen, near Prague, in the Czech Republic has fi-nancial support to cover between 15% and 50% of rent and other oper-ational costs. Some incubators used a fixed scale and all tenants are charged rent on the same basis. Some use a sliding scale using as a basis a range of measures such as sales turnover, the firm's profits, the number of jobs cre-ated, and even the length of stay.

OTHER PHYSICAL FACILITIES

The rent may include other facilities such as those shown in the list below:

- conference rooms;
- restaurants and cafeteria;
- building security;
- furniture rental;
- office equipment rental (including Internet facilities);
- telephone equipment;
- library and reference material;
- vehicle rental;
- cleaning and maintenance;
- child-care; and
- overnight accommodation.

Not all of these facilities are available in many incubators, nor are they equally attractive to all prospective clients. In a study (Maryland 2000) conducted for the Maryland Technology Group, Internet access was ranked as being a high priority for 80% of all clients, whilst access to specialized equipment was only important to 42%. Child-care services were rated a low priority by 75% and of vital importance to none of their sample of 130 incubator companies.

Some incubators have sophisticated physical facilities. For example, the AREA Science Park in Trieste, Italy, a public body set up under the aegis of the Ministry for University and Science and Technology Research, has as one of its strong points the sharing of common resources. Tenants and non-tenants have the use of a wide range of services – the joint use of which considerably lowers the costs – and facilities with 'cutting-edge' equipment for conference and teaching activities. The conference and teaching facilities and an on-site guest-house are run by an external company called Smile Service, which also offers PR, organization and secretarial services, translations, text transcriptions, proof-reading and complete mailing services to the AREA Science Park tenants.

The Conference Centre is situated on the AREA Science Park campus. It contains auditoriums and congress halls of different sizes, a service for organizing conferences, a room for refreshments, a bank counter and cashpoint, public telephones and a newsagent. Next to the Congress Centre is the AREA Science Park guest house, which can also accommodate people taking part in conferences or visiting incubator companies.

So, when considering rents, it is important to check what is being offered, what is included in the rent, and what might be of real value in getting the business successfully launched. But, as in the case of Cyber-Care, Inc. any help with facilities may be more than welcome. Cyber-Care, Inc. (formerly CyberCare.com) has come a long way since its days of foraging for basic office furniture. The company was started at Georgia Tech's business incubator, the Advanced Technology Development Centre (ATDC), thanks to a collaborative effort begun in 1995 between the Medical College of Georgia and Georgia Institute of Technology. The two institutions developed the technology behind an electronic house-call device, thanks to grant funding of about $1.8 million from the Army and the Georgia Research Alliance. Once clinical trials were complete and patents had been filed for, a buyer was sought for the commercially viable technology. John Haines was the entrepreneur who took on the project, and he chose ADTC's incubator as the place to get the business off the ground, setting up shop in 1997.

Haines claimed to be a classic example of how beneficial the ATDC can be. He was awarded the contract in August 1997 and the company was incubated right after that. The business took the space recently vacated by MindSpring, complete with concrete block walls and surplus furniture, which they appreciated, as it meant they could put all their money into developing the business. They also got immediate legal and accounting support. Georgia Tech and the Medical College kept equity stakes in the company, and continued an ongoing research and development relationship with Cyber-Care whilst they were incubating.

The electronic house call concept that Cyber-Care delivers is based on its Care Management System, a multimedia PC- and Internet-based system featuring a touch-screen user interface. Chronically ill patients can track their own medical conditions and access care-givers whenever needed, and monitoring and measurement devices can be controlled from either end of the networked connection. Results are automatically collected, charted, placed in permanent records and available for future consultations. Video and conferencing features are also offered in both the home and institutional product versions.

This commonsense yet innovative approach to coping with the some 2.5 million chronically ill patients in the US and overseas comes at an attractive price: $8 for the electronic form of interaction, as opposed to the average $85 for home-care visits. With some 35 percent of all U.S. health care dollars spent annually on this population alone, that makes a big and attractive difference to the market.

Whilst in the incubator, Cyber-Care's sales increased dramatically, as shown in Figure 14.1.

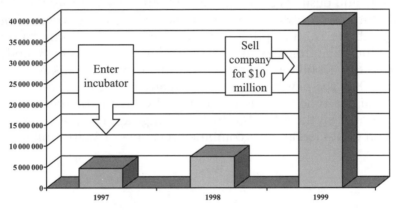

Figure 14.1   Cyberspace for Cyber-Care. Source: company accounts.

The company was acquired by Medical Industries of America in 1999 for $10 million in stock, and is now traded on the NASDAQ as CYBR (Cyber-Care, Inc.). They are on the verge of revolutionizing the delivery of healthcare in America.

Note on ATDC

Since ATDC opened in 1980, MindSpring, Theragenics, and nearly 100 other member and graduate companies have added some 4100 jobs and over $351 million in annual revenues to the Georgia economy. In one year alone, ATDC member companies attracted more than $100 million in investment. The value that ATDC creates with its clients and their business partners goes beyond these numbers, however. It can be summed up in three key ideas: focus, connections, and sense of place.

Working with selected fast-track companies, ATDC provides business assistance to help them bring innovations to the marketplace more quickly. Member companies develop products and services in advanced technology areas, including telecommunications, digital media, software, Internet applications, biotechnology, robotics, electronics, environmental technologies, manufacturing and materials processing.

Typically, these companies target emerging, high-growth markets. Success in these markets can bring stellar rewards for the entrepreneurs and their stakeholders. To make it there, however, entrepreneurs must master the uncertainties of relatively unknown markets, customers, channels, and competition. ATDC provides just-in-time advice and expertise to help new companies meet these challenges.

ATDC can be a matchmaker, using its knowledge of Georgia's academic, technology and business communities to help bring together the elements needed to form successful new enterprises. The star performer from the ATDC incubator is MindSpring. Between 1994 and 2000 MindSpring Enterprises, Inc. went from having 32 non-paying customers and 8 modems to entering into a $3 billion merger with competitor EarthLink Networks. In February 2000, the newly combined company officially became Earthlink, Inc., and at the time was one of the world's largest Internet service providers. It trades on the NASDAQ stock exchange as ELNK, serves more than 3.1 million customers and has combined revenues of $670.4 million.

15

Business services

The provision of businesses services holds the key to the value-adding capability of most incubators. Since over a dozen services fit under this heading, to make it more digestible we will look at in two stages, looking first at general business services, followed by professional business services.

GENERAL BUSINESS SERVICES

The range of business services that an incubator might supply are given in the bullet list below:

- audio-visual equipment;
- shipping and receiving;
- mail services;
- photocopier, fax;
- reception services, messaging;
- word-processing, clerical and administration services; and
- access to laboratory and computer equipment.

The Maryland study (Maryland 2000) put these services as being a high or medium priority for 82% of incubator tenants. It clearly must make sense for small firms to spread such costs over a wider base than they might do if they were on their own. But having such services either incorporated into the rent or subsidized is fairly rare outside government-sponsored incubators. The PricewaterhouseCoopers study (1999) found that 18% of the incubators they researched offered some or all of these services for free, whilst 50% applied some level of subsidy. A third, however, charged a full commercial rate for all services provided whilst in the incubator.

A study by Mian (1996) of university-based incubators concluded that, with the exception of having access to a photocopier, most tenants did not perceive these services as being of major value. However, less than 15% saw them as being of no value at all.

PROFESSIONAL BUSINESS SERVICES

As long ago as 1985, Allen and Rahman identified a list of 38 possible incubator services. Few incubators provided all 38 of these services, and in many cases the services were delivered by a third party, usually listed as an approved supplier. The range of possible professional business services that are most likely to be on offer in an incubator is given below, and several of these areas are examined in more detail to illustrate how different incubators go about delivering these services:

- legal matters;
- intellectual property;
- accounting;
- book-keeping;
- recruitment and staff selection;
- education and training; and
- IT and Internet services.

LEGAL MATTERS

Although Allen and Rahman separated legal matters under a number of headings in practice, entrepreneurs are rarely aware from the outset of the range of legal matters that can beset a new business, and tend to cluster all legal matters under one umbrella heading. Drawing up partnership agreements, registering companies, preparing contracts of employment, drafting confidentiality agreements, vetting leases, filing patents, registering designs, and licensing technology are just some aspects of the legal minefield ahead of an entrepreneur starting up a new business. Not surprisingly, this area of professional service is valued highly by incubator tenants.

It is unusual, though not unheard of, to have legal experts on incubator staff. It is much more likely, however, that one or more law firms are brought in under the incubator's networking activities. The Canberra Business Centre incubator in Australia, for example, has a network of over 30 business advisers. Interest was initially stimulated in the Centre's activities through two small articles in a daily newspaper, *The Canberra Times*. Centre management always interview and vet any individuals who wish to join the advisory network. Members of the business adviser network are not paid by the Centre, however, an offer is made to reimburse any expenses in servicing Centre tenants. Some of the service providers in the network are professional accountants and lawyers. Typically, such business professionals provide their services free for the first and perhaps the second meeting with a tenant, but after this they normally begin to charge fees. The Canberra Business Centre plays an intermediary role during this transition by advising the professionals which firms can or cannot afford to pay full rates for their services.

EarthCare Systems, Inc. is one example of an incubator client making good use of the facility's legal services. They set up in the Genesis incubator, based in Fayettville, Arkansas, which was itself set up in 1986 by the University of Arkansas with assistance from the US Small Business Administration. Earth-Care's business proposition was a new concept in composting, consisting of a cocktail of microbes which it used to inoculate compost materials to significantly accelerate the composting process. Genesis, through its links with the University of Arkansas, helped to transform a good idea into a business system.

The university helped to identify the conditions and species of bacteria which would give optimal composting results. As a result of this analysis, a university research centre worked with the company to design and construct an agricultural scale machine, protected by patents, that provides the company with the capacity to convert material into compost. Genesis made critically important contributions to EarthCare Systems becoming a viable business. Without their technological input, the firm would have had an interesting idea, but no product. And without their legal expertise, delivered in part by an outside law firm in their network, EarthCare Systems would not have had any barrier to prevent other better-established firms in the sector stepping in first to capture the market.

The following is an unusual example of an incubator helping out a client business with a serious and unexpected legal issue, which amply demonstrates the unpredictable nature of such matters.

Austin-based Trilogy Software, Inc., a corporate incubator, turned to the courts to find the author of an online message that made negative claims about the financial health of CarOrder.com Inc., a former Trilogy incubator client which it still had a substantial interest (Fowler 2000). In February 2000, a Travis County District Court judge issued subpoenas to Edmunds.com, Inc., a California-based Internet service provider, and Hotmail, a Microsoft subsidiary that provides e-mail accounts. The subpoenas – which followed a court petition filed by Trilogy to investigate potential claims – request information aimed at discovering the identity of the person who posted the derogatory messages in question.

According to court documents, on 17 February someone using the name 'alex2001' posted a message on an Edmunds.com discussion group called 'CarOrder.com Experiences'. The message warned against buying cars through US-based CarOrder.com because of alleged financial troubles at the company, noting that '. . . the ship is going down'. The message also claimed that the company had been unsuccessful in finding investors and that buyers should try to back out of agreements to purchase cars through them. The author of the message posted an e-mail address hosted by Hotmail, inviting further questions by others on the message board.

In a second message posted that day, the same author claimed that he or she was a Trilogy employee, according to court documents, and that Trilogy had 'written off CarOrder [sic] as a risk investment that is beyond salvage.'

The author also criticized recent changes made by a new CarOrder.com executive, as well as the recent firing of customer service representatives. Company officials previously confirmed the termination of 35 employees as part of efforts to improve customer service.

'Unless CarOrder can get the substantial amount of money they need to buy the dealerships and turn their business model into a direct sales channel, CARORDER will parish [sic],' says the message, according to court documents. 'This is not an inner-company rumor – this is direct information from decision makers who unfortunately MUST remain anonymous.' A spokeswoman for Microsoft, Hotmail's parent company, says that the company occasionally receives requests from law enforcement officials for information about users, such as runaways. Although the company keeps no exact numbers on those types of requests or incidents, the spokeswoman called them 'incredibly rare'.

Hotmail's e-mail users' privacy statement says that the company will not give e-mail accounts to users who do not provide their first and last names. The statement also says that the company will not release that information to third parties unless '. . . acting under a good faith belief that such action is necessary to: (1) conform to legal requirements or comply with legal process; (2) protect and defend the rights or property of Hotmail; (3) enforce the Hotmail Terms of Service; or (4) act to protect the interest of its members or others.'

RECRUITMENT AND SELECTION

Few small firms would pretend to be experts at recruiting and selecting staff. New firms have the added disadvantage of lacking credibility with the best candidates, who quite rightly see them as a risky proposition. Brian Stafford, launched his firm, CarOrder, in September 1999 as an online auto brokerage that delivered cars to customers' homes. But from the start, Mr Stafford had more ambitious goals than merely serving as a car broker. He planned to buy up to 100 traditional, rural dealerships close to metropolitan areas across the country. The idea was that these small dealerships would serve as CarOrder distribution centres, filling orders taken over the Internet. With direct access to manufacturers, the plan went, CarOrder could undercut traditional dealers on price and service. He raised $125 million in venture capital whilst in an incubator, which for most people would have seemed like a good enough result to commend incubation to anyone. But Brian Stafford rated the 'rapid access to world-class human capital' as the critical benefit that being in Trilogy's incubation process offered him to help his business get started. He had previously started two companies but a lack of talented people had starved them both. The situation was dramatically different this time round. He was able to hire approximately two-thirds of his technical employees through Trilogy's on-campus recruiting process, widely recognized as one of the most effective systems for finding elite technical graduates. In addition, Stafford made use of CollegeHire.com, a fellow company in the Trilogy incubation process which provides sophisticated online services to place high-tech college graduates.

Vinod Khosla is in an ideal position to discuss both the opportunities and the challenges facing entrepreneurs and their backers today. He is an accomplished entrepreneur himself, having co-founded Sun Microsystems in the early 1980s. And since joining venture capitalists Kleiner, Perkins, Caufield, & Byers in 1986, he has helped steer companies such as Amazon.com, Excite, Juniper Networks and Cerent to success. He has no doubt that recruiting people is the number one problem for small new businesses trying to exploit big opportunities.

He claims that his smoothest, best-executed deal was that involving Juniper Networks, a deal which he helped develop from day one. Pradeep Sindhu, Juniper's founder, had come up with a technological breakthrough in the way enterprise routers work. But he had never worked in the router business, and didn't recognize the full commercial possibilities of his ideas. He didn't see that enterprise routers could also serve as Internet routers. In an interview with David Champion and Nicholas Carr for the *Harvard Business Review* (Champion and Carr 2000) Khosla described how they incubated Juniper:

> So the first thing we did was help him define the market for Internet routers. Then we gave him a crash course in building a business. I had him take an office for three weeks next to Milo Medin, who was then at @Home. As Milo's shadow, he absorbed what it meant to run a public Internet-protocol network – what the big issues and problems were. It was a fast way to bring him up the learning curve.

The first thing we focused on was getting the right set of people for the company – the right gene pool. We started out on the technical end. Pradeep had helped architect the Ultrasparc processor at Sun, so he had strong skills in building technical architectures and could apply those skills to routers. But he needed somebody with experience in building and operating an IP network, and he needed somebody who'd done operating systems software for routers and somebody who'd done protocols for routers. So we drew out a map that said, 'Here are the ten different areas of expertise we need.' Then we made a list of the companies doing the best work in each area, and we listed the five people in each company who would make good targets. We went after those people, and piece by piece we assembled a multidisciplinary team that could make Juniper a leader.

On top of the technical layer, we put together a management layer, recruiting Scott Kriens, who'd founded StrataCom, as the CEO. We needed the technical layer in place first, because without it we couldn't have attracted the top management talent. At that point, the company was off and running, and I basically just got out of the way. There wasn't much else I needed to do. So from my point of view, it was the most bang for the least buck – the buck being my time. It was the perfect incubation. Our starting investment was $200 000, and now the company is worth many billions.

EDUCATION AND TRAINING

In general it is, unsurprisingly enough, the university-based incubators that have the strongest emphasis on training and developing entrepreneurs and their teams in the practical subjects that will give their venture a head start. But universities are by no means the only group who recognizes the role training has to play in business development. The following three examples show the type of training on offer in business incubators.

The Docklands Innovation Park

The Docklands Innovation Park is the business incubator arm of the Dublin Institute of Technology in Dublin, Ireland. In association with the Bolton Trust, they established the Small Enterprise Seed Fund in 1995. This is one of the very few incubators to offer seed-level funds of between £50 000 to £100 000 to companies. To date, the fund has raised £1.3 million from private investors and has placed the money with around 16 small companies that have either started up or grown out of their incubation process. The Innovation Park has a range of training programmes which companies based on the Park are generally expected to take, but which are also open to non-Park entrepreneurs. The Enterprise Development Programme is a one-year support structure for graduate-led businesses. More than 250 new businesses have been created through this programme, and over 800 jobs. By international standards the survival rates of these businesses is high, with 76% in operation after three years, and 56% after five years. Overall it is a very successful programme and is the core activity of the Park. Just over one-fifth of companies taking part in the programme end up being categorized as 'fast growth' firms achieving a much higher rate of growth than other comparable local firms (Hogan and Foley 1996).

The Fast Growth Programme is also a one-year scheme designed to help owner/managers facing the challenges of growth, e.g. cash flow management, building a management team, etc. This programme was funded under the Small Businesses Operational Programme. The scheme was established in 1996, and 47 companies went through the programme in the following three years. The results claimed are impressive, with turnover increased, on average, by 150%, profits by 300% and with the creation of an additional 300 jobs.

Enterprise Development, Inc.

Enterprise Development, Inc. at Case Western Reserve University, Cleveland, Ohio is also strong on training. The Edison Technology Incubator is based in Enterprise Development, Inc. (EDI). That was formed in April 1987 by combining the Centre for Venture Development (CVD) and the Entrepreneurial Assistance Group (EAG). Both organizations were founded in 1983, CVD by a joint task force of Cleveland Tomorrow (a committee of 44 business leaders committed to Greater Cleveland's economic development) and the Council of Smaller Enterprises (a division of the Greater Cleveland Growth Association), and EAG by the Weatherhead School of Management (WSOM) at Case Western Reserve University.

Enterprise Development, Inc.'s programme elements include:

- the operation of The Edison Technology Incubator for technology-based start-ups;
- business counselling for entrepreneurs;
- a minority assistance programme;
- courses and conferences on entrepreneurial topics; and
- a public information and education programme.

EDI offers access to the standard array of shared administrative services. In addition, conference and meeting rooms, kitchen facilities, a commercial loading dock, service lift, and 24-hour building security are available at a low or no cost. Office, laboratory, light assembly/manufacturing, and storage space is available on an annual lease basis, with no minimum space or monthly rental amount required.

For entrance into EDI's incubator programme, one of five Thomas Edison Incubators located throughout the State of Ohio, entrepreneurs must have a commercially focused concept for a technology-oriented business. Periods of tenancy differ from business to business; however, tenants are expected to graduate to the Greater Cleveland business community within three years of joining the incubator programme. EDI sponsors a number of conferences and courses throughout the year on issues of interest to entrepreneurs who have recently started a business (or are about to do so) as well as other members of the business community. Since 1987, EDI has offered over 20 different but related courses to managers in start-ups or emerging growth companies, and well over 400 entrepreneurs have signed up to take them.

Courses are normally offered once a week for four or more consecutive weeks in the autumn and in the spring on topics such as strategic marketing, innovation in management, and leadership as a management tool. Entrepreneurs from the local business community are brought in as lecturers and/or course leaders. Feedback from course participants often determines the topics that are offered. Conferences on entrepreneurial subjects are held two or three times a year and have continued to attract a diverse group of people within the business and professional communities. Conferences have been held on entrepreneurial banking and finance, growth capital, mergers and acquisitions, and technology transfer. Altogether, the conferences have attracted over 2000 attendees.

In each of the courses EDI runs, there is one place reserved for a Weatherhead School of Management MBA student. In return for free entry to the course, the students trade their note-taking ability, thus allowing the participants to focus on the content and interaction.

One MBA student characterized the value of the EDI courses by recounting, 'I learned more practical knowledge and techniques from the eight-week EDI marketing course than the six courses in marketing I have taken during my MBA. I learned things that I could use tomorrow if I were running a business.'

Cranfield

The Innovation Centre and the Internet incubator, Cranfield Creates, share premises on the Technology Park at Cranfield in the UK. Both facilities offer advice, expertise and resources to help individual entrepreneurs and early-stage growing businesses. The incubator has all the range of services that could reasonably be expected on a postgraduate science-based university campus: state-of-the-art premises, good access, a business angel investment network and close collaboration with university departments. The Cranfield School of Management is located on this campus, and incubator clients have access to the full range of enterprise programmes developed by the school. The school's interest in entrepreneurship education predates the creation of the incubator facility by a decade.

Cranfield enterprise training covers everything from start-up through early growth and finally to their latest programme, value creation, which covers exit routes and paths to a public share issue. The central programme, which a number of incubator tenants take each year, is the business growth and development programme, which takes in 65 entrepreneurs for 8 2-day sessions at Cranfield to help them develop a fast growth strategy. Participants also receive counselling from Cranfield faculty and have the use of an MBA team to carry out a business audit of the entrepreneur's strategic options as an aid to their decision-making. The counselling process is a powerful training tool akin to a professional sports player having a personal coach. A number of business incubators have adopted the counselling approach to training and development. For example, the Genesis incubator discussed earlier in this chapter, uses SCORE (Service Core Of Retired Executives) Association, which has its area office based in the incubator itself. (SCORE is a national, non-profit association with 11 500 volunteer members and 389 chapters throughout the US and its territories. It is a resource partner with the US Small Business Administration. Their statistics are impressive and go some way towards explaining why the business formation process works better in the US than in many other parts of the developed world. More than 4.2 million clients have been given SCORE counselling since 1964; more than 1.2 million volunteer hours have been donated to assist entrepreneurs; more than 300 000 entrepreneurs have been assisted with counselling and workshops; and more than 6000 workshops or seminars have been conducted nationwide.)

Genesis, the Thomas Edison incubators, the science and technology park-based incubator at the West Bohemian University in Plzen near Prague in the Czech Republic, and The Docklands Innovation Park in Dublin all offer financial assistance to entrepreneurs in their incubators to cover the cost of training. The level of subsidy can vary from a few percent to as much as 45%, as in the Czech Republic's incubators, for example.

DOES TRAINING PAY?

Numerous studies (Bates 1990, for example) have argued that the performance of new and small firms is significantly improved by improving the level of development of the people in the business. Likewise, a study on profitability (Hall 1995) in small firms concluded that 'a well-educated work force was the variable most strongly associated with growth'. The corollary of this argument may also be true. It's a fact that most small firms spend little or no time or money on training, seeing such expenditure as a luxury open only to big firms. Just as a football team can be coached and trained into the top division, so a business team can be trained to deliver superior performance.

The trouble is that fewer than one in eight small firms in the UK invests five or more days per year in training their management team (see Figure 15.1).

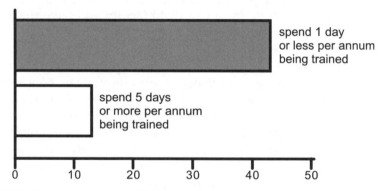

Figure 15.1   How much do small firms train?

There is little evidence to support the belief that entrepreneurs are any more inclined towards training elsewhere. Since so few small firms spend either time or money on training, there must be some doubt in their owners' minds as to whether training is worthwhile. One study at Cranfield (Barrow 1999) has documented changes in the performance of companies where such training takes place. The study compared firms in the years before training took place and afterwards against a 'control' sample. The control sample was, in effect, the whole small business population of similarly sized independent firms that had filed full accounts for the whole period of the study. These 3000 firms were assumed to represent the UK Small Firms Sector (UK-SME). Since so few small firms do any significant amount of training this control group was taken as a fair approximation of the results that are likely to be achieved by entrepreneurs who do not train their staff (Figure 15.2).

Whilst the 3000 companies in the general study grew sales and profits at 8% and 11% respectively on average over the last five years, Cranfield business growth and development programme participants grew sales by 19% and profits by 36% each year – a performance between 200 and 300% better

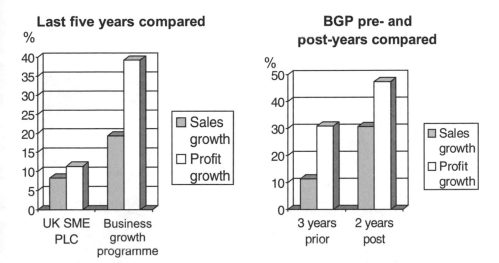

Figure 15.2   Small firms that train their staff generally do better than those who don't.

than the average of SME-UK plc. Sales and profit per employee in the Cranfield sample were also higher at £81 913 and £4149 per head, compared with £72 367 and £3302. The comparison between performance before and after attending the business growth programme of this sample is equally significant. Profit growth in the two years after attending the programme averaged 47%, compared with just 31% in the three prior years. Average sales growth was 30% after the programme, up from 11% in the years prior to attending the programme. The message here is clear – owner/managers can learn to improve themselves and their business dramatically.

In another study (Barrow *et al.* 1997) small firms were clustered into four groups: *companies in decline*, whose profits and sales were dropping; *unprofitable growers*, those whose sales were growing whilst their profits were not; *profit enhancers*, those whose profits were growing on relatively static sales; and the final group we called *champions* – those firms whose sales and profits were growing rapidly. Firms with HR (human resource) functions, which invested significantly in people and training, were then compared with those who did not. Virtually no companies in the former category were in decline, and the majority were either champions or profit enhancers. Those firms which did not invest in training and developing people, by contrast, were most likely to be in decline or to be an unprofitable grower (see Figure 15.3).

Perhaps the most optimistic view that can be taken of these findings is that entrepreneurs using a business incubator are more likely to be exposed to training and learning opportunities than entrepreneurs in general, which can only be beneficial for themselves and their businesses.

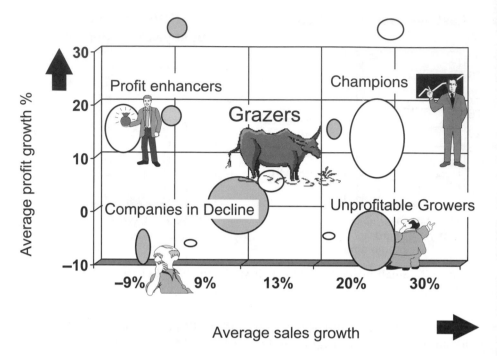

Figure 15.3   Growth profiles of SMEs in general compared to those with HR functions, investing in people.

16

Management and business strategy services

The area in which the new generation of 'accelerator' incubators aim to make the greatest impact on their protégés is in delivering management and business strategy services. Internet Incubation.com's founder, Abe Schwartz, who claims 25 years experience as a successful software entrepreneur, clearly demonstrates the importance of this aspect of incubator support. He makes no claims for the physical aspects of his incubator and spends no time expounding the virtues of shared facilities or general business services. Members of the Internet Incubation.com's management team possess 'unique skills in strategic planning and understanding how to conceptualize, develop and implement good ideas and turn them into profitable and valuable businesses'. The list below shows that this incubator sees business plan development and marketing planning as representing a major portion of its capacity to add value to clients.

1. Technology assessment
- R&D strategies
- Competitive positioning
- Patents and IP protection
- Technology partnering

2. Business plan development
- Critical success factors
- Revenue models
- Wealth generation strategies
- Exit strategies

3. Marketing plan
- Launches
- Alliances and partnerships
- Sales and distribution strategies
- PR campaigns

4. Corporate finance
- Capital raising
- Mergers and acquisitions
- IPOs

Management and business strategy services can be clustered into eight or so main areas (see list below), but it is the first three or four of these that occupies the energies of most incubator managements.

- preparation of business plans;
- marketing and business strategy formulation;
- public relations;
- research and development;
- employee relations including employee share ownership issues;
- international trade;
- government relations including procurement; and
- networking.

BUSINESS PLANNING

A research paper (Fry 1987) identified a clear difference between companies that were in business incubators and those that were not, in terms of their business planning and strategy characteristics. For example, 39% of incubator tenants had a written strategic plan, 48% had a written operational plan and 53% had a mission statement. For companies not in an incubator, these figures were, 29%, 25% and 42% respectively. When it came to financial strategy and planning, the differences were more marked. Sixty per cent of incubator tenants had a financial plan for future funding, whilst only 33% of non-incubator firms had such plans.

In the same study, Fry established that as early as 1987 over 70% of incubators offered their tenants help and advice with business and financial plans and help in developing strategic plans. Today the figure would probably be higher still. Often, help with business planning starts as part of the 'application' process to get into the incubator in the first place. For example, HatchAsia, whose primary mission is to 'become a "womb-to-tombstone" provider of management and technology expertise, business infrastructure and capital access to Asian technopreneurs', puts business planning at the centre of their offer. They provide website visitors with the following four helpful pointers towards better business planning:

1. The most effective way to grab the attention of incubators, VCs, and potential investors is to write a brilliant **Executive Summary.** To view information that will help you come up with one, click here.
2. If you are interested in software packages that will enable you to write a brilliant business plan, click on www.PaloAlto.com or www.Adarus.com.

3. To receive Internet-based professional business plan consulting, click on www.BizPlanIt.com or www.PlanPro.com.
4. To attend an online business plan workshop, click here.

DOES BUSINESS PLANNING PAY?

The research literature on planning has generally shown a positive relationship between planning and business performance. Thure and House (1970) studied 92 firms with sales of over $75 million. Formal planners in this study outperformed informal planners in the percentage increase in sales, the percentage increase in earnings per share, the percentage increase in stock price, and the percentage return on either equity or total capital. They also found that firms performed better after they started formal planning than they did before they started formal planning. Herold (1972) studied the same firms four years later and found that the differences between the two groups had widened since the Thure and House study.

More than a decade later Rhyne (1985) studied 89 Fortune 500 companies. Those with strategy-oriented planning stystems exhibited superior performance both relative to their industry and in absolute terms. Although most research studies have found a positive link between planning and performance, this is not a universal experience. Rue and Fulmer (1973), in a study of 386 firms in 16 industries, did not conclude that planners performed better than non-planners. Shrader *et al.* (1984) reviewed a number of studies focusing on the planning/performance relationship. Although they concluded from their literature review that there is a relatively strong relationship between planning and performance at both the corporate and business level, 11 of the 31 studies they reviewed did not find a strong positive relationship between the two variables. The relationship between planning and performance also has been shown to exist for small businesses. Bracker and Pearson (1986) studied 265 owner/managers of dry-cleaning establishments. The significance of their study is that it used a large sample of firms in a single, homogeneous, mature industry. In this way distorting factors caused in other studies using cross-industry samples or using differing time periods when the economic climates were dissimilar, were eliminated. They found that firms which did structured strategic planning outperformed others. In addition, those with long planning histories outperformed those with shorter planning histories. They found that an increased level of planning sophistication was the key to financial performance, and they concluded that planning requires a comprehensive commitment to the planning process.

Robinson *et al.* (1986) investigated planning around 81 small independent food retailers. They found that 13 planning activities accounted for 82%

of the variance in the performance of food stores, and 7 activities accounted for 37% of the variance. These factors – analysing customers, competitive analysis, making sales projections, cashflow analysis, setting labour cost standards, and inventory control – were seen as important contributors to both return on sales and managers' perceived performance in the stores.

Orpen (1985) separated his sample of 58 various small business firms into high performers and low performers. Although he found little differences in the amount of time that high and low performers spent planning, he did find substantial differences in the quality of planning between the two groups. For example, he found that nearly 80% of the higher performers had developed a set of long-range plans. Only half of the low performers had similar long-range plans. High performers updated their plans more frequently than low performers did. Almost 60% of the higher performers conducted detailed analyses of the firm's competitive position compared to only one-quarter of the low performers. Perhaps the most significant difference was that 85% of the high performers had a planning horizon of two or more years, while less than half of the low performers looked that far into the future.

A cross-Europe study at Cranfield of over 2000 small firms (Burns 1994) reached the same conclusions. This study looked only at firms which were growing faster than others in their industry. The aim of the study was to see if 'good' businesses could be made better still. The sample was divided into 'adaptors' who claimed to have no long-term plan, but changed their strategy to suit prevailing conditions. The 'planners' were those firms who made long-term plans and used their best endeavours to achieve them. The conclusions (see Figure 16.1) were an impressive endorsement of the value of business planning.

Fry, in his study on business planning in incubators, reached an interesting conclusion. He found that the planning activities of incubator tenants *cannot* be easily increased simply by having planning services available. Small business owners need strong encouragement to do something that they see as 'something to do if they ever have sufficient time'. Education once again is the key. But incubators certainly perform a valuable service when they insist on entrepreneurs having a business plan, of sorts, to get in, and a much worked on and well thought-out business plan to raise finance and move on.

MASTERS OF STRATEGY

The core thinking behind business plans and their eventual implementation is strategic analysis. This refines or confirms the entrepreneur's view of what is unique about their proposition; or, to put it another way, 'why on

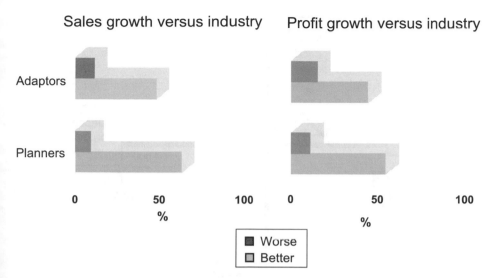

Figure 16.1   Business planning pays.

earth would anyone want to pay enough for this to make me rich?' Every business needs a clear mission, vision, objectives and a business plan. A survey of 475 global firms published by US management consultants Bain confirmed that 74% had mission and vision statements (this figure was higher in the US), and used the process to revitalize and direct growth. After the analysis comes the strategy itself: how will we get to market and achieve our goals?

This is the point at which the big divide occurs between incubators that work largely on a contingency basis and take an equity stake to secure their reward, and the more gentlemanly incubators run by some universities, government agencies and even property developers, who get their rewards and benefits in some other way. This latter group are primarily concerned that the business survives and can pay the rent or give students opportunities to study entrepreneurs in near-laboratory conditions and reflect well on the business incubator.

Business incubators run by venture capital firms, business consultants and the major accountancy firms all want to have a hand in shaping the core strategy of the companies they incubate. However politely they dress up their 'recommendations', they want their investments to pay off, and to pay off well. Both parties know something of the risks involved, though the incubator client undoubtedly is less well informed. Both want the same outcome; stardom at almost any price. Firms in incubators may well not experience any side-effects for some time after 'graduating', but unpleasant side-effects there usually are. Four strategies are most likely to be advanced by equity incubator players, and sometimes all four are advocated for the same client (see Figure 16.2).

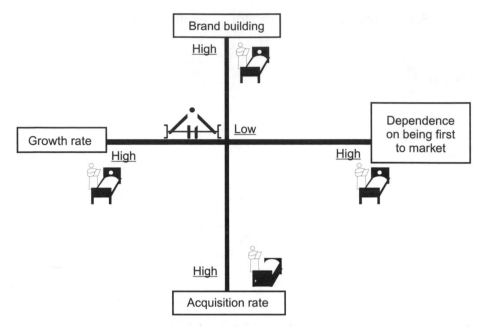

Figure 16.2   Strategies most likely to be recommended by 'for profit' incubators.

Cyberstart, a US 'for profit' incubator, makes no bones about its commitment to helping its clients to be first to market. Its list of six benefits it offers incubator clients includes:

- first-mover advantage;
- ability to achieve profitability within two years; and
- synergies with other CyberStart portfolio companies.

That language is fairly transparent and can surely be read to mean, let's get you to market first, ramp up the business as fast as we can, and if necessary we'll merge your business with other similar ventures to create critical mass through synergies. That's not to suggest that the 'for profit' incubators are not knocking on open doors. Entrepreneurs are not unsophisticated or inexperienced. Perhaps they don't need or deserve the protection a consumer of any other financial product would expect. The case study below shows that entrepreneurs are as eager to be first to market, go for growth, build a brand and buy up any business in sight as the consultants are to persuade them these are the best strategies.

DIGITAL EQUIPMENT

For Jamey Harvey, the founder of Digital Addiction, the choice between developing his firm in a for-profit or not-for-profit incubator was easy. His philosophy is that 'cash is king' when you start a business, and any deal that he can make that costs him nothing is a good deal in the short run. He started Digital Addiction with the proceeds from the sale of a patent – less than $100 000 in cash – and wanted to make that money go a long way. Harvey looked at using a not-for-profit incubator run by the High Tech Council of Maryland. The four-year-old Montgomery County Technology Enterprise Center occupies about 10 000 square feet of a two-storey building on Gaither Road. Their start-up businesses in the county incubator pay about $11 per square foot in rent, with a 10% increase for each year a firm stays in incubation. The Center collects fees for telephone use; photocopies cost 5 cents per page, outgoing faxes are 15 cents per page and Internet access costs $20 per month. When firms graduate from the programme, they can either pay back the subsidy they have received from the Center (about $25 000 for a three-year stay) or give the Center a small stock option. The center does not want to become a 5% owner or a 10% owner in a company. It just wants to help their businesses become a success, and then perhaps get some of that investment back.

In the for-profit incubator Harvey paid no rent. He had free use of photocopiers and fax machines, and got free legal, accounting and human resources advice. But, instead of cash, Harvey had to part with a sizeable chunk of the firm's equity at the outset. As for surrendering an equity stake in his firm, he believed the benefits outweighed the costs. For one thing, it gave the incubator management team a real stake in seeing his business succeed, because they wouldn't get paid if Digital Addiction didn't succeed. But, as much as the cash free services, he liked the speed at which the incubator team got his operation up and running. To understand why this is important, it helps to know a bit about his product, a game called '12 Arcana'. The game presents a series of battlefields in which competing general/wizards use armies of elves, dwarves and gargoyles to capture each other's castles. They draw magic from 12 houses, called the House of the Dead, the House of Hope, the House of Despair, etc. Harvey planned to give the game away for free, and then sell software objects to enhance game play – virtual spells, for instance, that will boost a wizard's powers. The concept is based on the card-collection game 'Magic: The Gathering', which had only just exploded into a billion dollar a year business as Harvey was setting up his venture. Harvey reckoned it would only be only a matter of time before someone got the digital equivalent of that successful product on to the market, and he was determined it would be his company. He spent three years as president and CEO of Digital Addiction before leaving in 1999 to start a new Internet community company called iKimbo, Inc. Since 1998, Ethan Ham, Harvey's long-time friend, has been president of Digital Addiction.

DO THESE STRATEGIES PAY OFF?

Each of the four strategies most likely to be on offer by equity-taking incubators has a low probability of success even when being executed by management teams with much more experience under their belts than most incubating firms are likely to have. So the value of such advice must be open to serious question, and may itself explain why so few Internet and high-tech firms succeed or, for that matter, survive. There seem to have been an awful lot of successful operations in which the patient has died! Exploring each of these in turn, we can see the areas of risk that high-tech and Internet firms are exposing themselves to.

FIRST TO MARKET

Gaining 'first mover advantage' is one of the most enduring ideas in business theory and practice. Entrepreneurs and established giants are always in a race to be first. Research from the 1980s that shows that market pioneers have enduring advantages in distribution, product-line breadth, product quality and, especially, market share underscores this principle.

This centrepiece of battles such as those being waged between Amazon and Barnes & Noble. Beguiling though the theory of first mover advantage is, it is probably wrong. A thorough review of the research studies that supported this theory was published four years ago by Tellis and Golder (1996), and the findings were found to be flawed. Amongst the many errors in earlier research, the authors revealed that the questions used to gather much of the data were at best ambiguous, and perhaps dangerously so. For example the term 'one of the pioneers in first developing such products or services', was used as a proxy for 'first to market'. The only compelling evidence from all the research was that nearly half of all firms pursuing a first-to-market strategy were fated to fail, whilst those following fairly close behind were three times as likely to succeed.

To emphasize their point, Tellis and Golder challenge their readers to name the biggest chain of franchised restaurants, the first company to market with disposable nappies and the pioneer of personal computers. If you think that McDonalds, Pampers and Apple are the answers, then you are mistaken. Howard Johnson was first to market with a chain of highway restaurants, but were overtaken by McDonalds in the 1970s. CHUX was the first brand in the disposable nappy business. Introduced in 1935, it was still ranked the best in a survey in 1961. Pampers, now the market leader, didn't even get a look-in. Micro Instrumentation and Telemetry Systems (MITS) so dominated the PC market in 1976 that *Business Week* referred to them as 'the IBM of home computers'. The magazine went on to say that their early lead had made them the 'industry standard'. A decade later Apple was referred to as the 'pioneer of personal computers', a firm that now has a single-figure share of that market and falling fast. This can be compared to the following story: in the country that is now Syria, one of the the earliest examples of the printed word was discovered a few decades ago. It is around 5000 years old. But in Syria today, the very place that had given the world this elegant script, half the population is still illiterate.

BUYING TO GROW

Growth by acquisition is the cornerstone of the strategy of Cisco and a host of other e-business firms. Cisco's top management claims such expertise in the acquisition process as to have a steady stream of management consultants visiting them to learn how it should be done. But here too the jury is out on acquisition strategy as a route to creating shareholder value. A review of the literature by this author (Barrow 1998) does not support the view that growth by acquisition is a winning strategy for anyone other than the shareholders of the company being acquired. They usually make a gain, whilst the buyers mostly lose value. The drivers of acquisitions are the desire for growth by investment analysts, the chance to make millions in fees whatever the outcome by corporate finance departments, and the egos of CEOs in acquiring firms, who see the acquisition process as a proxy for gladiatorial combat. For-profit incubators have the unfortunate knack of having an abundance of relationships with the main proponents of this type of strategy. There is evidence that some conditions are less favourable than others to the creation of shareholder value via a strategy involving acquisitions. For example, both bidders and targets lose in stock-financed deals, as opposed to those financed by cash (according to Myers and Majluf (1984), Krasker (1986), Asquith *et al.* (1986), and Masulis and Korwar (1986)). Yet Internet and high-tech IPOs often cite an acquisition strategy as a primary reason for coming to market. There is also strong evidence that firms with increased amounts of managerial ownership are more costly to acquire (according to Stulz (1988), Stulz *et al.* (1990), and Song and Walkling (1993)). Internet and high-tech firms almost invariably have heavy managerial ownership. Indeed, such ownership is one of their main attractions. At the same time, greater ownership gives company managers more control of the company, a power which can then be used to resist acquisitions. Managers often resist bids, even when the bid looks likely to create greater shareholder value (according to Ruback (1988) and Sudarsanan (1991)). There is also evidence from Walkling and Long (1984) to show that managers are likely to resist when the personal wealth gain from being taken over is not great enough to compensate for their loss of office.

Most high-tech acquisitions meet many of the conditions that seem guaranteed to deliver poor shareholder value to the acquirer. Whilst investors are content to value Internet firms on multiples of sales rather than profits, then any acquisition will be seen as beneficial. But when sanity returns and profit again becomes the measure of economic worth, most of these 'growth by acquisition' strategies will be unmasked as extravagant failures.

BUILDING A BRAND

The third strategy pursued by many Internet firms is the desire to build a brand, usually a global brand, and so have the advantages of price premium and customer loyalty. But creating a brand is not done overnight, nor can it be done without a clear understanding of both the market segment being served and the image to be created. Simply spending large sums of money or having hundreds of thousands of subscribers does not constitute a valuable brand. Whilst petrol companies spend heavily to create an image, they rely on 'give-aways' in their efforts to generate repeat purchases. Kotler (1988) asserts that brand beliefs built up from a range of attributes all contribute to a brand image. For a certain segment, that investment can create added value. The benefits conferred on teenagers drinking the 'real thing' rather than a substitute product such as Virgin Cola are crystal clear to members of that age group, as Virgin's sales figures clearly demonstrate. How the Amazon brand is supposed to operate, however, is far from clear. Once a book or CD reaches the end user its 'consumption' is invisible to the outside world. And lastminute.com's proposition seems the antithesis of a true brand, where people are being invited to buy cheap(er) services, such as hotel rooms and holidays that are surplus to the provider's level of demand. It's hard to see how consumers will feel in any way 'special' using such a service, which in any event is also invisible (although their main selling points are that they are cheap, and offer good value for money).

Unlikely commodities such as Perrier water can be turned into a valuable brand. But, Meldrum and McDonald (2000) assert that most products and services endowed with the tittle of 'brand' do not deliver value, do not deliver sustainable competitive advantage and do not add to the asset value of an organization when it is sold. The desultory price that Boo.com fetched (£350 000) after an investment of £80 000 in its 'brand' demonstrates how difficult this task can be.

ACCELERATED GROWTH

The notion that businesses can be grown at any rate you like as long as enough resources are chucked at them is tantalizing as an idea, and certainly one that incubators relate to. However, it is almost definitely fallacious. Children do not grow seamlessly from babies through to adulthood. They pass through phases: infancy, adolescence, teenage years and so on. Businesses also move through phases, if they are to grow successfully. Each of these phases is punctuated by a 'crisis', a word which derives from Chinese and translates loosely as 'dangerous opportunity'. Researchers such as Greiner (1972) and Churchill and Lewis (1983) have identified each distinctive phase in a firm's growth pattern, and provided an insight into the changes in organizational structure, strategy and behaviour that are needed to move successfully on to the next phase of growth. Figure 16.3 shows the phases of growth identified by these researchers.

Typically a business starts out by taking on any customers it can get, operating informally, with little management and few controls. The founder, who usually provides all the ideas and drive, makes all the decisions and signs the cheques, becomes overloaded with administrative

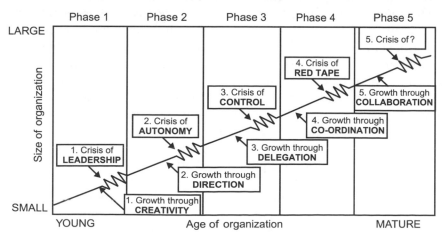

Figure 16.3   The organizational phases of growth.

details and operational problems. Unless the founder can change the organizational structure of his business, any further growth will leave the business more vulnerable. The crises of leadership, autonomy and control loom large. Over time, the successful owner-manager tackles these crises: finds a clear focus, builds a first-class team, delegates key tasks, appraises performance, institutes control and reporting systems, and ensures that progress towards objectives is monitored and rewarded. The firm itself consistently delivers good results. Another Microsoft, or Cisco Systems, has been born.

There is no set time that each of these phases should last. An old economy company may take decades to pass through each phase. IBM, for example, took over 70 years to hit the buffers of Phase Four growth. But for new economies, the luxury of this marathon approach has been supplanted by a series of stressful sprints.

Each phase of growth calls for a different approach to managing the business. Sometimes strong leadership is required, while at others a more consultative approach is appropriate. Some phases call for more systems and procedures, some for more co-operation between staff. Most entrepreneurs and most incubator managers operate as though these stages of growth do not exist. They believe the problems of growth can be solved by taking on another salesperson, a few hundred square metres of space or another large shot of venture capital. This approach is rather like suggesting that the transition from infancy to adulthood could be accomplished by simply providing larger clothes. For larger clothes, substitute faster burn rate, and you could easily be forgiven for thinking the only thing that prevents an Internet or high-tech business from realizing its potential is cash. That's certainly the view taken by many incubators, but experience is proving them wrong. However hard you try to accelerate high-tech ventures through the stages of growth, there seems to be a natural force at work, just as there is in life itself, that restrains and arrests the business until a minimum period has elapsed. As one former employee of failed e-tailor, Boo.com, who worked in their finance department said: 'When I joined it was the coolest place to work. But though the management had great vision they had no idea how to get there. It was extremely chaotic and spending went out of control.' It almost always takes five years to get a business through the first two phases of growth and up to a stage of maturity where it has become a valuable entity rather than the 'hobby farm' that nine out of ten firms gravitate towards being. But that horizon is too distant for the equity model adopted by some incubators.

What is also clear is that it's not just the organization that has difficulty adapting to a fast rate of growth. The market for new products and services has also got powerful forces restraining its capacity to accept large volumes of anything new, quickly. There is a predictable acceptance cycle to be gone through before the full market can be accessed (Figure 16.4).

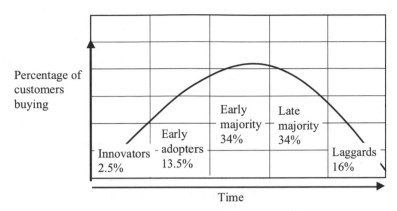

Figure 16.4   How quickly new and innovative products and services are adopted.

Let's suppose you have identified the market for your Internet flower-sending service. Initially your market has been constrained to affluent men within five miles of your base because of initial difficulties with delivery. So if market research shows that there are 100 000 people that meet the profile of your ideal customer and they have regular access to the Internet, the market open for exploitation at the outset may be as low as 2500. Only the Innovators, generally the more adventurous types who try out new things early on, are initially likely to buy. The Early Adopters will only start buying when the product or service has been given the seal of approval from the Innovators, and so on down the chain, until you reach the Laggards. It's quite probable that the market for any new product, however many people are identified as potential users, will therefore be very small for three to five years until this natural process has been followed through. However much money is spent on marketing, it will make little difference to the rate of sales growth until you get through to the majority of the market.

Now, this does not mean that no first-to-market strategy or one based on branding or acquisition can be made to work. Nor is it true that no firm can be accelerated through the stages of growth and propelled quickly to great stature. Hotmail showed that by using viral marketing, a new concept reliant on the Internet, but akin to the more conventionally recognizable 'craze', it is possible to grow exponentially in months rather than years. Hotmail's founder insisted that every e-mail sent by a Hotmail user should incorporate the message: 'Get your free web-based e-mail at Hotmail'. By clicking on this line of text, the recipient would be transported to the Hotmail home page. If this e-mail had been sent by the company itself, it would not have had much effect, but at the foot of an e-mail sent by a business colleague or friend it made a powerful impact. The very act of sending a Hotmail message constituted an endorsement of the product, and so the current customer was selling to future customers on the company's behalf by simply communicating with them. The recipient of a Hotmail message learnt that the product worked, but also that someone they respected or liked was a user. You only have to see how quickly a harmful computer virus can spread to cover the whole world in hours and days to see the potential of viral marketing. But whilst these high-powered strategies may work in certain cases, they are more likely to fail and, in so doing, to bring down the company in question. Firms that are accelerated into and out of incubators are rarely given enough fuel to do any more than show their potential. If stunning potential does not come through quickly no more fuel (money) will be forthcoming, and the business will plunge back to earth.

OTHER MANAGEMENT AND BUSINESS STRATEGY SERVICES

Whilst business planning and formulating strategy are likely to be the most significant management services on offer in an incubator, they are by no means the only ones. Research and development, opportunities for government contracts and help with getting into overseas markets can all be invaluable to certain types of company and those at a particular stage in their development. However, the earlier two subjects are of vital importance to every business at every stage in its development. Public relations (PR) is certainly a help in getting a new and unknown business in front of the various publics that it has to influence if it is to succeed. Managing the media is indisputably a central issue to all for-profit incubators, if only for their own self-interest. For example, eConception, a Nashville-based Internet incubator, saw 500 business plans before backing Logic Media Group, who planned to rewrite the rulebook for obtaining PR services not only by using the Internet, but by offering PR à la carte, a departure from the approach of traditional full-service firms. eConception then used Logic Media Group to generate publicity for themselves and their other incubator clients. In all probability, eConception have recovered the $2 million they invested in the company in press coverage alone. Joe Freedman, eConception founder, has acknowledged that 'we've gotten a tremendous amount of national press'. Whilst Logic Media already has some notable traditional clients such as the National Foundation for Cancer Research, the John Templeton Foundation, London-based *Science & Spirit* magazine, and the Hilton

Suites Nashville, they are working with all of the eConception-funded companies.

Networking in every sense of the word is also a useful service. Incubators often offer preferred rates and terms from two-tier service providers, enabling enterprises in the incubator to enjoy certain economies of scale. Although the Internet has made it easier for new firms to quickly generate their own network of suppliers and other contacts, entrepreneurs still face large opportunity costs in the form of hours spent finding, negotiating and contracting for products and business services. Many entrepreneurs (Hansen *et al.* 2000) spend upwards of half their time for the first six to nine months setting up the basic infrastructure to run their businesses. Incubators can cut down the time needed and hassle of getting up and running. In fact Hansen and his colleagues go so far as to argue that one type of incubator, which they have christened a *networked incubator* represents a fundamentally new and enduring organizational model uniquely suited to growing businesses in the Internet economy. Its key distinguishing feature is its ability to give start-ups preferential access to a network of potential partners. Such incubators institutionalize their networking. That doesn't mean that incubatees get preferential treatment; it only means that they have built-in access to partnerships that might not have existed without the incubator.

Hansen cites Hotbank, the incubator managed by Softbank Venture Capital (SBVC) situated in Mountain View, California, as the model network incubator. The first Hotbank incubatee was Model E, a start-up formed in September 1999 that offers build-to-order vehicles and a web-based comprehensive service package that includes vehicle registration, finance, insurance and delivery scheduling. Model E's founder, George Kim, acknowledges that the bundle of benefits obtained from Softbank and its incubator enabled his company to accelerate its development. As well as getting premises, help with recruiting staff was provided by Korn/Ferry, a leading recruitment firm, and Softbank's network of family members, over 150 Internet companies, helped with everything from preparing the business plan to sitting on their advisory board. This was in addition to providing referred suppliers for almost every management service they required.

17

Financing and financial consulting

There is little doubt that finance is at the heart of every new business. Exactly how much money is needed may vary, but that some is needed is unlikely to be a point of dispute. Apart from the pure property incubators, all the rest offer some help in these areas. The list below shows the kinds of help on offer:

- government grants and loans;
- equity financing arrangements;
- debt financing arrangements;
- business tax; and
- risk management and insurance.

In fact, raising finance is seen as such a vital aspect of getting a business incubated that most new incubators start from that perspective, even those based in universities. The London Business School (LBS) is a good example of this phenomena. Their incubator, the Gavron Business Centre, was set up in 2000 and has all the usual incubator paraphernalia; serviced office space near the business school, with Internet connections, networked computers, voicemail, photocopiers and the like. Hot desks are provided as well as offices, meeting rooms and a boardroom. They have an innovative tenancy agreement that only commits tenants to a month at a time. The sting in the tail is that companies can only stay for 12 months, or until they have 25 members of staff. But the centrepiece of the incubation process is Sussex Place Investment Management (SPIM), named after the business school's main London address. SPIM is the business school's in-house venture capital arm, also formed in 2000, and it has raised £21.5 million to back entrepreneurial ventures that can be supported in the Gavron Business

Centre. The funding on offer covers everything from pre-seed money to validate a concept or business opportunity, through seed financing to get a business up and running, and first round financing to get the first stage of serious growth underway. For pre-seed financing, up to £50 000 is on offer, in return for which they want 10–20% of the ordinary shares of the company concerned. For the other stages of investment they can go to £200 000 and £500 000 respectively.

SPIM only backs alumni, though that term can be pretty widely stretched to include, for example, 'a business committed to recruit an LBS graduating student to the team in an executive capacity'. Taking on one of their alumni might be a shrewd move in any event. Their graduates, as with Cranfield graduates and those of other major business schools, will have had a thorough grounding in getting a new venture up and running during their period of study. Companies going through the LBS incubator include Homepro.com, a web- and mobile phone-based service offering an 'approved' database of trade professionals to home owners, and Global Workplace, an online recruitment firm targeting the alumni of the world's leading business schools. Both these businesses have strong international dimensions, with Homepro.com having operations in the UK, France and Germany, and Global Workplace signing exclusive agreements with 24 business schools covering four continents. As well as raising money from SPIM, these two ventures have had heavyweight backing from other sources. Hompro.com raised £2.6 million from Carphone Warehouse and Atlas Ventures, and Global Workplace has a joint venture operation in Japan with Softbank Corporation. The LBS incubator has a few more obviously high-tech ventures in it too. Bodymetrics is developing a 3D body scanner able to capture highly accurate body size data and Hidden Footprints has patent pending technology that uniquely marks each user copy delivered from a single original via multicasting, over the Internet.

No self-respecting new incubator would start up without having help in financial matters high on its agenda of benefits. On 6 May 1999, over enchiladas at a taco stand near Disney's Burbank studios, Sky Dayton and Jake Winebaum decided to create eCompanies. Dayton and Winebaum had each spent the last five years building industry-leading Internet businesses: Deyton founded EarthLink, assembled a management team and oversaw its growth into one of the world's largest Internet service providers (ISPs). At Disney, Winebaum had built and run the media company's various Internet businesses, which included Disney.com, ABCNews.com, ESPN.com and Go.com. Disney is today ranked number five on the Internet in traffic, the only non-technology company in the list of top ten most-visited websites.

The eCompanies incubator was created to rapidly launch Internet start-ups that will grow into profitable, lasting businesses. What separates eCompanies from incubators such as idealab!, CMGI and eHatchery, according to Winebaum, is the infrastructure he and Dayton claim will make it possible for a start-up to go from zero to launch in 90–180 days. Start-ups channel through a seven-step programme, from business plan and hiring a CEO to marketing. The incubator provides the critical services start-ups need in seven disciplines: strategy, finance, recruiting, creative, technology, business development and marketing. eCompanies has hired blue-chip executives in each discipline, so entrepreneurs can get advice from a whole team of Internet veterans. But the key to the whole incubation process is access to money. eCompanies raised $160 million from Accel Partners, Credit Suisse First Boston, Disney, EarthLink, Goldman Sachs, Kohlberg Kravis Roberts, Soros Fund Management, Sprint, Sun America and Times Mirror as well as pumping money in themselves.

eCompanies claim that an entrepreneur typically spends 90% of his time when starting a business raising money, securing partners, finding talent, and countless other activities associated with forming a company. He spends the remaining 10% on product development and marketing, the two activities that will make the company win in the market. So in addition to help from an array of Internet veterans, eCompanies provides its start-up CEOs with all the services they need, including help in raising all types of finance so they can concentrate on getting to market quickly with the right product.

eCompanies is located by the ocean in Santa Monica, California, a city that the founders believe is poised to become the world's next Internet hotbed. The companies in eCompanies' existing portfolio include Efavorites, a product recommendation service; Ememories, a photo-sharing company; online content company Icebox; small-business M&A company USBX; back-office management firm Ledgent; and the high-profile business portal Business.com, in which they have invested $7.5 million alone.

Most of those running incubators and accelerators start from the premise that financing and financial issues are an important, perhaps the most important, benefit that their skills can bring to help make a new venture successful. But these financial talents may be nowhere near as valuable as they might like to think.

IS FINANCE REALLY THAT IMPORTANT?

In an interview published in *The Industry Standard* (US Edition) 7 December 2000, eCompanies confirmed that all of the cash it had raised had been committed to a portfolio of more than 20 start-ups, many with a consumer slant. Up to then, however, none of the companies in eCompanies' venture portfolio had completed an initial public offering – and there is little prospect of that changing any time soon. So much for the much vaunted 180-day in-and-out cycle for their incubator. That's left the company little room to manoeuvre in what remains a difficult environment for both incubators and consumer-oriented net companies alike. eCompanies operates two incubators, one of which focuses on wireless companies, the other on 'wireline' Internet companies. The latter group has suffered layoffs, and has stopped creating new companies.

These developments at eCompanies are not unique. They just add to the growing troubles in the Internet incubation business. Walker Digital, founded by Priceline.com creator Jay Walker, has had to lay off staff and has reduced its operations. Publicly traded Internet investment companies Internet Capital Group (ICGE), CMGI and Divine InterVentures have recently seen their stocks plunge in value. Garage.com and idealab! have postponed planned IPOs.

The big question now is, apart from making a series of suspect investments, were they barking up the wrong tree anyway? Research available to anyone starting an incubator when eCompanies and all the other new wave of incubators started up suggested that money was not anywhere near as high on an entrepreneur's shopping list as incubator management teams thought it was.

In Mian's (1996) study the perceived value added from such matters as raising finance, accessing government grants and loans, or getting advice on risk management and insurance was not that high. Help in finding outside capital, for example, was only considered of major value by about a quarter of companies in incubators, about the same proportion as saw value in getting advice on tax planning. In fact, a higher proportion of people in this study felt that help in all matters to do with finance were of no value at all than felt they were of major value. Mian's research was not, however, confined to high-tech or Internet companies; indeed, back in 1995 there would have been no such sector as Internet companies, but he took his sample from six incubators; Advanced Technology Development Centre (ATDC), Technology Advancement Programme (TAP), Technology Innovation Centre (TIC), Ben Franklin Technology Innovation Centre (BFTI), Edison Technology Incubator (ETI) (all of which could reasonably be assumed to contain a high proportion of technology-based enterprises), and the Ben Craig Centre (BCC), which at the time of the study may or may not have done so. So it seems reasonable to accept Mian's findings as representing those of high-tech firms in incubators.

One even more surprising result from Mian's work is in what low regard they held getting help to access government loans and grants, areas that one could be forgiven for thinking would be high on the agenda of an

entrepreneur with a capital-intensive high-tech venture in mind. Forty percent of those surveyed rated this incubator service as of no value at all,
although some 32%, saw it as being of major value. Yet help with financial
strategy is still one of the main benefits touted by new incubators and some
older incubation processes such as that in LBS. It's just possible that they are
playing the wrong game altogether.

Part Four

Could incubation work for you?

From the entrepreneur's point of view, business incubation would appear at first sight to provide superb benefits. It's less certain that those incubators provide such great results for their sponsoring bodies. As we have already seen, the growth of many new VC model incubators is in decline, and few are showing any discernable return on their investments. But that fact need not concern a would-be incubator entrant. Today's high-profile incubators promise to develop entrepreneurs' ideas into compelling business plans, assemble world-class management teams, build working organizations, create products and services, acquire strategic partners and customers, and, finally, prepare their fledgling companies for further funding, acquisition, or public equity markets. And they aim to accomplish all this within three to six months, the time it takes an entrepreneur, working alone, to address such basic start-up needs as office space, telephone services, network operations and staffing. The reality may be a little short of that ideal, but there seems little doubt that most entrepreneurs get a good deal from being incubated.

The research, such as it has been, broadly confirms that view. Mian (1996) in his conclusion said 'the vast majority of the respondents [incubator tenants] believed that the services they were receiving were adding value to their fledgling firms'. When compared with previous fragmented research findings (Allen and Levine 1986; Allen and Bazan 1990), Mian's findings confirm that incubators add value to their client firms, and that 'university technology business incubators in particular are specifically suitable for developing new technology-based firms'. In fact, there are some grounds for believing that entrepreneurs are more satisfied than they are letting on. Allen and Bazan (1990) confirmed what most who have anything to do with business starters already knew: 'entrepreneurs are not a particularly appreciative group, and their high degree of autonomy and self-esteem shade their perceptions of how much they are really being helped'.

Notwithstanding this endorsement, there are drawbacks and dangers for an entrepreneur in a business incubator, and a price somewhat higher than expected may have to be paid. Also, some of the promises made by incubators in their attempts to woo companies may not live up to expectations.

In Part 4 we will review the main potential benefits for an entrepreneur of locating in an incubator, discuss whether the process is right for your business, and then look at how to get into and out of an incubator.

18

What are the real benefits to be gained from locating in an incubator?

As we have seen, incubators have a wide range of services on offer to prospective clients. The key questions for a potential entrant to ask are, are the benefits real and are they worth having? This section will discuss the key benefits in turn.

SURVIVAL

Small and new firms are notoriously vulnerable to an early death, and few grow very much or very fast (Barrow and Brown 1997). Greater Hamilton Technology Enterprise Centre (GHTEC) is typical of business incubators in making claims about what it can do to improve business survival rates for its client companies. Operated by the Regional Municipality of Hamilton-Wentworth, Canada, GHTEC is a business incubator assisting potential entrepreneurs to form technology-based businesses. It operates out of a 40 000 square-foot air-conditioned building, opened in 1993, funded totally by the Regional Municipality and 'conceived and developed to diversify the economy of the region and add wealth to the community through job creation by new entrepreneurs'.

The opening statement on GHTEC's website states:

The biggest challenges facing entrepreneurs are getting started quickly, staying focused on the core business and achieving positive cash flow. Nationwide statistics show that 80% of companies starting in an enterprise centre survive four times longer than the national average.

There is no reliable research to support this claim, which has been repeated time and time again by incubators around the world. Past studies have tended to conclude that business incubators do improve the probability of survival for new business ventures (Campbell *et al.* 1988; Lyons 1990; Tornatzky *et al.* 1995; Molnar *et al.* 1996). But Allen and Bazan's conclusions (1990) sum up the feelings of most researchers trying to establish the truth in this area. 'Firms that graduate from incubators have a slightly lower failure rate compared to non-incubated firms'. Sherman (1999), in one of the most recent comprehensive research studies covering survival rates for incubator companies, comes to a much more bullish conclusion. His study showed that 87% of firms that had graduated from their incubator programmes were still in operation five years later. This compared favourably with the SBA (1997) report only two years before Sherman's study. The SBA showed that 53% of all new businesses failed in the first five years.

Even taking Sherman's results as being representative of other researchers' findings (which they are not) it would be difficult to support the argument that firms born via incubators are four times more likely to survive than firms born outside incubators. Australia is the only place that has produced research that might support the 'four times more likely to survive hypothesis' (OECD 1999), where it is claimed that an estimated 8% of incubator tenants fail in the first year compared with a national average of around 32%. It is, however, a more believable hypothesis that entrepreneurs going into incubators are more thoughtful and reflective than the entrepreneurial population in general, and thus more likely to carefully plan their strategy. As a sub-group, they probably have a slightly better than average chance of survival in or out of incubation than others business starters. If this is true, then a higher than national average business survival rate could be expected of this group whether or not they start up in incubators.

PROFITABLE GROWTH

This too is a questionable outcome for companies coming through the incubation process. Sherman (1999) in his study of 310 incubator graduates, showed that their average sales were $30 000 in their first year and $150 475 some five years later. This he claims as an impressive 501% growth rate. But in fact this is only a 38% compound rate of sales growth which, considering the amount of effort put into such ventures, is hardly meteoric. The high-tech component of his sample did rather better, growing sales by a compound 47% over the five-year period. Even firms, mostly propelled from the VC and consultancy incubators, that have achieved meteoric growth have plunged to earth again quickly enough. idealab!'s e-Toys, beauty e-tailor Eve.com and employment service Refer.com all grew their sales impressively for the brief period of their ascent, but made no profit in the process. Sherman's sample show only an average of $27 000 annual profits five years after incubation.

Jeremy Quitter (2000) spent two months speaking to dozens of researchers, incubator managers and the NBIA, concluding rather wryly, 'yet no one could point me to clear data demonstrating that incubators are as effective as so many in the industry say'. He went on to pose another challenging question for the incubation business: 'if they dramatically improve a small business' chance of success, it would seem likely that in the last 20 years, at least one would have produced a large, profitable company'.

The big success story incubator proponents point to is Peapod, the online grocery store. Peapod operated at the Technology Incubation Center (TIC) in Evanston, Illinois, which is affiliated with Northwestern University, from 1989 to 1996 (more than twice the length of time that most businesses stay in incubators). It went public in June 1997, and had $60 million in revenues in 1998. Peapod employs about 1200 people nationally and 400 in the Chicago area. It didn't stay in the town that fostered it, though. Faced with doubling rent, Peapod left Evanston for cheaper Skokie as soon as it graduated. Andrew Parkinson, president and chief executive of Peapod, claims the chief benefit of the incubator was 'office space at a very cheap rent' and moral support from other start-ups. Access to Northwestern University's mainframe computers was also a plus: 'it was a nice way to tap [university] brain power'. TIC's prestige also gave Peapod credibility when it approached Jewel Foods, its first supplier and now an investor. Parkinson, a former Procter & Gamble manager of such brands as Pringles (potato chip makers), Duncan Hines (choc-chip cookie makers), and Parkay (margarine company), set the firm up along with his younger brother Thomas, a software designer. Peapod began to deliver groceries in the Chicago area and then expanded to deliver in San Francisco, Houston, Dallas, Austin, Boston, Atlanta, and other regions filled with high-tech, high-income, time-crunched people. By its eleventh anniversary in 2000, more than 120 000 households were ordering through the service, and Peapod was posting annual revenues of close to $100 million. Yet its quarterly operating loss had more than doubled to nearly $13 million (Figure 18.1).

Peapod built the country's best-known online grocery brand through local advertising, attracting press coverage, and sending out America Online-type mass mailings of millions of free sign-up diskettes to potential customers in its target metro areas. Its tag line (America's Internet Grocer) and its slogan ('Smart Shopping for Busy People') seem to say exactly what it is and does. Yet despite its name recognition, its market value and overall

	Quarter ended 31 March 2000	1999
Statement of operations	$000	$000
Net sales	24 914	18 008
Cost of sales	19 216	14 366
Gross profit	5698	3642
Operating expenses:		
Fulfilment operations	8931	4872
General and administrative	2039	1573
Marketing and advertising	1340	1238
System development and maintenance	1189	723
Depreciation and amortization	664	474
Pre-opening expenses	–	280
Non-recurring expenses	4118	–
Total operating expenses	18 281	9160
Operating loss	(12 583)	(5518)

Figure 18.1   Peapod's quarterly financial summary (1999–2000).

financial performance have been immensely disappointing. In 1997, Barron's, the weekly publication for investors from the publisher of the *Wall Street Journal*, honoured Peapod with the distinction of being the worst-performing web-related initial public offering (IPO) of the year.

As Peapod has grown, signing up more and more households in more markets, this business model has become a near-perfect paradox. The more successful companies are, the more money they lose. In a recent four-year period, net losses have increased every year to a terrifying total of more than $50 million, with nearly $18 million of that occurring in the half-year to 31 March 2000. Peapod's latest CEO, William Malloy, left suddenly in March 2000, leaving a further round of financing in jeopardy, and a number of angry recent purchasers of their stock telephoning their lawyers. On 28 February 2001 Peapod Inc. announced that it had secured an additional $30 million in financing from Dutch grocer Royal Ahold, which owns 50% of the company. The previous week, Peapod had reported its biggest quarterly loss yet, $23.8 million, and announced it would run out of cash by the year end without additional financing. The company also announced the closure of its distribution centre serving San Francisco and ended its supply arrangement with Chicago-based supermarket retailer Jewel-Osco, and in another change of tack it began to procure certain dry goods and health and beauty aids through Ahold subsidiaries, including Cleveland-based Tops Market. In April 2001, Royal Ahold N.V. agreed to pay $75 million for a 51% stake in Peapod which, together with warrants they own for additional shares, could take them up to 75% ownership, giving them almost total control.

It's difficult to see how a potential incubator entrant could draw much comfort from the results attained by Peapod, in terms of either the robustness of its strategy or its performance in terms of profitable growth.

FUNDING

Getting into an incubator in the first place, unless it is a pure property incubator, is the most difficult part, and one we will examine in Chapter 20. But once in, it does seem that raising money is a less painful process than raising capital on the outside. Business incubators often provide access to the kind of early-stage capital that emerging companies desperately need. According to the ten-year survey of NBIA members (NBIA 1996), 83% of incubators provide access to seed capital. Seventy-six per cent provide assistance with obtaining federal grants, 74% assist with preparing financing proposals, 60% can help obtain royalty financing and the same proportion have direct access to their own network of business angels, and 57% can lend a hand in obtaining purchase-order financing.

The Sherman (1999) study showed that high-tech firms had raised on average $129 801 of capital in the year they entered an incubator, and by the fifth year of their lives had raised $552 246. Since few of these firms were reporting significant profits, it seems reasonable to assume they had been successful in raising more funds. But you have to remember that the advisers make money by helping firms to raise money. A small firm will end up paying out dearly (in terms of its equity) to raise money from VCs and business angels. Any debt they raise will have to be paid back, and even grants usually come with strings attached.

A more interesting question to ask is, do you really need to raise all that money in the first place? For example, Degrftour, the French Internet company bought in August 2000 by lastminute.com had operated profitably since it's first year of trading. Degrftour and lastminute.com are in broadly similar lines of business and are much the same size, yet the former makes a million pounds profit a year whilst the latter loses a million pounds a week. lastminute.com was pumped full of expensive VC money from the outset and then went to the stock market to raise hundreds of millions of pounds more to fund its growth. Degrftour needed only the equivalent of £50 000 to create a profitable venture. In the year to March 2000, lastminute.com grew revenues by 34% and lost money. Degrftour grew by 31%, just 3% less, and made money. (For a comprehensive review of funding likely to be open to companies in incubators, see Barrow 2001.)

HELP ON TAP

The incubator manager plays a critical role in developing contacts, building networks, managing facilities, and consulting with tenants. It's difficult to find the whole range of skills needed to succeed in all these areas in just one person, but incubators are rarely managed by more than one or two people on a full-time basis. Sherman's (1999) study indicates that there is a more profound problem. Incubator staff often don't have enough time to provide the one-to-one, tailored counselling and consulting that they claim to offer. Over 70% of incubator managers reported spending less than 50% of their time doing consulting and referrals for their clients, and 48% reported that they spent less than 25% of their time on these areas.

The PricewaterhouseCoopers report (1999) also had incubator managers spending less than a quarter of their time on 'tenant interaction'. Managers spent more time on matters relating to the incubator structure itself, such as fund-raising, property management or committee meetings with sponsoring organizations. The PricewaterhouseCoopers study also made another revealing finding. Tenant failure rates were nearly twice as high in incubators less than two years old when compared with those that had been in operation for five years or more. The inference was that incubator managers had settled into their role, had the infrastructure of the incubator itself under control and now had enough time to devote to their tenants.

EVERYBODY PULLS TOGETHER

Learning from your peers while you all grow your businesses is a key incubator selling-point. Rick Gibson ran a web content publishing company called FeatureCast in idealab!'s first batch of incubatees in 1996–7, with another dozen budding entrepreneurs such as CitySearch's Charles Conn and eToys' Toby Lenk. Gibson recalls weekly breakfast meetings held to bounce ideas and war stories off each other. They even worked on each others' products. But soon it became apparent that some incubator tenants were more likely to succeed than others. When that happened the winners got most of the incubator management attention, which is hardly surprising, but galling for the entrepreneurs left out in the cold. Gibson's business dissolved quickly and quietly, unlike the businesses of some of those who shared idealab!'s breakfast table, who went out with a bang a few years later. Gibson later used his experience in idealab! to set up his own incubator, HOTventures, in Tucson, Arizona.

Bill Gross, idealab!'s founder, recognized the problem caused by companies getting left behind. He wanted all the owners of companies in his incubators to actively share ideas and knowledge with one another. A disciplined approach to such synergistic relationships only got underway when they all had a stake in each others' success when Gross (1998) cut incubatees in on idealab!'s equity, so that everyone stood or fell together.

WILL YOU STILL BE RUNNING THE SHOW?

A fundamental reason for setting up in business, from the entrepreneur's perspective, is to run his own business in his own way. Making money features fairly low down the list of motivations (Barrow 1998). Business incubators, as we have seen, have a very different agenda. The for-profit incubators have making money at the top of their agenda. It's often so far up the agenda that the entrepreneur is almost an incidental part of the process. Jan Gapinski, the founder of the Swedish incubator, Speedventures, who we looked at in an earlier chapter, discusses his view of the relationship between himself and a business starter in his incubator (Leleux 2000): 'We don't just want to be part of new companies, we want to be in the driver's seat.' Reach, an incubator we have already looked at, shares some of Gapinski's vision. Reach claims that its environment is so complete that they are capable of launching businesses with nothing more than an idea. They say that they can provide everything including an interim CEO to take over as soon as it becomes clear the founder cannot deliver, or they can provide a full-time permanent CEO to handle more sensitive issues such as an IPO. Advanced Technology Development Center, the Georgia-based incubator, took in MindSpring's founder Charles Brewer in 1994, but by March 1996 a bland statement in the company's accounts showed that he had passed control to a new CEO. By March 2000, the accounts showed that Charles Brewer had 'resigned from the company to pursue other interests'. Sky Dayton, a seasoned professional, had assumed the role of chairman of the board in time for MindSpring's next stage of growth. The not-for-profit incubators are less likely to take a route involving effectively removing the founder, but they too have their own agendas and are unlikely to support failing ventures for long.

This does not mean that moving the founder out, or at least out of the driving seat, is not a healthy thing to do. Few business founders are the right people to take their business much beyond the launch stage (Barrow *et al*. 2001), but moving over and out within a few years of starting up may not be what the founder has in mind in starting up in the first place. If it isn't, then an incubator may not be the right place for him to be.

THE WORD 'INCUBATOR' OPENS ALL DOORS

Once upon a time, the word 'incubator' opens all doors may have been true. In 1995, when Mark Kopcha was starting up Novient with little more than a business plan, being located in the ATDC incubator allowed him to 'look like a company'. Kopcha reckons that he could never have pulled off any deals with big corporate firms if he had been operating from his basement. Now with 125 employees and a client list which includes Hewlett-Packard and Siemens-Nixdorf, his situation is a little different.

But the kudos associated with the hotter accelerators and incubators has all but gone. VCs have a low opinion of them. One Californian VC claims that all incubators do is shove entrepreneurs into cubes with a computer and a high-speed Internet link and say, 'make me money'. Few publicly quoted incubators are making any money; those with four-year track records such as CMGI are, as we have already seen, delivering indifferent performance when it comes to making money for their shareholders.

Intranet.com, an idealab! company, has used that relationship to grab 200 000 customers and a global partnership with a Japanese firm, Hikari Tsushin. But one of its competitors, Planet Intra, who did not start up via the incubation route, captured 22 000 paying customers in its first eight months and it too has a tie-up in Japan, this time with trading company Itocha. Planet Intra's subscribers brought in an average of $420 per month, whilst idealab!'s protégé brings in nothing (Carbonara and Overfelt 2000).

19

Is incubation right for you?

S teve Crummey was well satisfied with the results he got from Gross's idealab! incubator. But not everyone necessarily feels the same way, even if their results are satisfactory. A key part of going through the process of starting a business is being exposed to the hazards and learning how to deal with them. Incubators may provide too soft an experience in that regard, making their incubated clients too delicate to survive in the outside world. Answering the following questions should make it clear whether being in an incubator will work for you (or your client).

ARE YOU A TEAM PLAYER?

To get the best out of the process, you have to be able to share your inner-most business hopes and fears with others, as well as be prepared to listen to others. The pressure of peer review is a powerful learning tool. There is a tendency to listen to and respect the views of others who have gone or are going through the same experience as yourself. But many entrepreneurs are secretive and operate better as soloists rather than as members of an orchestra. For the former, incubation could be a painful experience.

ARE YOU A GOOD LISTENER AND LEARNER?

People with great business ideas have usually arrived at them after much hard work and deliberation. They are likely to be so passionate and com-mitted to their idea that they have difficulty in listening to or taking advice that deviates from their original vision. Part of the trouble is that develop-ing anything new forces an entrepreneur into a sceptical environment where they are inevitably put on the defensive. Even friends who respect you may have difficulty in taking your big idea seriously. This is how a friend and colleague reacted to Bill Gross's plans to start idealab!: 'After Steve Crummey got off the phone in 1996 with his old Lotus crony Bill Gross, he turned to his wife and said, "That guy's crazy! Have you ever heard of a crazier idea?" Gross, who had become very rich and had acquired an aura of entrepreneurial genius when he sold his company, Knowledge Adventure, for $100 million that year, had just tipped off Crummey about idealab!, his planned Internet incubator' (Carbonara and Overfelt 2000). So if you are not open to modifying and perhaps even radically changing your business idea, forget incubation.

DO YOU MIND SHARING OWNERSHIP?

Any incubator, with the exception of one that provides little more than a premises. The property-based incubator Regus, and others like it, are likely to want a share of the future worth of your business. The reasoning behind this is fairly straightforward. The more potential your business shows once in the incubator, the more effort the incubator staff will feel inclined to invest in helping you realize that potential. This also means that the gap between any rent and payment for services being used in the incubator and the cost of providing such services will be wide. The only economic way for the incubator to bridge that gap is by taking an equity stake: the larger the gap, the greater the stake. Now entrepreneurs appear to divide into two neat camps, those that want 100% of what they have, however small that may be, and those that are happy to have a smaller, perhaps even a substantially smaller, stake in a much larger enterprise. No amount of reasoning or logic can move the former into the latter camp, so if that's where you fit, stay away from incubators.

DO YOU LIKE MILESTONES?

Incubation is intended to be a short-term process lasting, ideally, a few months, and a year or so at most. The way an incubator team keeps track of how close their eggs are to hatching is by having a series of measurable goals. Miss a goal and you are on the danger list, miss a few goals and you are out of the incubator. In the real world, a business can be measured in a more tra- ditional way. Sales growth, profits achieved, new markets entered are all conventional measures. But in incubators most activity is concealed beneath the 'shell', so keeping track of progress means agreeing to achieving certain results within an agreed period of time. Get the patents filed within two months, get the product literature ready in three months and a sales team in place by the same time. The incubator manager will have regular meetings with tenants to make sure these milestones are being met. This can be an irksome process, as some of the milestones appear bureaucratic and seem to be more to do with the incubator's problems than the entrepreneurs'. But the incubator manager has a boss too, and his sponsors need to know that their investment is being managed. If you are the type of person who responds badly to imposed targets and timescales, then incubation is not for you.

DO YOU WANT TO BE RICH?

As we have already seen, most businesses start small and stay that way. Few owner-managers ever get much richer working for themselves than they might have done working for someone else. Barely 250 firms in every million will ever see their annual profits hit the £1 million mark (Barrow 2000).

If all you want to do is to make a living, then the chances are that no self-respecting incubator will want you in their facility. VCs want to IPO their clients and make millions, universities want a lucrative outlet for their technologies, and corporate venture firms want big opportunities to replace their dying old businesses and carry their existing burden of overheads. Only governments quixotically committed to encouraging new business start-ups, with little concern about what happens to them afterwards, are likely to offer a safe haven for the unambitious.

DO YOU NEED HELP?

If you don't need help in any of the areas discussed in this book and re-capped below, then you should certainly question whether going into a business incubator is worthwhile.

Product and service development: Do you need to move from prototype to manufacturing model? Do you need to perform product testing and evaluation?

Sales and marketing: Do you need guidance in looking at and developing your target market? Does your company need better access to distribution channels? Do you need help in developing an advertising campaign? Frequently, early stage entrepreneurs need most assistance in the sales and marketing areas.

Finances: Do you have enough money to get your business off the ground? Remember that you will never have all the money to do everything on your wish-list. Also remember that no money comes without strings. Do you need a chief financial officer (CFO)? Have you set a realistic timetable for when the company will generate a positive cash flow? Do you need additional resources to carry the company through start-up and product development until it generates cash?

Management: Successful companies have an effective management team that works co-operatively and consists of members selected to provide a range of knowledge and skills. Will your company need to build or strengthen its management team?

Strategic relationships: Would your business benefit from being able to forge good working relationships with larger and well-established businesses?

DO YOU WANT TO RUN THE SHOW?

As we have already seen, there are a number of circumstances under which the founder of a business can end up being ousted from running his own business, if he enters an incubator. The paradox here is that both success and failure often merit the same reward; an early 'retirement' from the top job. Grow too slowly, or fail to perform in some other way, and the incubator team will be on hand to recruit your replacement. Succeed beyond everyone's wildest dreams, and you may not be the right person to run a big business. lastminute.com, whose share price collapsed by 60% within a month of their IPO, found themselves in this situation. Their VCs 'encouraged' them to introduce a new tier of senior management to run the day-to-day business almost immediately after their float, to steady the nerves of their investors if nothing else. Often the skills needed to create a company in an incubator just aren't the same as those needed to build it into an industry giant.

HAVE YOU CONSIDERED THE ALTERNATIVES?

You don't have to locate in a business incubator to get many of the advantages an incubator can offer. A less formal arrangement in a virtual incubator may suit you better. Alternatively, you can get most of the benefits by picking and choosing from the range of services that most incubators make available to entrepreneurs in any event. Almost all the education, training and networking events are open to anyone who takes the trouble to find out about them. You may well have to pay, but then so will incubator tenants. At least you will only have to pay once: those inside the incubator who have parted with a share of their business will have to go on paying forever for those transient benefits.

20

Getting into an incubator

There is almost invariably an application process to getting into any business incubator. All that varies is the process itself. Some incubators positively invite and encourage the informal approach, some are highly structured, some have their own models and techniques which they believe can separate the wheat from the chaff. All application processes take time and, if they didn't you would have cause for concern. After all, if they take in just anyone without any serious consideration as to what they can do to help their businesses, that particular incubation process is unlikely to be of much value.

Most application processes require some sort of a business plan. This may be little more than an executive summary to be done in line with your application, or it may be a more comprehensive written document setting out your latest thinking on what is so special about you and your big idea. Then comes the interview and, after that, the decision. This chapter will discuss each of these areas in turn.

THE INFORMAL APPROACH

The Springfield Enterprise Center (SEC) based in Western Massachusetts on the STCC Technology Park is a good example of the more relaxed style of incubator application process. They invite applicants to:

> . . . call us first and talk it over. We'll tell you if you're ready to apply. Associates at the SEC need to have established the beginning of a track record. Maybe you've been working out of your house for the past year or so, and now you're ready for the next step. You have a business plan, and have already started to establish a client base. You've built up a satisfactory credit history and have the ability to pay rent at the SEC. Now you're ready

for the incubation process, ensuring strong and healthy growth to sustain your business into the future.

Your application will be evaluated by a sub-committee of the SEC Advisory Board, tailored to your concept. If you've begun a business in computer repair, software development or web page design, there will be a successful computer-related business person on your sub-committee, along with a small business finance specialist, probably a marketing consultant, perhaps an accountant and a management consultant. These people will be the 'guidance squad' for your business as it goes through the incubation process, devoting time on a *pro bono* basis to give you the advice and assistance you need to succeed.

Resident businesses and guests can join the monthly pizza parties at the Center, where associates and affiliates can talk over what they're trying, what works, what doesn't, and why. Sometimes the group is joined by experts, from the SEC Advisory Board or from other elements of the business community, for discussions of entrepreneurial topics. At the bottom of the page of services on offer is free parking for incubator residents and their guests. Once you have been to see a few successful incubators you will know just how valuable that can be.

ASSESSING INNOVATIONS

An inevitable part of the application process will be an assessment of any technology involved in the business proposition. It is unlikely that the incubator staff will always have the necessary state-of-the-art knowledge themselves, but invariably they will know someone who does. Also, as in the case study below, they will have a process for assessing the innovation itself, as well as trying to gauge if the applicant has what it takes to make the grade.

The Sydney Business Enterprise Centre (SBEC), in Sydney, Australia, is supported by the state government to provide a three-tiered service targeted at inventors. The three tiers are a self-assessment service for inventors, a counselling service and a technical assessment. All three form a part of the overall assessment as to whether or not an applicant should be accepted for incubation. But as with many incubator application processes, there is an element of value added for the would-be entrepreneur in the process itself.

The Self-assessment Service consists of a computer-based questionnaire of 32 questions relating to the technical status of an inventor's concept and his knowledge of the marketplace in which customers for the invention might be found. The profile of the inventor's answers to the questionnaire generate a response from the computer which predicts the likelihood of commercial success. In essence, the Self-assessment Service provides a structured checklist for the inventor inexperienced in the commercialization of new concepts. Inventors are provided with an interactive counselling session with one or two experienced business advisers for a fee of A\$50, paid by the inventor. The fee is nominal and is simply intended to eliminate frivolous applicants, of which there are many. The counsellor reviews the technical and business concept proposed by the inventor and provides feedback. Where appropriate, the counsellor refers the inventor to one of SBEC's advisers or broader network members with skills of particular relevance to the product or service in question.

The value the inventor derives from the counselling is largely dependant on the counsellor's ability to link the inventor into appropriate business development training and support offered by SBEC, or links to services offered by its network with government agencies, industry associations, universities or other organizations. SBEC commissions a written technical assessment of the invention proposed for commercialization. The assessment is carried out by an engineering consultant registered with the New South Wales State Government. The purpose of the technical assessment is to provide the inventor with a credible technical review by an independent third party where it is felt that this may assist the inventor to secure the interest of a prospective commercial partner.

This three-tiered process is deliberately structured as a screening device. Those inventors lacking in the personal qualities of determination, persistence, willingness to learn (all criteria used by SBEC in its evaluation process) required to successfully commercialize an invention do not normally pass through the stages where increasing commitment of personal time and resources are required.

TECHNIQUES AND DEVICES

SBEC's questionnaire approach is one example of the proprietary methods that many incubators use to evaluate prospects. Many have had to adopt computer-based methods simply to handle the sheer volume of applicants. That is particularly true of all VC, business angel, and management consultant-based incubators.

Duff (1993) discovered that state-sponsored incubators in Australia had adopted a five point Likert scale (a unidimensional scaling method) for assessing the suitability of applicants. The seven areas measured are listed below. The maximum score for each area is 5, as is the maximum average score. No one scoring less than 3 on the Likert scale would be considered suitable.

1. Ability to pay rent.
2. Compatibility with incubator objectives.
3. Completion of application package.
4. Demonstrated business capability of principals.
5. Projected growth potential.
6. Completion of comprehensive business plan.
7. Potential for royalty or equity income to incubator.

Novell Ventures, a US firm who run a VC incubation process, have developed a mapping system to see if applicants are likely to 'fit' in with the incubator house style. They are selective and only look for development-stage companies that have (1) demonstrated a strategic fit with Novell; (2) have a management team with the ability to execute in a changing market; (3) at the very least, have developed a fully functional prototype networking or distributed computing software product; (4) a business plan that describes a winning strategy, detailing its business model, future development, marketing, sales, production and support; and (5) financials that reasonably project significant market potential and return on investment.

Candidates for incubation are screened using a five-dimensional model (see Figure 20.1). Each factor is scored between 0 and 5. Successful candidates have to score values higher than 2 in each factor.

The areas listed in Figure 20.1 will now be discussed in turn.

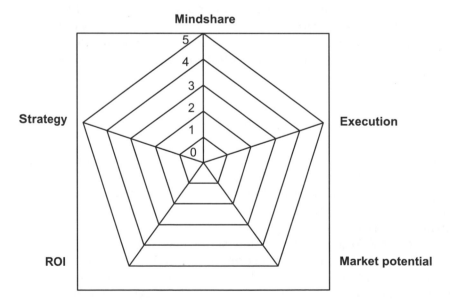

Figure 20.1   Mapping into an incubator.

Mindshare: Successful candidates have to demonstrate their ability to increase or enhance public awareness of key Novell strategies, products or initiatives. Scored subjectively, Mindshare analysis will answer how well the candidate has demonstrated his ability to influence or drive the direction of the industry and/or key players, and to what extent the candidate might persuade developers to use his products.

Strategy: Successful candidates have to demonstrate their strategic fit with Novell in two ways. First, candidates are expected to meet certain strategic prerequisites. Second, candidates will need to demonstrate commitment to Novell's strategy. Strategic fit is determined subjectively by answering how well each candidate will 'showcase, complement, or enhance the NDS ubiquity strategy, or if the candidate's strategy enables Novell to better serve its customers'.

Market Potential: Successful candidates have to demonstrate that they have chosen their businesses well, that the chosen businesses have revenue growth potential averaging between 20–40% annually, and significant diversification potential, i.e. the ability to use the specific knowledge gained in its current business to create or segue to a new business.

ROI: Successful candidates have to be able to project a return on investment over three years of at least 20% annually.

Execution: Successful candidates have to demonstrate the ability to execute their strategies and the ability to successfully conclude one or more business transactions with Novell that have lasting internal support. This factor is subjectively determined by Novell management.

Some incubators use a two-axis four-point scale to assist in identifying appropriate clients. In Figure 20.2, the x-axis represents the stage of management team development. For example, 0 would be an idea with no accompanying entrepreneur, while 4 would signify a fully-formed management team holding all the skills required to develop a successful venture together with extensive experience relevant to the technology/market niche. The y-axis illustrates the level of maturity of product development with 1 signifying a concept with some drawings and proof of concept prototype, and 4 indicating a profitable new product.

Using this framework, (0.5, 0.5) would be the scoring for a technical inventor with an idea. On the other hand, (4 ,4) would indicate a mature company with a fully developed management team, and with more than one product in the marketplace.

Government and local government-backed incubators usually see themselves as targeting (2, 2) companies. That is, two people with some business experience with a concept (and, ideally, a prototype) with some understanding of the market potential of the concept. The ideal stage of development for a client, for these incubators, is that the venture should be

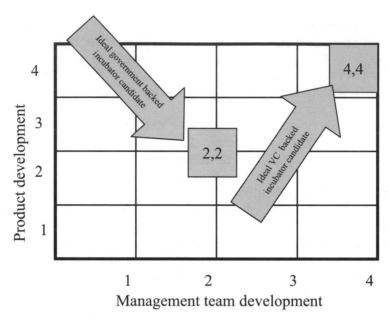

Figure 20.2   Incubator client screening matrix.

more mature than simply a concept, but much less mature than a company that a venture capital firm or a consultant-backed incubator would be willing to consider.

THE BUSINESS PLAN

Both the start and end of the incubation process are marked with a business plan of some description. The plan at the end should be rather more professional, or at any rate more convincing, than the first version used in the application process. On incubator websites you are likely to be faced with questions along these lines:

The executive summary   This may be all the incubator manager reads. The executive summary pulls together the key elements of your proposition: how big the market is, why everyone needs your product or service, and why you are the team to do it. In truth, few business ideas are unique. People and teams with talent, drive, passion and energy, and business savvy are what's really in short supply. That you have these attributes in abundance has to come through in both the plan and the executive summary.

Applying via a website you may only have a hundred words to get all this over. If you are asked to send your plan in hard copy, keep it down to one page. Figure 20.3 shows an extract from an incubator's website.

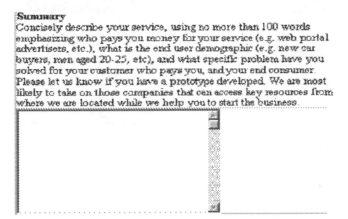

Summary
Concisely describe your service, using no more than 100 words emphasizing who pays you money for your service (e.g. web portal advertisers, etc.), what is the end user demographic (e.g. new car buyers, men aged 20-25, etc), and what specific problem have you solved for your customer who pays you, and your end consumer. Please let us know if you have a prototype developed. We are most likely to take on those companies that can access key resources from where we are located while we help you to start the business.

Figure 20.3   The executive summary.

What do you plan to do and who will you do it for?   You need to spell out exactly what is it you do, who you are doing it for, and why that matters.

The following statements have the ring of practical authority about them:

> Our website makes ordering office supplies for small businesses simple. It saves the average customer five hours a week browsing catalogues and £5000 a year through bank discounts not otherwise available to firms this size. We have surveyed 200 local small firms, who rate efficient purchasing as a key priority.

> We will provide a complete outsourced customer loyalty management solution to electronic businesses and traditional companies seeking to enhance their customers' online and offline experience before, during and after a purchase.

Figure 20.4 shows another example from an incubator's website, this time showing a list of business concepts and models from which entrepreneurs must choose.

You also need to spell something out about the size of the market. VC-sponsored incubators are generally only interested in big markets. Jim Clarke's Healtheon Venture was focused on the $1.5 trillion a year health market. About a third of that was wasted on paperwork. Healtheon's proposition was that the Internet was ideal as a means of bringing all parties to any healthcare transaction together – doctors, patients, health authorities

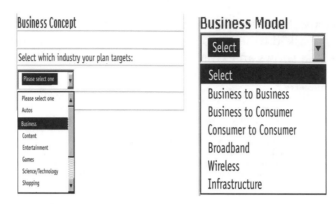

Figure 20.4   Business model or concept.

and pharmacists – without paper. Healtheon would take a slice of these savings.

Amazon.com started up in the $25 billion book market. AOL and Yahoo are in the $200 billion advertising business. Small percentages of these markets may be hard to achieve – but if it works, at least they are worth achieving. Going for 10% of a market measured in millions rather than billions may come to the same number but it won't be as interesting. Outside of the VC world and as long as the incubator you are heading for is not taking an equity stake in your company, they may well just be reassured that you know something about the market beyond a single sentence statement such as 'we are going into the software market'.

The business plan, in detail   Next come the business plan proper. Applying on an incubator's website, you may only have space for 300 words. The hard-copy version could run to ten pages (but, as with HatchAsia, the chances are there will be plenty of online help with putting your plan together.) Figure 20.5 shows an extract from a website asking for plan details.

Who are you and who are the team?   You need to demonstrate a track record of accomplishments in past jobs or past companies. People are now amazed that Boo.com's team were given £80 million with barely a business plan, yet alone a great idea. But Boo's ace in the hole was that two of their founders had started up and sold out a successful Internet book business one year earlier.

Non-executive directors are a useful addition to a young team, but they need to have relevant experience or be able to open doors and do deals. They need to be interested in you and your business and able to offer insights into how things really work in your industry. Figure 20.6 shows a typical extract from an incubator's website asking for team details.

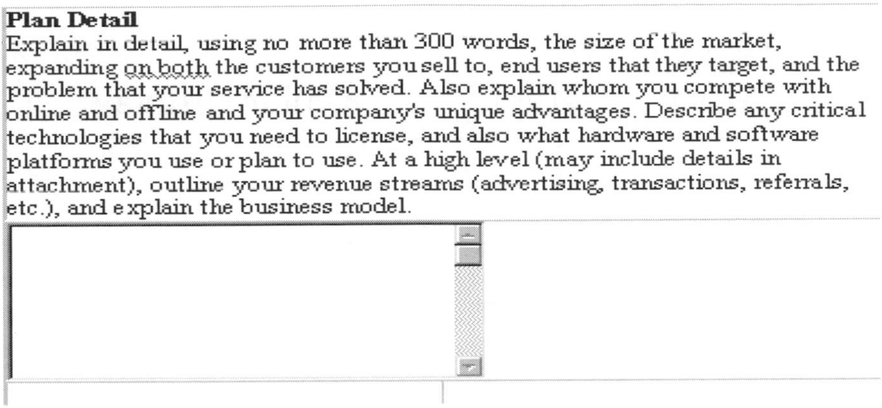

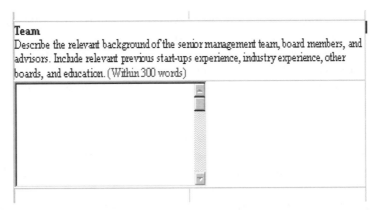

Plan Detail
Explain in detail, using no more than 300 words, the size of the market, expanding on both the customers you sell to, end users that they target, and the problem that your service has solved. Also explain whom you compete with online and offline and your company's unique advantages. Describe any critical technologies that you need to license, and also what hardware and software platforms you use or plan to use. At a high level (may include details in attachment), outline your revenue streams (advertising, transactions, referrals, etc.), and explain the business model.

Figure 20.5   The business plan in detail.

Team
Describe the relevant background of the senior management team, board members, and advisors. Include relevant previous start-ups experience, industry experience, other boards, and education. (Within 300 words)

Figure 20.6   Who are your team?

Who are the competitors and why are you better than them?   Nothing puts an incubator off a business proposition as much as an entrepreneur who doesn't know everything about their competitors. You need to know about their products, prices, advertising channels, who works for them, and why what you plan to do is better or different, in a way that matters to them. Figure 20.7 shows an online box showing competitors' details to be completed.

The financials   You need to explain precisely what you need the money for and when it will be needed: build website, hire CFO, advertising budget, product development, and so forth. Despite media hype, no one will throw money at your business without asking questions first. And in any event the market is maturing. The days when VCs knew nothing about technology

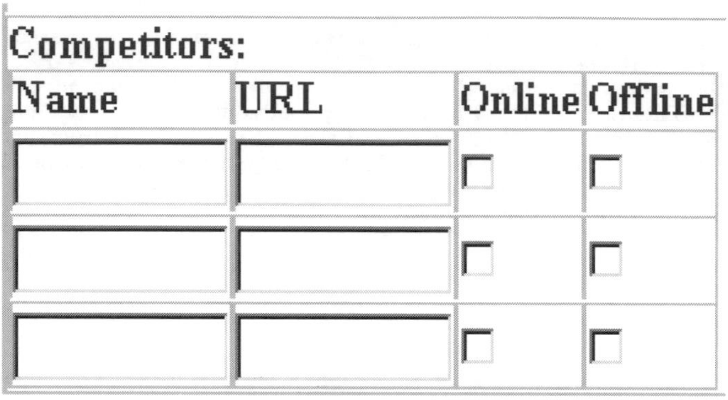

Competitors:

Name	URL	Online	Offline
		☐	☐
		☐	☐
		☐	☐

Figure 20.7   Who are your competitors?

are long gone. They now wear T-shirts when making house calls and would feel at home with any group of IT engineers.

You need projected cash flows, profit and loss accounts and balance sheets for at least the next three years. No one believes them after Year One, but the thinking behind them is what's important. Looking further ahead in technology or in the Internet world is difficult: Netscape went from being a browser company to an enterprise software maker to a Web portal in less than three years, and sold soon after that.

Your profit margins will be key numbers in your projections, alongside your sales forecasts. These will be probed by any VC. Amazon makes 25% gross margin on books. If your plan suggests 55%, you had better have a convincing reason for it. Figure 20.8 shows an example from a typical incubators' site of the financial information requested.

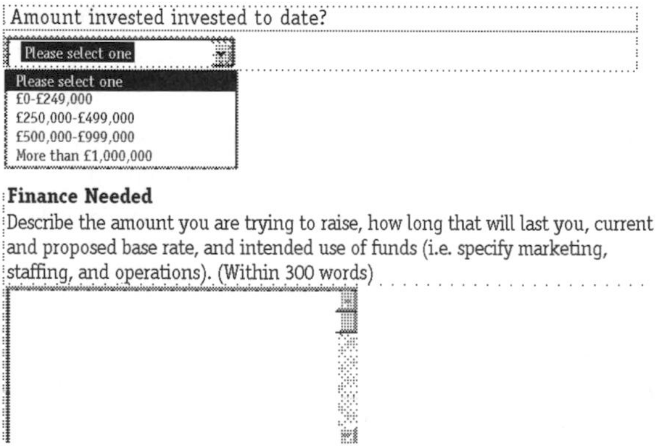

Amount invested invested to date?

Please select one

Please select one
£0-£249,000
£250,000-£499,000
£500,000-£999,000
More than £1,000,000

Finance Needed

Describe the amount you are trying to raise, how long that will last you, current and proposed base rate, and intended use of funds (i.e. specify marketing, staffing, and operations). (Within 300 words)

Figure 20.8   The financials.

CONFIDENTIALITY

Before submitting a business plan via the Internet you will be asked to agree to certain terms. By submitting a plan or idea to a website, you are agreeing to the company's terms. The terms will look something like these:

- Our incubator expects to receive a large number of plans, and we reserve the right to review only those plans that we believe fit our criteria for being accepted into our incubator.
- We also reserve the right to reject plans at our sole discretion, and we are under no obligation to return any plans to the sender.
- If we elect at our sole discretion to pursue a plan or idea with you, we may discuss with you an acceptable business arrangement. The plans or ideas submitted to us are not subject to limitations or restrictions on our use.
- We expect to receive many similar plans and ideas. Therefore, you understand that your idea may already have been submitted to us or be under consideration by us. We are not limited or restricted in any way from pursuing opportunities with others or on our own.
- Please do not send us anything that constitutes a trade secret or confidential and proprietary information. We are not in a position to accept such information, nor can we agree to obligations of non-disclosure or confidentiality with regard to submitted plans or ideas. Please note that by sending us your plan or idea, you are acknowledging that such materials do not include any trade secrets or confidential and proprietary information.
- By submitting your plan or idea to us, you acknowledge that they are original to you and owned by you. You also acknowledge that you are not violating anyone's legal rights by submitting the plan/idea to us.
- Finally, we have to be selective about the businesses that we select. Therefore, you understand that we are not committed to select your plan, to make an investment in your business, or otherwise to commit any resources to the business you propose.

SHOW-TIME

If you get beyond the first stage by submitting a short 'application' type business plan, you will be interviewed by the incubator manager, or perhaps by a panel of people with some experience in your sector. Anyone backing a business does so primarily because they believe in its management. They know from experience that things rarely go to plan, so they must be confident that the team involved can respond effectively to changing conditions. You can be sure that any incubator manager you are presenting to will have read dozens of similar plans, and will be well rehearsed. He may even have taken the trouble to find out something of your business and financial history.

Keep the following points in mind when preparing for your interview.

1. Rehearse your presentation beforehand, having found out how much time you will have. Allow at least as much time for questions as for your talk.
2. Use visual aids and, if possible, bring and demonstrate your product or service. A video- or computer-generated model is better than nothing.
3. Explain your strategy in a businesslike manner, demonstrating your grasp of the competitive market forces at work. Listen carefully to comments and criticisms, avoiding a defensive attitude when you respond.
4. Make your replies to questions brief and to the point. If they want more information they can ask. This approach allows time for the many different questions that must be asked either now or later before an investment can proceed.
5. Your goal is to create empathy between yourself and your listeners. Whilst you may not be able to change your personality, you could take a few tips on presentation skills. Eye contact, tone of speech, enthusiasm and body language all have a part to play in making a presentation go well.
6. Wearing a suit is never likely to upset anyone. Shorts and sandals could just set the wrong tone! Serious money calls for serious people, and the Internet world is growing up.

Without appearing too critical, this is also your chance to interview the incubator. You have to satisfy yourself that they can add value to your business proposition.

HOW LONG WILL IT ALL TAKE?

Incubator managers try to at least get an e-mail response back quickly to prospective companies. But as you can see from Figure 20.9, there are a few hoops to jump through first. However entrepreneurial the incubator, unless it is run by a business angel with his own funds, there is an inevitable degree of bureaucracy. No one person will make the final decision, so an internal review has to take place. The review committee may meet weekly or monthly, so that could add more time to the equation. Then you will be given a chance to present before a panel. Diary clashes (yours and theirs) could build more time in here. Then the incubator has to review how they feel you have done in your presentation. The whole process is likely to take around six weeks, and it could even be longer. Use that time to good effect by strengthening your business proposal.

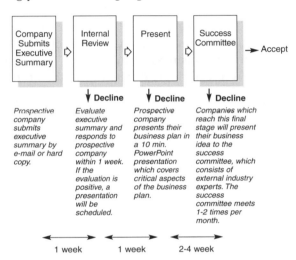

Figure 20.9   Incubator acceptance timeframe.

HOW MUCH WILL INCUBATION COST?

If you are just paying rent and for services as you use them, then the cost of being in an incubator is transparent. But if giving an incubator an equity stake in your business is involved, then the final cost can run from the incubator being a near-charity to being outrageously expensive. It's not always clear that the more you pay the more value you get. It depends on your business needs and the scale of the opportunity you want to exploit. Not-for-profit incubators are usually aimed at non-business-educated people who have good ideas for creating traditional small businesses, usu-ally with little technology involved. These incubators are frequently government-funded; are often in underdeveloped cities; provide mentor-ing, business development, and office space. The typical equity stake re-quired ranges from none to nominal (some require CEOs to give back to the community). Batavia Industrial Center (Batavia, New York) and Women's Technology Cluster (San Francisco) are examples of this type of incubator.

For-profit VC, angel or consultant-run incubators are in it more for the money. The smallest and least experienced of these will go for around a 20% stake and probably will not go down much from that figure. The average for firms such as CMGI, McKinsey, BainLab, Anderson and PwC will be up-wards of 20% and could be nearer 35%. However, incubators formed around serial entrepreneurs with big names provide office space, web ser-vices, strategic advice, seed funding, and a promise of market-leading suc-cess – all in exchange for a huge piece of your company, often a majority stake, and maybe the loss of your CEO slot. They are looking for well above 35% and may even hanker after more than 50%, especially if they don't really need you to run the business. eCompanies (Los Angeles), idealab! (Pasadena), and Oxygen (Cambridge, England), might fit into this bracket.

21

Getting out of an incubator

Once in, you really only have five possible exit routes. You could shut down, if your business idea turns out to be a dud. You could be pushed out for non-performance. You could move on yourself once the business becomes viable. You may find that your business is sold off to another larger firm in the incubator network of companies. Or it's just possible that your business becomes so successful it's groomed for a flotation on a stock market. This chapter looks at each of these in turn.

BEING PUSHED OUT

Most incubators will have some type of monitoring and review process to make sure firms are performing to an acceptable standard. Even a not-for-profit incubator wants to retain only those businesses that have a serious chance of success. The Center For Business Innovation (CBI), Kansas City, Missouri, for example, has established a system which includes weekly reporting to clients on the status of tasks, identifying who is responsible for tasks, when they must be completed and which criteria the completed task must satisfy. This weekly information provides clients with a confirmation of the amount and nature of the work being performed for it by CBI. At monthly intervals, CBI meets with clients to review progress against clear, measurable milestones, usually set three months in advance. In turn, these three-monthly milestones are related to the milestones and objectives which appear in each client's business plan. Thus, due to the intensive, hands-on mode of working with its clients, CBI has an intimate knowledge of not just the apparent financial performance of the firm, but the inner workings of the enterprise. This detailed understanding of a firm's progress places CBI in a strong position to judge how strongly a firm is growing and what prospects it has for generating returns to the incubator. CBI experience indicates that longer-term goals (set at yearly intervals, for example) are too abstract and distant to be an effective management tool.

Other incubators have time or size restrictions which they impose to keep a healthy flow of new ventures in and out of the process.

SHUTTING DOWN

The first stages of a business' life can be seen as an extended market research exercise. No amount of desk research can substitute for a few months of selling real things to real people. Even if you were to accept the wildest claims made by incubators of their ability to prevent businesses from folding, at least one in five of their eggs are not going to hatch. In all probability, this figure will be higher still. Failure comes in all shapes and sizes. If you have gone into a big name incubator they may not want to sustain anything short of a superstar, in which case they may withdraw support and render your business unviable in its present shape. There may still be a smaller or more modest enterprise lying beneath the surface which can be brought to life in some other form. Or it may just be that the business idea has some fatal flaws. Most of the first generation of Internet businesses seem to have suffered from one or two flaws. Either not enough people in their chosen market were already on the Internet and so couldn't become customers, or, and more usually, the service offered nothing unique, except for actually being on the net.

If your first idea is not a success, don't despair. Henry Ford had gone bankrupt twice and was over forty before he got his successful motor business off the ground. The key thing is to learn from your mistakes and build that learning into your next attempt.

MOVING ON

The majority of firms going in for incubation are neither superstars nor failures. They become healthy self-sufficient ventures able to go their own way, creating jobs and wealth in the communities in which they were 'hatched'.

The Genesis incubator at the University of Arkansas has what they call 'the Exodus committee'. It is comprised principally of people with financial management experience. The committee performs two key tasks. The first is to monitor the advancement of tenants via their monthly reporting. The second is to assist firms in successfully making the transition from Genesis tenant to independent, growing company. Each month, each client is interviewed and their progress against milestones in their business plan is monitored. Companies supply financial information in the form of a balance sheet, profit and loss statement and sales journal and this is reviewed against the business plan and the requirement for working and expansion capital. Each client which graduates from the Genesis programme is thoroughly prepared by the Exodus committee. On exiting the programme, a detailed questionnaire of over 60 items is completed in an interview with the director.

SELLING UP

About 15 000 trading companies change hands each year in the US. Setting that against the few hundred that float on a stock market, even in a good year, you can see why selling up is a popular route for a for-profit incubator to take to recoup some of its investment. It may not be such a bad thing for you either as, whilst you may no longer be running the show, you will probably be worth more than when you went into the incubator. The example below shows how this process might come about.

Nutravida.com, the natural health products e-tailer, launched in November 1999 with £1 million of funding from eSouk, the Internet incubator, and Oyster Partners. It then spent much of 2000 looking for second-round funding, without success. The company – which was rated number 50 in *The Sunday Times'* 'e-league' in August 2000 – suffered from the general apathy in the Internet sector. But one thing Peter Brockbank, Nutravida's managing director, did get out of his time with the incubator was the ability to network. To survive, the company first formed a trading alliance with Apotheke 20–20, a highly successful complementary healthcare retailer, holistic health and wellbeing centre based in Chiswick, London, in November 2000. Under the new deal Apotheke will carry out all the customer service and fulfilment aspects of the business, whilst Nutravida will continue to maintain a fully functional and transactional website. The site will have fewer products than the original, but it will concentrate on the best brands.

Then in April 2001 the Neutralife Group, headed by Barrie Smith, took a controlling interest in the company, pumping some very welcome money into their website. The joint venture and eventual trade sale has meant that the company has finally become viable, just 15 months after eSouk got involved.

FLOTATION

If you set up shop in a for-profit incubator then sooner or later the subject of a stock market flotation will come up. A perfectly respectable private business that might have sold on a multiple of six times annual profits could sell for anything between two and three times that sum. Why? Well the logic is fairly simple. Placing shares on a stock market makes the company's equity liquid. In other words, shareholders can buy and sell at will, or nearly so (there will be an embargo on 'insiders' selling their shares for between six months and two years. That can be pretty painful if the market turns. Andrew Rickman, founder of Bookham Technologies, and graduate of the Cranfield enterprise system, saw his personal fortune sink from over $1 billion to about $150 million in a year because of this.)

There are two types of stock markets on which to gain a public listing. A full listing on the London stock exchange, the New York stock exchange or any other major country's exchange calls for a track record of making substantial profits with decent seven-figure sums being made in the year you plan to float. A full listing also calls for a large proportion of the company's shares to be put up for sale at the outset. In a 'frothy' market these rules can be sometimes be set aside.

However, if an IPO (Initial Public Offering) appeals to you and your main shareholders, which probably includes the incubator you are in, the US market may be the best place to float. The NASDAQ is the powerhouse of the IPO machine. Once a 'stodgy' exchange, the NASDAQ has recently launched NASDAQ Europe and NASDAQ Japan, and forged a partnership with Softbank, the giant of Internet investment. The value placed on new companies on a NASDAQ market is between three and five times that of UK and European markets (see Figure 21.1).

Market	Number of stocks	Flotation cost	Entry requirements	Minimum market capitalization	Comparable Price Earnings (P/E) ratios
Alternative Investment Market (AIM)	350	£0.5m	Low	None	1
London Stock Exchange	2500	£1m+	High	£1m+	1
techMARK	200	£0.75m+	High	£50m+	×3
New York Stock Exchange	2600	£7m	Very high	£12m+	×2
NASDAQ	5500	£6m	Very high	£10m+	×5

Figure 21.1   Where to float . . . and why it matters (source: Exchange details).

Junior markets such as London's Alternative Investment Market (AIM), or the Nouveau Marché in Paris are a much more attractive proposition for entrepreneurs seeking equity capital. Formed in the mid-to-late-1990s specifically to provide risk capital for new rather than established ventures, these markets have an altogether more relaxed atmosphere. The AIM market is the largest junior market in Europe. Over 300 firms are listed and some £2 billion of new equity capital has been raised. The AIM is particularly attractive to any dynamic company of any size, age or business sector which has rapid growth in mind. The smallest firm on AIM entered at under £1 million capitalization and the largest at over £330 million. The formalities are minimal, but the costs of entry are high and you must have a nominated adviser, such as a major accountancy firm, stockbroker or banker. Your incubator will have a number of such advisors in its network.

Internet-based Direct Public Offerings (DPOs) are a relatively new US phenomenon which has the potential to change the face of financing for small firms. These involve small companies offering their stock direct to would-be investors over the Internet. There are two ways of doing this: one is to use a service, the other is for firms to use their own websites to go direct to the public. There are already some Internet-based listing services for DPOs in the US. The Access to Capital Electronic Network (ACE-NET) was set up in 1997 by the Small Business Administration as a public-private partnership to lower the legal barriers for small businesses needing financing of up to $5 million. The filing form satisfies federal and many states' securities regulations, with 37 states recognizing it, and it is relatively cheap at only $450 for an annual listing. The offering document can be completed online and can be changed in real time, allowing the entrepreneur the flexibility to modify his offer. Only accredited investors (who have over $1 million to spend) can invest.

Direct Stock Market is a similar, private service that was set up in 1993 and where a listing costs from between $2000 to $4000 for 90 days. Firms have to file their own paperwork offline with the states in which they wish their listing to be registered (unlike the ACE-NET service). Potential investors from Europe thus cannot participate in companies listed under such schemes. It is almost certain that regulations mean that these Internet services cannot sell securities in non-US firms. However, this does not prevent a European entrepreneur from creating a US company to exploit the fundraising potential of such services. What difficulties in the US in establishing this sort of service have amply demonstrated is the need for regulation at a federal level rather than state level, if the service is to be successful. This suggests that, were such a service to be established in Europe, it would be appropriate to regulate it at a European level in order to offer similar sums of money and geographic spread.

US firms may also decide to go direct and battle their way through various state legislation hoops. The up-side of this for firms is that this method overcomes barriers of geography and information, and that small investors are unlikely to carry out due diligence or download prospectuses. DPOs allow small investors access to genuine possibilities without paying fees to either a matchmaking service or a venture capital firm, and they allow much smaller investments (from $500 upwards). The down-side of Internet DPOs is that they are time-consuming and high-risk for the angel, (or micro-angel), and it is difficult to distinguish between genuine companies and fraudsters. For the firm, there are a raft of different state legislations in operation to protect investors from scams which can seriously disrupt the offer process. In the US 83 individuals have already been charged with Internet securities fraud, 26 for entirely fictional deals.

The main problem here might be that multiples are lower on Internet exchanges, so the valuation placed on the firm is low. However incubators desperate to unlock some value in their fledging firms may tempt you in this direction.

THE TIMETABLE OF AN IPO

An IPO used to take about six months to execute, but now it is routinely being done in 13 weeks. Though it may vary from exchange, to exchange the timetable looks broadly like this:

Week 1
Pick underwriters to take your company to market. This involves listening to a dozen or more bankers tell you why they are the best at doing your type of IPO. At the rate of three a day, this can be a wearying experience, listening to depressingly similar presentations. The bankers will all have done successful IPOs before, probably by the dozen, so you will probably be looking more for empathy than technical competence. At the end of the week you need to have chosen a lead and probably a couple of co-managers, to help spread the good word about your business to the share-buying community. Your incubator team will have a strong opinion on who should lead the process, but as long as you still own the majority of the shares it's still your business and your call.

Week 2
Lead manager begins to draft the company's prospectus. This involves sucking you, your management team and your accountants dry of background

information. Your CFO will be involved full-time in this process, so it's best to get some financial back-up in place to deal with routine matters.

Week 3
You and your bankers collaborate on the prospectus. By now, fairly junior staff will be handling the process. The stars you met on week one's presentations have moved on to sell the next deal. This process can involve several eight-hour days with people from your law, banking and accounting firms going through the documentation line by line. This involves a delicate balance between outlining the risks whilst simultaneously describing the business and the investment prospects in a way that will appeal. You can see how other companies have gone about this process by looking at their filings on the Securities and Exchange Commission (SEC) website (www.sec.gov/). This due diligence process should flush out any worries and concerns about you or your business.

Week 4
Lead manager files the registration document, known in the US as an S1, with the SEC (or its equivalent in whichever country you plan to list).

Weeks 5–8
Lead bankers, you and your team prepare the roadshow presentation and wait for the SEC to digest your documents.

Week 9
SEC responds with 20 pages of questions: 'What do you mean by "online response times"?' and, 'Can you provide evidence that your client "x" is one of the largest drinks manufacturers in Spain?'

There may well be a second round of questions a few weeks later, but by now you will know how to reply.

Probity is important in this process. What is required is transparency. The World Online float on the Amsterdam Exchange (AEX) in the spring of 2000 is a salutary warning on disclosure. The company was, at the time, Europe's largest Internet service provider. They generated an enormous amount of interest among Dutch private investors, the company's home base, with 150 000 people subscribing in the March IPO at a price of €43. Within six weeks the price was down to €14.80. The reason given for the slump in price was that World Online's chairman, Nina Brink, had disposed of some of her shares to US private equity fund Baystar Capital in December 1999, three months before the float. The price she sold at was €6.04 and Baystar sold the shares in the first few days of trading at over €30. Brink was accused of allegedly making misleading statements during the offer period, and was forced to resign on 13 April. Unhappy shareholders not unsurprisingly took legal advice, but the company's bankers claimed there had been no wrongdoing.

Week 10

Lead manager plans the roadshow. You go to the bank and sell the company to their institutional sales force. They then get to work with their clients to persuade them to subscribe for your stock. Everyone is bound by what are known as 'the rules'. Rule 174 of the Securities Act governs the 'Quiet Period', which extends from due diligence to 25 days after the IPO. Over this period the company must be careful about not hyping the stock or doing anything that would lead to speculation about your firm's performance in the press.

Rule 135 explains exactly what you can and cannot say to the press. It's generally best to say nothing. If one of your competitors is doing an IPO, their Quiet Period is a good time to hit out at them in the press, or to go out and buy a business you know they might want. They are, in effect, in limbo and cannot retaliate.

This is where the institutional sales team come into their own. Via an ancient ritual of winks, nudges, passive verbs, rhetorical questions and comparisons, they get their story across. The lead bank's sales team can also be a powerful force. Goldman Sachs, for example, has some 400 front-line sales people in its IPO team, and that can result in a message reaching a lot of potential investors.

Weeks 11–12

A glorified travel agent in the bank fixes up a punishing schedule, known as the 'road-show'. This is the reverse of week one, when people were selling to you. Now you are selling the stock to institutional investors. This could involve as many as 80 meetings across 3 continents in 13 days. A lot can be said at roadshow meetings, but the only document that can be handed out is the S1 prospectus. Anything else could be a violation of Section 5 of the Securities Act.

Commitments start to come in from institutions: 'I'll take 250 000, but only if it's priced below $20. At $25 I'll only take 100 000.' The bank's syndicate manager has to make sense of this anticipated demand to come up with an IPO price.

Week 13

The day of the IPO. Assuming the NASDAQ has not gone into one of its habitual nosedives, the bank's market-maker figures out the highest price someone will sell and someone will buy at and sets a price, usually above the opening price and the price at which the institutions have bought. One entrepreneur likened doing his IPO to childbirth: painful, glorious, but not to be done again.

Your company is now public, the bank collects 7% of the proceeds, your incubator and VCs have cleaned up, your employees are rich and you now have the funds and credibility to get out of the incubator and continue growing the business.

If the market-maker has got the price too high, and the shares plunge quickly it will leave a sour taste in everyone's mouth. The pre-float share-holders can't realize their gain for months after the float, and having a paper profit slashed in half (as for example with lastminute.com's float) will not endear you to your staff.

The institutions will be sitting on a loss, and whilst they are grown up enough to take it on the chin, they will be very wary when you come back for more money. It is usually best to set the price at a rate that will see the shares rising in the weeks and months following a float. This also leads to better press coverage, which inevitably impacts favourably on customers, suppliers and potential employees.

A FINAL WORD OF CAUTION

If the NASDAQ has plunged or for any other reason you have to pull out of the IPO, this can be likened to slipping down a long snake back to the bottom of the Snakes and Ladders board. You may get another crack at it in six months, or perhaps never.

Only one in ten companies that withdraw IPOs ever go public, according to Craig Dunbar (2000), a finance professor at the University of Western Ontario and an expert on failed IPOs. After studying every cancelled IPO between 1980 and 1995, Dunbar discovered that only 10% managed to go public at a later date. 'Withdrawing an IPO is usually a crippling event, even if the company doesn't realize it at the time,' he says.

Since the beginning of 1997, just 5% of the companies that have with-drawn IPOs have been able to sell stock at a later date. In 1998, 155 com-panies withdrew, and just 13 of those are now public. Last year, 125 companies withdrew IPOs and only three of those are now public.

Why the low survival rate? Part of the problem is the notoriously short attention span of technology investors. In less than a year, the market has cycled through a half-dozen different business models. E-tailing, business-to-business, Linux services, and wireless all had their moments in the sun, only to be discarded when something new, such as photonics, came along. The fickle nature of the market means that even if the overall demand for IPOs is strong, companies actually have an extremely narrow window of opportunity for filing an IPO. This is particularly so for a company that is not a leader in its sector. When it comes to IPO withdrawals, it seems that what doesn't kill a company really can make it stronger. That's one explanation for why second-chance IPOs seem to fare so well. Another is related to valuation. The second time around, many companies are forced to accept a lower valuation – either on an absolute basis or relative to earnings or revenue – than they had sought the first time they tried to go public. As a result, these stocks may have more room to grow than IPOs that start off with sky-high stock prices.

Part Five

World directory of incubators

THE UK

Institution	Description	Contact address	Telephone/e-mail/website
Aberdeen Science and Technology Park	Developed jointly by Grampian Enterprises and Aberdeen City Council with the active support of the local Higher Education Institutions (HEIs). The Aberdeen Science and Technology Park has a number of facilities for emerging knowledge-based businesses, including the Software Development Centre, the Biotechnology Incubator and the Balgownie Technology Centre	Anthony Aldhous, Aberdeen Science and Technology Park, 27 Albyn Place, Aberdeen, AB10 1DB	00 44 1224 575100 00 44 1224 213417 tony.aldhous@scotent.co.uk astp.co.uk
Animal Health Technology Transfer Complex	This new incubator on the University of Glasgow campus will specialize in support for technology start-ups, particularly those with a link to the veterinary sector, as well as offering professional research support. The project is supported by Glasgow Development Agency with ERDF (European Research and Development Foundation) funding.	Sylvia Morrison, Animal Health Technology Transfer Complex, University of Glasgow Veterinary School, Bearsden Road, Glasgow	00 44 141 330 2690 00 44 141 942 7215 (fax) S.Morrison@vet.gla.ac.uk
AntFactory	Founded by a group of Internet veterans in 1999. Collectively the founders have made over 100 investments in Internet and related start-ups since then.	AntFactory, Prospect House, 80–100 New Oxford Street, London, WC1A 1HB	00 44 207 947 5000 00 44 207 947 5001 (fax) uk@antfactory.com antfactory.com
Aston Science Park	Established science park and innovation centre. Developed by Birmingham City Council, Aston University and Lloyds Bank in central Birmingham, next to Aston University. Innovation Centre opened in 1983.	Derek Harris, Aston Science Park, Love Lane, Birmingham, B7 4BJ	00 44 121 250 3500 00 44 121 359 0433 (fax) derekh@astonsciencepark.co.uk astonsciencepark.co.uk
Babraham Bioincubator		David J Hardman, Babraham Bioincubator, Babraham Hall, Babraham, Cambridge, CB2 4AT	00 44 1223 496205 00 44 1223 496020 (fax) dj.hardman@babraham.co.uk bi.bbsrc.ac.uk

Institution	Description	Contact address	Telephone/e-mail/website
Bangor Innovation and Technology Centre	A 20000 sq ft purpose-designed building for innovative businesses in their start-up phase to include a full reception service, conference facilities, refectory and meeting rooms. A variety of unit sizes is available, from 200 sq ft to 1000 sq. ft. for office and laboratory-based activities. Business support measures and financial incentives will be available.	James Goodman, Bangor, Innovation and Technology Centre, c/o Snowdonia BIC, Llys y Fedwen, Parc Menai, Bangor, LL57 4BF	00 44 1248 671101 00 44 1248 671101 (fax) jamesG@Gwynedd.gov.uk
Barnsley Business and Innovation Centre Ltd	BBIC provides incubator space and services for innovative/ technology-based start-up companies plus a range of innovation programmes to offsite individuals and companies.	Tim Milburn, Barnsley Business and Innovation Centre Ltd, Innovation Way, Barnsley, S75 1JL	00 44 1226 249590 00 44 1226 249625 (fax) postbox@bbic.co.uk bbic.co.uk
Bio Adventures™	Bio Adventures™ was created by Dunbartonshire Enterprise as a key component in generating economic development through the introduction of commercial biotechnology to Dunbartonshire. Bio Adventures™ is a biomedical business incubator and exists to increase the number of successful company start-ups. It does this by providing laboratory and office accommodation linked to a high level of equipment, facilities and business management support during companies' initial period of operation.	Dr Shane Booth, Bio Adventures™, 5 South Avenue, Clydebank Business Park, Clydebank, G81 2LG	00 44 141 951 3450 00 44 141 951 3451 (fax) admin@bioadventures.com bioadventures.com
Bioincubator York Ltd	Bioincubator York Ltd is a joint venture company between the University and ML laboratories plc. They provide a mechanism for identifying, appraising and selecting innovative pharmaceutical, life science and biotechnology projects with the aim of progressing commercially viable projects through to start-up companies.	Julian White, Bioincubator York Ltd, Institute for Applied Biology, PO Box 373, University of York, York, YO10 5YW	00 44 1904 433206 00 44 1904 433030 incubate@york.ac.uk york.ac.uk/org/bioincubator

Name	Description	Contact	Details
Bioscience Innovation Centre	This incubator was completed in November 1999 and is situated at St John's Innovation Park. Office and laboratory accommodation is provided for up to 12 start-up bioscience companies as well as a full range of business support services and access to sources of finance, in particular seed capital.	David Best, Bioscience Innovation Centre, St. John's Innovation Centre, Cowley Road, Cambridge, CB4 4WS	00 44 1223 421867 00 44 1223 421873 (fax) bioscience@mmigroup.co.uk mmigroup.co.uk
Bioscience Innovations (SouthEast) Ltd	This incubator is located within an established 54-acre research park. It offers assistance to bioscience and technical R&D start-up companies within a 30000 sq. ft. purpose-built facility.	Robert Williams, Bioscience Innovations (SouthEast) Ltd, Sittingbourne Research Centre, Woodstock House, Winch Road, Sittingbourne, ME9 8AG	00 44 1795 411500 00 44 1795 411511 rwilliams@bio-innovations.co.uk src-uk.com
Birmingham Research Park	Birmingham Research and Development Ltd (BRDL) manages the commercial development of new technology generated by research work at the University of Birmingham.	Simon C A Freeman, Birmingham Research Park, Vincent Drive, Edgbaston, Birmingham, B15 2SQ	00 44 121 471 4988 00 44 121 472 5739 (fax) BRPL@bham.ac.uk
Brainspark	They seek to recreate the network of professional services available in Silicon Valley.	Brainspark PLC, The Lightwell, 12/16 Laystall Street, London, EC1R 4PA	00 44 207 843 6600 00 44 207 843 6601 (fax) brainspark.co.uk
British Steel (Industry) Ltd	The innovation centre is located on the University of Sheffield campus and is targeted at technology companies and university spin-outs.	David Pilling, British Steel (Industry) Ltd, The Innovation Centre, 217 Portobello Road, Sheffield, S1 4DP	00 44 114 224 2424 00 44 114 224 2222 (fax) innovation.centre@bsi.onyzxnet.co.uk innovation-centre.co.uk
Brunel Science Park	Brunel is an established science park developed by the university on its campus in Uxbridge, West London. Incubation is encouraged within university departments when space permits.	Peter Russell, Brunel Science Park, Brunel University, Cleveland Road, Uxbridge, UB8 3PH	science-park@brunel.ac.uk brunel.ac.uk/scipark
Campus Ventures	Campus Ventures is a business incubator unit established to encourage, nurture, support and train technologists with the initiative and potential to start their own businesses.	Prof David Auckland, Campus Ventures, University of Manchester, Oxford Road, Manchester, M13 9PL	00 44 161 273 5110 00 44 161 273 5111 (fax) dauckland@campus-ventures.co.uk campus-ventures.co.uk

Institution	Description	Contact address	Telephone/e-mail/website
Cardiff Business Technology Centre	CBTC provides accommodation for innovative high-tech companies. The centre is situated on the edge of Cardiff's civic and city centre university campus.	Eileen Turner, Cardiff Business Technology Centre, Senghennydd Road, Cathays, Cardiff, CF24 4AY	00 44 2920 372311 00 44 2920 373436 (fax) eturner@cbtc.co.uk
Cardiff Medicentre	Incubator accommodation for the medical and healthcare sectors, a joint venture of Cardiff County Concil, University of Wales College of Medicine, University of Wales NHS Trust and the Welsh Development Agency.	Eileen Turner, Cardiff, Medicentre, Heath Park, Cardiff CF14 4UJ	00 44 2920 757744 00 44 2920 750239 (fax) eturner@cardiffmedicentre.co.uk
Carrington Business Park Ltd	Established following the closure of major petrochemical facilities, the park provides workspace (offices, workshops, storage) and central services for a wide range of SMEs.	William Taylor, Carrington Business Park Ltd, Carrington, Manchester, M31 4DD	00 44 161 776 4000 00 44 161 775 8995 (fax) will@cbpk.com
Centre for Advanced Industry	CAI is managed by the North of England Microelectronics Institute. NEMI is a public-private partnership initiative and has links with local universities. The CAI building focuses on support for small businesses at the higher end of the technology spectrum.	John R Williams, Centre for Advanced Industry, NEMI, Royal Quays, North Shields, NE29 6DE	00 44 191 293 7000 00 44 191 293 7001 (fax) jrw@nemi-cai.co.uk nemi-cai.co.uk
Cherwell Innovation Centre	Developed by Oxford Innovation, Cherwell District Council and the North Oxfordshire Consortium on the former US Air Force base at Upper Heyford with EU Konver funding.	Anne-Sophie Vallier, Cherwell Innovation Centre, 77 Heyford Park, Upper Heyford, Bicester, OX6 3HD	00 44 1869 223800 00 44 1869 238001 (fax) cichp@oxtrust.org.uk oxfordinnovation.co.uk
Chilworth Business Incubator	Chilworth Business Incubator will accommodate new or recently formed knowledge-based companies in any branch of science or technology. Units will range from 300 sq. ft. to 1200 sq. ft. Business mentoring will be available. The incubator will benefit from privileged access to facilities provided by the University of Southampton.	Don Fox, Chilworth Business Incubator, Chilworth Research Centre, Chilworth, Southampton, SO16 7JF	00 44 2380 767420 00 44 2380 766190 dpf@soton.ac.uk

Name	Description	Contact	Details
CIRCE Ltd	CIRCE stands for the Chemical Industries Regional Centre of Excellence. It offers a service which helps businesses in the chemicals sector to prosper and grow. A range of chemical analysis, process safety and environmental testing services are offered to improve businesses. Industry-focused training courses are also tailored to companies' needs.	Steve Napier, CIRCE Ltd, Wheldon road, Castleford, WF10 2JT	00 44 1977 712712 00 44 1977 712713 (fax) infor@circe.co.uk circe.co.uk
CMGI	A leading global Internet operating and development company with 12 majority-owned companies. Providers of Internet technologies to enterprises.	Dave Hooker, CMGI, Sygnus Court, Market Street, Maidenhead, Berks, SL6 8AD	00 44 1628 588504 00 44 1628 588519 (fax) dhooker@cmgi.co.uk cmgi.com
Cornwall Science Park	An entirely standalone facility, close to Cornwall College, Cornwall Business School and Camborne School of Mines. One wing has seven industrial units, another has 28 high-tech units, and there is also an incubation wing with 4 industrial and 16 high-tech start-up units. The central concourse has meeting rooms, café, exhibition space and computer booths.	John Ager, Cornwall Science Park, South West Investment Group, Trevint House, Strangeways Villas, Truro, TR1 2PA	00 44 1872 223883 00 44 1872 242470 (fax) swigservicesltd@btinternet.com
Coventry University Technology Park		Glen Barrowman, The Technology Centre, Coventry University Technology Park, Puma Way, Coventry, CV1 2TT	00 44 2476 838 140/145 00 44 2476 221 396 (fax) g.barrowman@coventry.ac.uk
Cranfield Creates.com	Cranfield Creates.com helps Cranfield people to progress their Internet business start-up ideas as quickly as possibly from idea to launch. The centre focuses on early-stage ideas helping entrepreneurs to produce business plans, develop pilot websites, obtain seed-corn funding and begin trading. It operates from within the Cranfield School of Management, where students can make use of the incubator during their MBA programme, and as a feeder to the Cranfield Innovation Centre.	Gerard Burke, Cranfield Creates.com, Cranfield Innovation Centre, Cranfield Technology Park, Cranfield, MK43 0BT	00 44 1234 751122 00 44 1234 752636 (fax) gerard-burke@cranfield.ac.uk cranfieldcreates.com

Institution	Description	Contact address	Telephone/e-mail/website
Cranfield Innovation Centre	Incubator designed to help ambitious, growing knowledge-based businesses. Supportive, hands-on staff help their clients to maximize their potential. It is a thriving business community and is fully let. However, help is also extended to businesses who are not yet ready to move into the centre. Its aim is to graduate clients on to the Cranfield Technology Park.	Hermant Amin, Cranfield Innovation Centre, University Way, Cranfield Technology Park, Cranfield, MK43 0BT	00 44 1234 756000 00 44 1234 752514 (fax) cranfield.org
DDL Internet Incubator	Dawnay Day Lander (DDL) is one of the new breed of Internet incubators being established in the UK. It is a high-tech investment boutique which operates in the UK, Europe and the Middle East. DDL also invests in start-up and early stage Internet companies, particularly where they are either too small or too young for traditional investors.	Jonathan Lander, DDL Internet Incubator, Dawnay Day Lander Ltd, 8–10 Grosvenor Gardens, London, SW1H 0DH	00 44 20 7979 7575 00 44 20 7979 7585 (fax) infor@d2L.com d2L.com
DERA – Haslar	Marine Technology Park based at DERA Haslar, the Ministry of Defence's marine technology establishment.	Dr John Dering, DERA-Haslar, Gosport, PO12 2AG	00 44 23 9233 5024 00 44 23 9233 5114 (fax) John_Dering@compuserve.com dera.gov.uk
Doncaster Business Innovation Centre	Barnsley & Doncaster Training and Enterprise Council (TEC) are behind this new technology incubator. It will be approximately 20000 sq. ft. and will accommodate up to 33 businesses.	Emma Hutton, Doncaster Business Innovation Centre, Barnsley and Doncaster TEC, Innovation Way, Barnsley, S75 1JL	00 44 1226 248088 00 44 1226 291625 (fax) emma.hutton@bdtec.co.uk bdtec.co.uk
Dundee Incubator Co Ltd	Dundee Incubator Ltd is a joint venture company opened by the University of Abertay Dundee, University of Dundee, Dundee City Council and Scottish Enterprise Tayside. It offers a mix of purpose-built laboratory space, supported by a team of experienced scientists and technology entrepreneurs. The company is currently assisting several teams to develop the commercial potential of discoveries in the bio-technology and medical fields.	Alan J Muir, Dundee Incubator Co Ltd, Technopole House, PO Box 6932, Dundee, DD2 5YE	00 44 1382 360226 00 44 1382 360226 (fax) a.j.muir@dundeeincubator.co.uk dundeeincubator.co.uk

Edinburgh Technology Transfer Centre	ETTC provides serviced accommodation to new spin-out businesses in the knowledge-based industries during their pre-investment phase. Tenants must have a link with the university of Edinburgh and would normally be seeking to commercialize technologies from the university. A limited range of support services are available from the university's commercialization team.	Keith Winton, Edinburgh Technology Transfer Centre, Kings Buildings, Mayfield Road, Edinburgh, EH9 3JL	00 44 131 472 4700 00 44 131 662 4678 keith.winton@ed.ac.uk
Elvingston Science Centre	Elvingston Science Centre (ESC) acts as a catalyst for economic development in the region. ESC offers a 'total lifestyle' incubation concept, located in the grounds of historic Elvingston estate. All current tenants are knowledge-based, leading-edge software, opto-electronic or hardware-based companies.	Janice Simpson, Elvingston Science Centre, Elvingston, near Gladsmuir, EH33 1EH	00 44 1875 408000 00 44 1875 408001 enquiries@elvingston.co.uk elvingston.co.uk
Farnborough Innovation Centre	An innovation centre close to Defence Evaluation and Research Agency (DERA) research complex and airfield. Developed by Rushmoor Borough Council, DERA and Business Links Hampshire as a way of transforming defence technology into the commercial field.	Harry Steer, Farnborough Innovation Centre, DEM Room 101, X92 Building, DERA, Farnborough, GU14 0RX	00 44 1252 550000 00 44 1252 550001 (fax)
Flintstone	Flintstone plc is an aggressive high-tech incubator and business accelerator with a mission to identify applied research that may be utilized to create multiple product- and/or service-based businesses operating in the Internet, consumer products and industrial sectors.	Mr I Woodcock, Flintstone, 8–10 Malew Street, Castletown, Isle of Man, IM9 1AB	00 44 1624 825472 00 44 1624 825660 (fax) info@flintstone.com flintstone.com
Framlingham Technology Centre	This new project opened in 2000. It is a 17 000 sq. ft. town centre incubator development which can accommodate a maximum of 17 start-up companies.	Tony Stockman, Framlingham Technology Centre, Station Road, Framlingham, Woodbridge, IP3 9EE	00 44 1728 727003 00 44 1728 724318 (fax) tony@minima.co.uk
Generics Group (see also US, Sweden, Switzerland)	Generics – now a subsidiary of Swedish firm Catella – was co-founded in 1986 by Gordon Edge at Cambridge University, and invests in intellectual property and capital only.	The Generics Group AG, Harston Mill, Harston, Cambridge, CB2 5NH	00 44 1223 875200 00 44 1223 875201 (fax) generics.co.uk

Institution	Description	Contact address	Telephone/e-mail/website
Harris Knowledge Park	The incubator is located on a 14-acre parkland development close to the main university campus in Preston. It has been designed to house a wide range of activities relating to the two-way transfer of knowledge between the university, its strategic partners (in further education, NHS Trusts, and other public/private sector organizations) and business. The Harris Knowledge Fund is a seed-corn fund created by the university and BNFL Enterprise Ltd. The fund manager is resident on the park and can provide assistance to entrepreneurs in developing robust business plans for presentation to the fund.	Dr Bill Walmsley, Harris Knowledge Park, Adelphi Building, University of Central Lancashire, Preston, PR1 2HE	00 44 800 195 0055 00 44 1772 892 994 (fax) w.m.walmsley@uclan.ac.uk uclan.ac.uk/hkp
Himalaya	Himalaya comes from the website development space. It animates a virtual learning space called e-lab to study emerging technology trends.	Himalaya UK, 1 Kemp House, 152–160 City Road, London, EC1V 2NP	00 44 207 608 8530 00 44 207 608 8539 (fax) himalaya.fr
Huddersfield Business Generator	The business generator is primarily for graduates wishing to start up their own businesses in the creative industries sector. The centre provides partitioned workspace, desks, computers, filing cabinets, on-site management, free business training and staggered rents.	John Edmonds, Huddersfield Business Generator, Suite S14, 2nd floor, The Kirklees Media Centre, 7 Northumberland Street, Huddersfield, HD4 7BQ	00 44 1484 346780 00 44 1484 346781 (fax) ejohn@architechs.com hud.ac.uk/busgen
IdeaLab-Europe (see also US)	Founded in 1996, it currently has 50 businesses in various stages of development.	Idealab-Europe, 58–59 Haymarket, 5th Floor, London, SW1Y 4QX	00 44 207 968 4700 00 44 207 930 4310 (fax) idealab.com
Ideashub	Launched in 1999 by a group of proven Internet entrepreneurs to found a powerful new organization and network. Their aim is to bring together finance and a full range of business skills, services and expertise.	Ideashub, 40 Portman Square, London, W1H 6LT	00 44 207 487 1300 00 44 207 487 1301 (fax) infor@ideashub.com ideashub.com
Imargo Ltd	A without-walls incubator that focuses on building businesses. Imargo works with individuals and teams to start companies with growth potential.	James Macfarlane, Imargo Ltd, Aston Science Park, Love Lane, Birmingham, B7 4BJ	00 44 121 333 3848 00 44 121 333 3858 (fax) admin@imargo.co.uk

Name	Description	Contact	Phone/Email
Imperial College Company Maker Ltd	ICCM is dedicated to the creation and support of spin-out companies from Imperial College and was formed in 1998 with the backing of a DTI BMI Challenge Award. Its management team has experience in the creation of new ventures, and strong links with venture capital groups, business angels and other sources of early-stage finance. ICCM services spin-outs by adding value to the investment proposal which is finally presented to investors. It also operates a business-mentoring network, which pulls in the expertise of patent agents, accountants, tax consultants, and insurers as well as legal experts.	David Holbrook, Imperial College Company Maker Ltd, Imperial College, 47 Prince's Gate, Exhibition Road, London, SW7 2QA	00 44 207 594 6597 00 44 207 594 6561 (fax) d.holbrook@ic.ac.uk icimnovations.co.uk
Internet Capital Group (Europe)	Floated in the summer of 1999. ICG reached a market capitalization at its peak of $51 billion. Focus is on B2B e-commerce companies across traditional industries.	ICG, Cassini House, 57 St James's Street, London, SW1A 1LD	00 44 207 959 1100 00 44 207 959 1199 (fax) internetcapital.com
Inverness Business Technology Centre	The Inverness Business Technology Centre provides 19 incubator units, in a range of sizes, to growing companies in the technology sector. Central support services and commercial/financial advice are provided by an experienced managing agent on behalf of Inverness and Nairn Enterprise.	Bill Sylvester, Inverness Business Technology Centre, Inverness and Nairn Enterprise, The Green House, Beechwood Business Park North, Inverness, IV2 3BL	00 44 1463 713504 00 44 1463 712002 (fax) thegreenhouse@hient.co.uk business-incubator.co.uk
London Lee Valley BIC Ltd	Developed by Enfield Council and Middlesex University with EU funding, in partnership with local economic development organizations. Part of European Business Network of Innovation Centres. Aims to create and develop innovative, technology-based SMEs.	Gareth Osborne, London Lee Valley BIC Ltd, Business Innovation Centre, Innova Park, Mollison Avenue, Enfield, EN3 7XU	00 44 181 350 1350 00 44 181 350 1351 (fax) lvbc@lvbc.demon.co.uk Lvbic.demon.co.uk
Malvern Hills Science Park	The Malvern Hills Science Park (MHSP) development is a pioneering collaboration between the Defence Evaluation and Research Agency (DERA) and Malvern district local economic development agencies. It has been established to benefit start-up, growth and established companies in relocating to Herefordshire and Worcestershire.	Mark Glossop, Malvern Hills Science Park, Geraldine Road, Malvern, Worcester, WR14 3SZ	00 44 1684 585200 00 44 1684 585201 (fax) manager@mhsp.freeserve.co.uk mhsp.co.uk

Institution	Description	Contact address	Telephone/e-mail/website
Manchester Innovation Centre Ltd	The incubator, which is financed by Manchester University and has EU grant finance, stands next to the university's School of Biological Sciences. It supports commercial R&D in the bioscience sector and provides the means to nurture early-stage businesses, corporate venturing and the commercialization of research. It provides turnkey laboratories, plus office/write-up areas and additional services and business support plus mentoring.	Dr Maire Smith, Manchester Innovation Ltd, Incubator Building, Grafton Street, Manchester, M13 9XX	00 44 161 606 7200 00 44 161 606 7300 (fax) mail@manbio.com maninv.com
Merlin Ventures	Merlin co-founds new biotechnology companies around leading edge science with international commercial potential. Since 1996 Merlin has helped to found seven companies which cover a diverse range of activities within the biotech sector. Having identified leading edge science, Merlin will work closely with scientists and, where applicable, technology transfer offices to form a start-up company. Merlin will then provide the initial seed funding out of its own resources.	Peter Keen, Merlin Ventures, 12 St Jame's Square, London, SW1Y 4RB	00 44 207 849 6003 00 44 207 976 1444 (fax) mailbox@merlin-ventures.co.uk merlin-ventures.co.uk
Merseyside Innovation Centre Ltd	Developed in 1981 to encourage technology start-ups in association with two Liverpool universities.	Trevor Reese, Merseyside Innovation Centre Ltd, 131 Mount Pleasant, Liverpool, L3 5TF	00 44 151 708 0123 00 44 151 707 0230 (fax) denis.salamon@micltd.co.uk micltd.co.uk
Metro New Media	New project aimed at developing early-stage media businesses alongside training and design courses.	Nick Crombie, Metro New Media, 35 Kingsland Road, London, E8 2AA	00 44 207 729 9992 00 44 207 739 7742 (fax) nickcrombie@mnm.co.uk metronewmedia.co.uk
Milton Park Innovation Centre	Milton Park Innovation Centre is specifically for small or start-up businesses which have an innovative idea or product. The innovation centre offers these businesses a soft start in their commercial life by providing accommodation on very flexible terms, by minimizing administration	Mandy Bennett, Milton Park Innovation Centre, 68 Milton Park, Abingdon, OX14 4RX	00 44 1235 437100 mandybennett@ oxfordinnovation.co.uk oxfordinnovation.co.uk

and providing a comprehensive range of back-up services. It is run by Oxford Innovation, which is part of the Oxford Trust charitable foundation.

Name	Description	Contact	Telephone/email
MRC Collaborative Centre	The MRC Collaborative Centre is a not-for-profit technology-transfer organization (a UK registered charity) affiliated to the UK Medical Research Council. It acts as an interface between the MRC's research base and the pharmaceutical and biotechnology industries.	Catherine Kettleborough, MRC Collaborative Centre, 1–3 Burtonhole Lane, Mill Hill, London, NW7 1AD	00 44 208 906 3811 00 44 208 906 1395 (fax) c-kettle@nimr.ac.uk cc.mrc.ac.uk
New Media Spark	One of Europe's leading investors in early-stage companies in the technology, media and telecoms sectors.	New Media Spark PLC, 3rd Floor, 33 Glasshouse Street, London, W1R 5RG	00 44 207 851 7777 00 44 207 851 7770 (fax) enquiries@newmediaspark.com newmediaspark.com
North East of England Business Innovation Centre	The objective of the BIC is to create jobs through the establishment and growth of innovative companies. All of the business support infrastructure is located on-site so the BIC acts as a one-stop shop for all businesses in the Sunderland area, in addition to tenant companies on site.	Arnold Raine, North East of England Business Innovation Centre, Wearfield, Sunderland Enterprise Park, Sunderland, SR5 2TA	00 44 191 516 6023 00 44 191 516 6143 (fax) arnoldraine@northeast-bic.co.uk Sunderlandtec.uk.com
North Lanarkshire Business Incubation Centre	Provision of office suites, boardrooms and lecture halls for 'graduates' of the Lanarkshire Entrepreneurship Programme.	Campbell Murray, North Lanarkshire Business Incubation Centre, The Atrium Business Centre, North Caldeen Road, Coatbridge, ML5 4EF	00 44 1236 702020 00 44 1236 702021 (fax) cmurray@monklandsenterprise.com
Oxford Centre for Innovation	The centre is managed by The Oxford Trust, a charity which promotes the study and application of science and technology. The Oxford Trust first established business incubation in Oxfordshire in 1985.	David Baghurst, Oxford Centre for Innovation, The Oxford Trust, Mill Street, Oxford, OX2 0JX	00 44 1865 728953 00 44 1865 793165 (fax) octi@oxtrust.org.uk oxtrust.org.uk
Oxfordshire BiotechNet Ltd	Oxfordshire BiotechNet is a business mentoring/incubation network for the bioscience sector in Oxfordshire. It has established a new incubator called the Oxfordshire BioBusiness Centre with funding from a DTI BMI Challenge Award.	David Baghurst, Oxfordshire BiotechNet Ltd, Oxford BioBusiness Centre, Littlemore Park, Littlemore, Oxford, OX4 4SS	00 44 1865 405100 00 44 1865 405101 (fax) david.baghurst@biotechnet.co.uk biotechnet.co.uk

Institution	Description	Contact address	Telephone/e-mail/website
Pentlands Science Park	Managed by New Park Management Ltd., Pentlands Science Park offers the veterinary, pharmaceutical and biotechnology industries access to R&D and commercial/financial expertise.	Ian Leslie, Pentlands Science Park, Penicuik, EH26 0PZ	00 44 131 445 6116 00 44 131 445 6256 (fax) ian.leslie@newparkk.co.uk
Peterborough Workspace Ltd	A city council-managed workspace project for small businesses with fifty workshops and offices of various sizes.	Rodney Britten, Peterborough Workspace Ltd, 28/29 Maxwell Road, Woodston, Peterborough, PE2 7JE	00 44 1733 390707 00 44 1733 390622 (fax) admin@peterborough-workspace.co.uk peterborough.workspace.co.uk
Plus Technology Ltd	Plus Technology was established in 1998 as a 'without walls' incubator for emerging companies at the interface between medicine and engineering. It provides hands-on management and financial assistance to those companies which meet their investment criteria. Their focus is on technology-based companies, and they only assist those companies to which they can add value through a partic-ipative role. They currently support three such companies. Plus Technology is made up of a group of five senior executives who have proven track records in managing high-growth, biomedical technology companies in Europe and the US. As well as finance, they provide help with business plans, mentoring and advice on raising finance.	Michael Brand, Plus Technology Ltd, Joseph Wright House, 34 Iron Gate, Derby, DE1 3GA	00 44 1332 368568 00 44 1332 368768 (fax) info@plus-tech.com
Portsmouth Enterprise Centre	One of three enterprise centres in the Portsmouth area (see also the Challenge Enterprise Centre and Victory Business Centre).	John Barton, Portsmouth, Enterprise Centre, Quartremaine Road, Portsmouth, PO3 5QT	00 44 2392 661598 00 44 2392 673647 (fax)
Progeny Bioventures	Set up with the support of a DTI BMI Challenge Award to mentor and assist in the formation of new companies in the biotechnology sector across the UK.	Dr Wiliam Mullen, Progeny Bioventures, Angle Technology, Surrey Technology Centre, Guildford	00 44 7712 191810 00 44 1483 295836 (fax) progeny@angletechnology.co angletechnology.com
Scottish Micro-electrcnics Centre	Incubator units for high-tech companies developing new products that require semi-conductor process support.	Iain Hyslop, Scottish Microelectronics Centre, Kings Buildings, Mayfield Road, Edinburgh, EH9 3JL	00 44 131 650 6023 00 44 131 662 4678 (fax) iain.hyslop@ee.ed.ac.uk scotmicrocentre.co.uk

Name	Description	Contact	
Sheffield Science and Technology Park (city centre site)	Sheffield Science and Technology Park is split between two sites (city centre and Don Valley). The aim of the park is to contribute to regeneration and job creation in Sheffield through enterprise by encouraging the development of technology- and knowledge-based businesses.	Brian Thompson, Sheffield Science and Technology Park (city centre site), The Cooper Buildings, Arundel Street, Sheffield, S1 2NS	00 44 114 221 1800 00 44 114 221 1801 (fax) bthompson@sci-tech.org.uk sci-tech.org.uk
Sheffield Science and Technology Park (Don Valley site)	Sheffield Science and Technology Park is split between two sites (city centre and Don Valley). The aim of the park is to contribute to regeneration and job creation in Sheffield through enterprise by encouraging the development of technology- and knowledge-based businesses.	Brian Thompson, Sheffield Science and Technology Park (Don Valley site), 60 Shirland Lane, Sheffield, S9 3SP	00 44 114 221 1800 00 44 114 221 1801 (fax) btompson@sci-tech.org.uk sci-tech.org.uk
Snowdonia Business Innovation Centre	A Special New Product Development Centre in north-west Wales, dedicated to stimulating new product development and business innovation. The centre provides facilities for the design and development of new products and technologies. It is situated between the Snowdonia National Park and the Menai Strait.	Osborn Jones, Snowdonia Business Innovation Centre, Parc Menai, Bangor, LL59 4BF	00 44 1248 671101 00 44 1248 671102 (fax) osborn@bic-eryri.wales.com Bic-eryri.wales.com
Software Business Network	The SBN is a self-help, collaborative network which brings together the key elements for developing successful software businesses. The aim of the network is to accelerate the growth of the high-tech industry in the UK.	Andrew Wilder, Software Business Network, CSSA, 20 Red Lion Street, London, WC1R 4QN	00 44 207 395 6739 sbn.org.uk
South Wiltshire Incubator and Biotechnology	SWIBTECH is a joint venture between DERA (Porton Down), New Sarum Enterprises (NSE) and Great Western Commerce and Enterprise (GWCE). It was recently awarded a DTI BMI Challenge grant. The project will provide a mentoring network and services through NSE, and 220 days support for developing bioscience companies per year on the Porton Down Science Park site, with flexible easy-in-easy-out bases for developing companies. Property management expertise and access to Business Link support initiatives will be provided through GWCE.	Judy McArdell, South Wiltshire Incubator for Biotechnology, 8 Centre One, Old Sarum Park, Salisbury, SP4 6BU	00 44 1722 415026/7 00 44 1722 415028 (fax) nse@dial.pipex.com

Institution	Description	Contact address	Telephone/e-mail/website
Springvale Innovation Centre	The Springvale Innovation Centre opened in January 2000 and is a joint venture between ICL and the University of Ulster. It will focus on Internet and e-commerce businesses.	Ken Magee, Springvale Innovation Centre, Millennium House, 1 Millennium Way, Springvale Business Park, Belfast, BT12 7AL	00 44 2890 288836 00 44 2890 288850 ken@synergycentres.org
St Johns Innovation Centre Ltd	Established in 1987 by St John's College Cambridge to promote the growth of early-stage technology-based businesses. Provides business services, mentoring and a range of support services and contacts. Located on St John's Innovation Park on the outskirts of Cambridge.	Walter Herriott OBE, St Johns Innovation Centre Ltd, Cowley Road, Cambridge, CB4 0WS	00 44 1223 420252 00 44 1223 420844 (fax) wjherriott@stjohns.co.uk stjohns.co.uk
StarTech Partners Ltd	StarTech Partners Ltd is a private limited company which exists to support the early-stage development of Scottish-based technology businesses. It offers an infrastructure and environment which is geared to achieving rapid transition from start-up project to viable independent company.	Gordon Eadie, StarTech Partners Ltd, 4 Woodside Place, Glasgow, G3 7QF	00 44 141 353 5230 00 44 141 332 2928 gordon.eadie@startech.co.uk startech.co.uk
Stirling University Innovation Park Ltd	An established innovation centre on the Stirling University campus. Its aim is to promote commercialization of research, create new products/processes and encourage new ventures.	Tom Ogilvie, Stirling University Innovation Park Ltd, Scion House, Stirling University Innovation Park, Stirling, FK9 4NF	00 44 1786 448333 00 44 1786 458033 infor@forthright.co.uk stir.ac.uk/innovation_park/innpark.html
Strathclyde University Incubator Ltd	The Strathclyde University incubator was established to address three primary objectives (a) the creation of a supportive structure for new companies; (b) deal flow for commercial investors; and (c) to encourage the transfer of technology out into the commercial world from the University of Strathclyde.	Gillian MacAulay, Strathclyde University Incubator Ltd, 141 St James Road, Glasgow, G4 0LT	00 44 141 552 7287 00 44 141 552 3886 gm@sui.scotnet.co.uk
Sussex Innovation Centre	The innovation centre was established in 1996 on the University of Sussex campus as the flagship of the 'Sussex Academic Corridor'. At present it provides 20 000 sq. ft. of incubator space with plans to extend to 40 000 sq. ft. in future. The centre	Michael Herd, Sussex Innovation Centre, Science Park Square, Falmer, Brighton, BN1 9SB	00 44 1273 704400 00 44 1273 704499 (fax) info@sussexinnovation.co.uk sussexinnovation.co.uk

Name	Description	Contact	Details
	provides further innovation services to both clients of the centre and to companies throughout Sussex.		
Tamar Science Park Ltd	Joint venture between Plymouth City Council, the University of Plymouth and PROSPER, partly financed by EU and English Partnerships. Aims to help start-up and existing science and technology-oriented companies to grow through provision of office, management and business support.	Richard Morgan, Tamar Science Park Ltd, IITC, Tamar Science Park, 1 Davy Road, Deriford, PL6 8BX	00 44 1752 772200 00 44 1752 772227 (fax) tamarsp@ittc.infotrade.co.uk tamar.org.uk
Tapton Park Innovation Centre	New development of workspaces from 200 sq. ft. to 1600 sq. ft., with a supporting central office providing a range of services. The centre is targeted at innovative small businesses with growth potential.	Richard Harvey, Tapton Park Innovation Centre, Brimington Road, Tapton, Chesterfield, S41 0TZ	admin@tapton.co.uk tapton.co.uk
Technology House Business Incubation Unit	Technology House is owned by the University of Salford and operated via University of Salford Enterprises Ltd. The provision of manager workspace for knowledge-based SMEs at commercial rents underpins two other key tasks: (a) the provision of low-cost incubation workspace; and (b) a range of businesses.	Mike Cantello, Technology House Business Incubation Unit, Technology House, Lissadel Street, Salford, M6 6AP	00 44 161 278 2552 00 44 161 278 2421 (fax) m.j.cantello@salford.ac.uk technology-house.com
TEDCO Business Centre	Provides workspace plus management support to a mixed range of early-stage businesses.	John Oldham, TEDCO Business Centre, Viking Industrial Park, Jarrow, NE32 3DT	00 44 191 428 3300 00 44 191 428 3388 (fax) John.Oldham @TEDCO.btinternet.com
The Challenge Enterprise Centre	One of three centres in Portsmouth (see also the Portsmouth Enterprise Centre and Victory Business Centre).	John Barton, The Challenge Enterprise Centre, Sharps Close, Portsmouth, PO3 5RJ	00 44 2392 651701 00 44 2392 651801 (fax)
The Foundation for Entrepreneurial Management	The London Business School aims to build a leading centre of entrepreneurship with a support network for dynamic fast-growing new businesses.	John Bates, The Foundation for Entrepreneurial Management, London Business School, Sussex Place, Regents Park, London, NW1 4SA	00 44 207 262 5050 00 44 207 724 7875 (fax) jbates@lbs.ac.uk lbs.ac.uk

Institution	Description	Contact address	Telephone/e-mail/website
The Hothouse	The Hothouse was launched in February 2000 and is a Merseyside-based business incubator. It provides an environment for entrepreneurs to fully develop potential, high growth and innovative businesses, which build upon technology and leading edge expertise. The Hothouse offers a unique support process, which combines ingenuity from the Merseyside knowledge base, quality business management mentoring, and access to public and private sector business start-up financing.	Chris McLinden, The Hothouse, Peter Jost Enterprise Centre, Byrom Street, Liverpool, L3 3AF	00 44 151 231 2136 00 44 151 231 2486 (fax) c.j.mclinden@livjm.ac.uk thehothouse.org.uk
The Luton and Dunstable Innovation Centre	The site has 15 000 sq. ft. of incubator space with plans for a further 40 000 sq. ft. The innovation centre is to be developed by the university and local council with SRB funding. The aim is to develop early-stage technology-based (particularly IT, environmental and engineering) businesses. The centre provides accommodation, a range of services and small grants to technology-based businesses wishing to establish themselves in the Luton-Dunstable conurbation.	Mike Anstey, The Luton and Dunstable Innovation Centre, The Spires, 2 Adelaide Street, Luton, LU1 5DU	00 44 1582 743700 00 44 1582 743701 (fax) mike.anstey@luton.ac.uk luton.ac.uk
The Oxford Science Park	The Park's first phase developed as a joint venture between Magdalen College (Oxford University) and property developer (The Prudential). The Park's incubator centre opened in 1991 with a focus on IT/biotech businesses.	Heather Knight, The Oxford Science Park, Robert Robinson Avenue, Oxford, OX4 4GA	00 44 1865 784000 00 44 1865 784004 (fax) rcq03@dial.pipex.com
The Surrey Research Park	The innovation centre was developed by the University of Surrey on its science park in the mid-1980s to support early-stage technology-based businesses. Once established, space is available for expansion on the science park.	Malcolm Parry, The Surrey Research Park, 30 Frederick Sanger Road, The Surrey Research Park, Guildford, GU2 5YD	00 44 1483 579693 00 44 1483 568946 (fax) m.parry@surrey.ac.uk surrey.ac.uk/research_park.html
The Turnpike	Conveniently located office and meeting facilities, actually and virtually housing start-up and spin-out new businesses. There is a specialist 'virtual' UK base package (Catalyst Springboard) available for non-UK	Bob Ashton, The Turnpike, Marketing Catalyst Ltd, Suton, Wymondham, Norfolk, NR18 9SS	00 44 1953 605000 00 44 1953 605800 bob@marketing-catalyst.co.uk marketing-catalyst.co.uk

Name	Description	Contact	Phone/Email
	companies wishing to enter this market. Occupants can benefit from service support (telephone, book-keeping etc) and the synergy of sharing a building with similar businesses. Specialist marketing support is available from host company, Marketing Catalyst Ltd. Tenants include e-commerce specialists Apex Web Solutions Ltd.		
The Valleys Innovation Centre	The Valleys Innovation Centre (VIC) is a workspace-led initiative designed to support the development of new technology- and innovation-based businesses. The accommodation includes incubator units which are supported by a range of services provided by the council's Economic Development Unit and the Valleys Innovation Partnership.	Stephen Jones, The Valleys Innovation Centre, Economic Development Unit, Rhondda Cynon Taff CBC, Valleys Innovation Centre, Navigation Park, Abercynon, CF45 4SN	00 44 1443 665000 00 44 1443 665001 (fax) invest@rhondda-cynon-taff.gov.uk invest.rhondda-cynon-taff.gov.uk
The Victory Business Centre	One of the three Enterprise Centres in the Portsmouth area (see also the Challenge Enterprise Centre and Portsmouth Enterprise Centre).	John Barton, The Victory Business Centre, Victory House, Somers Road North, Portsmouth, PO1 1PJ	00 44 2392 826225 00 44 2392 864023 (fax)
The WHEB Partnership	The WHEB Partnership provides specialist business advice to early-stage companies in the environmental technology and services sector. Its focus is on helping companies overcome the barriers to innovation through mentoring and maximizing access to sources of finance.	Robert Wylie, The WHEB Partnership, 213 The Foundry, 156 Blackfriars Road, London, SE1 8EN	00 44 207 721 7285 00 44 207 721 7286 (fax) wheb.partnership@virgin.net whebpartnership.co.uk
Univentures International Ltd	Univentures helps to create new technology-based businesses by forming business teams around businesses licensed from elsewhere in the UK and internationally.	Andre Burton, Univentures International Ltd, Woodhouse Business Centre, Wakefield Road, Normanton, WF6 1BB	00 44 1924 891125 00 44 1924 892207 (fax) univentures@lmu.ac.uk univentures.co.uk
University of Exeter	The University of Exeter's new incubator will provide serviced accommodation for up to 15 business clients in a purpose-built innovation centre which is located next to state-of-the-art manufacturing pilot facilities and testing equipment. A full range of business support services is available as well as access to seed finance and links with local business angel groups.	Sean Fielding, University of Exeter, Northcote House, The Queen's Drive, Exeter, EX4 4QJ	00 44 1392 263 181 00 44 1392 263 187 (fax) business@ex.ac.uk ex.ac.uk

Institution	Description	Contact address	Telephone/e-mail/website
University of Leeds	The University of Leeds is establishing its new innovation centre as a joint venture with Shepherd Development Co Ltd. The first of three phases in this development will provide around 25 000 sq. ft. of accommodation in a new building attached to the business school.	Prof A D Day, Pro-Vice Chancellor, University of Leeds, Leeds, LS2 9JT	00 44 113 233 4121 00 44 113 233 3988 (fax)
University of Reading Innovation Centre	Office and laboratory space in purpose-built premises on the University of Reading campus.	Alison Ansell, University of Reading Innovation Centre, University of Reading, Reading, RG6 6AH	00 44 118 931 8978 00 44 118 931 8979 (fax) a.ansell@reading.ac.uk reading.ac.uk/rsg
University of Wales Swansea Innovation Centre	The primary function of the UWS innovation centre is to act as a business incubator for SMEs, providing property in small affordable units. It provides an instructive and supportive environment to the technology- and knowledge-based sector at start-up and during the early stages of development.	Nia Edwards, University of Wales Swansea Innovation Centre, University of Wales Swansea, Singleton Park, Swansea, SA2 8PP	00 44 1792 295562 00 44 1792 295613 (fax) innovation@swansea.ac.uk
University of Warwick Science Park BIC Ltd (Coventry)	A joint venture formed by the University of Warwick Science Park, Coventry City Council and the Coventry and Warwickshire Chamber of Commerce and TEC to create a business innovation centre for high-growth, innovation-led start-up businesses. The companies receive business support, access to capital and mentoring from the Science Park and Business Link Partners.	John Barnes, University of Warwick Science Park BIC Ltd (Coventry), Barclays Venture Centre, Sir William Lyons Road, Coventry, CV4 7EZ	00 44 2476 323000 00 44 2476 323001 (fax) john.barnes@uwsp.co.uk uwsp.co.uk
University of Warwick Science Park Innovation Centre Ltd (Warwick)	The innovation centre was developed by Warwickshire County Council and the University of Warwick Science Park on the existing technology park. A second phase was completed in 1998, and is now fully let.	Jo Seale, University of Warwick Science Park Innovation Centre Ltd (Warwick), Warwick Technology Park, Gallows Hill, Warwick, CV34 6UW	00 44 1926 623000 00 44 1926 623001 (fax) uwsp@uwsp/co.uk uwsp.co.uk

University of Westminster Innovation Studios – New Media Knowledge	The innovation studios have been set up to provide incubation opportunities for companies working in the new digital media. They are supported by the New Media Knowledge Project. Other sector support projects are being set up which will have incubation units attached to them.	Stephen Whaley, University of Westminster Innovation Studios – New Media Knowledge, Harrow Campus, Watford Road, Harrow, HA1 3TP 00 44 208 357 7303 00 44 208 357 7326 (fax) stephen.whaley@nmk.co.uk nmk.co.uk
UUTECH Incubators at the University of Ulster	Business incubators at the University of Ulster campuses offer high-tech companies central clerical and management support, access to specialist facilities and expert professional advice. Life and health technologies is the focus at the Coleraine site and the Magee site specializes in software companies. Plans are being developed for an engineering/IT incubator at the Jordanstown and a medical technologies incubator at the Springvale site. The incubators support 'spin-out' companies as well as 'spin-in' companies.	James Curran, UUTECH Incubators at the University of Ulster, 2F19, University of Ulster at Jordanstown, Shore Road, Newtownabbey, BT37 0QB 00 44 1232 368019 00 44 1232 366802 (fax) jp.curran@ulst.ac.uk ulst.ac.uk/research/uutech/techtran.html
Wandsworth Youth Enterprise	Wandsworth Youth Enterprise (WYE) was set up in 1988 in response to the growing problems of unemployment, social exclusion and lack of opportunity for young entrepreneurs. Since inception, WYE has supported over 2000 young people and helped hundreds to successfully set up and develop their own businesses.	Michael Manning-Prior, Wandsworth Youth Enterprise, Broadway Studios, 28 Tooting High Street, London, SW17 0RG 00 44 208 672 2832 00 44 208 767 3247 (fax) wyec@wyec.org.uk wyec.org.uk
Wellpark Enterprise Centre	Wellpark is a centre of excellence committed to the growth and development of women in business.	Clare Mooney, Wellpark Enterprise Centre, 120 Sydney Street, Glasgow, G31 1JF 00 44 141 550 4994 00 44 141 550 4443 clare@wellpark.co.uk wellpark.co.uk
Westlakes Ventures Ltd	Westlakes Ventures Ltd (WVL) exists to provide investment risk-funding together with legal and management expertise to assist new technology-based start-up companies to become established in Cumbria. It provides office space on the science park and is currently home to six companies.	Fred Wright, Westlakes Ventures Ltd, Westlakes Science & Technology Park, Moor Row, Cumbria, CA24 3JZ 00 44 1946 690 960 00 44 1946 591 141 (fax) wvl-westlakes@dial.pipex.com wvl-westlakes.co.uk

WESTERN EUROPE

Austria

Institution	Description	Contact address	Telephone/e-mail/website
BIC Burgenland GmbH	Provider of full range of services, focusing on innovation for industry or services to industry.	Johann Binder, BIC Burgenland GmbH, Technologiezentrum, 7000 Eisenstadt, Austria	00 43 2682 704 220 00 43 2682 704 2210 (fax) office@bice.at burgenland.at
March Fifteen	The Vienna-based outfit headed by C Wolff plans to become the gateway for Eastern European investments.	March Fifteen, Austria Tuchlauben 12, a-1010, Vienna	00 43 1512 3917 00 43 1512 391720 (fax) office@marchfifteen.com marchfifteen.com
RIZ NO Holding GmbH	Provider of full range of services focusing on innovation for industry or services to industry.	Karin Platzer, Rudolf Schiessl, RIZ NO Holding GmbH, Professor Stephan Koren Strasse, 10, 2700 Wiener Neustadt, Austria	00 43 2622 26326 00 43 2622 2632699 (fax) office@riz.co.at riz.at

Belgium

Institution	Description	Contact address	Telephone/e-mail/website
Bureau Economique de la Province de Namur	Provider of full range of services focusing on innovation for industry or services to industry.	Jean M Bouvry, Bureau Economique de la Province de Namur, Avenue Sergent Vrithoff, 2, 5000 Namur, Belgium	00 32 81 81 71 71 37 00 32 81 81 71 71 00 (fax) jbo@bep.be bep.be
CEII Heracles	Provider of full range of services focusing on innovation for industry or services to industry.	Philippe Chevremont, CEII Heracles, Avenue General Michel 1E, 6000 Charleroi, Belgium	00 32 71 27 03 11 00 32 71 31 67 35 (fax) heracles@heracles.be heracles.be

Name	Description	Contact	Phone/Email
CEII ID Scrl	Provider of full range of services focusing on innovation for industry or services to industry.	Michel Preud'Homme, CEII ID Scrl, Avenue Leon Champagne, 2, 1480 Saintes-Tubize, Belgium	00 32 2 390 92 72 00 32 2 390 93 86 (fax) id.bw@skynet.be agenceid.be
CEII Socran	Provider of full range of services focusing on innovation for industry or services to industry.	Robert Frederic, CEII Socran, Parc Industriel du Sart-Tilman, Avenue Pre aily, 4031 Angleur, Belgium	00 32 4 367 83 11 00 32 4 367 83 00 (fax) info@socran.be socran.be
Centre de Developpement de Projets CDP	Provider of full range of services focusing on innovation for industry or services to industry.	Daniel Gheza, Centre de Developpement de Projets CDP, Dreve de l'Arc-en-Ciel 98, 6700 Arlon, Belgium	00 32 63 23 18 11 00 32 63 23 18 95 (fax) idelux.aive@idelux.be idelux.be
Centre de Technologie et de Gestion des Affaires	Managed by the Company of Regional Development of Brussels (SDRB), in close co-operation with the Université Libre de Bruxelles. Companies are subjected to an approval procedure which utilises economic urbanistic and technological criteria.	CTGA, Rue de l'Industrie 20, 1400 Nivelles	00 32 67 88 36 11 00 32 67 88 36 88 (fax) jcetting@ulb.ac.be ulb.ac.be
Innotek	Provider of full range of services focusing on innovation for industry or services to industry.	Luc Peeters, Innotek, Cipalstraat 3, 2440 Geel, Belgium	00 32 1457 05 70 00 32 1457 05 60 (fax) innotek@innotek.be innotek.be
Interface Entreprises Universite	To promote collaborations between the University of Liege and local companies	Interface Entreprises Universite, Quai Van Beneden 25, 4020 Liege	00 32 43 49 85 10 00 32 43 49 85 20 (fax) interface@ulg.ac.be ulg.ac.be
Maison de l'Entreprise	Provider of full range of services focusing on innovation for industry or services to industry.	Patrice Thiry, Maison de l'Entreprise SA, Parc Scientifique Initialis Rue Descartes 2, 7000 Mons, Belgium	00 32 65 36 11 15 00 32 65 36 17 46 (fax) patrice.thiry@idea.be fme.be
SailPort	Sailport is the new incubator concept part of SailTrust, the Flanders fund.	SailPort, Westhoek Online, Auris Centre, Flanders Language Valley 1, B-8900 Ieper, Belgium	00 32 057 421985 info@westhoek.be sail.com

Institution	Description	Contact address	Telephone/e-mail/website
SPI+	Created in 1970, the park is dedicated mainly to sciences and high-tech companies	SPI+, Rue Lonhienne, 14, 4000 Liege	00 32 4 230 11 11 00 32 4 230 11 20 muriel.albert@spi.be liegeonline.be
Union Miniere	Technologically evolved non-ferrous companies. Management activity supports the creation of an environment that unleashes talents by driving responsibility and ownership through the organization.	Union Miniere, Zine Straat, 1 2490 Balen	00 32 14 91 91 14 00 32 14 81 91 99 (fax) marc.oner@um.be um.be

Denmark

Institution	Description	Contact address	Telephone/e-mail/website
BIC Nord	Provides SMEs with a full range of services.	Freddy Rano, BIC Nord, Niels Jernes Vej 10, 9220 Aalborg O, Denmark	00 45 96 35 44 30 00 45 96 35 44 25 (fax) bic@bic-nord.dk bic-nord.dk
IncMediator	Business incubation.	IncMediator, Sundvaenget 45, DK-2900 Hellerup, Denmark	00 45 2095 8566 incmediator@usa.net
Innovations Centeret	Business development, research-based industrial innovation, knowledge diffusion within entrepreneurship and industrial innovation.	The Technical University of Denmark, Hoersholm Science Park, Frederiksborg County	innovation.dk
Regional Development Company Ringkjoebing County	Provider of full range of services focusing on innovation for industry or services to industry.	Soren Holm Pederson, Eura A/S, Vester Strandsbejerg, 4A, 6950 Ringkjoebing, Denmark	00 45 9732 5000 00 45 9732 5044 (fax) eura@eura.dk eura.dk

Finland

Institution	Description	Contact address	Telephone/e-mail/website
BIC Botnia	Provider of full range of services focusing on innovation for industry or services to industry.	Jarmo Myllyla, PO Box 810, 65101 Vaasa, Finland	00 358 6 282 82 80 00 358 6 282 82 99 (fax) jarmo.myllyla@merinova.fi merinova.fi
BIC Carelia	Provider of full range of services focusing on innovation for industry or services to industry.	Pirkka Aula, BIC Carelia, Lansikatu 15, Carelian Science Park, 80110 Joensuu, Finland	00 358 13 263 72 10 00 358 13 263 71 11 (fax) pirkka.aula@carelian.fi carelian.fi
BIC Kareltek	Provider of full range of services focusing on innovation for industry or services to industry.	Markku Kivisto, BIC Kareltek, Laserkatu, 53850 Lappeenranta, Finland	00 358 5 624 11 00 358 5 412 09 49 (fax) info@kareltek.fi kareltek.fi
Speedventures (see also Netherlands, Spain, Sweden)	Speedventures NV is a venture-capital investment firm that began operating in the spring of 1998 and now has £70 million at its disposal. Speedventures takes a percentage of the start-ups' equity and a seat on its board.	Teams looking for funding and operational support should send an e-mail to any one of the countries listed. Industrial companies interested in possible joint ventures should email: newindustries@speedventures.com. Investors looking for investment opportunities should e-mail: staffan.thorstensson @speedventures.com	Funding-Helsinki@ speedventures.com
StudioVillage Ltd	A company created to promote development in the Kemi-Tornio region. It specializes in environmental technology, electronics and applied information technology.	StudioVillage Ltd, Tietokaitu 6, 94600 Kemi	00 358 16 22 851 00 358 16 228 552 (fax) kimmo.heikka@tokem.fi kemi.fi

France

Institution	Description	Contact address	Telephone/e-mail/website
@viso	Atviso is a joint venture between Vivendi and Softbank, aimed at helping US Internet companies gain rapid market entry into continental Europe. Atviso's regional expertise and 'toolbox' of services enable clients to team up with the most successful Internet partners in each local market.	Daniel Scolan, Tour Cedre, Paris La Défense, 7 allee de l'Arche, 92677 Courbevoie	00 33 171 77 12 51 00 33 171 77 30 92 daniel.scolan@atviso.com atviso.com
Agoranov	The Pierre and Marie Curie University (Paris 6), the Dauphine Paris University (Paris 9), the Higher Teacher training school (ULM) and the nine Parisian schools of engineers have joined to create Agoranov, an incubator whose vocation is to develop the capacity of creating innovating and viable companies, from projects of scientific and technological laboratories.	Daniel Blondel, Agoranov, 31 Bd de la Tour, Maubourg, 75007 Paris	00 33 144 18 07 15 00 33 145 51 20 88 (fax) info@agoranov.org agoranov.org
Agroparc	Agroparc offers the potential for harmonious growth and expansion to French and foreign businesses and research centres. Among its assets a strong food industry sector and a fast-growing, dynamic computer engineering and communication sector. Agroparc is home to research centres, technical institutes and internationally renowned technology transfer institutions.	Marie-Josée Roig, Agroparc Bâtiment Agriscope BP 1205, 84911 Avignon, Cedex 9	00 33 490 23 80 50 00 33 490 23 80 59 (fax) agricope@agroparc.com agroparc.com
Agropole	Agropole is a science and technology park specializing in the food processing sector and providing a complete range of services. It offers superb business facilities on the 173-acre site including logistical infrastructures, special services for business start-ups with the active support of economic decision-makers, financiers, and the region's public bodies.	Daniel Soulage, Agropole Services BP 102, 47931 Agen, Cedex 9	00 33 553 77 20 00 00 33 553 77 21 00 (fax) agropole@agropole.com agropole.com

Name	Description	Contact	Phone / Email
Alimentec	Primarily a meeting point for skills and services in agribusiness and biotechnology. Alimentec has a dual vocation: to meet the needs of small and medium enterprises; and to offer high-level skills in the field of applied research. Alimentec's strength lies in its ability to link together in one network all the partners in the agribusiness and biotechnology processing industries, equipment manufacturers, distributors, and connected services.	Henri Guillermin, Alimentec, Syndicat Mixte du Technopôle, Alimentec rue Henri Boissieu, 01060 Bourg-en-Bresse, Cedex 9	00 33 474 45 52 00 00 33 474 45 52 01 (fax) ggarin@alimentec.com alimentec.com
Angers Technopôle	This incubator has close ties with the Université d'Angers. They provide those wanting to start up a business with practical help in putting together their business plan. Specifically, they provide advice on marketing, finance, business law and technology, and market research. Amongst their expertise is a particular strength in botanic ventures. They also help with finding business partners.	Jean-Claude Antonini, Angers Technopôle, Maison de la Technopôle 8, rue Le Nôtre, 49066 Angers, Cedex 01	00 33 241 72 04 04 00 33 241 48 90 39 (fax) contact@angerstechnopole.com angerstechnopole.com
Anticipa	Anticipa, primary centre of the French optic and telecommunications industry, owns about 45% of French research in telecommunications.	Robert le Gouguec, Anticipa, Agence de Développement, Industriel du Trégor Maison des entreprises, Aéroport BP 155, 22302 Lannion	00 33 296 05 82 50 00 33 296 05 82 55 (fax) adit@technopole-anticipa.com technopole-anticipa.com
Atlanpole	Innovation network around the Nantes-Saint-Nazaire metropolitan area. Networking and partnership engineering.	François Fillon, Atlanpole, Château de la Chantrerie Route de Gachet, BP 90702, 44307 Nantes, Cedex 3	00 33 240 25 27 29 00 33 240 25 10 88 (fax) atlanpole@atlanpole.fr atlanpole.fr

Institution	Description	Contact address	Telephone/e-mail/website
Biopole Auvergne Technologie	Auvergne aims at developing the life science sector. It provides property solutions to start-ups in bio-industry activities, connected with the thematic parks of Auvergne (Bioparc–Vichy, Biopôle de Haute Auvergne–Aurillac). The members of the science park, universities, research centres, companies and local authorities provide entrepreneurs with a complete tool dedicated to the creation and the development of their companies.	Jean-Claude Jourdan, Biopole Auvergne Technologie, Biopôle Clermont-Limagne, 63360 Saint-Beauzire	00 33 473 64 43 30 00 33 473 64 43 44 (fax) biopole@aol.com pro.wanadoofr/biopole
Carrefour Entreprise Sarthe	Offers a variety of actions within a global policy aiming at creating activities and employment in La Sarthe.	Patrick Choisy, Carrefour Entreprise Sarthe, 75 Bd Alexandre-Oyon, 72100 Le Mans	00 33 243 57 72 72 00 33 243 87 01 02 (fax) ces@cybercable.tm.fr sarthecom/carrefour-entreprise
CEEI Aditec	Forms, with the business incubators of the Pas-de-Calais area, a consulting network specializing in innovation. Each business incubator offers to existing or creating firms solutions adapted to their needs.	Philippe Olejnik, CEEI Aditec, Pas-de-Calais, Rue de l'université Technoparc Futura, 62400 Bethune	00 33 321 63 15 15 00 33 321 63 15 16 (fax) contact@aditec.org aditec.org
CEEI de Nimes		Michel Vindry, CEEI de Nimes, Siège social, 12 rue de la République, 30032 Nimes, Cedex 1	00 33 466 76 33 04 00 33 466 04 73 24 (fax) ceei@nimes.cci.fr ceei.nimes.cci.fr
CEEI Provence	The Business Innovation Center provides an extensive and comprehensive suite of solutions to fully implement innovations inside companies. This implementation consists of monitoring start-ups with a wide range of services and the ability to host start-ups in an incubator.	Jean-Michel Decaudin, CEEI Provence, Europôle de l'Arbois, Domaine du Petit Arbois, BP 88, 13545 Aix en Provence	00 33 442 97 18 18 00 33 442 97 18 19 (fax) info@ceei-provence.com ceei-provence.com

CEEI Synergie	The business and innovation centre (BIC) Synergie, born in 1985, is today a branch of the Moselle's Chamber of Commerce and of Industry. Thanks to its methods of selection, analysis, accompaniment and follow-up, the rate of survival of incubated companies is over 85%.	Maurice Grunwald, CEEI Synergie, Centre Européen d'Entreprise et d'Innovation, 13 rue Claude-Chappe, 57070 Metz Thechnopole	00 33 387 76 36 36 00 33 387 76 23 03 (fax) synergie-ceei.com
CEEI Theogone	The Theogone business innovation centre offers several services for innovative companies.	Daniel Blonde, CEEI Theogone, Parc Technologique du Canal, 10 Av de l'Europe, 31520 Ramonville, Saint Agne	00 33 561 28 56 56 00 33 561 28 56 00 (fax) theogone-martres@wanadoo.fr
Chateau Gombert Technopôle	The Marseille Provence Technopôle at Château-Gombert has been in operation since 1989.	Jean-Claude Gaudin, Chateau Gombert Technopôle, Maison du Développement Industriel, Rue Joliot Curie, 13452 Marseille, Cedex 13	00 33 491 10 01 25 00 33 491 11 79 69 (fax)
Cicom Organization	At CICA (on a 14 000 square metre surface) in Sophia Antipolis, in the heart of the first European science park, CICOM Organization provides information technology, telecommunications and audiovisual/broadcasting resources, as well as technical assistance and an ergonomic working environment.	Alain Andre, Cicom Organization, Centre International de Communication Avancée, 300 route des Crêtes Sophia, Antipoli, 06500 Valbonne	00 33 493 00 60 00 00 33 493 00 60 01 (fax) cica.fr
Clermont La Pardieu Parc Tech-nologique	Clermont-Ferrand lies at the centre of an urban area with some 300 000 inhabitants and is proud of its role as a regional capital. From here a network of good roads and motorways spans the region, making the city the focal point for business meetings. It specializes in the tyre and mechanical industries and advanced technological and food industry companies, not forgetting health and pharmaceutical specialists.	Jean-Yves Gouttebel, Technopôle Clermont La Pardieu, Parc Technologique, Service de Développement Economique de la Ville de Clermont-Ferrand, 27 rue Jean Claret, 63063 Clermont-Ferrand, Cedex 1	00 33 473 28 72 72 00 33 473 28 72 82 (fax)

Institution	Description	Contact address	Telephone/e-mail/website
Crealys	Crealys is an incubator financed by the French government, Rhône-Alpes Region and Greater Lyon. Its objective is to increase the number of start-ups from the region's universities or laboratories.	Joël Rochat, Crealys, 78 Bd du 11 Novembre 1918, 69100 Villeurbanne	00 33 437 47 83 83 00 33 437 47 83 87 (fax) contact@eurasante.com eurasante.com
Ester	Businesses setting up at Ester Research Park enjoy direct links to leading-edge research teams, the resources of established technology transfer centres, and a host of qualified subcontractors and suppliers.	Alain Rodet, Ester, Délégation pour le développement de la technopole BP 6901, 87069 Limoges	00 33 555 42 60 00 00 33 555 42 60 05 (fax) ester@tech-limoges.fr tech-limoges.fr
Eurasante	Eurasante is a regional agency dedicated to the development of biotechnology- and healthcare-related activities. It assists French and foreign companies wishing to set up in the Lille/Nord-Pas de Calais Region.	Alain Demaille, Eurasante, 310 Av Eugène Avinée, 59120 Loos	00 33 328 55 90 60 00 33 328 55 90 61 (fax) contact@eurasante.com eurasante.com
Europole Méditerranéen de l'Arbois	The Europôle Méditerranéen de l'Arbois is a hosting site for environmental firms, which are given the option to become integrated into technology transfer networks.	Europole Méditerranéen de l'Arbois, Domaine du Petit Arbois BP 67, 13545 Aix-en-Provence, Cedex 04	00 334 42 97 17 00 00 334 42 97 17 07 (fax) info@europole-med-arbois.org europole-med-arbois.org
Futura Corse Technopôle	Concentrates most of its regional incubator activities around the N.T.I.C., Environmental and Agroalimentary themes. It created over 50 jobs in the N.T.I.C. business in 1999. Ensam is now sheltered by Futura Corse Technopôle, thus increasing its role in terms of renewable energies and protection of the environment.	René Lota, Futura Corse Technopôle, Parc Technologique de Bastia, 20601 Bastia	00 33 495 30 96 00 00 33 495 30 96 01 (fax) futura.technopole@wanadoo.fr
Futuroscope Technopôle	80 minutes from Paris by high speed train, Futuroscope's Teleport is a 200-hectare technology complex with laboratories (800 researchers), training centres (3000 students), 130 companies and a conference centre along with hotel facilities.	Gérard Biette, Hôtel d'Entreprises, 3 Bâtiment B Téléport 1 BP 10133, 86961 Futuroscope	00 33 549 49 42 42 00 33 549 49 00 65 (fax) dev-eco@cg86.fr futuroscope-technopole.com

Genopole	Six project managers responsible for incubating companies for Genopole. They take on projects, from day one (the initial idea that could lead to the creation of a business) to the first round of financing by investors.	Pierre Tambourin, Genopole, 2 rue Gaston Crémieux CP 5723, 91057 Evry	00 33 160 87 83 00 00 33 160 87 83 01 (fax) genopole.com
Grand Lyon Technopôle	Supported by a very strong industrial, scientific and educational web: 2000 high-tech firms, 9000 researchers, 450 laboratories, 10 technical centres, 4 universities and 25 high schools and 100 000 students.	Jacques Moulinier, Grand Lyon Technopôle, Communauté urbaine de Lyon, Direction des affaires économiques et internationales, 20 Rue du Lac, BP 3103, 69399 Lyon	00 33 478 63 40 99 00 33 478 14 38 74 (fax)
Incubateur En Reseau Nord-Pas de Calais du Gip Miti	Incubateur en reseau nord-pas de Calais du Gip Miti brings together regional skills from the public and private universities of the region, including the prestigious Institut Pasteur of Lille, to help entrepreneurs through the whole business start-up process.	Jacques Duveau, Incubateur en Reseau Nord-pas de Calais du Gip Miti, Espace Recherche Innovation, 2 rue des Canonniers, 59800 Lille	00 33 328 38 50 10 00 33 328 38 50 11 (fax) miti@miti.fr miti.fr
Incubateur Lorrain	Responsibilities: project assessment in collaboration with university researchers and associated organizations; logistical support for entrepreneurs and new companies; managerial, legal, industrial, financial, and organizational support.	Pierre Bardelli, Incubateur Lorrain, 101 av de la libération, 54000 Nancy	00 33 383 97 84 50 00 33 383 97 84 51 (fax)
La Regie Departementale des Ruches d'Entreprises du Nord	A network of eight incubators located throughout the north of France. Its main skill is the promotion of entrepreneurship. More than 400 projects are helped per year. Today, 136 companies are involved, which generate 491 jobs.	Jean-Jacques Candelier, La Regie Departementale des Ruches d'Entreprises du Nord, Siège social, 54–56 rue Jean Sans Peur, BP 1291, 59014 Lille	00 33 320 63 57 59 00 33 320 63 58 85 (fax) reseau.ruches@wanadoo.fr
Laval Mayenne Technopôle	Laval Mayenne Technopôle plays an active role in helping entrepreneurs start up businesses in the region. Their help includes networking with local chambers of commerce and industry, venture-capital firms and universities. They have a business	Jean Heaume, Laval Mayenne Technopôle, 6 rue Léonard de Vinci, BP 0102, 53001 Laval	00 33 243 49 75 00 00 33 243 49 75 70 (fax) technopole@laval-technopole.fr laval-technopole.fr

Institution	Description	Contact address	Telephone/e-mail/website
	centre that provides premises and services to newly set-up firms.		
Lorient Technopôle Innovations	Lorient Technopôle Innovations (LTI) plays an active part in the economic development of the greater Lorient area. It is committed to setting up links between industrial companies, R&D, higher education and companies.	Thierry Fauvet, Lorient Technopôle Innovations, Espace Média Parc Technologique de Soye, 56270 Ploemeur	00 33 297 88 23 23 00 33 297 88 23 20 (fax) info@lorient-technopole.com lorient-technopole.com
Marne-la-Vallée Technopôle	Designed in the 1960s, the development scheme for Marne la Vallée is based on encouraging economic growth.	Michel Dresch, Marne-la-Vallée Technopôle, EPA Marne, 5 bd Pierre Carle-Noisel, 77426 Marne la Vallée	00 33 164 62 44 44 00 33 164 62 44 61
Mediterranée Technologies	Involved with Technology Advisors Network; has created a database of locally available technology.	François Kourilsky, Mediterranée Technologies, Les Docks, 10 place de la Joliette, BP 62004, Atrium 10.2, 13002 Marseille	00 33 488 66 01 00 00 33 488 66 01 01 (fax) info@mediterranee-technologies.com mediterranee-techologies.com
Montpellier Mediterranée Technopôle	Montpellier is the town in France with the fastest-growing population; it also has the highest concentration of knowledge-based activities. It has a wealth of research facilities and innovative companies, and many new companies in cutting-edge sectors such as ICT and biotechnology are choosing to locate here.	Georges Freche, Montpellier Mediterranée Technopôle, 50 place Zeus, La Coupole, BP 9531, 34045 Montpellier	00 33 467 13 60 99 00 33 467 13 61 10 (fax) mlrt@mlrt.fr tech-montpellier.com
Nîmes Rhône Cevennes Technopôle	Involved in all economic development sectors.	Vincent Maurel, Nîmes Rhône Cevennes Technopôle, CCI c/o EERIE Parc Scientifique et Technique Georges Besse, 30035 Nîmes, Cedex 1	00 33 466 38 40 88 00 33 466 04 73 23 (fax) nrce@idgd.org idgd.org
Orleans Technopôle	Involved with companies in economic and scientific development who work with local universities, etc.	Jean-Pierre Sueur, Orleans Technopôle, Centre d'Innovation, 16 rue Léonard de Vinci, 45074 Orleans, Cedex 2	00 33 238 69 80 98 00 33 238 69 80 42 (fax) ot@tech.orleans.fr tech.orleans.fr

Name	Description	Contact	Details
Parc D'Activités Techno-logiques Europarc	Créteil has quickly expanded and offers the optimal conditions for developing companies.	Stéphanie Ursulet, Parc d'Activities Technologiques Europarc, Direction des Affaires Economiques de la Ville de Créteil, 1 allée des Rochers, 94045 Créteil	00 33 149 80 38 04 / 00 33 149 80 38 06 (fax) / info@ville-creteil.fr / ville-creteil.fr
Parc d'Innovation d'Illkirch Strasbourg Technopôle	Designed to accommodate high-tech companies and public labs, the 420-acre park takes advantage of the strong scientific and research potential of the Strasbourg metropolitan area, which provides the best opportunities for the development of new activities.	Catherine Trautmann, Parc d'Innovation d'Illkirch, Strasbourg Technopôle, SERS (Société d'Aménagement de la Région de Strasbourg), 10 rue Oberlin, 67080 Strasbourg	00 33 388 37 88 88 / 00 33 388 37 88 77 (fax) / sers@compuserve.com
Reims Technopôle	ADER (Association for the Economic Development of Reims), is designed to foster economic growth, thus encouraging the expansion and the competitiveness of industries and companies in Reims.	Serge Kochman, Reims Technopôle, ADER, 13 rue Chanzy, 51100 Reims	00 33 326 77 10 90 / 00 33 326 77 10 95 (fax) / ader@reims-ader.com / reims-ader.com
Rennes Atalante	This science park hosts 220 companies employing 12 700 persons, and acts as a federating body for all the high-tech companies in Rennes (Western France). Its success is based on the IT sector led by famous public and private research centres such as France Télécom, Thomson Multimedia (RCA), Mitsubishi Electric, Lucent Technologies, Alcatel, Acterna, Harris Communication, Philips Semiconductors, and Canon.	Jacques D de Certaines, Rennes Atalante, 11 rue du Clos, Courtel, 35700 Rennes, Rennes Atalante	00 33 299 12 73 73 / 00 33 299 12 73 74 (fax) / technopole@rennes-atalante.fr
Savoie Technolac	Located in Chambéry-Aix-les-Bains, Savoie Technolac has from the beginning, focused its actions on the quality of life. It is equipped with many services, such as telecommunications and Internet access.	Jean-Pierre Vial, Savoie Technolac, Bâtiment L'Horloge 16, voie B, BP 234, 73374 Le Bourget du Lac	00 33 479 25 36 36 / 00 33 479 25 36 97 (fax) / technopole@savoie-technolac.com / savoie-technolac com
Sicoval Technopôle Toulouse Sud-Est	It includes 800 companies (18 000 jobs) in four parks. Through its high quality networks, offers relationships with universities, educational institutions, research laboratories and major contractors.	François-Régis Valette, Sicoval Technopôle Toulouse Sud-Est, Rue du chêne vert, BP 136, 31676 Labege	00 33 562 24 02 02 / 00 33 561 39 20 45 (fax) / info@sicoval.fr / sicoval.fr

Institution	Description	Contact address	Telephone/e-mail/website
Synergia Techncpôle Caen/Normandy	Synergia, the science park of Caen-Normandy, will put you in touch with other businesses, with training centres and research centres. Through the EBIC (European Business Innovation Centre), it helps companies to launch projects, and create and develop new activities.	Jean-Baptiste Durieux, Synergia Technopôle Caen/Normandie, Unicité 12, rue Alfred Kastler, 14053 Caen	00 33 231 46 73 73 00 33 231 46 73 74 (fax) technopole@synergia.fr synergia.fr
Technopôle Brest-Iroise	Missions: Development and reinforcement of our key assets; Creation of innovative new businesses; and technological, scientific and industrial asset promotion of the region by proactive marketing (business conventions, seminars, exhibitions, etc).	Pierre Maille, Technopôle Brest-Iroise, 40 rue Jim Sévellec, BP 10804, 29608 Brest	00 33 298 05 44 51 00 33 298 05 47 67 (fax) tech-brest-iroise.fr
Technopôle de la Region de Mulhouse	This incubator is focused on the region's three main industries; cars, chemistry and logistics. In addition, it has close ties with the city's university which has 18 research laboratories, covering fields as diverse as data processing and textiles.	Bernard Meyer, Technopôle de la Region de Mulhouse, 40 rue Marc Seguin, BP 2118, 68060 Mulhouse	00 33 389 32 76 76 00 33 389 32 76 31 (fax) technopole@evhr.net
Technopôle de l'Aube en Champagne	Locating your business in the Aube Technopolis means joining a dynamic series of networks to share skills and experience. Close links exist between the Université de technologie de Troyes and companies in the incubator and the business park. Synergies are created, stimulating people and sparking new ideas. The Aube Technopolis offers a full range of services to entrepreneurs to facilitate their business, whatever their stage of development. The technology and science park is the perfect place for firms at the leading edge of new technology in every sector of activity.	Jacques Rigaud, Technopôle de l'Aube en Champagne, BP 1064, 10009 Troyes	00 33 325 83 10 10 00 33 325 83 21 80 (fax) technopole@netchampagne.com technopole-aube.fr
Technopôle du Mans	This incubator is based on partnerships between local industry.	Jean-Claude Boulard, Technopôle du Mans, Syndicat Mixte d'Aménagement et de promotion de la Promotion de la Technopôle du Mans, Hôtel de Ville Place, Saint Pierre, 72039 Le Mans	00 33 243 47 47 47 00 33 243 47 40 02 (fax)

Name	Description	Contact	Contact details
Technopôle Helioparc Pau Pyrenees	This incubator, established over 10 years ago under the local council's initiative, brings together research teams, innovative project developers and companies, in close proximity to the university.	Jean Gougy, Technopôle Helioparc Pau Pyrenees, 2 avenue Pierre Angot, 64053 Pau	00 33 559 02 48 48 00 33 559 84 42 96 (fax) heliantis.fr/helioparc
Technopôle Lille Metropole	This is the link between the high-tech research development dynamics at work in the region and the regional network of technological development.	Gerard Caudron, Technopôle Lille Metropole (MACC), Cite scientifique, 59650 Villeneuve d'Ascq	00 33 320 91 02 70 00 33 320 47 28 28 (fax) lot@nordnet.fr nordnet.fr
Technopôle Metz 2000	Metz Technology Park offers companies research and education courses in software, telecommunications, multimedia applications, industrial engineering, electrical engineering and international trade and management.	Nathalie Griesbeck, Technopôle Metz 2000, SEM Technopôle Metz 2000, 4 rue Marconi, 57070 Metz	00 33 387 20 41 70 00 33 387 74 67 59 (fax) technopole2000.georgiatech-metz.fr
Technopôle Nancy Brabois Innovation	This is an innovation centre focused mainly, but not exclusively, on helping the region's technology- and knowledge-based businesses start up successfully. They have close ties with local universities, venture-capital providers and the chamber of commerce and industry.	Gérard Rongeot, Technopôle Nancy Brabois Innovation, 10 rue Victor Poirel, BP 516, 54008 Nancy	00 33 383 17 42 28 00 33 383 17 42 30 (fax) nancytechnopole.com
Technopôle Quimper Cornouaille	The mission of this incubator is the economical development of the area through technology and innovation. It supports new business creation, technology transfer, and manages infrastructural projects. Main industrial sectors of activity are the food industry, the packaging industry and IT.	Bernard Poignant, Technopôle Quimper Cornouaille, 2 rue Guillemot, 29000 Quimper	00 33 298 10 02 00 00 33 298 10 02 01 (fax) technopole@tech-quimper.fr tech-quimper.fr
TEMIS (Technopôle Micro-technique et Scientifique de Besançon)	They help entrepreneurs to start up and grow businesses in the region. Their help includes having close links with local chambers of commerce and industry, venture-capital firms and universities. They have a business centre that provides premises and services to newly set up firms.	Robert Schwint, TEMIS (Technopôle Microtechnique et Scientifique de Besançon), Mairie de Besançon, 2 rue Mégevand, 25034 Besançon	00 33 381 50 46 95 00 33 381 53 21 75 (fax) anthony.jeanbourquin@ens2m.fr TEMIS.org

Institution	Description	Contact address	Telephone/e-mail/website
Valmaris Technopôle	Activities include: risk, safety and environment. Aims: to organize networks; to encourage and to increase innovation, technological transfers and starts-ups; to increase employment levels; to develop and promote the technological area and the science park.	Jacques Ozanne, Valmaris Technopôle, Route de la Chapelle, Réanville, BP 2265, 27950 Saint-Marcel	00 33 232 53 63 18 00 33 232 53 64 66 (fax) valmaris-technopole@wanadoo.fr
Vannes Technopôle	Vannes Technopôle plays an active role in helping entrepreneurs to start up businesses in the region. Their help includes networking with local chambers of commerce and industry, venture-capital firms and universities. They have a business centre that provides premises and services to newly set up firms.	Marcel Fourmestraux, Vannes Technopôle, Parc d'Innovation Bretagne Sud, Le Prisme, CP 1, 56038 Vannes	00 33 297 68 14 23 00 33 297 68 14 01 (fax) vipe@pays-de-vannes.com intervenetes.com
Zirst	Situated in the suburbs of Grenoble, Zirst has an enviable geographical position. Its strategic location allows easy communication between major centres of technology, industry and finance throughout the Gresivaudan Alpine valley.	Jean-François Simon, Zirst, 18 chemin du Vieux Chêne, 38246 Meylan	00 33 476 90 41 57 00 33 476 90 21 11 (fax) prozist@zirst.com zirst.com
Zoopole Development	Since 1989, Zoopole has been dedicated to technological activities related to public health, from livestock breeding to food safety. Today more than 600 people work at Zoopole where there are 10000 m² of analysis and research laboratories, training institutes and companies. Zoopole development supports: technological innovation, in particular in SMEs; partnerships with national and international companies; incubation and the creation of high-tech companies; research programmes; and exhibitions and international symposiums.	Jean Gaubert, Zoopole Development, Rond-point du Zoopôle, BP 7, 22440 Ploufragan	00 33 296 76 61 61 00 33 296 76 61 69 (fax) zoopole.com

Germany

Institution	Description	Contact address	Telephone/e-mail/website
Apollis	Apollis is an independent company founded by the leading global investor in information technology, Internet and Internet-enabling businesses. Their mission is to develop a family of companies in the field of mobile solutions that have the potential to become global leaders.	Apollis AG, Tal 24, 80331 Munich, Germany	00 49 89 2423 21200 00 49 89 2423 21297 (fax) apollis.com
BIC Frankfurt (Oder) GmbH	Provider of full range of services focusing on innovation for industry or services to industry.	Uwe Hoppe, BIC Frankfurt (Oder) GmbH, Im Technologiepark 1, 15236 Frankfurt (Oder), Germany	00 49 335 557 11 00 00 49 335 557 11 10 (fax) info@bic-ffo.de bic-ffo.de
BIC GIZ & Tele-Service GmbH	Provider of full range of services focusing on innovation for industry or services to industry.	Renate Ciba, BIC Giz & Tele-Service GmbH, Obermarkt 24, 63671 Gelnhausen, Germany	00 49 6051 8280 00 49 6051 828 20 (fax) arb3@tele-service-center.de bic-giz.de
BIC Kaiserslautern	Full range of services focusing on innovation for industry/services to industry.	Marc Beisel, BIC Kaiserslautern, Opelstrasse 10, 67661 Kaiserslautern, Germany	00 49 6301 7030 00 49 6301 703 119 (fax) marc.beisel@bic-kl.de bic-kl.de
BIC Zwickau GmbH	Full range of services focusing on innovation for industry/services to industry.	Hans-Jurgen Uhlmann, BIC Zwickau GmbH, Lessingstrasse 4, 08058 Zwickau, Germany	00 49 375 54 10 00 49 375 54 13 00 (fax) bic@bic-zwickau.de bic-zwickau.de
IGZ BIC Altmark GmbH	Full range of services focusing on innovation for industry/services to industry.	Georg Naumann, IGZ BIC Altmark GmbH, Arneburge Strasse 24 Technologiepark, 39576 Stendal, Germany	00 49 3931 681 440 00 49 3931 681 444 (fax) bic@altmark.de bic-altmark.de

Institution	Description	Contact address	Telephone/e-mail/website
New Media Spark	New Media Spark is one of Europe's leading investors in early stage companies in the technology, media and telecoms (TMS) sector. New Media Spark has already made over 50 investments in early-stage companies in Europe, India and the US.	New Media Spark GmbH, Friedrichstrasse 76, D-10117 Berlin	00 49 30 2094 7200 00 49 30 2094 7201 (fax) berlin@newmediaspark.com newmediaspark.com
Pixel Park	Pixel Park lives up to the promise of the European roll-out. The company went public in late 1999.	Pixel Park, Rotherstrasse 8, 10245 Berlin	00 49 3 050 580 00 49 3 050 581 (fax) pixelpark.com

Greece

Institution	Description	Contact address	Telephone/e-mail/website
BIC of Attika	Full range of services for industry/services to industry.	Dimitris Karachalios, BIC of Attika, Stadiou Street 7, 8th Floor, 105 62 Athens, Greece	00 30 1 331 42 30 00 30 1 331 42 32 (fax) bicofatttika@hol.gr bicofattika.gr
BIC of Epirus	Full range of services for industry/services to industry.	Aikaterini Filippou, BIC of Epirus, Domboli, 30, 45332 Ioannina, Greece	00 30 651 44 447 00 30 651 44 457 (fax) bicepirus@ioa.forthnet.gr bicepirus.gr
BIC Patras	Full range of services to industry/services for industry.	Andreas Papavlasopoulos, BIC Patras, Michalakopoulou Street 58, 26221 Patras, Greece	00 30 61 622 711 00 30 61 277 830 (fax) ksmme@patrascc.gr patrascc.gr
Serres EC-BIC	Full range of services to industry/services for industry.	Christos Karaghiannis, Serres EC-BIC, 9 Amynta Street, 69124 Serres, Greece	00 30 321 49 442 56 029 00 30 321 46 443 (fax) bic@bic.the.forthnet.gr bic.the.forthnet.gr

Iceland

Institution	Description	Contact address	Telephone/e-mail/website
IceTec-Technological Institute of Iceland	Primary aims are to strengthen the Icelandic economy through development, innovation and increased productivity.	Andres Magnusson, IceTec, Keldnaholد, 112 Reykjavik, Iceland	00 354 570 7100 00 354 570 7111 am@iti.is iti.is

Ireland

Institution	Description	Contact address	Telephone/e-mail/website
Ballymun Partnership	Provides incubation space for early-stage start-up companies.	Terence Kavanagh, Ballymun Partnership, North Mall, Ballymun Town Centre, Ballymun, Dublin 11, Ireland	00 353 1842 3612 00 353 1842 7004 (fax) bmunparc@indigo.ie guinness-enterprisectr.com
Business Incubation Centre	Provider of incubation space for early-stage start-up companies.	Rory O'Meara, Business Incubation Centre, Richmond Business Campous, North Brunswick Street, Dublin 7, Ireland	00 353 1872 7190 00 353 1872 6252 (fax) richmond@iol.ie ireland.iol.ie guinness-enterprisectr.com
Dublin Business Innovation Centre	Set up in 1987 with private, public, educational and EU support. Assists and provides advice to new business projects.	Desmond C W Fahey, Dublin Business Innovation Centre, The Tower, IDA Enterprise Centre, Pearse Street, Dublin 2, Ireland	00 353 16 71 41 11 00 353 16 71 33 30 (fax) info@dbic.ie dbic.ie
		Dolores Dempsey, The Dublin Business Innovation Centre, Incubation Centre, Fourth Floor, Burton Hall, 19–22 Dame Street, Dublin 2, Ireland	00 353 1670 9389 00 353 1670 9399 (fax) damedbic@indigo.ie indigo.ie guinness-enterprisectr.com

Institution	Description	Contact address	Telephone/e-mail/website
Innovation Centre Limerick	Ireland's first digitally networked business incubation centre.	Alice Morgan, Innovation Centre Limerick, National Technological Park, Limerick, Ireland	00 353 61 33 81 77 00 353 61 33 80 65 (fax) morgana@shannon-dev.ie shannon-dev.ie
West BIC	Established in 1988, WestBic is concerned with the generation of regional economic growth. Client base embraces a range of industry sectors.	Joe Greaney, West BIC, Hardiman House, Eyre Square 5, Galway, Ireland	00 353 91 56 79 74 00 353 91 56 80 (fax) bicgwy@iol.ie westbic.ie

Italy

Institution	Description	Contact address	Telephone/e-mail/website
Agenzia Lumetel	Services to enterprises include development, technology transfer, export, takeovers, representation abroad, information centres, consultancy.	Luciano Consolati, Agenzia Lumetel, Via Mazzini 92, 25065 Lumezzane, Italy	00 39 030 82 51 010 00 39 030 89 21 420 (fax) consolati@lumetel.it lumetel.it
Agenzia per lo Sviluppo del Golfo (CEII)	Provides full range of services to businesses.	Antonino Iozza, Agenzia per lo Sviluppo del Golfo, Via Filippo Morello 3, 93012 Gela, Italy	00 39 0933 92 56 97 00 39 0933 92 56 97 (fax) Bicgela@tin.it
BIC Calabria	Provides full range of services to businesses.	Francesco Samengo, BIC Calabria, Corso d'Italia 166, 87100 Cosenza, Italy	00 39 0984 39 14 55 00 39 0984 39 15 07 (fax) Info@biccal.it biccal.it
BIC Omega	Provides full range of services to businesses.	Francesco Di Pietrantonio, BIC Omega, 64010 Ancarano, Italy	00 39 0861 80 561 00 39 0861 86 246 (fax) Bicomega@bicomega.it bicomega.it
BIC Varese	Provides full range of services to businesses.	Marco Bossi, BIC Varesa, Vicolo Molino 2, 21052 Busto Arsizio (Varese), Italy	00 39 0331 32 46 11 00 39 0331 63 94 87 (fax) Info@pstl.it pstl.it

Luxembourg

Institution	Description	Contact address	Telephone/e-mail/website
Centre de Recherche Public Henri Tudor	Provides a wide range of facilities and support services to high-tech entrepreneurs, innovators, SMEs and manufacturing companies.	Claude Wehenkel, Centre de Recherche Public Henri Tudor, 6, rue de Coudenhove-Kalergi, 1359 Luxembourg	00 352 42 59 91 1 00 352 43 65 23 (fax) Claude.wehenkel@crpht.lu crpht.lu

Netherlands

Institution	Description	Contact address	Telephone/e-mail/website
BIC Noord-Nederland	The Zernike Group is a young international dynamic company in the field of technology transfer, patenting and licensing.	Bob Hiemstra, Bic Noord-Nederland, Zernikepark 4, 9747 An Groningen, Netherlands	00 31 50 57 45 750 00 31 50 57 36 247 (fax) Bhiemstra@freeler.bl zernikegroup.com
BIC Twente	BIC-Twente promotes and supports the start-up and growth of innovative enteprises at the Business and Science Park, Enschede.	Gijs van Driem, BIC Twente, Hengelosestraat 705, PO Box 545, 7500 AM Enschende, Netherlands	00 31 53 483 63 53 00 31 53 433 74 15 (fax) Info@btc-twente.nl btc-twente.nl
Speedventures (see also Finland, Spain, Sweden)	Speedventures NV is a venture-capital investment firm that began operating in the spring of 1998 and now has £70 million at its disposal. Speedventures takes a percentage of the start-ups' equity and a seat on the board.	Teams looking for funding and operational support should e-mail any one of the countries listed. Industrial companies interested in possible joint ventures should e-mail: newindustries@speedventures.com. Investors looking for investment opportunities should e-mail staffan.thorstensson@speedventures.com	Funding-Amsterdam@speedventures.com

Norway

Institution	Description	Contact address	Telephone/e-mail/website
Forskning-sparken As	The Oslo Research Park has provided a central arena for the development of new media in Norway over the last few years. It aims to be one of the leading centres in Europe for innovation and industrial development.	Torp Svenning, Forskningsparken As, Gaudstadalleen 21, 0371 Oslo, Norway	00 47 22 95 85 33 00 47 22 60 44 27 (fax) Svenning.torp@sposlo.no fposlo.no

Portugal

Institution	Description	Contact address	Telephone/e-mail/website
BIC Algarve Huelva	Provides full range of services to businesses.	Dario Dias, BIC Algarve Huelva, Av. Dr Bernardino da Silva 65–2 Dto, 8700 Olhao, Portugal	00 351 289 70 79 20 00 351 289 78 11 21 (fax) Geral@bic-ah.com bic-ah.com
Centre of Companies & Innovacao – BIC Wood	Services to enterprises.	Mr Padron, Centre of Companies & Innovacao – BIC Wood, Tecnopolo wood Path of the Combed one, 900 Funchal – Wood, Portugal	00 351 91 723000 00 351 91 720030 (fax) ceim@madinfo.pt madinfo.pt/ceim

Spain

Institution	Description	Contact address	Telephone/e-mail/website
Barcelona Activa SA	Local development agency for implementing policies of the Council of Barcelona in terms of economic promotion, business corporation and fostering of entrepreneurial services.	Josep Maria Marques Ferrer, Barcelona Activa SA, Llacuna 162, 08018 Barcelona, Spain	00 34 93 401 98 00 00 34 93 300 90 15 (fax) Josep.marques@barcelonactiva.es bcnactiva.bcn.es

Beaz SA	Specializes in SME development in the industrial and service to industry sectors.	Jose Ignacio Izurieta Mendieta, Beaz SA, Alameda Recalde 18–6, 48009 Bilbao, Spain	00 34 94 423 92 28 00 34 94 423 10 13 (fax) Javier.barcina@beaz.net beaz.net
BIC Berrilan	Processors of innovative business ideas, and development projects serving industry.	Maria-Louisa Arriola, BIC Berrilan, C/Barrenengua, 3, 20600 Eibar, Spain	00 34 94 320 07 26 00 34 94 320 11 07 (fax) Correo@bicberrilan.com bicberrilan.com
CEEI Aragon	Main aim is to identify the necessities and objectives of customer/entrepreneurs, enterprises and institutions.	CEEI Aragon, Maria de Luna, Poligono Actur, 50015, Zaragoza, Spain	00 34 976 733 500 00 34 976 733 719 (fax) Ceei.z@ceeiaragon.es ceeiaragon.es
Eurocei	Offers a range of services and assistance on a transnational level.	Enrique M Piriz, Eurocei, Autovia Sevilla-Coria s/n Apdo de Correos 76, 41920 San Juan de Aznalfarache, Seville, Spain	00 34 95 41 79 210 00 34 95 41 71 117 (fax) Eurocei@eurocei.com eurocei.com
San Sebastian Technology Park	The park is a generator of economic and social development.	San Sebastian Technology Park, Passeo Mikeletegi 53. E-20009 San Sebastian, Spain	00 34 943 30 90 00 00 34 943 30 91 30 (fax) Miramon@miramon.es miramon.es
Speedventures (see also Netherlands, Finland, Sweden)	Speedventures NV is a venture-capital investment firm that began operating in the spring of 1998 and now has £70 million at its disposal. Speedventures takes a percentage of the start-ups' equity and a seat on its board.	Teams looking for funding and operational support should e-mail any one of the countries listed. Industrial companies interested in possible joint ventures should e-mail: newindustries@speedventures.com. Investors looking for investment opportunities should e-mail: staffan.thorstensson@speedventures.com	Funding-Milan@speedventures.com

Sweden

Institution	Description	Contact address	Telephone/e-mail/website
BIC Mid Sweden AB	A regional resource for business development for growth and export SMEs.	Nils Karlsen, BIC Mid Sweden AB, Terminalvagen, 10, 861 36 Timra, Sweden	00 46 60 19 09 00 00 46 60 10 09 09 (fax) Info@bicmid.se bicmid.se
BIC Norr AB	Partnership area for the project RIS North Sweden.	Niklas Gustavsson, BIC Norr AB/ Sweden, Box 7980, S-901 86 Umea	00 46 90 15 49 82 00 46 90 15 49 85 (fax) N.gustavsson@bicnorr.se bicnorr.se
BIC Sweden West AB	The first certified BIC organization in Sweden in 1995, BIC was owned by a non-profit organization for the first five years.	Olof Halbert, BIC Sweden West AB, Kurodsvagen 1, 451 55 Uddevalia, Sweden	00 46 522 65 66 40 00 46 522 39 93 0 (fax) Bic@bic.se bicwest.se
Generics Group (see also UK, Switzerland, USA)	Generics, now a subsidiary of Swedish firm Catella (www.catella.se) was co-founded in 1986 by Professor Gordon Edge at Cambridge University and invests in intellectual property and capital only. It initially offered only high-tech consultancy and research services. Starting in 1992, Generics began to hatch its own start-ups, providing them with a supportive but challenging intellectual environment, financial support and flexibility.	Catella Generics AB, Veddestavagen 7, S-175 62 Jarfalla, Sweden	00 46 8 445 7960 00 46 8 445 7999 (fax) catella.se
New Media Spark (see also UK, Germany)	New Media Spark is one of Europe's leading investors in early-stage companies in the technology, media and telecoms (TMS) sector. New Media Spark has made over 50 investments in early-stage companies in Europe, India and the US.	New Media Spark Stockholm, Hightech building 111, S-101 52 Stockholm, Sweden	00 46 0 8 566 159 00 00 46 0 8 566 159 09 (fax) pjp@newmediaspark.com newmediaspark.com

Institution	Description	Contact address	Telephone/e-mail/website
Speedventures (see also Netherlands, Finland, Spain)	Speedventures NV is a venture-capital investment firm that began operating in the spring of 1998 and now has £70 million at its disposal. Speedventures takes a percentage of the start-ups' equity and a seat on its board.	Teams looking for funding and operational support can e-mail any one of the countries listed. Industrial companies interested in possible joint ventures should e-mail: newindustries@speedventures.com. Investors looking for investment opportunities should e-mail: staffan.thorstensson@speedventures.com	Funding-Stockholm@speedventures.com

Switzerland

Institution	Description	Contact address	Telephone/e-mail/website
Business Incubateur EPFL	Specializes in SME development.	Business Incubateur, EPFL, Park Scientifique, EPFL, 1015 Lausanne	00 41 21 693 46 65 00 41 21 693 46 75 (fax) Pse@epfl.ch epfl.ch
Donation Futur	Offers companies free places during their start-up phase.	Peter Schneider, Donation Futur, University Rapperswil, Upper Maritime Route 10, 8640 Rapperswil, Switzerland	00 41 55 222 44 03 00 41 55 222 44 44 (fax) Peter.schneider@hsr.ch futur.ch
E-Tower, Thun	Focuses on e-business, e-commerce and Internet start-ups.	Stefan Linder, E-Tower, C F L Lohnestr.24, 3601 Thun, Switzerland	00 41 33 221 60 21 00 41 33 221 60 20 (fax)
Generics Group (see also UK, Sweden, USA)	Generics, now a subsidiary of Swedish firm Catella (www.catella.se) was co-founded in 1986 by Professor Gordon Edge at Cambridge University and invests in intellectual property and capital only. It initially offered only high-tech consultancy and research services. Starting in 1992, Generics began to hatch its own start-ups, providing them with a supportive but challenging intellectual environment, financial support and flexibility.	Generics AG, Bodmerstrasse 7, CH-8002 Zurich, Switzerland	00 41 206 4151 00 41 206 4152 (fax) generics.ch

Institution	Description	Contact address	Telephone/e-mail/website
Internet Business Park	Focuses on Internet companies.	Walter Cadosch, Internet Business Park, Headquarters for Economic Questions, Telli Multistoried Building, 5004 Aarau, Switzerland	00 41 62 835 24 40 00 41 62 835 24 19 (fax) Stabsstelle.wirtschaftsfragen@ag.ch hightechvalley.ch

CENTRAL EUROPE

Belarus

Institution	Description	Contact address	Telephone/e-mail/website
Gomel Business Innovation Centre	Supported by Gomel Technical University – main activity of BIC is support of R&D companies.	Gomel Business Innovation Centre, 48 Oktyabrya Avenue, Gomel 246000, Belarus	00 375 232 497 487 (phone/fax) sme.home.by
Lida Business Incubator	Information technologies, cable TV, software, motor repairs.	Lida Business Incubator, 43 Sovetskaya Street, Lida, Grodno Region 231300 Belarus	00 375 1561 284 39 00 375 1561 204 13 (fax) lidabi@mail.ru sme.home.by
Minsk Business Incubator	Activity areas include optics, electronics, laser instrumentation, T&M equipment manufacturing and software.	Minsk Business Incubator, 19 Sharagovicha Street, Minsk 220018, Belarus	00 375 17 259 07 92 (phone/fax) sme.home.by

	Description	Contact address	Telephone/e-mail/website
Molodechno Business Incubator	Activities include medical equipment, food processing, cardboard manufacturing and security systems.	Molodechno Business Incubator, 2 Metallistov Street, Molodechno, Minsk Region 222310, Belarus	00 375 273 702 60 (phone/fax) sme.home.by
Mozyr Business Incubator	Manufacturers of furniture, heating equipment, clothing.	2 Kirova Street, Mozyr 247760, Belarus	00 375 2351 240 59 00 375 2351 235 47 (fax) mozyrbc@mail.ru sme.home.by
United Nations Development Programme	A joint venture with the government of Belarus 'creating small business support and development infrastructure'.	UNDP, 11 Oranskaya Street, Minsk 220033, Belarus	00 375 17 216 28 42 00 375 17 216 28 43 00 375 17 216 28 44 00 375 17 221 41 41 00 375 17 210 26 53 (fax) sme@un.minsk.by sme@un.minsk.by

Bulgaria

Institution	Description	Contact address	Telephone/e-mail/website
Bulgarian Association of Regional Development Agencies (BARDA)	Established in 1997 by six regional development agencies in Bulgaria. Its main aim is to serve as an umbrella association of independent regional and local economic development agencies and SME support centres in Bulgaria.	BARDA, Bulgaria, Sofia 1000, 4 Vitosha Blvd., fl 6	00 359 2 983 03 35 00 359 2 983 03 41 (fax) BARDA@barda.net barda.bg

Czech Republic

Institution	Description	Contact address	Telephone/e-mail/website
BIC Ostrava	Focusing on innovation for industry or services to industry.	BIC Ostrava, Mostarenska 1, 703 00 Ostrava-Vitovice	00 420 292 61 58 00 420 69 292 67 51 (fax) bicova@ostrava.czcom.cz bicova.cz

Institution	Description	Contact address	Telephone/e-mail/website
BIC Plzen	Supporters of new businesses; assists in the development of existing businesses, networking, information services, development of business plans and financial resourcing.	BIC Plzen, Riegrova 1, 301 16 Plzen, Czech Republic	00 420 7235379 00 420 19 7235320 (fax) Bic@bic.cz bic.cz
Business Development Agency	Offers services for SME activities.	Business Development Agency, Letenska 3, 11800 Prague 1	00 420 25 30 289 00 420 25 37 949 (fax) agentura@arp.cz agentura.cz
Prague Science and Technology Park (Czech Technical University)	Objective is to set up an integrated technological municipal zone, utilizing the latest technologies including environmental technology, power supply systems, material engineering, biomedical engineering, biotechnology, electronics precision, automation, software engineering etc.	P. Komarek, BIC CVUT, Prague, Plenska 221, 150 00, Prague 5	00 420 2 558 812 00 420 2 524 330 (fax) Komarek@BIC.CVUT.cz cvut.cz
Society of Science and Technology Parks of the Czech Republic	N/A	Pavel Svejda, Society of Science and Technology Parks of the Czech Republic, Novotneho Lavka 5, CZ-11668 Praha 1	00 420 2 21 08 22 74 00 420 2 21 08 22 76 (fax)
Technology Park Brno	A low-density development providing modern business premises for technology companies in a business park environment.	Technology Park Brno, Technicka 15, 616 00 Brno, Czech Republic	00 420 5 4119 11122 00 420 5 4119 1133 (fax) info@technologypark.cz technologypark.cz
The Science and Technology Park (Ostrava)	The technology park offers business development and employment in the area of high-technologies. The park covers 10 hectares and three phases of development are planned to the year 2005.	Jaromer Dudek, Vedecko-Technology Park (Ostrava), 17 Listopadu 15, 708 33 Ostrava-Poruba, Czech Republic	00 420 69 6996304 00 420 69 6996159 (fax) mmo.cz

Hungary

Institution	Description	Contact address	Telephone/e-mail/website
Ajka and Regional Business Development Centre	Involved with furniture manufacturing, tailoring, insurance, transportation, glassworks, and commerce.	Anna Somogyi, Ajka and Regional Business Development Centre, Esze Tamás u. 1 8400 Ajka	00 36 88 312987 00 36 88 201818 (fax) ajka-ti@veszzprem-hvk.hu
Bacs-Kiskun County Business Development Foundation	Industry, services, trade technology training, databases etc.	Mr Tamas Tokovics, Business Development Foundation, Ipoly u. 1/a, 6000 Kecskemet	00 36 76 485679 00 36 76 485684 (fax) info@bacslea.hu
Baranya County Business Development Foundation	Internet services, consulting, commerce.	Ms Gyongyi Farkas, Baranya County Business Development Foundation, Felsomalom ut 13, 7621 Pecs	00 36 72 214050 00 36 72 214050 (fax) omvk@mail.matav.hu
Bivak Budapest Youth Enterprise Centre	Marketing, installations and decorations, hostess service, fashion, software and hardware, IT, web design, e-commerce, pottery and ceramics, telecommunications.	Mr Miklos Mlynarik, Bivak Budapest Youth Enterprise Centre, Balasz Bela u. 18, 1094, Budapest	00 36 1 456 9090 00 36 1 456 9190 (fax) byec@matav-net.hu bivak@mail.poli.hu
Entrepreneurial Centre of Bekescsaba Ltd Business Incubator Centre	The incubator supports the following industries: car service, retail, commerce, dentistry, architecture, and transportation.	Mr Janos Sztanko, Innostart National Business and Innovation Centre Ketegyhazi ut 3, 5600 Bekescsaba	00 36 66 442720 00 36 66 442720 (fax) bic@bekes.hungary.net
Hungarian Association for Innovation	Providers of help and assistance with the development of new products and processes.	Hungarian Association for Innovation, Oktober huszonharmadika u. 16, H-1117 Budapest	00 36 118 69 61 5 00 36 118 52 18 1 (fax)

Institution	Description	Contact address	Telephone/e-mail/website
Innonet Innovation and Technclogy Centre	Software, mechanical engineering, industrial services, communications, commerce.	Mr Laszlo Buddavari, Innonet Innovation and Technology Centre, Gesztenyefa ut 4, 9027 Gyor, Ipari Park	00 36 96 5006900 00 36 96 506901 (fax) lbudavari@innonet.hu innonet.hu
Innostart Hungary National Business and Innovation	Full range of services/services to industry.	Kinga Garab, Innostart Hungary National Business and Innovation, Fehervari ut 130, 1116 Budapest	00 36 1 382 15 00 00 36 1 382 15 10 (fax) garab@innostart.hu innostart.hu
Innostart National Business and Innovation Centre	Metallurgy, technology, software, book-keeping, consulting.	Ms Erzsebet Szegner, Innostart Business and Innovation Centre	00 36 1 3821500 00 36 1 3821510 (fax) innostart@innostart.hu innostart.hu
Innotech Technical University Innovation Park	Electrical engeering, software, environment technologies, clothes manufacturing, commerce.	Mr Zoltan Szalai, Innotech Technical University Innovation Park	00 36 1 2084629 00 36 1 2084636 (fax) innotech@mail.matav.hu
Jasz-Nagykun-Szolnok County Business Development Centre	Woodwork, IT, computer software, SME consulting, etc.	Mr Gyorgy Hegmann & Mr Laszlo Turkus, Jasz-Nagykun-Szolnok County Business Development Centre, Jozsef A ut 83, 5000 Szolnok	00 36 56 423134 00 36 56 412319 (fax) info@jnszvfa.hu
Kazincbarcika Business Development Centre	Publishing, advertising, security, consulting.	Mr Lajos Agonas, Kazincbarcika Business Development Centre, Ipoly u. 1/a, 6000 Kecskemet	00 36 76 485679 00 36 76 485684 (fax) Info@bacslea.hu

Name	Services	Contact	Telephone/Fax/Email
Labirintus Office Centre and Incubator Ltd	N/A	Ms Timea Merteny, Labirintus Office Centre and Incubator Ltd, Lonyai u. 3, 1093 Budapest	00 36 2 216220 00 36 1 2162362 (fax)
Nograd County Business Development Foundation	Construction planning, technology, commerce.	Mr Gusztav Brunda, Nograd County Business Development Foundation, Rakoczi ut 36, 3100 Salgotarjan	00 36 32 520300 00 36 32 520304 (fax) nmva@elender.hu
Ozd Enterprise Centre Incubator Foundation	Catering services, commerce.	Mr Bela Torok, Ozd Enterprise Centre Incubator Foundation, Jaszi Oszkar ut 3, 3600 Ozd	00 36 48 473626 ovk@mail.matav.hu
PRIMON Business Incubation Centre	Sound and light technology, laser technology, catering, legal services, book-keeping.	Mr Istvan Zsukk, Primom Business Incubation Centre, Cavi Mihaly u 41, 4400 Nyiregyhaza	00 36 42 502101 00 36 42 502102 (fax) nyirinku@szabinet.hu
Progress Business Development Foundation	Production: metal and building elements; services: repair of utilities, commerce.	Mr Ferenc Renko, Progress Business Development Foundation, Tisza L krt 63, 6722 Szeged	00 36 62 441111 00 36 62 483233 (fax) info@lea-szeged.hu
Somogy-Flandria Business Incubators	Software, transportation, design, car dealership, financial services, commerce and information technology.	Mr Zoltan Csordas, Somogy-Flandria Business Incubators, Ond vezer u. 1, 7400 Kaposvar	00 36 82 500700 00 36 82 500787 info@somogy-hvk.hu
Szekesfeharvar Entrepreneur Centre	Building industry, information technology, software, publishing, etc.	Mr Istvan Annus, Szekesfehervar Entrepreneur Centre, Seregelyesi ut 113, 8000 Szekesfehervar	00 36 22 328102 00 36 22 328110 (fax) titkarsag@szvk.hu

Institution	Description	Contact address	Telephone/e-mail/website
Tolna County Business Development Foundation	IT, commerce.	Mr. Marton Braun, Tolna County Business Development Foundation, Augusz Imre ut 1–3, 7100 Szekszard	00 36 74 319166 00 36 74 311410 (fax) vallkozp@terrasofl.hu
Vallalkozok Haza	Legal services, real estate agency, driving school insurance, financial consulting, commerce.	Mr Sandor Ravasz, Vallalkozok Haza, Arpad ut 21, 2900 Komarom	00 36 34 344485 (phone/fax) komarom@Kemhvk.hu
Vas County & Szombathely Regional Business Development Centre	Engineering, commerce, book-keeping, communications.	Mr Ferenc Bocskei, Vas County & Szombathely Regional Business Development Centre, Petofi S.u 1/B.Pf. 198 9700 Szombathely	00 36 94 326049 00 36 94 326048 (fax) vas-lea@savaria.hu
Veszprem Regional Innovation Centre	Chemical engineering, commerce.	Mr Zoltan Repasy, Veszprem Regional Innovation Centre, Jozsef A. u. 34, Pf. 459 8200 Veszprem	00 36 88 407258 (phone/fax) veszpremti@veszprem-hvk.hu
Welfare Service Foundation – Sumeg Zalaerdod	Workshop, clothing manufacturers, commerce.	Mr Jozsef Bodis, Welfare Service Foundation – Sumeg Zalaerdod, Rendeki u. 14, Pf. 17 8330 Sumeg	00 36 87 350421 (phone/fax)
Zala County Business Development Foundation	Insurance, Federation of International Private Transporters, TNT, Worldwide Express.	Ms Livia Domok, Zala County Business Development Foundation, Koztarsasag ut 17 8901, Pf. 116 8900 Zalaegerszeg	00 36 92 316033 00 36 92 316062 (phone/fax) info_zmva@mail.sienet.hu

Institution	Description	Contact address	Telephone/e-mail/website
Zala County Business Development Foundation Incubator House Lenti	N/A	Mr Andras Horvath, Zala County Business Development Foundation Incubator House Lenti	00 36 92 551850 00 36 42 352285 lenti_zmva@zalasz.am.hu
Zala County Entrepreneur Centre Incubator House	Commerce.	Ms Zsuzsanna Part, Zala County Entrepreneur Centre Incubator House, Csany I u. 2, 8790 Zalaszentgrot	00 36 83 360410 (phone/fax) sztgrot_zmva@zalaszam.hu
Zemplen County Business Development Foundation	Bakery, consulting, commerce, publishing, mobile communications.	Mr Sandor Szabadka, Zemplen County Business Development Foundation, Rakoczi u. 18, 3980 Satoraljaujhely	00 36 47 523080 00 36 47 322919 (fax) zrva@mail.matav.hu

Latvia

Institution	Description	Contact address	Telephone/e-mail/website
Latvian Association of Technological Parks, Innovation Centres and Business Incubators	Services to SME/entrepreneurs in set regions.	Janis Stabulnieks, Latvian Association of Technological Parks, Aizkrauklesstr. 21, LV-1006 Riga	00 371 225 58 66 3 00 371 275 41 21 8 (fax)

Lithuania

Institution	Description	Contact address	Telephone/e-mail/website
Association of Lithuanian Innovation Networks	N/A	Association of Lithuanian Innovation Networks/co/Kaunus Innovation Centre, K. Donelaicio Street. 73, LT-3006 Kaunas	00 370 7 300 691 00 370 7 300 692 (fax) p.milius@cr.ktu.lt ediaclit.vtk.ktu.lt
KUT Innovation Centre	KUT are keen to become partners in the field of SME support, technology transfer and commercialization, regional development, etc.	KUT Innovation Centre, K. Donelaicio 73, LT-3006 Kaunas	00 370 7 300691 00 370 7 300690 (fax) idc@cr/ktu.lt idc.ktc.lt

Poland

Institution	Description	Contact address	Telephone/e-mail/website
Centre for Advanced Technology	The technology park is spread over 66.48 hectares. Managed by the Centre for Advanced Technology.	Centre for Advanced Technology – Krakow, ul. Studencka 7/3a, 31–216 Krakow	00 48 12 4284980 00 48 12 4226525 cztk@czt.cc.pl czt.cc.pl
Polish Business and Innovation Centres Association	The idea was modeled by those in Western Europe and the US. Incubator sites are Innovation Centre Ltd in Gdansk, Centre for Emerging Technology Enterprises in Warsaw, Progress and Business Incubator in Cracow.	Ul Polanka 6, 61–131 Poznan, Poland PBICA, Rubiez 46, PL-61612 Poznan	00 48 61 86 59 65 1 00 48 61 86 59 56 8 (fax) soipp@soipp.org.pl soipp.org.pl
Progress & Business Foundation (P & B Incubator Ltd)	Founded in 1991 due to needs and circumstances of a free economy – volunteers required to provide assistance in scientific research, technology transfer consultancy, promotion, educational advice and fund-raising.	Progress & Business Foundation, ul. Miechowska 5b, 30–041 Krakow, 16	00 48 12 6360100 00 48 12 6368787 pbf@agh.edu.pl pbf.pl

Institution	Description	Contact address	Telephone/e-mail/website
Solarex ul	Consultancy firm specializing in market research projects such as consumer goods, industrial products, telecoms and e-business enables your business to profit from expansion into Poland.	Solarex ul. Kasztanowa 27, 10–156 Olsztyn, Poland	00 48 533 1013 00 48 89 533 3978 (fax) info@solarex.pl solarex.pl
Technology Transfer Centre	Founded in 1997 in recognition of the growing trend in technology for the Polish economy. The centre advises innovative Polish companies, in areas such as high-tech solutions and innovations, economics, finance, training, legal assistance, business planning, etc.	Tomasz Dyras, Technology Transfer Centre, ul. Miechowska 5B, 30 041 Kracow	00 48 12 636 0100 00 48 12 636 8787 pbf@agh.edu.pl pbf.pl

Russia

Institution	Description	Contact address	Telephone/e-mail/website
Russian National Business Incubators Association Academy of Management and the Market	Providers help and advice to SMEs.	Veniamin Sh. Kaganov, Russian National Business Incubators Association, Zazepa Street, 41, RUS-113054 Moscow	00 7 95 56 48 18 3 00 7 95 95 57 93 7 (fax) kagan@morozov.ru morozov.ru

Slovakia

Institution	Description	Contact address	Telephone/e-mail/website
BIC Banska Bystrica	Range of services to businesses.	Mirtoslav Ursiny, BIC Banska Bystrica, Serverna 5, 97401 Banska Bystrica, Slovakia	00 421 88 412 42 24 00 421 88 412 42 20 (fax) Bicbb@psgnetbb.sk psgnetbb.sk

Institution	Description	Contact address	Telephone/e-mail/website
BIC Bratislava	Range of services to businesses.	Roman Linczenyi, BIC Bratislava, Zochova 5, 811 03 Bratislava, Slovakia	00 421 7 544 11 195 00 421 7 544 17 522 (fax) Femirc@bicba.sk bicba.sk
BIC Prievidza Ltd	Full range of services to businesses.	Frantisek Vrtak, BIC Prievidza Ltd, Hviezdoslavova 3, 971 01 Prievidza, Slovakia	00 421 8625 424 101 00 421 8625 426 733 (fax) Bicpd@bb.telecom.sk prievidza.sk
BIC Spisska Nova Ves	Full range of services to businesses.	Katarina Krotakova, BIC Spisska Nova Ves, Zimna 72, 05201 Spisska Nova Ves, Slovakia	00 421 965 44 26 254 (phone/fax) Bicsnv@spisnet.sk
Cassovia BIC	Full range of services to businesses to provide direct support to existing and newly created SMEs.	Ivan Pezlar, Cassovia BIC, Napajadla 2, 04012 Kosice, Slovakia	00 421 95 674 09 11 00 421 95 729 99 81 3 (fax) Bicke@napri.sk box.sk/bicke

Slovenia

Institution	Description	Contact address	Telephone/e-mail/website
BSC Kranj	To assist new and established SMEs, support businesses, network etc.	BSC Kranj, Lubljanska Cesta 24A, 6400 Kranj	00 386 64 33 11 33 00 386 64 33 13 13 (fax) bsc.kranj@siol.net bsc.net
Technology Park Ljubljana	Provides support to technology companies as well as assisting in the development of new technologies, products and services.	Technology Park Ljubljana, Jamova 39, SI–1000 Ljubljana	00 386 1 477 66 13 00 386 1 477 66 00 00 386 1 426 18 79 (fax) info@tp-lj.si tp-lj.si

Ukraine

Institution	Description	Contact address	Telephone/e-mail/website
Ukrainian Business Incubators and Innovation Centres Association	N/A	Igor Leleka, Ukranian Business Incubators and Innovation Centres Association, Petscherski Spusk 3, UA-01023 Kiew	00 380 44 23 56 210 (phone/fax) Igor@prime.net.ua

THE US

Institution	Description	Contact address	Telephone/e-mail/website
Advanced Technology Development Center	The Advanced Technology Development Center exists to help technology-based entrepreneurs who reside in Georgia. Within the Center's mission of supporting technology business is an educational component – to help provide the starting point for the entrepreneurial novice to begin climbing the steep learning curve that, in time, can produce a competitive technology business.	Advanced Technology Development Center, 430 10th Street, NW Suite N-116 Atlanta, GA 30318	001 404 894 3575 001 404 894 4545 (fax) atdc.org
Alameda Center for Environmental Technology	Alameda Center for Environmental Technology focuses on the promotion of environmental technology and is committed to nurturing new environmentally-related businesses; providing 'wet' laboratories for environmental entrepreneurs; transferring innovative and new technologies from the national laboratories; and offering incubator services that help small businesses grow and prosper.	Alameda Center for Environmental Technology, Acet Corporation, 851 West Midway Avenue, Building 7, Alameda Point, Alameda, CA 94501–5085	001 510 749 3977 001 510 749 6862 (fax) acet@greenstart.org greenstart.org

Institution	Description	Contact	Telephone/e-mail/website
Appalachian Center for Economic Networks	The Appalachian Center for Economic Networks (ACEnet) is a community-based economic development organization. ACEnet's purpose is to work with others in the area to create a healthy regional economy with many successful businesses and good jobs. ACEnet's goal is for people with low incomes to move out of poverty permanently through employment or business ownership.	Appalachian Center for Economic Networks, 94 Columbus Road, Athens, OH	001 740 592 3854 001 740 593 5451 (fax) acenetworks.org
Applied Process Engineering Laboratory	The Applied Process Engineering Laboratory is a state-of-the-art technology business start-up centre with engineering and manufacturing scale space as well as wet labs, bio labs, and business start-up space. You can start up your business, plug in your prototype or pilot plant to their utilities, services, and permits and be up and running. You can develop and validate your new ideas in their labs and test spaces.	Chuck R Allen, Applied Process Engineering Laboratory, 350 Hills Street, Suite #101, Richland, WA 99352	001 509 372 5146 001 509 372 5153 (fax) crallen@wnp2.com apel.org
Arco-Butte Business Incubation Center	The Arco/Butte Business Incubation Center (BIC) was started to assist existing and start-up businesses increase job opportunities in Butte County. The BIC assists existing businesses in the community and works on community projects such as grant writing, assisting schools, working with local community groups and assisting the City of Arco and the County with infrastructure improvements.	Arco-Butte Business Incubation Center	001 208 527 3060 001 208 527 3036 (fax) bic@atcnet.net businessidaho.org
Arizona Technology Incubator	Alumni include BuyingDecisions, Inc., Echotech International, Inc., Leading Edge Technologies ProLink, Inc., Grid Data, Inc., The Rouse Companies.	Sandie Hunter, Arizona Technology Incubator	ati@gpec.org accessarizona.com

Name	Description	Address	Contact
Austin Technology Incubator	The Austin Technology Incubator (ATI), as a part of the IC2 Institute and the University of Texas at Austin, was created in 1989 to facilitate the growth and development of technology companies. While supporting Austin by creating jobs and diversifying the economy, ATI also provides educational value for University of Texas faculty and students. Fifty companies have 'graduated' from ATI including five which have gone on to have IPOs.	Austin Technology Incubator, 3925 West Braker Lane, Austin, TX 78759	001 512 305 0000 001 512 305 0009 (fax) ic2.org
Bonner Business Center	The Bonner Business Center (BBC) is a small business incubator created to encourage and assist the development of new businesses in North Idaho. The BBC provides affordable, ready-to-go facilities and a place where new and/or early-stage businesses can operate and prepare for long-term success.	Bonner Business Center, 804 Airport Way, Sandpoint, ID 83864	001 208 263 4073 001 208 263 4609 (fax) sandpoint.org
Boulder Technology Incubator (Colorado)	Alumni include Basonics Fatty Tuna, LLC Freeflyr, Automation CDM, Optics, Inc., PatientFile.com Sales, Data Solutions, Inc.	Boulder Technology Incubator (Colorado), Marine Street Science Building, 3215 Marine Street, Boulder, CO 80303	001 303 492 8585 001 303 735 4499 (fax)
Business Center of Decatur	The Business Center of Decatur is a business incubator in which a number of new and growing businesses operate with affordable rents, shared office services and access to professional, technical and financial assistance during early, critical stages of development.	Business Center of Decatur, 2121 S. Imboden Court, Decatur, IL 62521	001 217 423 2832 001 217 423 7214 (fax) decaturcenter.com
Business Cluster Development	The Business Cluster Development (BCD) was created to assist communities in developing incubators or business clusters and to help start-up businesses to obtain inexpensive office space, services, and management assistance. BCD uses an innovative model which utilizes donated facilities and furniture to provide low-cost and rapid creation of incubators.	Business Cluster Development, 1600 N Castanya Menlo Park, CA 94028	001 650 854 1707 jarobbins@aol.com clusterdevelopment.com

Institution	Description	Contact	Telephone/e-mail/website
Business Innovation Center (Center for Entrepreneurial Excellence)	This BIC is a multi-tenant facility sponsored by Mobile County, the City of Mobile and the Mobile Area Chamber of Commerce. The incubator provides an ideal environment to nurture and launch new business concepts.	Lynn Stacey, Director, Business Innovation Center, 1301 Azalea Road, Mobile, AL 36693	001 334 660 7002 ceebic@ceebic.org ceebic.org. mobilechamber.com
Business Resource Center (McLennan Community College Small Business Development Center)	The Business Resource Center is an organized effort to bring together new and existing organizations and programmes to provide support systems that promote successful development of business. Designed to meet the needs of just about anyone who owns a small business or is interested in starting a business, the Business Resource Center houses several business assistance programmes at the same location.	McLennan Community College Small Business Development Center, Business Resource Center, 401 Franklin Avenue, Waco, TX 76701 – 2108	001 254 714 0077 001 254 714 1668 (fax) sbdc@sbdcc-waco.com mccweb.mcc.cc.tx.us
Business Technology Center of Los Angeles County	The BTC seeks to help reestablish businesses and employment opportunities in industries impacted by aerospace and defence cutbacks, by assisting firms in the fields of communications, Internet, and software development.	Business Technology Center of Los Angeles County Susan J Prado, 2400 Lincoln Avenue, Altadena, CA 91001	001 626 296 6301 001 626 296 6300 (fax)
CALSTART Advanced Transportation Business Incubators	The purpose of CALSTART Advanced Transportation Business Incubators is to serve as a fertile breeding ground for new companies with good ideas. The incubators are designed to nurture the next generation of leaders in the advanced transportation industry.	CALSTART Advanced Transportation Business Incubators, 2181 East Foothill Boulevard, Pasadena, CA 91107	001 626 744 5600 calstart.org

Name	Description	Address	Contact
Cambridge Incubator	Founded in 1999, Cambridge Incubator (CI) is the first and largest seed-stage Internet incubator in New England. CI invests in promising business concepts and accelerates their market launch by offering such services as product architecture, marketing, fund-raising, and recruitment of key personnel. CI refers to this process as Active Incubation™.	Tim Rowe, Cambridge Incubator, 238 Main Street, Suite 324, Cambridge, MA 02142	001 617 491 8968 001 617 491 8970 (fax) cambridgeincubator.com
Center for Applied Competitive Technologies (San Diego)	Since 1990, the Center for Applied Competitive Technologies (San Diego) has served over 300 local firms, using a database of professional and technical experts to deliver high quality client services. The Center provides assistance in gaining access to resources for technology development, technical training, computer integration, shop floor management, and a wide range of services.	Joan A Stepsis PhD, Center for Applied Competitive Technologies, San Diego City College, 1313 Twelfth Avenue, San Diego, CA 92101	001 619 230 2588 001 619 230 2080 (fax) jstepsis@sdccd.cc.ca.us bmpcoe.org
Chicago Southland Enterprise Center	The Chicago Southland Enterprise Center is a small business incubator owned and operated by Chicago Southland Development, Inc., a not-for-profit corporation. As a member of the National Business Incubation Association, the enterprise centre constantly stays abreast of any sources for business assistance and legislative developments that affect the entrepreneur.	Chicago Southland Enterprise Center, 1655 Union in Chicago Heights, IL	001 708 754 6960 001 708 754 8779 (fax) DeYoung@enterprisecenter.org enterprisecenter.org
CMGI	CMGI has a market capitalization in excess of $15 billion and a network of 65+ internet businesses.	CMGI Corporate, 100 Brickstone Square, Andover, MA 1810	001 978 684 3600 001 978 684 3658 (fax) cmgi.com
College of Southern Idaho Business Incubator	The College of Southern Idaho Business Incubator offers assistance to start-up businesses by providing affordable rent, flexible space and lease options, business services and equipment, and consulting in the areas of management, book-keeping, marketing and financing. In addition, the incubator provides its tenants with the opportunity to 'network' with other businesses and agencies.	College of Southern Idaho Business Incubator, 315 Falls Avenue, PO Box 1238, Twin Falls, ID 83303–1238	001 208 733 9554 001 800 680 0274 csi.edu

Institution	Description	Contact	Telephone/e-mail/website
Colorado Advanced Technology Institute	Through a number of public/private partnerships governed by industry-led boards, the Colorado Advanced Technology Institute (CATI) fosters high-tech industrial growth through academic research and new business formations. CATI programmes encompass applied research, industry/university seed grants, product and process development laboratories for students to work with industry, and business incubators.	Jeff Richardson, Colorado Advanced Technology Institute	001 303 620 4777 jefr@cati.org bcn.boulder.co.uk
Colorado Venture Centers, Inc.	Gonex, Inc, Universal Infusion Technology, LLC Daystar Energy Corp., TherapyZone.com, Inc., GeneThera, Inc., and Mortgageline.com, Inc.	Colorado Venture Centers, Inc., 1610 Pierce Street, Texas Building, Lakewood, CO 80214	001 303 237 3998 001 303 237 4010 (fax)
Communications Technology Cluster	Zimba, Xplica, Ultima, WomensRadio.com, QTrademark.com, SnailGram.com.	Communications Technology Cluster 2201, 300 Frank Ogawa Plaza, 2nd Floor, Oakland, CA 94612	001 510 836 8985 001 510 836 8987 (fax) kkim@ctcluster.com ctcluster.com
Contra Costa Software Business Incubator	The Contra Costa Software Business Incubator (CCSBI) is a non-profit educational and charitable corporation whose mission is 1) to create new job opportunities for local residents and, 2) to further the economic development goals of local governments. CCSBI uses the proven process of business incubation as its primary means of achieving these objectives. CCSBI's educational and business assistance programmes are designed to support entrepreneurial development and business ownership in order to assure the long-term economic stability and quality of life in the region.	Contra Costa Software Business Incubator, 2440 Stanwell Drive, Concord, CA 94520	001 925 681 1855 001 925 691 7019 (fax) ccsbi.com

Name	Description	Address	Contact
CSI Business Incubator	The CSI Small Business Incubator focuses specifically on the education and training of businesses that are in need of specialized business counselling. The Incubator provides a 'protected' environment until the client is able to make an educated decision regarding their success in the business arena. The Incubator aids start-up businesses with education and support.	Business Incubator, College of Southern Idaho, 315 Falls Avenue, P.O. Box 1238, Twin Falls, ID 83303–1238	001 208 733 9554 Ext. 2450 001 208 733 9316 (fax)
Dunn-Richmond Economic Development Center	Designed to house three types of businesses – light manufacturing, research and development, and service. The Center provides a nurturing environment for start-up and emerging businesses by providing flexible work areas, cost-effective production space, counselling and mentoring by experienced individuals in business, and by utilizing shared resources such as Fax, Xerox, message centre, mail drop-off, and meeting rooms.	Marianne Lather, Co-ordinators of Scheduling Office of Economic and Regional Development, Southern Illinois Unviersity, Carbondale, Carbondale, IL 62901	001 618 536 4047 001 618 453 5040 (fax) mlather@siu.edu siu.edu
Early Bird Capital	Focuses on the globalization of portfolio companies.	Early Bird Capital, One State Street Plaza, New York, NY 10004	001 212 792 8100 001 212 269 3787 (fax) info@earlybirdcapital.com earlybirdcapital.com
EC²@USC (University of Southern California)	Egg Company 2 (EC²), the new high-tech business incubator at the University of Southern California's Annenburg Centre for Communication. EC² offers its occupants a complete support system for up to three years to enhance entrepreneurial success.	EC²@USC, 746 West Adams Boulevard, Los Angeles, CA 90089-7727	001 213 743 2344 001 213 746 1226 (fax) info@ec2.edu ec2.edu
eCompanies	efavorites.com, ememories.com, eParties, Icebox, Business.com, Change.com.	ECompanies, 2120 Colorado Avenue, 4th Floor, Santa Monica, CA 90404	001 310 586 4000 001 310 586 4005 (fax) info@ecompanies.com ecompanies.com

Institution	Description	Contact	Telephone/e-mail/website
Enterprise Center (Massachusetts)	The Enterprise Center is a mixed-use business park with space available to established companies and those seeking their first commercial address. The Center features on-site support services, as well as an unusual business incubator programme and an entrepreneurs' network to help new and emerging businesses develop and thrive.	Springfield Enterprise Center, One Federal Street, Springfield, MA 01105	001 413 755 4367 001 413 739 5066 (fax) fandrews@stcc.mass.edu eship.org
Enterprise Center (Missouri)	The mission of the Enterprise Center is to provide information, training, and skills building programmes that aid the residents of the state of Missouri in reaching their business and employment goals.	Missouri Enterprise Business Assistance Center, 800 West 14th Street, Suite 111, Rolla, MS	001 800 956 2862 missourienterprise.org
Enterprise Center (Pennsylvania)	The Enterprise Center is a non-profit organization whose mission is to stimulate economic growth in West Philadelphia through entrepreneurship. Founded in 1989, it operates a small business incubator, providing entrepreneurs with offices, technical assistance, and a formal system of business development.	Enterprise Center (Pennsylvania) Contact: Della Clark, 4548 Market Street, Philadelphia, PA 19139	001 215 895 4000 wpec.org
Enterprise Center of Johnson County	Its mission is to stimulate business creation and employment in Johnson County by providing value-added resources and services to early-stage, high growth-oriented companies.	Enterprise Center of Johnson County, 9875 Widmer Road, Lenexa, KS 66215	001 913 438 2282 001 913 888 6928 (fax) info@ecjc.com ecjc.com
Enterprise Center of Louisiana	Its mission is to provide an environment in which a new or small emerging business can learn effective business practices while engaging in business operations, with the end result of creating jobs and diversifying the economy.	Stephen E Durrett, Enterprise Center of Louisiana, 3419 NW Evangeline Thruway, Carencro, LA	001 337 896 9115 001 337 896 8736 (fax) acadianabiz.com
Enterprise North Florida Corporation	ENFC is an independent not-for-profit corporation committed to its mission of nurturing job growth in North Florida's high-technology and manufacturing industries. To accomplish this, ENFC provides its clients with services critical for start up and growth.	Enterprise North Florida Corporation, 7400 Baymeadows Way, Suite 201, Jacksonville, FL 32256	001 904 730 4700 001 904 730 4711 (fax) teonline.com

Name	Description	Address	Contact
Entrepreneurial Center (previously Birmingham Business Assistance Network)	Dedicated to helping small service and light manufacturing businesses develop, grow and succeed. By providing business plan counselling, a strong support network and affordable space and services to start-up businesses, BBAN encourages entrepreneurship while minimizing some of the risk.	Entrepreneurial Center, 110 12th Street North, Birmingham, AL 35203	001 205 250 8000 001 205 250 8013 (fax) entrepreneurialctr.com
Florida/NASA Business Incubation Center	The Florida/NASA Business Incubation Center is a business incubator serving the location needs of early-stage technology-based entrepreneurs. The Center seeks to encourage and stimulate technology-based small business formation, growth, and success. Through offering affordable space, shared office equipment and services, the Center makes it possible to reduce many of the costs associated with establishing and operating a business.	Florida/NASA Business Incubation Center, 5195 South Washington Avenue, Titusville, FL 32780	001 321 269 6330 001 321 383 5260 (fax) admin@trda.org trda.org
Fort Worth MedTech Center	The Fort Worth MedTech Center, Inc. is a privately funded non-profit business incubator that provides specialized and industry-specific business assistance to medical and high-tech start-up companies. This economic development effort provides a mechanism that facilitates the growth and development of emerging medical and technology companies in Fort Worth.	Fort Worth MedTech Center, 2912 West Pafford Street, Fort Worth, TX 76110–5830	001 817 207 8550 001 817 207 8545 infor@medtech.org medtech.org
Generics Group (UK, Sweden, Switzerland)	Generics (now a subsidiary of a Swedish firm Catella) was co-founded in 1986 by Gordon Edge at Cambridge University. Invests in intellectual property and capital only. See also European listings.	The Generics Group, Inc., 1601 Trapelo Road, Waltham, MA 02451	001 781 290 0500 001 781 290 0501 (fax) generics.com
Genesis Medical Technology Inc, 11403 Cronhill Drive, Suite B, Ownings Mills, Baltimore, MD 21117	001 410 654 0090 genesismedical.com
Genesis Business Centers, Ltd.	Offers a programme of rent combined with valuable professional services in exchange for a negotiated equity position in your company. Genesis is looking for the best and the brightest of the new high-tech start-ups in Minnesota.	Harlan T. Jacombs, Genesis Business Centers Ltd., 3989 Central Ave NE, Suite 630 Columbia Heights, MN 55421	001 763 782 8576 001 763 782 8578 (fax) genesiscenters.com

Institution	Description	Contact	Telephone/e-mail/website
Genesis (at the University of Arkansas)	Companies incubated here include Bioengineering Resources, DayCo, EarthCare Technologies, ElectroMap, Inc., Tangent Computers and Vector, Inc.	Genesis (at the University of Arkansas), 1 University of Arkansas, Fayetteville, AR 72701–1201, Physical Address: 700 Research Center Boulevard, Fayetteville, AR 72701	001 501 575 7227 001 501 575 7446 (fax) genesis@cavern.uark.edu
Golden Triangle Enterprise Center	The Golden Triangle Enterprise Center was established to assist new, high-tech companies in overcoming the hardships of starting a new business. Currently the Center is home to software development, geographical information systems, web page design and services, online cattle auction, graphic design, and design simulation companies.	Golden Triangle Enterprise Center, One Research Boulevard, Suite 201, Starkville, MS 39759	001 662 320 3990 info@gtec.org gtec.org
Gorilla Park	Gorilla Park is an incubator and idea-generator for high-tech entrepreneurs who want to create Internet companies and grow them quickly into world-class organizations.	Gorilla Park, San Francisco, 576 Folsom Street, San Francisco, CA 94105	001 415 357 1889 001 415 683 7193 (fax) info@gorillapark.com gorillapark.com
Ground Floor Ventures	Ground Floor Ventures was established as a high-tech business incubator that closes the gender gap. GFV provides women-founded, owned, or operated software and e-businesses with an environment where they can thrive. It is the place women can choose when they want a fair shot at the resources needed to get their businesses started.	Ground Floor Ventures, 720 Monroe Street, Suite E-209, Hoboken, NJ 07030	001 201 420 4446 001 201 420 9176 (fax) groundfloorventures.com
Hampton Roads Technology Incubator	The purpose of the HRTI is to promote economic development of Hampton Roads through the commercialization of new technologies developed at NASA's Langley Research Center, local universities, and other regional government and industrial R&D laboratories. The mission of the HRTI is to: increase the number of successful technology-based companies originating in,	Marty Kaszubowski, Hampton Roads Technology Incubator, Hampton Roads, 24 Research Drive, Hampton, VA 23666	001 757 865 2141 001 757 865 0298 (fax) hr-incubator.org

Name	Description	Address	Contact
	developing in, or relocating to the Hampton Roads area; help technology-based companies gain access to the technologies that will help them better compete in a global marketplace; and sponsor and administer programmes to nurture new entrepreneurs in establishing and operating their companies.		
Health-Medical Enterprise Center	The Health-Medical Enterprise Center (H-MEC) is a business incubator for fast-track health and medical-related business owners. The H-MEC uses business development and entrepreneurial education programmes pioneered by the Entrepreneurial Development Center, Houston's first and Texas's oldest business incubator, to accelerate business growth for entrepreneurs in emerging businesses.	Services Co-operative Assocation, 9600 Long Point Road, Suite 150, Houston, TX 77055	001 713 932 7495 001 713 932 7498 (fax) service@serviceSCA.org servicesca.org
High Technology of Rochester	The mission of High Technology of Rochester (HTR) is to enhance working relationships between government, industry, academia, and professional organizations in ways that will facilitate business development and growth. HTR can also provide assistance to start-ups in the field of innovation regarding interactive multimedia.	High Technology of Rochester, 5 United Way, Rochester, NY 14604	001 716 327 7920 infor@htr.org htr.org
Idaho Innovation Center	Companies incubated include MeltTran, Environmental Research and Development (ERAD), Applied Engineering Services, SSR Technology, Inc., and Control Vision.	Idaho Innovation Center, 2300 North Yellowstone Highway, Idaho Falls, ID 83401	001 208 523 1026 001 208 528 7127 (fax) henry@micron.net epa.gov
Ideacubator	Ideacubator was founded in October 1998 by Anthony E Bayer to develop start-ups globally by bringing together talented management and entrepreneurs from emerging markets to develop the next generation of start-ups.	Ideacubator, 1135H Mason Ct, Treasure Island, San Francisco, CA 94130	001 415 765 9904

Institution	Description	Contact	Telephone/e-mail/website
idealab! (see also UK)	Founded in March 1996 by Bill Gross, currently has 50 businesses in various stages of development. idealab! generates ideas for new Internet businesses and creates, capitalizes and operates a separate company to conduct each new business.	idealab! HQ, 130 West Union Street, Pasedena CA 91103	001 626 585 6900 001 626 535 2701 (fax)
		idealab! Boston, 181 Newbury Street, Boston, MA 02116	001 617 867 7000 001 617 867 7001 (fax)
		idealab! Silicon Valley, 380 Portage Avenue, Palo Alto, CA 94306	001 650 251 5500 001 650 251 5501 (fax)
		idealab! New York, 675 Avenue of the Americas, New York, NY 10010	001 212 420 7700 001 212 929 4423 (fax) idealab.com
I-Group HotBank NE, a SoftBank Affiliate	I-Group HotBank focuses on three primary areas that are critical to the success of entrepreneurial companies and provides business strategy, access to initial customers and executive recruiting.	I-Group HotBank NE, 355 Commonwealth Avenue, Boston, MA 02115 P	001 617 638 3000 i-group.com
i-Hatch	Matches experienced practitioners in the Internet space with the founding teams of Internet ventures; injects seed capital; and provides hands-on support.	i-Hatch Ventures, 200 Park Avenue, 17th floor, New York, NY 10166	info@i-Hatch.com
Incubator, Inc.	The company's key objectives are: to identify promising Internet-related technologies and ideas, and partner with the best and brightest to turn those great ideas into great companies, generate attractive returns for their investors; promote entrepreneurship at UC Berkeley by dedicating a portion of their net profits towards the various programmes and schools on campus.	Incubator, Inc., 2437 Durant Ave., Suite 206, Berkeley, CA 94704	001 510 848 6048 sparky@reel- time.com incubator-inc.com
Innovation Factory	Innovation Factory is in the mentor capital business. They find promising new companies, then give them hands-on business development support, plus state-of-the-art infrastructure and money.	Innovation Factory, 201 Sabine Avenue, Narberth, PA 19072	001 610 227 2100 001 610 617 9316 (fax) innofactory.com

Name	Description	Address	Contact
Intend Change	Incubated companies include: Electron Economy, InveSmart, HyCurve, HardCloud.	Intend Change, 87 Encina Ave, Palo Alto, CA 94301	001 650 289 6600
International Business Center	The International Business Center (IBC) is a business incubator for fast-track importers, exporters and international business owners. The IBC uses business development and entrepreneurial education programmes pioneered by the Entrepreneurial Development Center, Houston's first and Texas' oldest business Incubator, to accelerate business growth for entrepreneurs in emerging businesses.	Services Co-operative Association, 9600 Long Point Road, Suite 150, Houston, TX 77055	001 713 932 7495 / 001 713 932 7498 / service@serviceSCA.org / servicesca.org
International Business Incubator	The International Business Incubator (IBI) is designed to be the first home for international companies expanding to the US for the first time. IBI has furnished space to house more than 45 resident clients who are ready to open their first US office. Resident clients rent on month to month leases and can stay at the IBI for up to two years.	International Business Incubator, 111 N Market Street, San Jose, CA 95113	001 408 351 3300 / 001 408 351 3332 (fax) / intlinc@aol.com / ibi-sv.org
iStart Ventures	Seattle's first Internet business accelerator, providing early-stage concepts with mass (people and resources) and momentum (capital and expertise) to rapidly accelerate the growth of tomorrow's most promising Internet concepts, and allowing entrepreneurs to focus their energies on the execution of their business plans.	iStart Ventures, PO Box 4309, Seattle, WA 93104	001 205 254 7500 / 001 205 254 3557 (fax) / istartventures.com
iVention Group	Its purpose is to identify, create and fund start-up business ventures in the Internet, technology and telecommunications industries.	iVention Group, 5704 Merriam Drive, Merriam, KS 66203-2500	info@ivention.com
i-Web Corporation	Incubated companies include: WebMRI.com, LLC radiology.com, DM Products, TVipo.com, Radioipo.com, FixedLoans.com, iMatters.com, Indipics.com.	James West, President iWeb Corporation, 2034 Cotner Ave, 4th Floor, Los Angeles, CA 90024	001 310 914 9700 / 001 310 914 4567 (fax) / jwest@iwebcorp.com

Institution	Description	Contact	Telephone/e-mail/website
Kansas Innovation Corporation	The Kansas Innovation Corporation (KIC) is a non-profit organization whose mission is to stimulate the creation and growth of technology-based, high-impact businesses in north-east Kansas, and facilitate technology transfer from the region's academic and entrepreneurial communities. Through a formal client relationship KIC provides these companies with strategic and operations assistance including market research, business plan writing and financial planning.	Jeff Alholm, Kansas Innovation Corporation, 1617 St Andrews Drive, Suite 210, Lawrence, KS 66047	001 785 832 2110 001 785 832 8234 (fax) jeff@kic.org, kic@kic.org kic.org
LaunchPower	LaunchPower is an Altos Ventures Incubator focusing on getting early-stage companies with hot ideas to market within six months.	LaunchPower, 167, Hamilton Ave, Fourth Floor, Palo Alto, CA 94301	001 650 566 6600 001 650 321 3274 (fax) jim@launchpower.com
Lewis Incubator for Technology	A business incubator designed to nurture new and emerging technology businesses. LIFT is a co-operative effort of the NASA Lewis Research Center, the Ohio Department of Development, Enterprise Development, Inc., the Great Lakes Industrial Technology Center, and BP America. LIFT's primary objectives are to create business and jobs in the state of Ohio, and to increase the commercial value of technology developed at the NASA Lewis Research Center.	Lewis Incubator for Technology, 16651 Sprague Road, Strongsville, OH 44136	001 440 260 3300 001 440 260 3301 (fax) liftinc.org
Long Island High Technology Incubator	The Long Island High Technology Incubator is a place where start-up companies can begin work immediately. It is also the centre of an economic development network of affiliations with strong ties to technology-related organizations in both the public and private sectors.	Long Island High Technology Incubator, 25 East Loop Road, Stony Brook, NY 11790–3350	001 631 444 8800 001 631 444 8825 (fax) inbox@lihti.org lihti.org
Louisiana Business & Technology Center	The Louisiana Business & Technology Center (LBTC) began in 1988 as a joint venture between LSU, the Greater Baton Rouge Chamber of Commerce and the Louisiana Public Facilities	Charles D'Agostino, Louisiana Business & Technology Center, South Stadium Drive, Baton Rouge, LA 70903–6100	001 225 334 5555 001 225 388 3975 (fax) bus.lsu.edu

	Authority. The LBTC is part of LSU's E.J. Ourso College of Business Administration. There are three parts to the LBTC: 1) the small business incubator provides administrative assistance and overhead facilities to start-up companies allowing them to concentrate on marketing and production; 2) the management assistance office (MAO) assists with business plans, feasibility studies, marketing strategies, and financial, operational and general management consulting; and 3) the Louisiana technology transfer office (LTTO) is run under a contract with the Louisiana Department of Economic Development to be a window for Louisiana businesses to tap into the vast pool of technology developed by federal laboratories.	
Manoa Incubation Center	Incubated companies include CyberCom Logical System Services, Inc, Dimensia, Inc., Oceanic Imaging Consultants, Inc., Ergo Linguistic Technologies, Pacific Area Networks, Inc., FlexNet Inc.	Manoa Innovation Center (MIC), 2800 Woodlawn Drive, Suite 100, Honolulu, Hawaii 96822 — 001 808 539 3600, 001 808 539 3611 (fax), micmgr@htdc.org
Massachusetts Innovation Center	The mission of the Massachusetts Innovation Center is to provide flexible space with unparalleled Internet connectivity, business and technical support services, and a dedicated investment fund. The Center uses a variety of 'harvesting' techniques including, acquisition, royalty and licensing fees, and equity appreciation.	Massachusetts Innovation Center, One Oak Hill Road, Fitchburg, MA 01420 — 001 978 424 2500, info@massinnmass innovation.com
MBI International/ Bio-Business Incubator of Michigan	The MBI International/Bio-Business Incubator of Michigan (BBIM) is an independent non-profit subsidiary created to meet the requirements of start-up biotechnology firms. BBIM offers tenants access to R&D expertise and link to marketing and shared service and support resources.	MBI International/Bio-Business Incubator of Michigan, 3900 Collins Road, Lansing, MI 48909–0609 — 001 517 336 4617, 001 517 337 2122, rivers@mbi.org, isa-usa.org

Institution	Description	Contact	Telephone/e-mail/website
Meridian Technology Center for Business Development	The Meridian Technology Center for Business Development is a business innovation facility designed to encourage the development of new and emerging companies. The Center is a 15 000 square foot facility with private offices, work space and light manufacturing areas. This environment provides entrepreneurs, early-stage technology companies, service companies and companies seeking to commercialize new products the support and strategic assistance necessary to realize their business ideas.	Meridian Technology Center for Business Development, 1312 South Sangre Road, Stillwater, IK 74074–1899	001 405 377 3333 001 888 607 2509 info@meridian-technology.com meridian-technology.com
Mid-America Commercialization Corporation	The Mid-America Commercialization Corporation (MACC) was established to help develop, transfer, and commercialize new technologies. Its objective is to create high-value jobs and increase prosperity in Manhattan and the outlying regions of Kansas. MACC is governed by a board of directors comprised of community, academic, and government leaders, and staffed by internationally experienced managers, with proven track records.	Ron Sampson, Mid-America Commercialization Corporation, 1640 Fairchild Avenue, Manhattan, KS 66502	001 785 537 0110 001 785 537 0226 (fax) macc@kansas.net oa-usa.org
NASA/Ames Incubation Center	The ATCC is a physical and virtual small business incubator, located in San Jose, California, providing opportunities for start-up companies utilizing NASA technologies to grow and become robust high-tech businesses. It uses a lab-to-market approach which takes the technological output of Ames' laboratories and pairs that technology with appropriate markets to create and foster new industry and jobs.	NASA/Ames Incubation Center, 650 Saratoga, San Jose, CA 95117	001 408 557 6700 001 408 557 6799 (fax) ctoserver.arc.nasa.gov
North Central Idaho Business Technology Incubator	The North Central Idaho Business Technology Incubator is a new $1.8 million facility, with over 17 000 square feet of space. The incubator provides affordable space and an array of support services for young, growing companies.	North Central Idaho Business Technology Incubator, University of Idaho, 121 Sweet Avenue, Moscow, ID 83843	001 208 885 2832 001 208 885 3803 (fax) uidaho.edu

Name	Description	Address	Contact
Northeast Alabama Entrepreneurial System	The Northeast Alabama Entrepreneurial System is a business incubation programme for start-up service and light manufacturing businesses. It supports business ideas from the early stage of company development until the graduation stage of growth.	Giles McDaniel, Northeast Alabama Entrepreneurial System, 1400 Commerce Blvd., Suite 1, Anniston, AL 36207	001 256 831 5215 001 256 831 8728 (fax) neaes.org
Northwestern University/ Evanston Research Park	The mission of the Northwestern University/ Evanston Research Park is to accelerate technology transfer from the laboratory to the marketplace by means of a research environment that combines the resources of a major university, a progressive community, and private industry. The park has three major research thrusts: materials and manufacturing technology; biotechnology, including pharmaceutical research; and software development, particularly in the areas of artificial intelligence, robotics, and Internet applications.	Northwestern University/ Evanston Research Park, 63 Clark Street, Evanston, IL 60208	parkinfo@researchpark.com researchpark.com
Oakland Communications Technology Cluster	See Communications Technology Cluster.		
Odessa College Business Incubator	Odessa College opened its business incubator to help small businesses and to diversify the economy of Ector County. A business may be a tenant in the incubator for up to three years, then it must 'graduate' or spin off into the regular business community.	Odessa College Business Incubator, 619 N. Grant Avenue, Odessa, TX 79764	001 915 333 7409 001 915 333 7413 (fax) fgibson@odessa.edu odessa.edu
Office for the Advancement of Developing Industries	The Office for the Advancement of Developing Industries (OADI) is a business incubator that assists high-tech companies in marketing and commercializing their products and services. OADI's mission is to provide Birmingham-based, technology-oriented entrepreneurs with a unique environment that will enhance their start-up companies' chances of success.	Office for the Advancement of Developing Industries (OADI), 2800 Milan Court, Birmingham, AL 35211	001 205 943 6560 001 205 943 6563 (fax) main.uab.edu

Institution	Description	Contact	Telephone/e-mail/website
Ohio University's Innovation Center Program	A business incubator for high-tech firms. It serves as a means to address the university's regional economic development mission, and to provide an outlet for the commercialization of university technology.	Ohio University's Innovation Center Program, 20 E Circle Drive, Suite 190, Athens, OH 45701–3751	001 740 593 1818 001 740 593 0186 (fax) ictto.ohiou.edu
Oregon Innovation Center	The Oregon Innovation Center is a support centre for technology-based companies and entrepreneurs. Utilizing existing and emerging technologies, the Center provides virtual and physical incubator space, capital sourcing, economic facilities, and a wide range of support services to the technological businesses of the future.	Oregon Innovation Center, Millside Building, Suite 204, 231 Scalehouse Loop Bend, OR 97702	001 541 312 5785 001 541 312 5787 (fax) info@innovationcenter.org oregoninnovation.org
Owatonna Business Incubator	Since 1988, the Owatonna Business Incubator has been helping to foster small business growth by creating an environment conducive to entrepreneurial success. Businesses that locate in the Incubator have the resources – loading docks, high ceilings, electrical power, conference room, modern offices, parking – of an all-in-one facility built specifically as a business incubator.	Owatonna Business Incubator, 1065 SW 24th Avenue, PO Box 505, Owatonna, MN 55060	001 507 451 0517 001 507 455 2788 (fax) owatonnaircubator.com
Pacific Technology Center	The Pacific Technology Center is an incubator in support of emerging high-tech companies at various stages of development. The Center is a collaborative development of Bramant Development Company and many Santa Barbara small-business support organizations.	Pacific Technology Center, Patterson Avenue, Santa Barbara, CA 93111	ptc.santabarbara.com
Panasonic Digital Concepts Center	Incubated companies include AudioBasket.com, 2 Roam, Inc., Dynaptics, eMentoring.com, Graphic Gems, IntAcct, InterActual, FortNocs, MagicBeanStalk.com, Vistify.	Panasonic Digital Concepts Center, 19925 Stevens Creek Blvd., Suite #200 Cupertino, CA 95014	001 408 861 3950 001 408 861 3955 (fax) AnitaReynolds@vc.papanasonic.com

Photonics Development Center	The Photonics Development Center (PDC) is a part of the STARTech Business Development Center and is dedicated to the creation of new high-tech start-up companies based on rapidly emerging photonics applications. The PDC is a joint alliance developed by STARTech in assistance with several global information technology companies, university resources, and venture capital firms. STARTech and the PDC alliance are committed to promoting and developing Texas as a key region for development of applications and new companies based on this important technology.	Rob Carruthers, Photonics Development Center, 911 E Arapaho, Suite 190, Richardson, TX 75081	001 972 671 1612 001 972 671 1625 (fax) info@photonics-center.com photonics.-center.com
Product Development Center	The Product Development Center (PDC) is a business incubator for fast-track investors seeking opportunities and inventors seeking commercialization of a product or an idea. The PDC uses business development and entrepreneurial education programmes pioneered by the Entrepreneurial Development Center, Houston's first and Texas's oldest business incubator centre, to accelerate business growth for entrepreneurs in emerging businesses.	Services Co-operative Association, 9600 Long Point Road, Suite 150, Houston, TX 77055	001 713 932 7495 001 713 932 7498 (fax) service@serviceSCA.org servicesca.org
Recycling Development Incubator	The Recycling Development Incubator (RDI) is a non-profit effort to help create a stronger local market for hard-to-recycle materials such as mixed colour glass, plastic waste, low-grade mixed paper, and many other potential recyclables.	Recycling Development Incubator, PO Box 260789, Lakewood, CO 80226–0789	001 303 988 5518 001 303 988 5589 (fax) recycling-incubator.org

Institution	Description	Contact	Telephone/e-mail/website
Rensselaer Polytechnic Institute Incubator Program	The Rensselaer Polytechnic Institute Incubator Program provides a uniquely supportive environment for nurturing new technological ventures. The incubator leases low-cost office, laboratory, and light manufacturing space to participating new ventures; provides shared office equipment and services; connects entrepreneurs to university and community resources; facilitates access to a broad-based network of business, financial and technical experts; and provides education and training programmes to enhance the knowledge and experience of participating entrepreneurs	Simon Blint, Rensselaer Polytechnic Institute Incubator Program, 1223 Peoples Avenue, Troy, NY 12180	001 518 276 6658 001 518 276 6380 (fax) incubator@rpi.edu rpi.edu
Research and Technology Park, Washington State University	Innovative ideas and technology developed by WSU's accomplished faculty members make their way into the commercial environment from this incubator. The easy-to-manage environment, access to the resources of a distinguished institution of higher education, and the university's strong organizational support for the park's tenants make WSU's Research and Technology Park one of the premiere locations in the nation for start-ups.	Cheryl Dudley, Research and Technology Park, Washington State University, Pullman, WA 99164–1802	001 509 335 1216 001 509 335 7237 (fax) wabio.com
Rural Development Center	The Rural Development Center's mission is to strengthen and diversify the rural economy of Maryland's Eastern Shore. It strives to increase incomes, the local tax base and jobs by providing technical assistance to counties, communities, and businesses. It collaborates with local higher education institutions, governments and the private sector to accomplish this mission.	Davniel Kuennen, Rural Development Center, Richard A. Henson Center, Room 2147, UMES, Princess Ann, MD 21853	001 410 651 6183 001 410 651 6207 (fax) skipjack.net

Name	Description	Address	Contact
Rural Technology Incubator	The Rural Technology Incubator is designed to help innovators and entrepreneurs grow their businesses. The incubator assists start-ups by providing them with supportive, creative places in which to work as a team. Located next to the University of North Dakota campus in Grand Forks, the Rural Technology Incubator offers university talent, technology, training, and technical assistance to help business start-ups develop and test-market new products, ideas, technologies, and ventures.	Bruce Gjovig, Rural Technology Center, 4300 Dartmouth Drive, PO Box 8372, Grand Forks, ND 58202–8372	001 701 777 3132 001 701 777 2339 (fax) innovators.net
San Diego Enterprise Center	The San Diego Enterprise Center (SDEC) is dedicated to promoting the entrepreneurial success of its client companies. SDEC provides a one-stop source for the rapid development of new and emerging technology-based businesses. Starting with office space, SDEC strives to provide a full range of entrepreneurial development resources.	San Diego Enterprise Center, 10401 Roselle Street, Suite 200, San Diego, CA 92121	001 619 587 9974 localbusinesses.com
San Diego Technology Incubator	The Center for Applied Competitive Technologies-San Diego (CACT-SD), located at San Diego City College, is one of 12 regional advanced technology centres designated by the State of California to assist regional manufacturers in modernizing their management of manufacturing and production technologies.	San Diego Technology Incubator, 1313 Twelfth Ave, San Diego, CA 92101	001 619 230 2080 001 619 230 2162 (fax) info@cact-sd.org
San Jose Software Business Cluster	Incubated companies include Waiter.com, Haggle Online, Online Anywhere, Kids Lab, Inc., Agile Software Corporation, and BroadQuest Callidus Software.	San Jose Software Business Cluster, 2 North First Street, fourth floor, San Jose, CA 95113	001 408 535 2701 001 408 535 2711 (fax) info@sjsbc.org
Santa Barbara Technology Incubator	SBTi provides more than just venture capital and angel investing to entrepreneurs. They finance, incubate and launch high-tech start-ups, and look for early-stage technology companies with an interest in locating in the greater Santa Barbara area.	Santa Barbara Technology Incubator, 320 Nopal St., Santa Barbara, CA 93101 3225	001 805 564 8005 001 805 564 7188 (fax)

Institution	Description	Contact	Telephone/e-mail/website
Small Business Incubator and Technical Assistance Center	The Small Business Incubator and Technical Assistance center (SBI) is a federally funded programme created to support the development of small businesses in Bexar County. The SBI programme serves as a resource centre and has fostered the ability for its participants to apply a variety of business concepts – from business plan development to enhancing their success in the world of business.	Clinton Bolden, Small Business Incubator and Technical Assistance Center, San Antonio Local Development Co., 215 South San Saba, San Antonio, TX 78207	001 210 207 8152 001 210 207 8151 (fax) operez@ci.sat.tx.us sba.gov
Small Business Incubator Facility	The Small Business Incubator Facility offers 16000 square feet of leasable space suitable for offices and/or light manufacturing. With below-market lease rates, shared office and business services and a wide range of technical assistance, the incubator provides tenants with a supportive and dynamic business environment.	Small Business Incubator Facility, Early Texas Chamber of Commerce, 104 East Industrial Drive, TX 76802	001 915 649 9317 ecoc@earlytx.com earlytx.com
Software Business Center	The Software Business Center (SBC) is a business incubator for fast-track software developers and computer-related businesses. The SBC uses business development and entrepreneurial education programmes pioneered by the Entrepreneurial Development Center, Houston's first and Texas's oldest business incubator centre, to accelerate business growth for entrepreneurs in emerging businesses.	Services Cooperative Association, 9600 Long Point Road, Suite 150, Houston, TX 77055	001 713 932 7495 001 713 932 7498 (fax) service@serviceSCA.org servicesca.org
South DeKalb Business Incubator	The South Dekalb Business Incubator (SDBI) is a non-profit incubator programme for service, distribution and light manufacturing businesses in the South Dekalb area. The purpose of SDBI is to assist small businesses in growing, developing, and providing employment opportunities.	Richard Younge, South DeKalb Business Incubator, Location 1 Service Site, 2632 Rainbow Way, Decatur, GA 30034 Location 2 Industrial Site, 1599 Memorial Drive, Atlanta, GA 30317	001 404 329 4500 sdbusinc.org

STARTech	STARTech is a for-profit business development organization that assists high-tech entrepreneurs and early-stage start-up companies. Entrepreneurial companies admitted into STARTech have access to seed funding, mentoring, coaching, business plan and market strategy assistance, connections with prominent venture capital firms, and contacts with leading technology corporations, service companies, and area universities.	STARTech Foundation, 1225 N. Alma Road, 2nd Floor, Richardson, TX 75083 2047	startech.org commercebynet.com
Stevens Technology Ventures Incubator	The mission of Stevens Technology Ventures Incubator (TVI) is to encourage and assist potential entrepreneurs with innovative ideas or commercially attractive technology to start their own companies on the campus of Stevens Institute of Technology in a supportive environment. TVI directs its efforts toward meeting the special needs of technological entrepreneurs by providing scientific and technical expertise, together with experienced business guidance, to assist in accelerating the commercial application of high-value technology.	Gina Boesch, Stevens Technology Ventures Incubator, Stevens Institute of Technology, 610 River Street, Hoboken, NJ 07030–5053	001 201 216 5366 001 201 420 9568 (fax) gboesch@stevens-tech.edu attila.stevens-tech.edu
Technology Advancement Program	The Technology Advancement Program is an incubator facility offering space and support services for early-stage companies engaged in developing technology-based products or services with commercial potential. Companies involved in the programme can adapt their research to market requirements while gaining business experience.	Technology Advancement Program, 387 Technology Drive, University of Maryland, College Park, MD 20742	001 301 314 7803 001 301 314 9592 (fax) tap@umail.umd.edu erc.umd.edu
Technology Commercialization Laboratory	The mission of the Technology Commercialization Laboratory is to facilitate and expedite the efforts of entrepreneurs, fledgling firms, and established firms to commercialize technology and information generated in programmes run by the College of Agricultural, Consumer and Environmental Sciences and other units of the University of Illinois.	Technology Commercialization Laboratory, 2004 South Wright Street, Urbana, IL 61802	001 217 244 7742 001 217 244 7757 (fax) tech.com

Institution	Description	Contact	Telephone/e-mail/website
Technology Development Center	The mission of the Technology Development Center is to help launch growing technology-based companies whose success will provide economic benefits and employment opportunities to the citizens of Nebraska. The center is a 23 000 square-foot building with approximately 14 000 square feet of lab, production, and office space available for lease.	Technology Development Center, University of Nebraska Technology Park, 4701 Innovation Drive, Lincoln, NE 68521–5330	001 402 472 4200 001 402 472 4203 (fax) info@unebtechpark.com unebtechpark.com
The Augusta-Richmond County Small Business Incubator	Companies incubated include Eastern Digital Resources, EZ, Money Mortgage, Mental Soup, LLC, Pirid Technologies, Inc., and Pixel Forest, LLC.	The Augusta-Richmond County Small Business Incubator, 3140 Augusta Tech Drive, Augusta, GA 30906–3381	001 706 792 9044 001 706 792 9905 (fax) info@arcsbi.com
The Ben Franklin Technology Partners	The Ben Franklin Technology Partners of Southeastern Pennsylvania (BFTP/SEP) is an independent, not-for-profit economic development corporation established in 1983. BFTP/SEP is one of the four regional partners of the statewide Ben Franklin Partnership, and administers the Ben Franklin programme in Bucks, Chester, Delaware, Montgomery and Philadelphia counties.	RoseAnn B. Rosenthal, 11 Penn Center, Suite 1100, 1835 Market Street, Philadelphia, PA 19103	001 215 972 6700 001 215 972 6700 (fax) sep.benfranklin.org
The CASE Center	The mission of the CASE Center is to develop a high-technology economy in New York State by leveraging the intellectual (and other) resources of Syracuse University, and by collaborating with New York State businesses and other economic development organizations. The Center currently offers business incubation services, as well as technology exploration, technology services, visiting researcher exchange, and information dissemination.	The CASE Center, 212 Center for Science and Technology, Syracuse University, Syracuse, NY 13244	001 315 443 1060 001 315 443 47445 (fax) info@cat.syr.edu cat.syr.edu

Name	Description	Address	Contact
The Enterprise Network (TEN)	TEN helps start-ups in three ways: through mentoring and advising; by providing a network of local resources; and by providing facilities and services to work clusters.	The Enterprise Network, 650 Saratoga Avenue, San Jose, CA 95129	001 408 557 6700 001 408 557 6799 (fax) ten-net.org
The Entrepreneurial Development Center (EDC)	EDC is Houston's first and Texas' oldest business incubator. The EDC pioneered business development and entrepreneurial education programmes to accelerate business growth for entrepreneurs in emerging businesses, providing the resources, methodology and environment to accelerate the business growth of client entrepreneurs. It is paid a development fee based on the success of the venture.	C Dean Kring, Services Co-operative Association, 9600 Long Point Road, Suite 150, Houston, TX 77055	001 713 932 7495 001 713 932 7498 (fax) service@serviceSCA.org servicesca.org
The Montgomery Incubator (Alabama)	Incubated companies include actworld.net, Monitech Leige Systems ProDriver, SCORE and New Vision.	The Montgomery Incubator (Alabama), 600 South Court Street, P.O. Box 79, Montgomery, AL 36101	001 334 240 6863 001 334 240 6869 (fax)
The Seminole Technology Business Incubation Center	The STBIC is a joint venture of Seminole County (Florida), Seminole County Port Authority and Seminole Community College, supported by grants from NASA and the Technological Research and Development Authority. The STBIC is participating as a member of the TRDA/NASA network of incubators.	The Seminole Technology Business Incubation Center, 1445 Dolgner Place, Sanford, FL 32771	001 407 321 3495 001 407 321 4184 (fax) hardyw@mail.seminole.cc.fl.us
The Women's Technology Cluster	Incubated companies include AgentArts, LevelEdge, LifeGuides, MsMoney.com, RosePlace.com, Tuzona.com, Vistify.	The Women's Technology Cluster, 1207 Indiana, Suite 4, San Francisco, CA 94107	001 415 970 5090 001 415 970 5095 (fax) info@wtc-sf.org
Tucson Technology Incubator	The Tucson Technology Incubator, Inc. (TTI) is a non-profit business incubator serving technology companies. TTI offers entrepreneurs, innovators and researchers a place where they can turn good ideas into new technology companies.	Carl Russell, Tucson Technology Incubator Inc, The University of Arizona Science and Technology Park, 9040 South Rita Road, Suite 1100, Tucson, Arizona 85747	001 520 663 3597 001 520 663 3593 mail@tucsonincubator.org tucsonincubator.org

Institution	Description	Contact	Telephone/e-mail/website
UMBC Technology Center	Located just one mile from UMBC, the Technology Center is a multi-tenant R&D facility housing a high-tech business incubator and office and lab space for technology companies.	Ellen Wiggins, UMBC Technology Center, University of Maryland, Baltimore County, 1000 Hilltop Circle, Baltimore, MD 21250	001 410 455 3222 001 410 455 1050 (fax) umbc.edu
Vanguard Incubators	Vanguard has developed and refined a unique incubator structure to provide a capital-efficient vehicle to convert leading-edge technology companies into viable businesses. Vanguard teams up with two or three venture funds and corporate partners with common interests. The incubators focus on specific markets where a perceived opportunity is large, but where a complete start-up team with a business plan, product and market strategy has not been assembled.	Vanguard Incubators, 1330 Post Oak Boulevard, Houston, TX 77057	001 713 877 1662 001 713 877 8669 (fax) info@vanguardventures.com vanguardventures.com
Venture Catalyst Partners	Provides a Silicon Valley presence for national and international companies seeking either to monitor development of cutting-edge Internet technologies or those seeking to make strategic alliances or strategic investments (corporate venturing) in pre-IPO companies.	Victor Anderson, Venture Catalyst Partners, 2 Sandstone, Portola Valley, CA 94028–8033	001 650 464 9925 001 650 292 2329 (fax) info@venturecatalyst.com venturecatalyst.com
Venture Center, Inc.	The main goal of Venture Center, Inc. is to assist the diversification of the Mid-Michigan economy through the development of new businesses and jobs. The Center draws together the region's business assistance resources to provide a nurturing environment for new enterprises.	Lansing Regional Chamber of Commerce, 300 East Michigan Avenue, Suite 300, Lansing, MI 48933	001 517 487 6340 001 517 484 6910 (fax) lansingchamber.org

Name	Description	Address	Contact
Virtual Business Incubator	This site, funded in part by the Office of Community Services, Administration for Children and Families, US Department of Health and Human Services, provides resources to help small businesses grow without having to locate in a bricks-and-mortar incubator facility. Information is available on accounting, banking, insurance, marketing and legal matters, along with stories of successfully assisted businesses and various tools: calculators, statements, business plan forms and lists of mistakes to avoid. There's also a section on county resources, and a search engine.	Kathy Kregel, Virtual Business Incubator, 125 South Howes, #150 Fort Collins, CO 80524	001 970 221 1301 001 970 498 8924 (fax) info@fortCollinsIncubator.org fortcollinsincubator.org
VirtualFund	Incubated companies include B2BXchange, Inc, XchangeERP, XchangeEDI, CareerHits.com, CompareData.com, Cybernetic Express, and DataQuarry.com	VirtualFund, 7090 Shady Oak Rd., Eden Prairie, MN 55344	001 612 941 8687 001 612 941–8652 (fax)
Western New York Technology Development Center, Inc.	The Western New York Technology Development Center is a private, not-for-profit corporation whose mission is to strengthen, expand, and diversify the technology and manufacturing base in Erie, Niagara, Allegany, Chautauqua and Cattaraugus counties. The Center's business incubation programme supports the creation and growth of new technical businesses by providing assistance to entrepreneurs.	Robert J Martin, Western New York Technology Development Center, Inc., Baird Research Park, 1576 Sweet Home Road, Amherst, NY 14228	001 716 636 3626 001 716 636 3630 (fax) rjmartin@acsu.buffalo.edu wynytdc.org
Women's Business Center	The Women's Business Center is a business incubator for contemporary, fast-track women business owners and career professionals. It was the first such incubator in the nation to teach entrepreneurship and intrapreneurship to women. It uses business development and entrepreneurial education programmes pioneered by the Entrepreneurial Development Center, Texas' oldest business incubator.	Women's Business Center Inc., 1001 Connecticut Avenue, NW, Suite 312, Washington, DC 20036	001 202 785 4WBC 001 202 785 4110 (fax) info@womensbusinesscenter.org womensbusinesscenter.org

REST OF WORLD

Australia

Institution	Description	Contact address	Telephone/e-mail/website
Australian Technology Parks (ATP)	ATP is owned by the Sydney Harbour Foreshore Authority. A key member is ATP Innovations which represents a consortium of four of Australia's leading universities. ATP Innovations conducts a business incubator programme and is responsible for promoting numerous research and development initiatives.	ATP Innovations, Suite 145, Level 1, National Innovation Centre, Australian Technology Park, Eveleigh, NSW 1430	00 61 02 9209 4444 i.soyer@atp.com.au atp.com.au
Coastal Business Centre	A blend of advice, services and support for SMEs.	Coastal Business Centre, PO Box 1616, Fremantle, WA 6959	00 61 8 9430 8569 00 61 8 9430 8579 (fax) coastal@vianet.net.au vianet.net.au
CSIRC	Involved in scientific research and development in all industry sectors. Expertise includes advice on science and technology, R&D to achieve market objectives, collaborative research and development arrangements.	Karl Armstrong, CSIRO Enquiries, Business Contact, Bag 10, Glayton South, VIC 3169	00 61 3 9545 2206 00 61 3 9545 2175 (fax) enquiries@csiro.au csiro.au
HatchingIT	Creators of a unique network of international incubator facilities such as awareness of foreign markets, contact, development, distribution, knowledge and technology, R&D, and joint ventures.	HatchingIT, The Vault, 257 Collins Street, Melbourne, Australia 3000	00 61 3 9663 9170 00 61 3 9650 9484 (fax) adam@hatchingit.com hatchingit.com
Tasmanian Technopark (Hobart)	Specializing in advanced technology research, the park provides appropropriate infrastructure to facilitate growth of technology- and innovation-based industries.	Technopark Manager, Tasmanian Technopark, Hobart, PO Box 149, Glenorchy, TAS 7010	00 61 3 6233 5588 00 61 3 6272 0768 (fax) dsd@dsd.tas.gov.au dsd.tas.gov

China

Institution	Description	Contact address	Telephone/e-mail/website
BitUnion.com	Target is to provide a whole solution to both investors and entrepreneurs at all levels. Information is our lifeline. Covering a wide range of up-to-date information related to domestic and overseas incubators, investors, development zones and companies in various trades and meanwhile maintaining close ties with them. In general, BitUnion is a bridge to incubators, venture investors and hi-tech industries to ensure the most efficient communication among them.	BitUnion.com, Rm 720, No. 618, Shangcheng Road, Pudong New District, Shanghai 200120	00 86 021 5888 9006 00 86 021 5888 4039 mkt@bitunion.com bitunion.com
e-Ventures .com.cn (China Web Ltd)	e-Ventures sees opportunities for a commercial non-governmental incubator network to be established in China adhering to international standards and practice.	e.Ventures.com.cn, 11th Floor, Prime Tower, 22 Chaoyangmenwai Dajie, Beijing, China	00 86 10 6588 8866 00 86 10 6588 5011 (fax) Technical support: admin@e-ventures.com.cn Investor queries: investor@e-ventures.co.cn Entrepreneur queries: entrepreneur@e-ventures.con.cn Website content: content@e-ventures.com.cn Other inquiries: services@e-ventures.com.cn To submit a business plan: plan1@e-ventures.com.cn or plan2@e-ventures.com.cn To submit an incubator proposal: consultant@e-ventures.com.cn Feedback: consultant@e-ventures.com.cn
HatchingIT	Creators of a unique network of international incubator facilities such as awareness of foreign markets, contact, development, distribution, knowledge and technology, R&D, and joint ventures.	Benjamin Tong, Hatchasia.com, 759A Chai Chee road, #07–02, Suite 3, Technopark at Chai Chee, Singapore 469001	00 65 446 4847 00 65 441 9983 00 65 441 9661 (fax) btiong@hatchasia.com hatchasia.com

Institution	Description	Contact address	Telephone/e-mail/website
Hong Kong Industrial Technology Centre Corporation	A statutory body set up by the Hong Kong government as part of its policy to stimulate the growth of high-tech industries.	Johnny Leung, Business Incubation Program, Hong Kong Industrial Technology Centre Corporation, 1/F, Hong Kong Industrial Technology Centre, 72 Tat Chee Avenue, Kowloon, Hong Kong, China	00 852 2788 4433 00 852 2788 4261 (fax) johnny@HK.Super.net sirius.com
Shanghai Zhangjiang HighTech Park	The enterprises in the park enjoy preferential policies of the Pudong Area.	Shanghai Zhangjiang Hi-Tech Park, Shanghai, People's Republic of China	china-zj.com
Suzhou New & High-tech Innovation Service Centre	Established in the late 1990s. The aim of the centre includes creating a favourable business environment by providing an all-round service which benefits technology innovation and in particular the development of technology-based start-ups.	(see telephone/email address)	Business Centre, Pioneering Park 00 86 512 8245635 Business Centre Incubator 00 86 512 825544 Business Centre Innovation Centre 00 86 512 9852195 Contact Mr Qu Changyou jcy@sibi.jsinfo.gov.cn Mr Bei Qi Bei@sibi.jsinfo.gov.cn csibi.com
Wuxi-Singapore Industrial Park (WSIP)	World-class facilities offer an excellent environment for high-tech and electronics manufacturing. Developed by a consortium led by SembCorp industries who also have management involvement in industrial sites in Vietnam and Indonesia.	WSIP Development Co Ltd, WSIP Administration Building, 178 Xi Xin Er Lu, Wuxi-Singapore Industrial Park, Wuxi, Jiangsu Province, People's Republic of China 214028	00 86 510 5210178 00 86 510 5218276 (fax) sembpark.com.sg

Egypt

Institution	Description	Contact address	Telephone/e-mail/website
Egyptian Incubator Association	This association has set a master plan for its Science and Technology Parks Programme.	Egyptian Incubator Association, 4-El-Obour Buildings, Salah Salem Street, 11th Floor, Cairo	00 20 2 403 4690 00 20 2 403 4691 (fax) eia@starnet.com.eg fei.org.eg
Social Fund for Development	Supporters of SME financing, networking, support mechanisms, IT.	Social Fund for Development, 1 Hussein Hegazy Street, Kasr El Aini, Cairo	00 20 2 354 00 77 00 20 2 355 06 28 (fax) sdfmis@powermail.intouch.com sfdegypt.org
Tabbin Technology Incubator	The facilities at the Tabbin Institute for metallurgical studies include a business community for SME, financial support, technical services, professional working teams, and monitoring facilities.	Dr Atef El-Shabrawy, Tabbin Institute for Metallurgical Studies, Cairo	00 20 2 501 0176 elshabrawy@yahoo.com fei.org.eg
Technology Incubator in Assiut	The incubator offers, management, financial, technical, marketing support and services.	Egyptian Incubator Association, 4 El-Obour Buildings, Salah Salem Street, 11th Floor, Cairo	00 20 2 403 4690 00 20 2 403 4691 (fax) eia@starnet.com.eg
Technology Incubator in Banha	To be found inside the Banha Institute. The aim is to exploit the strengths and facilities of research institutes and other centres of technology in the surrounding area. This incubator includes 25 units.	Egyptian Incubator Association, 4-El-Obour Buildings, Salah Salem Street, 11th floor, Cairo	00 20 2 403 4690 00 20 2 403 4691 (fax) eia@startnet.com.eg fei.org.eg
Technology Incubator (Mansoura University)	Facilities include a community for SMEs, support systems, technical services, use of laboratories, workshops, etc.	Egyptian Incubator Assocation, 4 El-Obour Buildings, Salah Salem Street, 11th Floor, Cairo	00 20 2 403 4690 00 20 2 403 4691 (fax) eia@startnet.com.eg fei.org.eg

India

Institution	Description	Contact address	Telephone/e-mail/website
Hatchasia.com	Provide e-commerce entrepreneurs with an incubation experience that reduces the risks of operating a high-tech start-up at Internet speed.	Benjamin Tong, Hatchasia.com, 759A Chai Chee Road, #07–02, Suite 3, Technopark at Chai Chee, Singapore 469001	00 65 446 4847 00 65 441 9983 00 65 441 9661 (fax) btiong@hatchasia.com hatchasia.com
ICICI Infotech Incubation Center	Infotech undertakes operational management of the centre and provides technical and managerial mentoring to selected SMEs. The incubation centre also provides pre-venture-capital support and integrated world-class facilities to Indian SMEs.	A A Baride, ICICI Infotech Incubation Center, Keshav Khade Marg. Mahalaxmi, Mumbai 400034	00 91 222 4906259 00 91 22 4923600 (fax) baride@icici.com icici.com
NurtureIT	Incubator assists entrepreneurs or incubation companies in the start-up stage.	NurtureIT,F-128 Mohammadpur, New Delhi-110066	00 91 98101 14544 00 91 11 4691573 (fax) achand:ittindia.com ittindia.com
Software Technology Parks of India (STPI)	The scheme is 100% export-oriented, for the development and export of computer software using data communication links.	Shri B V Naidu, Director, STPI Bangalore, Block III KSSIDC complex, Electronics City, Hosur Road, Bangalore 561 229, India	00 91 80 8520959 00 91 80 8520958 (fax) soft.net
STPI – Bhubaneswar	The scheme is 100% export-oriented, for the development and export of computer software using data communication links.	Manas Patnaik, Software Technology Parks of India, Priyadarshini Market, 2nd floor, CRP Square, Nayapalli, Bhubaneswar 751 012	00 91 674 560 250 00 91 674 560 261 (fax) manas@stpbh.soft.net stpbh.soft.net
STPI – Calcutta	The scheme is 100% export-oriented, for the development and export of computer software using data communication links.	Chiranjib Rudra, Software Technology Parks of India, SDF Building, Salt Lake Electronics Complex, Block-GP sector-V, Bidhannagar, Calcutta-91	00 91 33 357 9663 00 91 33 357 9664 (fax) webel@giase101.vsnl.net.in soft.net

STPI – Chennai	The scheme is 100% export-oriented, for the development and export of computer software using data communication links.	R Rajalakshmi, Software Technology Parks of India, 44/1, Kalaimagal Nagar, II Street, Ekkaduthangal, Chennai-600 097	00 91 44 232 6308 00 91 44 232 8582 (fax) stpc.soft.net
STPI – Delhi	The scheme is 100% export-oriented, for the development and export of computer software using data communication links.	S N Zindal, Director General, Software Technology Parks of India, Electronics Niketan, 6, CGO Complex, Lodi Road, New Delhi 110 003	00 91 11 436 2811 00 91 11 436 3436 (fax) zindal@stpi.soft.net taneja@stpi.soft.net stpi.soft.net
STPI – Gandhinagar	The scheme is 100% export-oriented, for the development and export of computer software using data communication links.	Ajay Sharma, Software Technology Parks of India, A/78/7 flatted Factory Shed, Electronics Estate, GIDC, Gandhinaga 382 044	00 91 2712 35856 00 91 2712 27207 (fax) aya@stpg.soft.net stpg.soft.net
STPI – Hyderabad	The scheme is 100% export-oriented, for the development and export of computer software using data communication links.	Vijay Kumar, Software Technology Parks of India, 6th Floor, 6Q3 Cyber Tower, Hitech City, Madhavnagar, Hyderabad 500 081	00 91 40 3100500 00 91 40 3100501 (fax) mvkumar@stph.soft.net stph.net
STPI – Jaipur	The scheme is 100% export-oriented, for the development and export of computer software using data communication links.	Shri Ajay Prasad Shrivastava, Officer in Charge, STPI Jaipur, 201–202 Gaurav Tower I, Bardiya Shopping Centre, Malviya Nagar, Jaipur 302 017	00 91 141 720062/65 00 91 141 720063 (fax) ajay@stpi.soft.net stpi.soft.net
STPI – Manipal	The scheme is 100% export-oriented, for the development and export of computer software using data communication links.	Girish Babu, Officer in Charge, STPI Manipal, TMA Pai Planetarium Building, opposite Women's Hostel, Manipal 576 119	00 91 8252 71917 (phone/fax) girish@stpm.soft.net soft.net
STPI – Mohali	The scheme is 100% export-oriented, for the development and export of computer software using data communication links.	Sanjay Tyagi, Software Technology Parks of India, B-99 'L-Top', Phase VIII, Indl. Area, SAS Nagar, Mohali 160 059, Punjab	00 91 172 253 498 00 91 172 254 062 (fax) sanjay@stpm.soft.net stpm.soft.net

Institution	Description	Contact address	Telephone/e-mail/website
STPI – Mumbai	The scheme is 100% export-oriented, for the development and export of computer software using data communication links.	Officer in Charge, Software Technology Parks of India, International Infotech Park Tower #7, floor #6, Vashi Railway Station Complex, Navi Mumbai 400 705	00 91 22 781 2102 00 91 22 781 2034 (fax) stpmum.soft.net
STPI – Mysore	The scheme is 100% export-oriented, for the development and export of computer software using data communication links.	Suresh Babu, Officer in Charge, STPI – Mysore, SJCE-STEP Campus, ManasaGangothri, Mysore 570 006	00 91 821 412 090 00 91 821 412 080 (fax) suresh@stpmy.soft.net soft.net
STPI – Noida	The scheme is 100% export-oriented, for the development and export of computer software using data communication links.	S K Agrawal, Software Technology Parks of India, Block 4, Sector 29, Ganga Shopping Complex, Noida	00 91 118 445 0408/0409 00 91 118 445 0405 (fax) sunil@stpn.soft.net stpm.soft.net
STPI – Pune	The scheme is 100% export-oriented, for the development and export of computer software using data communication links.	Shri S K Gupta, Polt No-P-1 Infotech Park, Hanhawadi, Pune 411 027	00 91 2139 32644/45 00 91 2139 32639 (fax) sushil@stpp.soft.net stpp.soft.net
STPI – Thiruvanan-thapuram	The scheme is 100% export-oriented, for the development and export of computer software using data communication links.	K Ramesh Kumar, Software Technology Parks of India, #5517, JV Centre Bakery Jn, Thiruvananthapura 695 034	00 91 471 321224/327371 00 91 471 330037 ramesh@stpt.soft.net stpt.soft.net

Indonesia

Institution	Description	Contact address	Telephone/e-mail/website
Batamindo Industrial Park	This facility is owned and developed by a Singapore/Indonesian consortium. BIP focuses mainly on electronics and skill-intensive industries and has attracted 90 international companies and $1 billion worth of investments.	PT Batamindo Investment Corporation, Wisma Batamindo, Jln Rasamala No.1, Muka Kuning, Batamindo Industrial Park, Batam 29433, Indonesia	00 62 770 611 222 00 62 770 611 432 (fax) kim.sohl@sembpark.com.sg sembcorp.com.sg

Institution	Description	Contact address	Telephone/e-mail/website
Bintan Industrial Park	A duty-free bonded zone on Bintan island. Offers investors many resources as well as access to world markets via Singapore's excellent transport and logistics infrastructure. Focuses mainly on electronics and resource-intensive light industries.	PT Bintan Inti Industrial Estate, Tanjung Uban, PO Box 020, Bintan 29152, Indonesia	00 62 11 770 696 833 00 62 11 770 696 832 (fax) indonesia.elga.net.id sembpark.com.sg
SembCorp Parks Management (see also Singapore, China, Vietnam)	Offers efficient infrastructure and one-stop services.	SembCorp Parks Management, 3 Lim Teck Kim Road, #12–02, Singapore Technologies Building, Singapore 088934	00 65 2215374 00 65 2221994 (fax) sembpark.com.sg

Israel

Institution	Description	Contact address	Telephone/e-mail/website
Biomedicom	Software-driven platforms that easily add on to existing 2D ultrasound equipment.	Biomedicom, Manachat Technology Park, Building 1, Malha, Jerusalem 91 487	00 972 2 679 6355 00 972 2 679 6358 (fax) info@biomedicom.com biomedicom.com
Britech (see also UK)	A British-Israel technology foundation, an organization providing active support for collaborative Israeli companies.	Britech in Israel, Gibor Sport Tower, 28 Betsal'el Street, 9th Floor, Ramat Gan 5251 Israel	00 972 3 754 9581 00 972 3 754 9582 (fax) britech@actcom.co.il britech.org
Nanonics Ltd	Nanonics began operations in 1995 to develop products in the field of scanned probe microscopy to scientists and technologies throughout the world.	Nanonics Ltd, The Manhat Technology Park, Malcha, Jerusalem 91487	00 972 2 678 9573 00 972 2 648 0827 (fax) info@nanonics.co.uk nanonics.co.il
Navitek	Founded in 1995, a subsidiary of Betatron Inc. of Delaware. The company is engaged in the development of trading methodologies for global financial markets, and employs staff with backgrounds in science and finance. The company possesses highly experienced management personnel, financial resources and an ability to host small to mid-sized high-tech companies.	Seth Jacobson, Navitek Ltd, Manachat Technology Park, Building 1, Jerusalem IL 96 951	00 972 2 679 7470 info@navitek.com navitek.com

Institution	Description	Contact address	Telephone/e-mail/website
The Manhat Technology Park in Jerusalem	Seventy per cent of available space to be rented out to high-tech industrial companies which have received official status of certified enterprises. Thirty per cent of the park will be rented out to industy-related services such as financial institutions, consultancy firms, etc.	The Manhat Technology Park, Jerusalem	00 972 2 679 4513/4 00 972 2 649 0601 (fax) techpark@intournet.co.il intournet.co.il

Japan

Institution	Description	Contact address	Telephone/e-mail/website
Okamoto & Company	An accounting firm that has added business incubation to its portfolio.	Okamoto & Company, Shinkojimachi Building 7F, 4–3 Kohimchi, Chiyoda-ku, Tokyo, Japan 102–0083	00 81 3 5276 0900 00 81 3 5276 0950 (fax) okamoto@okamoto-co.co.jp okamoto-co.co.jp

Malaysia

Institution	Description	Contact address	Telephone/e-mail/website
Malaysian Technology Park	Offers an opportunity for SMEs to carry out research and development. The park is equipped with modern facilities such as fibre optics technology, Internet access and facilities for developing companies.	Mimos Berhad, Technology Park Malaysia, 5700 Kuala Lumpur	00 60 3 8996 5000 00 60 3 8996 0527 (fax) ccd@mimos.my mimos.my

New Zealand

Institution	Description	Contact address	Telephone/e-mail/website
Industry New Zealand	Actively working with innovative New Zealand businesses. Providers of advice, investments, networking, etc.	Industry NZ, Level 9, 22 The Terrace, PO Box 2878, Wellington, New Zealand	00 64 4 495 5080 00 64 4 495 5081 (fax) info@industrynz.govt.nz industrynz.govt.nz

Singapore

Institution	Description	Contact address	Telephone/e-mail/website
SembCorp Parks Management	Industrial park whose mission is to plan, market, and manage companies. Offers efficient infrastructure and one-stop services.	SembCorp Parks Management, 3 Lim Teck Kim Road, #12–02, Singapore Technologies Building, Singapore 088934	00 65 221 5374 00 65 222 1994 (fax) sembpark.com.sg
Singapore Science Centre	Incubators of scientific knowledge.	The Singapore Science Centre, 15 Science Centre Road, Off Jurong Town Hall Road, Singapore 609081	sci-ctr.edu.sg

Vietnam

Institution	Description	Contact address	Telephone/e-mail/website
Vietnam Singapore Industrial Park	VSIP is differentiated from its competitors by its management board, which was specially set up by the Vietnamese government. The board has authority to issue investment licences for projects. Investors are assured of a supply of skilled workers coming from VSIP's own Technical Training Centre.	Vietnam Singapore Industrial Park JV Co Ltd, 8 Dai Lo Huu Nghi, Vietnam Singapore Industrial Park, Thuan An District, Binh Duong Province, Vietnam	00 84 650 743 898 00 84 650 743 868 (fax) sembpark.com.sg

USEFUL ADDRESSES

Association of Lithuanian Innovation
Networks
C/o Kaunas Innovation Centre
K. Donelaicio Street 73
LT – 3006 Kaunas
00 370 7 300 691
00 370 7 300 692 (fax)
P.Milius@cr.ktu.lt
www.ediaclit.vtk.ktu.lt

Baltic Association of Science/
Technology Parks & Innovation Centres
(BASTIC)
Ehitajatee 5
EE – 0026 Tallinn
00 372 620 20 13
00 372 738 30 41 (fax)
raivot@edu.ttu.ee
www.edu.ttu.ee

Bedrijfs Technologisch Centrum Twente
BV (btc)
Postbus 545
NL 7500 AM Enschede
00 31 53 48 36 35 5
00 31 53 43 37 41 5 (fax)
info@btc-twente.nl
www.btc-twente.nl

Britech (British-Israel Technology
Foundation)
Wyvols Court
Swallowfield
Reading
Berks RG7 1WY
00 44 118 988 0275
00 44 118 988 0375 (fax)
enquiries@britech.org
www.britech.org

European Business & Innovation Centre
Network
Avenue de Tervuren 168
B-1150 Brussels
00 32 2 77 28 90 0
00 32 2 77 29 57 4
info@ebn.be
www.ebn.be

ELAN Association des Dirigeants de
Peipinieres d'Enteprises
C/o Atecval, Prolgue Voie No.1
BP 27/01 Labege Innopole
F-31312 Labege Cedex
00 33 561 39 10 31
00 33 561 39 86 89 (fax)

France Technopoles
C/o Atlanpole Chateau de la Chantrerie
Chateau de la Chantrerie BP 90702
F-44307 Nantes Cedex 3
00 33 240 25 227 03
00 33 240 25 10 88 (fax)
balducchi@atlanpole.fr
www.atlanpole.fr

Hungarian Association for Innovation
Oktober huszonharmadika u.16
H-1117 Budapest
00 33 1 18 69 61 5
00 36 1 18 52 18 1 (fax)

IASP International Association of
Science Parks
C/o Parque Tecnologico de Andalucia
Sede Social
Maria Curie s/n
E-29590 Campanillas (Malaga)
00 34 95 26 19 19 7
00 34 95 26 19 19 8 (fax)
iasp@isapworld.org
www.iaspworld.org

Latvian Association of Technological
Parks, Innovation Centres and Business
Incubators
Aizkrauklesstr.21
LV-1006 Riga
00 371 2 25 58 66 3
00 371 2 75 41 21 8 (fax)

NBIA National Business Incubation
Association
20 East Circle Drive
Suite 190
Athens
Ohio 445701 USA
001 740 59 34 33 1
001 740 59 31 99 6 (fax)
dadkins@nbia.org
www.nbia.org

PBICA Polish Business & Innovation
Centres Association
Rubiez 46
PL-61612 Poznan
00 48 61 86 59 65 1
00 48 61 86 59 56 8 (fax)
soipp@soipp.org.pl
www.soipp.org.pl

Russian National Business Incubators
Association
Zazepa Streete 41
RUS-113054 Moscow
00 7 095 56 48 18 3
00 7 095 95 57 93 7 (fax)
kagan@morozov.ru
www.morozov.ru

Society of Science & Technology Parks
of the Czech Republic
Novotneho lavka 5
CZ-11668 Praha 1
00 420 2 21 08 22 74
00 420 2 21 08 22 76 (fax)

Spice-Group (ICECE)
C/o Zentrum am Zoo Geschaftsbauten
AG
Hardenbergplatz 2
D-10623 Berlin
00 4930 26 47 07 0
00 4930 26 47 07 33
zaz@zoobogen.de
www.zoobogen.de

Stiftung Technopark Zurich
(Club de Schweizer Technologieparks)
Technoparkstrabe 1
CH-8005 Zurich
00 41 1 445 10 10
00 41 1 445 10 01 (fax)

TII European Association for the
Transfer of Technology, Innovation and
Industrial Information
3 rue des Capucins
L-1313 Luxembourg
00 352 46 30 35
00 352 46 21 85 (fax)
tti@sitel.lu
www.sitel.lu

Ukrainian Business Incubators and
Innovation Centres Association
Petscherski Spusk 3
UA-01023 Kiew
00 38 044 23 56 21 0
00 38 044 23 56 21 0 (fax)
ligor@prime.net.ua
www.prime.net.ua

UKSPA (United Kingdom Science Park
Association)
Aston Science Park
Love Lane
Aston Triangle
Birmingham B7 4BJ
00 44 121 69 34 85 0
00 44 121 33 35 85 2
infor@ukspa.org.uk
www.ukspa.org.uk

United Nations Industrial Development
Organization
Head Quarters
PO Box 300
A-1400 Vienna
Austria
00 43 1 26026
00 43 1 2692669 (fax)
unido@unido.org
www.unido.org

VTO Vereinigung der
Technologiezentren Osterreichs
Wehrgrabengasse 1–5
A-4400 Steyr
00 43 7252 88 41 05
00 43 7252 88 41 11 (fax)
vtoe@inna.at
www.inna.at

References

PART ONE   A BRIEF HISTORY OF BUSINESS INCUBATION

Allen, D.N. (1988) Business incubator life cycles. *Economic Development Quarterly* **2**(1), 19–29.

Allen, D.N. and Weinberg, M. (1988) State investment in business incubators. *Public Administration Quarterly* **12**(2), 196–215.

Bates, T. and Nucci, A. (1989) An analysis of small business size and rate discontinuence. *Journal of Small Business Management* **27**(4), 1–7.

Birch, D. (1979) *The Job Generation Process*. MIT Programme in Neighbourhood and Regional Changes, Cambridge, MA.

Birch, D. (1987) *Job Creation in America: How our smallest companies put most people to work*. New York, The Free Press.

Bolton, J.E. (1971) *Report of the Committee of Enquiry on Small Firms*. 411, HMSO, London.

Campbell, C., Berge, D., Janus, J. and Olsen, K. (1988) *Change Agents in the New Economy: Business Incubators and Economic Development*. Report prepared for the Institute of Public Affairs, University of Minnesota, Minneapolis, MN.

Corporate Venturing Report (2000) September, Wellesley, MA.

Culp, R.P. (1996) A test of business growth through analysis of a technology incubator program. Unpublished doctoral dissertation, Georgia Institute of Technology, GA.

Duff, A. (1999) *Best Practice in Incubation Management*. AUSTEP Strategic Partnering Pty Ltd., Booragoon, Western Australia.

Fraunhofer Institut für Systematik und Innovation (1985) *Sieben Fragen zum Thema Gründer-und Innovationszentren*. Karlsruhe, Germany.

Gill D., Martin, C., Minshall, T. and Rigby, M. (2000) *Funding Technology: Lessons from America*. Wardour Communications, London.

Ginsburg, A. and Hay, M. (1995) Confronting the challenges of corporate venturing. *European Management Journal* **12**(4), 382–389.

Harley, B. (2001) Business incubators: good old models vs exciting new models. Conference paper presented at The First International Workshop on Technology Business Incubators in India, Bangalore, India, 29–31 January.

McKee, B. (1992) A boost for Start-ups. *Nations Business,* August, 40–42.

National Council for Urban Economic Development (1985) *Creating New Jobs by Creating New Businesses – The Role of Business Incubators.* Washington, DC.

National Science Foundation (1985) *Innovation and Enterprise: A Study of NSF's Innovation Center Program.* Washington, DC.

Reynolds, P.D. and Mitler, B. (1988) New Firms Study: An exploration of New Firms and their Economic Contribution. Centre for Urban and Regional Affairs, Minneapolis, MN.

Roure, J. and Keeley, R. (1990) Predictors of success in new technology-based ventures. *Journal of Business Venturing* **(5)**, 201–220.

Schumpeter, J.A. (1912) *The Theory of Economic Development.* (In German). Published in English in 1934 by Harvard University Press.

Shahidi, H. (1998) The impact of business incubators on entrepreneurial networking: a comparative study of small, high-technology firms. Unpublished doctoral dissertation, George Washington University, Washington, DC.

Sternberg R., Behrendt, H., Seeger, H. and Tamasy, C. (1997) Bilanz eines booms – Wirkunganalyse von Technologie – und Grunderzentren in Deutschland. Paper presented at RISE 1996 conference. *Dortmunder Vertrieb fur Bau und Planungsliteratur* **2**, Autflage.

Storey, D.J. (1985) Manufacturing employment changes in northern England. In *Small Firms in Regional Economic Development.* (ed. D.J. Storey) Cambridge University Press, Cambridge, UK.

Storey, D.J. (1994) *Understanding the Small Business Sector.* Routledge, London.

Swierczek, F.W. (1992) Strategies for business innovation: Evaluating the prospects of incubation in Thailand. *Technovation* **12**(8), 521–533.

PART TWO   WHO ARE THE PLAYERS?

Amirahmadi, H. and Saff, G. (1993), Science parks: a critical assessment. *Journal of Planning Literature* **8**(2), November, 16–21.

Autio, E. and Klofsten, M. (1998) A comparative study of two European business incubators. *Journal of Small Business Management* **36**(1), 30–43.

Bank Boston Economics Department (1997) *MIT: The Impact of Innovation.* Boston, MA.

Barrow, C. (2000) *How to Survive the E-Business Downturn.* Wiley, Chichester, England.

Barrow, C., Copin, G., Lange, J., Leleux, B., Paliard, R., Richardson, A. and St-Cyr, L. (1999) Valuing High-Growth Potential Companies: An International Comparison of Best Practices by Venture Capitalists and Underwriters. *Cranfield Working Papers,* Cranfield, England.

Baughman, G.W. (1981) *Research Parks Dimensioning Study.* Battelle Institute, Columbus, OH.

Biggadike, R. (1979) The risky business of diversification. *Harvard Business Review* **57**(3), 103–111.

Bygrave, W.D. and Timmons, J.A. (1992) *Venture Capital at the Crossroads.* Harvard Business School Press, Boston, MA.

Campbell, C., Kendrick, R. and Samuelson, D. (1985) Stalking the latent entrepreneur: business incubators and economic development. *Economic Development Review* **3**(2), 43–48.

Cave, R. (1999) UK Business Angels: Characteristics and Developments. Cranfield Working Papers, Cranfield, England.

Chen, Y. (1983) On the positive role of financial intermediation in allocation of venture capital in a market with imperfect information. *Journal of Finance* **XXXVIII**(5), 1543–1568.

Chesbrough. H., (2000) Designing corporate ventures in the shadow of private venture capital. *California Management Review* **42**(3), 31–49.

CMGI (2000) Annual report. Andover, MA.

Confederation of British Industry (CBI) (1999) *Connecting Companies*, London.

Creagh, M. (1999) From Home Birds to Virtual Eagles? An overview of the current and potential habits of business angels in the UK and USA. Cranfield Working Papers, Cranfield, England.

Danilov, V. (1971) The research park shake-out. *Industrial Research* (May), 44–47.

Davies, P. and Koza, M. (2001) Eating soup with a fork: how informal social networks influence innovation in high-technology firms. *Strategic Change* **10**, 95–102.

Drucker, P. (1985) *Innovation and Entrepreneurship*. Heinemann, London.

Duff, A. (1999) *Best Practice in Incubation Management*. AUSTEP Strategic Partnering Pty Ltd., Booragoon, Western Australia.

European Observatory for SMEs (1997) Fifth Annual Report. EIM Small Business Research Consultancy, Zoetermeer, The Netherlands.

Fast, N. (1978) *The Rise and Fall of Corporate New Ventures Divisions*. UMI Research Press, Ann Arbor, MI.

Financial Times, 7 April 2001, *Survey – Britain's Universities*, p. 1.

Forrester Research (2000) Technographics survey. Amsterdam, The Netherlands.

Foster, R. & Kaplan, S. (2001) *Why Companies That are Built to Last Underperform the Market – and How to Transform them Successfully*. Doubleday, Dell, US.

Galante, S.P. (1987) Business incubators adopting niche strategies to stand out. *The Wall Street Journal*, 13 April, p. 25.

Gaston, R.J. (1989) The scale of informal capital markets. *Small Business Economics* **1**, 223–230.

Grayson, D. (2000) Building networks. Chapter in *Mastering Entrepreneurship – the complete MBA companion in entrepreneurship* (eds S. Birley and D. Muzyka), FT Prentice Hall, London.

Greco, S. (1999) Get$$$NOW.com, *Inc*, September, 35.

Gross, W. (1998) The new math of ownership. *Harvard Business Review*, Boston, MA.

Harrison, R. and Mason, C. (1992) International perspectives on the supply of informal venture capital. *Journal of Business Venturing* **7**, 459–475.

Harrison, R. and Mason, C. (1996) Developing the informal venture capital market: a review of the Department of Trade and Industry's investment demonstration projects. *Regional Studies* **30**(8), 765–767.

Jackson, T. (1998) Determining the impact of discretionary development assistance: the Scottish Enterprise output measurement framework. *Regional Studies* **32**, 559–577.

Kauranen, I., Takala, M., Autio, E. and Kailla, M.M. (1992) *Kolme Ensimäistä Vuotta: Tutkimus Uuden Teknologiakylän ja sen Vuokralaisten Alkutaipaleesta*. Publication 2/1992, Otaniemi Science Park Publications, Espoo, Finland.

Kroll, L. (2000) Mad hatchery syndrome. *Forbes*, 17 April, 132–134.

Louis, K.S., Blumenthal, D., Gluck, M.E. and Stoto, M.A. (1989) Entrepreneurs in academe: An exploration of behaviours among life scientists. *Administration Science Quarterly* **34**(1), 110–131.

Mason, C.M. and Harrison, R.T. (1995). Informal venture capital and the financing of small and medium-sized enterprises. *Small Enterprise Research* **3**, 33–56.

Mason, C.M. and Harrison, R.T. (1997) Business angels in the UK: a response to Stevenson and Coveney. *International Small Business Journal* **15**(2), 83–90.

Massey, D., Quintas, P. and Wield, D. (1992) *High Tech Fantasies: Science Parks in Society, Science and Space.* Routledge, London.

Mathews, J. (1993) TCG R&D networks: the triangulation strategy. *Journal of Industry Studies*, October, 6–9.

Merrifield, D.B. (1993) Intrapreneurial corporate renewal. *Journal of Business Venturing* **8**(5), 383–389.

Mian, S.A. (1997) Assessing and managing the university technology incubator: An Integrative Framework. *Journal of Business Venturing* **12**, 251–285.

Midland Bank (1997) *Growing Success: Helping companies to generate wealth.* Enterprise Panel Report, Birmingham, England.

Miles, R.E. and Snow, C.C. (1995) The new network firm: a spherical structure built on a human investment philosophy. *Organisational Dynamics* **23**, Spring, 5–18.

Minshall, C. (1984) *An Overview of Trends in Science and Technology Parks.* Battelle Institute, Columbus, OH.

Molian, D. (2001) *Corporate Venturing: A Review of the Literature.* Cranfield Working Papers, Cranfield, England.

Monck, C. and Segal, N. (1983) University Science Parks and Small Firms. Conference Paper, Durham University, England.

Monck, C., Porter, D., Quintas, P., Storey, D. and Wynarczyk, P. (1990) *Science Parks and the Growth of High Technology Firms.* Routledge, London.

Money, M. (1970) University-related science parks. *Industrial Research* (May), 62–63.

Moore, B. and Spires, R. (1983) The Experience of the Cambridge Science Park. Organisation for Economic Co-operation and Development (OECD) Workshop on Research, Technology, and Regional Policy, Paris, France.

Moss Kanter, R. (1985) *The Change Masters.* Simon and Schuster, New York.

Mott, N. (1969) Committe Report. Cambridge University, England.

National Foundation of Women Business Owners (1996) Women business owners make progress in access to capital but still lag men-owned businesses in credit levels. Report by the National Foundation of Women Business Owners, US.

Nyprop, K. (1986) Business incubators as real estate ventures. *Urban Land* **45**(12), 6–10.

Oakley, R. (1984) British university science parks and high-technology small firms: a comment on the potential for high growth. *International Journal of Small Business* **4**(1), 58–67.

OECD (1999) Forum for Entrepreneurship and Enterprise Development. Organization for Economic Co-operation and Development, Paris.

Pacholski, R.L. (1988) Hatching an incubator: obtaining recognition of section 501(c)(3) status for incubator organisations. *The Tax Magazine* **66**(4), 273–283.

Pinchot, G. (1985) *Intrapreneuring.* Harper & Row, New York.

PricewaterhouseCoopers (1999) Department of Employment, Workplace Relations and Small Business, National Review of Small Business Incubators. *Final Internal Report.*

Ronstadt, R. (1984) *Entrepreneurship.* Lord Publishing, Dover, MA.

Roper, S. (1999) Israel's technology incubators: repeatable success or costly failure? *Regional Studies*, Cambridge University, England.

Salhman, W.A. (1990) The structure and governance of venture-capital organizations. *Journal of Financial Economics* **27**, 473–521.

Schollhammer, H. (1980) Analysis and assessment of internal corporate entrepreneurship strategies. Graduate School of Management, UCLA, CA.

Seglin, J. (1998) What angels want. *Inc*, 43.

Sherman, H. (1999) *Assessing the Intervention Effectiveness of Business Incubation Programs on New Business Start-Ups. Journal of Developmental Entrepreneurship* **4**(2), 26–33.

Shread, P. (2001) US Venture Returns. *Internet VC Watch*, US.

Smilor, R.W. (1987) Commercialising technology through new business incubators. *Research Management* **30**(5), 36–41.

Smilor, R.W. and Gill, M.D. (1986) *The New Business Incubator: Linking Talent, Technology, Capital and Know-How.* Lexington Books, MA.

Sykes, H. (1986) The anatomy of a corporate venturing program: factors influencing success. *Journal of Business Venturing* **1**, 275–293.

Teräs, J., Byckling, E. and Kaila, M.M. (1985) *Teknologiakylien Menestymiseeen Vaikuttavat Tekijät.* Otaniemi Science Park Publications, 1/1985, Espoo, Finland.

Wetzel, W.E. (1983) Angels and informal risk capital. *Sloan Management Review* **24**, 23–33.

Wetzel, W.E. (1987) The informal risk capital market: aspects of scale and efficiency. In *Frontiers of Entrepreneurship Research* (eds N.C. Churchill, J.A. Hornaday, B.A. Kirchoff, O.J. Krasner and K.H. Vesper), Babson Park, MA.

Wetzel, W.E. and Freear, J. (1988) Equity Financing for New Technology-based Firms. Babson Entrepreneurship Research Conference, Calgary, Alberta, May.

Williams, J. (1984) *Review of Science Parks and High Technology Developments.* Drivers Jones, London

PART THREE WHAT DO INCUBATORS REALLY HAVE TO OFFER?

Allen, D. N. and Rahman, S. (1985) Small business incubators: a positive environment for entrepreneurship. *Journal of Small Business Management* **22**(3), 12–22.

Asquith, P., Bruner, R. and Mullins, D. (1986) Equity issues and stock price dilution. *Journal of Financial Economics* **15**, 61–89.

Barrow, C. (1998) *The Creation of Value for shareholders: Do Mergers and acquisitions deliver?* G8 Management Conference, Lyon, France.

Barrow, C. (1999) Enterprise Culture. Cranfield Working Papers, Cranfield, England.

Barrow, C, Mayne, L. and Brewster, C. (1997) Taking people seriously: do SMEs treat human resource management as a vital part of their competitive strategy? Paper presented at the 12th Workshop on Human Resource Management, Turku, Finland.

Bates, T. (1990). Entrepreneurial human capital inputs and small business longevity. *Review of Economics and Statistics* **72**(4), 551–559.

Bracker, J.S. and Pearson, J.N. (1986) Planning and financial performance of small, mature firms. *Strategic Management Journal* **7**(6), 503–522.

Burns, P. (1994) Does Planning Pay? Cranfield Working Papers, Cranfield, England.

Champion, D. and Carr, C.G. (2000) Starting up in high gear: an interview with venture capitalist Vinod Khosla. *Harvard Business Review*, July/August.

Churchill, N.C. and Lewis, V.L. (1983) The five stages of small business growth. *Harvard Business Review*, May/June.

Fowler, T, (2000) Trilogy pursues author of anti-CarOrder posting. *Austin Business Journal*, 20 March, Austin, TX.

Fry, F.L. (1987) The role of incubators in small business planning. *American Journal of Small Business*, Summer, 51–61.

Greiner, L.E. (1972) Evolution and revolution as organisations grow. *Harvard Business Review*, July/August.

Gross, W. (1998) The new math of ownership. *Harvard Business Review*, Boston, MA.

Hall, G. (1995) *Surviving and Prospering in the Small Firms Sector.* Routledge, London.

Hansen, M.T., Chesbrough, H.W., Nohria, N. and Sull. D. (2000) Networked incubators: hothouses of the new economy. *Harvard Business Review*, September/October.

Herold, D.J. (1972) Long-range planning and organizational performance: A cross-validation study. *Academy of Management Journal* **15**(1), 91–104.

Hogan, T. and Foley, A. (1996) *Fast Growth Firms in Ireland: An Empirical Assessment.* DCUBS Research Papers 1995–1996, No. 5.

Kotler, P. (1988) *Marketing Management.* Prentice Hall, New Jersey.

Krasker, W. (1986) Stock price movements in response to stock issues under asymmetric information. *Journal of Finance* **41**, 93–105.

Maryland Technology Development Corporation (2000) *Incubator Focus Group Study.* Maryland.

Masulis, R.W. and Korwar, A.W. (1986) Seasoned equity offerings: an empirical investigation. *Journal of Financial Economics* **15**, 91–118.

Meldrum, M. and McDonald, M. (2000) *Key Marketing Concepts.* Macmillan Press, London.

Mian, S.A. (1996) Assessing value-added contributions of university technology incubators to tenant firms. *Research Policy* **25**, 325–335.

Myers, S.C. and Majluf, N.S. (1984) Corporate financing and investment decisions when firms have information that investors do not have. *Journal of Financial Economics* **13**, 187–222.

Orpen, C. (1985) The effects of long-range planning on small business performance: A further examination. *Journal of Small Business Management* **23**(1), 16–23.

PricewaterhouseCoopers (1999) Department of Employment, Workplace Relations and Small Business, National Review of Small Business Incubators, Final internal report.

Rhyne, L.C. (1985) The relationship of strategic planning to financial performance. *Strategic Management Journal* **4**, 319–337.

Rice, M.P. and Matthews, J.B. (1995) *Growing New Ventures, Creating New Jobs: Principles and Practices of Successful Business Incubation.* Quorum Books, Westport, CN.

Robinson, R.B., Salem, M.Y., Logan, J.E. and Pearce, J.A. II (1986) Planning activities related to independent retail firm performance. *American Journal of Small Business* **II**(1), 19–26.

Ruback, R. (1988) An overview of takeover defences. In *Mergers and Acquisitions* (ed. A.J. Auerbach) Chicago University Press, Chicago.

Rue, L. and Fulmer, R. (1973) Is long-range planning profitable? *Academy of Management Proceedings.* 66–73.

Shrader, C.B., Taylor, C.B.L. and Dalton, D.R. (1984) Strategic planning and organizational planning: A critical appraisal. *Journal of Management* **10**, 149–171.

Song, M.H. and Walkling, R.A. (1993) The impact of managerial ownership on acquisition attempts and target shareholder wealth. *Journal of Financial and Quantitative Analysis* **28**(4), 439–457.

Stultz, R.M. (1988) Managerial control of voting rights, shareholder wealth and the market for corporate control. *Journal of Financial Economics* **20**, 25–54.

Stultz, R.M., Walkling, R.A. and Song, M.H. (1990) The distribution of target ownership and the division of gains in successful takeovers. *Journal of Finance* **45**, 817–833.

Sudarsanan, P.S. (1991) Defensive strategies of target firms in UK contested takeovers. *Managerial Finance* **17**(6), 47–56.

Tellis, G.J. and Golder, P.N. (1996) First to market, first to fail? Real causes of enduring market leadership. *Sloan Management Review* **37**(2), 65–76.

Thure, S.S. and House, R.J. (1970) Where long-range planning pays off. *Business Horizons* **13**(4), 81–87.

Walkling, R. and Long, M. (1984) Agency theory, managerial welfare, and takeover bid resistance. *Rand Journal of Economics* **5**, 54–68.

PART FOUR   COULD INCUBATION WORK FOR YOU?

Allen, D. and Bazan, E. (1990) Value-added contributions of Pennsylvania's business incubators to tenant firms and local economies. Report prepared for Pennsylvania Department of Commerce, Pennsylvania State University, Park, PA.

Allen, D. and Levine, V. (1986) *Nurturing Advanced Technology Enterprises: emerging issues in state and local economic development policy*. Prager, New York.

Barrow, C. (1998) *The Essence of Small Business*. Prentice Hall, Hertfordshire, England.

Barrow, C. (2000) Barriers to Growth. Cranfield Working Papers, Cranfield, England.

Barrow, C. (2001), Managing Your Finances. Dorling Kindersley, London.

Barrow, C. and Brown, R. (1997) *Principles of Small Business*. International Thompson Press, London.

Barrow, C., Brown, R. and Clarke, C. (2001) *The Business Enterprise Handbook: A complete guide to profitable growth for entrepreneurs*. Kogan Page and the Sunday Times, London.

Campbell, C., Berge, D., Janus, J. and Olsen, K. (1988) *Change Agents in the New Economy: Business Incubators and Economic Development*. Report prepared for the Institute of Public Affairs, University of Minnesota, Minneapolis, MN.

Carbonara, P. and Overfelt, M. (2000) The dotcom factories. *Fortune.com*, 18 September.

Duff, A. (1993) State of the Industry Study: Business Incubators in Australia. AUSTEP Strategic Partnering, Booragoon, Western Australia.

Dunbar, C. (2000) Factors affecting investment bank initial public offering market share. *Journal of Financial Economics* **55**(1), 3–41.

Gross, W. (1998) The new math of ownership. *Harvard Business Review*, Boston, MA.

Leleux, B. (2000) Baby boom or blood bath? *European Business* **2**, Summer.

Lyons, T. (1990) *Birthing Economic Development: How Effective are Michigan's Incubators?* Michigan Center for the Redevelopment of Industrial States, Social Science Research Bureau, Michigan State University, MI.

Mian, S.A. (1996) Assessing value-added contributions of university technology incubators to tenant firms. *Research Policy* **5** 325–335.

Molnar, L., DePietro, R. and Gilliette, L. (1996) *Sustaining Economic Growth: The Positive Impact of the Michigan Incubator Industry, 1985–1995*. Ann Arbor, MI: University of Michigan Business School and the Michigan Business Incubator Association.

National Business Incubation Association (1996) *Tenth Anniversary Survey of Business Incubators, 1985–1995: A decade of growth.* Athens, OH.

Organisation for Economic Co-operation and Development (OECD) (1999) *Business Incubation: International Case Studies*, OECD, Paris.

PricewaterhouseCoopers (1999) Department of Employment, Workplace Relations and Small Business, National Review of Small Business Incubators. Final internal report.

Quitter, J. (2000), Can business incubators justify their existence? *Business Week Online*, 25/10.

Sherman, H. (1999) Assessing the intervention effectiveness of business incubation programs on new business start-ups. *Journal of Developmental Entrepreneurship* **4**(2), 26–33.

Small Business Administration Office of Advocacy (1997) *Small Business Answer Card.* Available at http:www.sba.gov/ADVO/stats/answer.html.

Tornatzky, L., Batts, Y., McCrea, N., Lewis, M. and Quittman, L. (1995) *The Art and Craft of Technology Business Incubation: Best Practices, Strategies and Tools from 50 Programs.* Athens, Ohio: National Business Incubation Association and the Ohio University Institute for Local Government and Rural Development.

Index